Praise for *The Last Bell*

'About life, death and boxing, McRae beautifully melds those constituent parts, then transcends them, to recount a profound journey through the human experience in a way that only a writer of his immense talent and humanity could. Exceptional and unique. I can't recommend it enough'
David Whitehouse, author of *About A Son*

'As with the sport itself, boxing writing is about so much more than physical combat – it's about the dark drama of life and death in their totality. That Donald McRae understands this implicitly makes him one of the very best writers working today. I'll read anything he turns his hand to'
Benjamin Myers, author of *The Offing* and *The Gallows Pole*

'*The Last Bell* is an unforgettable book. Its portraiture is akin to that of the finest novelists, and its reflections on life, death, loss and decency-under-duress are profound and moving. McRae unveils the grim realities of the industrialised brutality of boxing. He shows us the vain and cruel who seek to profiteer from and corrupt the sport, but he shows us also, with what amounts to brotherly love, those who act with daring, respect and honour. This book, which is laced through with bravery and tenderness, goes to the depths of life and death and back. Boxing, sport even, is fortunate to have a laureate such as this'
Adrian Duncan, author of *Sabbatical in Leipzig*

'A beautiful, gripping, always surprising book about sport, life, boxing, men, women, art, ageing, family and why we get lost in things. Don McRae is a champion of sports writing. This book is a relentlessly absorbing mix of detail, humour, sadness, wisdom and colour from a life lived in that world'
Barney Ronay, chief sports writer at the *Guardian*

'Nobody writes about boxing like Don McRae. But with *The Last Bell* he has written a book that moves beyond just boxing and grapples instead with what it truly means to fight. It is a book about knowing when to bite down and keep swinging, about knowing when to throw in the towel, a book about loss and defeat, and how we might, in the final reckoning, face those inevitabilities with a kind of a redeeming grace'
Keiran Goddard, author of *I See Buildings Fall Like Lightning*

'Donald McRae enjoys what boxing fans will hope is not one last successful run in the sport, chronicling it with the passion, depth and colour that only he can. *The Last Bell* is a personal look at the sport through a human lens and at the business of boxing with a critical eye and it shows how different both parts are. McRae proves, once again, that he is one of the great sportswriters of his time while reminding boxing fans how lucky they are to have him'
Tris Dixon, Boxing Scene, author of *Damage: The Untold Story of Brain Trauma in Boxing*

'If *Dark Trade* was about one man wanting to find out what it is to fight and how it feels to lose, *The Last Bell* is about a man who is now familiar with these things through personal experience using boxing as a reminder that he is not alone in feeling the emotions attached to them. McRae's eyes may be wearier and slightly narrower now, but when you see modern-day boxing through them there is a surprising and refreshing clarity to be found … McRae, twenty-nine years after *Dark Trade*, continues to write about boxing with an elegance, intelligence and maturity and again delivers the definitive text on where we are today. *The Last Bell* is a book plenty of people need to read but only one person could have written'
Elliot Worsell, Boxing Scene, author of *Dog Rounds: Death and Life in the Boxing Ring*

ALSO BY DONALD McRAE

Nothing Personal: The Business of Sex

Dark Trade: Lost in Boxing

Winter Colours: The Changing Seasons of Rugby

In Black and White: The Untold Story
of Joe Louis and Jesse Owens

Every Second Counts: The Extraordinary Race
to Transplant the First Human Heart

The Old Devil: Clarence Darrow,
The World's Greatest Trial Lawyer

Under Our Skin: A White Family's Journey
through South Africa's Darkest Years

A Man's World: The Double Life of Emile Griffith

In Sunshine or in Shadow: How Boxing
Brought Hope in the Troubles

THE LAST BELL

LIFE, DEATH AND BOXING

Donald McRae

**SIMON &
SCHUSTER**

London · New York · Amsterdam/Antwerp · Sydney · Toronto · New Delhi

First published in Great Britain by Simon & Schuster UK Ltd, 2025
Copyright © Donald McRae, 2025

The right of Donald McRae to be identified as the author of this work has been
asserted in accordance with the Copyright, Designs and Patents Act, 1988.

1 3 5 7 9 10 8 6 4 2

Simon & Schuster UK Ltd
1st Floor
222 Gray's Inn Road
London WC1X 8HB

www.simonandschuster.co.uk
www.simonandschuster.com.au
www.simonandschuster.co.in

Simon & Schuster Australia, Sydney
Simon & Schuster India, New Delhi

The authorised representative in the EEA is Simon & Schuster Netherlands BV,
Herculesplein 96, 3584 AA Utrecht, Netherlands. info@simonandschuster.nl

The author and publishers have made all reasonable efforts to contact
copyright-holders for permission, and apologise for any omissions or errors in the form
of credits given. Corrections may be made to future printings.

A CIP catalogue record for this book
is available from the British Library

Hardback ISBN: 978-1-3985-0418-9
Trade Paperback ISBN: 978-1-3985-3991-4
eBook ISBN: 978-1-3985-0419-6

Typeset in Caslon by M Rules

Printed and Bound in the UK using 100% Renewable Electricity
at CPI Group (UK) Ltd

MIX
Paper | Supporting
responsible forestry
FSC® C171272

For the family and friends of Patrick Day

CONTENTS

1

Resurrection

Sunday 2 December 2018

I wonder why I am up at such a bleak hour of the morning to watch two men hurt each other. At 3.45 a.m., the house is freezing and my family are asleep. Walking slowly downstairs, I still cannot shake everything that happened eleven weeks ago.

I open the living room door and hear the soft thud of our old cat as she jumps down from a chair onto the wooden floorboards. A red dot in the dark confirms my pay-per-view purchase of the boxing. When I turn on the television, to check that Tyson Fury and Deontay Wilder have not yet climbed into the ring for their world heavyweight title fight in Los Angeles, the room is illuminated by the glowering face of Cuba's Luis Ortiz. Slow-motion footage shows Ortiz pummelling the American journeyman Travis Kauffman.

Nine months earlier, Ortiz had almost knocked out Wilder before the WBC world champion did what he had done to thirty-nine of his forty vanquished opponents. Wilder's terrifying power made Ortiz stagger around the ring, dropping him twice. Fury will soon face the same danger.

I meander through the familiar routine in a daze. I turn on a lamp and feed Lola the cat. I switch on the kettle and spoon coffee into a mug. As I wait for the water to boil, I remember how fight nights had once felt very different.

In the late 1980s, and through the 1990s, I would stay up all night to watch Mike Tyson, Evander Holyfield, Riddick Bowe and Lennox Lewis fight in Las Vegas and New York. By the time the opening bell rang, I would be wired with excitement and more than a few drinks. From the early 1990s, my girlfriend Alison, who is now my wife, would stay up with me. Those nights were often crazy, and a party for two, because we would jump off the sofa and run around the room, screaming in disbelief as we surrendered to the mania of boxing.

In November 1993, we watched incredulously as a fan flew into the arena at Caesars Palace on a paramotor. He crashed into the ring in the middle of the seventh round of a rollicking world heavy-weight title rematch between Holyfield and Bowe. Then, in June 1997, we saw Tyson bite a chunk out of Holyfield's ear on an even more demented night.

We were married by then and Alison was used to me saying 'This is boxing, baby' or regaling her with uplifting moments from heavyweight history. I would reassure her that boxing had once held a political and cultural resonance which made it endlessly fascinating.

In the first half of the 20th century, heavyweight boxing broke previously unshakeable racial barriers as African American fighters, galvanised by the audacious Jack Johnson and bolstered by the stoical Joe Louis, swept aside inferior challengers peddled year after year as 'The Great White Hope'. Muhammad Ali did even more for Black America in the 1960s and '70s when, despite being banned from boxing for three years because he refused to fight in the Vietnam War, he resembled the King of the World.

Ali entranced a young white boy, living under apartheid in South Africa, and changed my life forever.

By the time I began watching boxing closely, and eventually

writing about it, the business had fragmented and collapsed into chaos. Nineteen years have now passed since there had last been an undisputed heavyweight champion of the world. I was ringside in Vegas on the night, in November 1999, when Lewis beat Holyfield to briefly unify the belts.

So much has changed since then. Alison and our two youngest kids, seventeen-year-old Jack and fifteen-year-old Emma, are asleep upstairs. Our eldest daughter Bella, who is nineteen, is away at university. They have grown up surrounded by my boxing habit and so there was no surprise when I said I would set my alarm for Fury and Wilder. But they don't quite understand why this fight suddenly means so much to me.

It is a hushed early Sunday morning in England and a raucous Saturday night at the Staples Center. The eight-hour time difference means it's 7.50 p.m. in LA on 1 December 2018, the year of my sister's death.

On 15 September, Heather had died suddenly and my family cracked open.

I drift into the living room, coffee in hand, and think of my dad, Ian, just outside Johannesburg. Two hours ahead of me, he will be awake and waiting for the nurses to help him get ready for another day. I imagine my dad lying on his side, watching my mother, his dying wife of sixty-three years. Even at eighty-nine, he retains his calm empathy.

Later this morning, my lovely old mom, Jess, devastated by Heather's death and with morphine muffling her senses more than the cancer inside her, will sit in her chair next to my dad in the Frail Care Centre. She will gaze at the sunshine streaming through the lace curtains.

Tyson Fury rises up on television. He is unlike most boxers as he does not possess a sculpted or tattooed body. Fury is a huge man and he does not mind being fleshy around his waist. He is still able to move with surprising speed and lightness. But it is hard to know if he will be quick and agile enough to evade the shocking power of Wilder for twelve long rounds. Fury looks briefly pensive as his hands are wrapped in the locker room.

I say hello quietly and ask Fury how he is feeling. I dream up such nonsense because I am a writer rather than a fighter. I am bulky rather than chiselled. I am white-haired rather than tattooed. I am shy rather than boisterous. I am old rather than young.

For fifty years, I have followed boxing, often obsessively. I've fallen for Ali, Mike Tyson and other great champions. Fury could join this pantheon if, somehow, he withstands Wilder's ferocity. I've given so much of my life to thinking and writing about the giants of boxing, and thousands of lesser fighters who will never scale their magnitude of achievement. I have been moved, amused, confused and enriched by these encounters. But it's embarrassing to admit the extent of my fixation because, to most people, boxing is barbaric. I have written about its corruption and damage but, for the past thirty-five years, I've mostly exalted the lonely courage of fighters and the thrilling drama of their best contests.

Yet even zealots grow weary. In recent years, my family and work, as well as books, movies and Arsenal, have filled my head as much as boxing. There has been a fleeting freedom from the ring.

Then, less than three months ago, death and grief unhinged me.

Earlier this week, I watched a documentary about Fury. The soft-focused imagery of the boxer with his wife and children gave way to the distressing maze of his mind. 'I prayed for death on a daily basis,' Fury said as he explained why depression, heavy drinking and drug dependence had kept him out of boxing for two-and-a-half years.

'I woke up and thought: *Why didn't I die in my sleep?*,' Fury continued in his throaty murmuring. 'I tried to drink myself to death. I attempted to crash into a bridge one time.'

It reminds me of my first interview with Fury seven years ago, in November 2011. He was twenty-three years old and, before revealing that he wanted to smash up the room where we sat, he said he was so sad that he wanted to take his own life.

Exactly four years later, in November 2015, Fury boxed like a chess grandmaster and dazzled Wladimir Klitschko in Germany to become the WBA, IBF and WBO world champion. He soon slipped over the edge into a new desolation and, having not fought since beating Klitschko, Fury vacated his heavyweight titles in October 2016. Then, in January 2018, Fury ended his silence and announced his return to boxing. Weighing almost 400 pounds, and with a broken mind, it seemed an impossible task.

But here we are, at 4.38 a.m., with Fury having lost 140 pounds and on his way to the ring again. His miraculous comeback has made him one of the most popular, if divisive, sportsmen in Britain.

I have not forgotten the bigotry Fury has spouted, or the positive drugs test, but I am adrift. At least I still have Alison and the kids. They give me great hope and resolve, but my original South African family is shrouded by death. I need to believe in boxing again.

It seems simple on the surface. Boxing is now a refuge of distraction from the loss – and the further loss I know is coming. But it is much more than this. I want to remember how boxing once made me feel so exuberant and so fucking alive. I know it is a bleak and dirty business but, at its best, it's like nothing else on earth. All life is here and it can be as beautiful as it is brutal, as glorious as it is painful. Fury is a reminder that boxing can offer light in the darkest of stories. He is a primary reason why I have turned back to it at one of the worst times of my life.

At 4.40 a.m., the camera cuts away to a tunnel where Fury wears an olive-green gown. His head is covered by a hood.

Ricky Hatton, the great old Manchester boxer who followed a similar dark path to Fury, leads him out, while Shane Fury, a bearded bear of a man, shouts in his brother's ear. 'C'mon Tyson!'

Fury holds up the crucifix draped around his neck. He kisses the figure of Christ.

Shane repeats his cry with gravel-voiced Lancastrian urgency. *'C'mon Tyson!'*

Fury bounces up and down as Gala's 'Freed From Desire', the

old Euro-screamer from 1996, echoes around the arena. The boxer whoops as the crowd join Gala in singing about people wanting more and more, freedom and love most of all, before reaching the thunderous chorus.

A jubilant Fury, resurrected from near death, whips the hood from his head. Two days before, he'd looked a biblical figure, with his Old Testament beard and fiery ranting at Wilder, but he seems born again now. He is clean and sleek, his shaven face dancing with life.

Just like boxing, Fury is a mass of contradictions, inspiring and disturbing in equal measure.

He keeps smiling and winking before, on the apron of the ring, he waves a bemused official away and, with one massive lift of his left leg, clambers over the ropes. He's back inside the ring where he feels so at home.

Wilder waits in the same tunnel. The unbeaten world champion wears a heavy gold mask, a gold crown on his head and a long black feathery gown. At his side, the rapper Jay Rock barks out the lyrics to 'Win' as he urges everyone to get the fuck out of his way.

Thousands of phones glow in the dark and there are booming pyrotechnics as a brass band emerges from different corners of the Staples Center. Inside the ring, Wilder turns his dead-eyed stare on Fury, who punches the air to stay loose.

After his trademark shout of 'It's showtime!', the suave old ring announcer Jimmy Lennon Jr turns to Wilder. 'Standing at six feet, seven inches, he weighed in at 212 and one-half pounds,' Lennon hollers. 'He is undefeated as a professional with a record of forty wins, no losses, thirty-nine big wins coming by way of knockout. Tonight, making the eighth defence of his title . . .'

Mark Breland, Wilder's trainer, removes the gown and the crown. He unclips the sequined mask when Lennon reaches his crescendo. 'Ladies and gentlemen, please welcome the hard-hitting and defending WBC heavyweight champion of the world . . .'

Wilder opens his jaws wide as Lennon roars, 'Introducing the Bronze Bomber . . . *DEONTAY WILDERRRRR!*'

Lennon turns to Fury. 'Standing at six foot nine inches and weighing 256 and one-half pounds, he, also, is undefeated with a record of twenty-seven wins, no losses, nineteen wins coming by way of knockout. Ladies and gentlemen, the former WBA, WBO and IBF unified heavyweight champion of the world and the current lineal heavyweight champion of the world ... The Gypsy King ...'

Shaking his head furiously, and waggling his long tongue, Fury is a carnival barker and hellfire preacher rolled into one. 'Introducing the undefeated ... *TYSON FURRRYYYYYY!*'

Stretching his right arm high above his head, while looking at the heavens, Fury nods as if he and the Almighty have a secret pact.

The referee Jack Reiss brings them together and, gripping each fighter's wrist, says, 'Obey my commands at all times. Protect yourself at all times. Fight hard, fight clean. Good luck.'

Slowly, the ring empties. Fury dances on the spot while Wilder glowers at him. I lean forward, lost in boxing again, willing Fury on at the end of a year riddled with illness and death.

Boxing makes me live in the moment. I want that feeling again.

The bell rings. Fury and Wilder walk towards each other.

In 1996, my book *Dark Trade* allowed me to become a full-time writer. I owe that gift to boxing. But our relationship is not easy. Boxing often disappoints and upsets me. It is as crooked and destructive as it is magnificent and transformative. All these years later, I am still trying to reconcile boxing's paradoxes of hope and despair, salvation and ruin.

At its finest, boxing transcends sport to become epic and electrifying before reminding us that, above all else, the humanity of fighters resonates most. I know what it is like to watch them ringside in London or Las Vegas, New York or Manchester. I know what it is like to hold a fighter's hand while he is crying and being wheeled away on a stretcher to an ambulance after a brutal bout. I know what it is like to see the joy pour out of a boxer in the dressing room after a great victory – and to remember how, in contrast, it had been so quiet and sombre an hour earlier while he waited to fight.

Boxing has a perverse way of turning every significant bout I see into something deeply personal. It echoes the small battles and little triumphs of real life when I write about boxing stories as profound as they are colourful. It happens when I am almost close enough to touch the ropes while watching boxers risk their lives. I fall for the gory drama once more.

It helps that I have history with Fury. In November 2011, on an ordinary Wednesday morning at his home in Morecambe, near Lancaster, Fury gave me one of the most disturbing interviews I have ever done.

It began with him stepping outside even before I knocked on his door. Fury walked down a narrow alley, carrying three bags of rubbish in each huge hand. 'Hello, mate, give me a moment,' he murmured, nodding towards two refuse collectors approaching his corner bungalow. 'It's binmen day.' After spending less than a minute talking to them about his fight later that month against Neven Pajkić, Fury offered me his hand. There was no knuckle-crushing welcome from a hard man. Instead, it felt like holding a cold and curling lettuce leaf.

Halloween had been two nights before, but a massive plastic pumpkin still blocked the front door of the house he shared with his twenty-one-year-old wife, Paris, and their two children, Venezuela and Prince, so he led me round the back.

Fury had won all sixteen of his professional fights while becoming the British and Commonwealth heavyweight champion, but he seemed diffident and there was no certainty he would eventually win a world title. I did not know what to expect from Fury either in the ring or our interview.

I had planned on starting in a predictable way by asking how he felt about facing another volatile fighter in Pajkić. The Bosnian heavyweight, who had emigrated to Canada, certainly did not seem to fear him. 'He has an ugly face,' Pajkić had said of Fury.

I'd warmed to the humour in Fury's response. 'I like his haircut, but when will he get it finished?'

Fury still had a full head of black hair then. At home in Morecambe, the dark stubble on his youthful face could not hide his contemplative expression as we sat with his family in their tiny front room. It soon became apparent that Fury was uninterested in a routine interview.

The sight of two-year-old Venezuela jumping around happily, and their four-week-old baby Prince sleeping in a pale blue pram, prompted a discussion of their exotic names. 'One night, while I was sleeping,' Fury said, 'I thought of Venezuela. My wife is called Paris. I'm Tyson and [gesturing to his son] he's Prince John James. If the girl had a normal name, it wouldn't fit, would it? I wanted to call the boy Patrick but the wife didn't want it.'

Paris gave me a knowing look. 'Ask him what name he really wanted for our son . . .'

'Jesus,' Fury said.

'That got a quick no from me,' Paris said with a sigh.

'Jesus Fury,' the fighter said wistfully. 'A lot of Mexicans are called Jesus.'

We discussed the remarkable story of how his father chose to call him Tyson. It sounded like an apocryphal tale, but Fury swore that every word told to him by his dad, the former pro heavyweight 'Gypsy' John Fury, was true. In August 1988, his mother had been taken to hospital in severe pain, even though she was not due to give birth for another eight weeks. John Fury was called early the next morning, at 3 a.m., as the baby had been born prematurely.

When he arrived at the special care unit, John Fury could have lifted the fragile infant up in one hand. He weighed less than two pounds.

'Miracles do happen,' the doctor told the new father, encouragingly.

'They will happen with my son,' John Fury replied. 'He'll live.'

'What are you going to call him?' the doctor asked.

'I'm naming him after the heavyweight champion of the world . . . Mike Tyson.'

The doctor smiled doubtfully. 'Forget the Michael,' John said. 'His name's Tyson. Tyson Fury will grow up to be heavyweight champion of the world.'

Fury had the knack of a born storyteller, but such knockabout fun was framed by darkness. His father was serving a prison sentence for an assault which cost another man his eye. 'He knew the guy,' Fury said. 'They bumped into each other at a car auction in Manchester. The guy started it. There were three of them against my father. The feller bit my dad on the face but, as he shoved him back, he punched the feller in the eye. And the feller lost his eye. He had to have the eye taken out because it got infected. The judge found my dad guilty of wounding with intent.'

Fury himself did not seem violent to me. 'I've never been in trouble,' he confirmed. 'I've not got a criminal record. Never had a fight outside boxing. So I'm very different to my dad.'

We relaxed and Fury suggested that 'boxing is a dying sport. Years ago, the world heavyweight champion could be said to have reached the highest pinnacle of sport. Even in this country, boxers were heroes. Henry Cooper was one and no footballer was bigger than Frank Bruno. I don't think it will get back to that – never in a million years. People look to celebrities now.

'In British boxing today, Joe Calzaghe's gone. Ricky Hatton's gone. I'm hoping I can bring it round. When I beat Derek Chisora in July, 3.2 million watched it on Channel 5. I've got an outspoken personality which gets people thinking, and my style of fighting is aggressive. In my fights, there's drama. So that can help.'

Fury would defend his Commonwealth title against Pajkić, Canada's heavyweight champion. 'I went ringside with Pajkić and shouted, "Oi, you and me, let's have a fight",' Fury said. 'He chucks this dirty ring towel at me and says, "C'mon, let's fight now". Everyone's jumping in and holding us back. It was pantomime.'

The big man's mood shifted. 'I went on national TV in Canada and said exactly what I thought of Pajkić. I'd watched his fight and thought it was rubbish. He started calling me and my family names. I know this is terrible, but I'm in the mode to do serious damage. When I go in there, I'm trying to put my fist through the back of his head. I'm trying to break his ribs and make them stick out the other side. I don't like this kid.'

Fury sounded ominously like Mike Tyson. His father's favourite fighter used to say, in the 1980s, that he aimed to hit his opponent on the tip of the nose 'because I try to drive the bone into the brain'. Fury had fast hands but, then, he had not yet learned how to plant his feet and become a destructive puncher. Those days would come but, back in 2011, he was inexperienced.

There was something about Fury, however, which made him seem very different to more ordinary heavyweights. Having interviewed Tyson in his most desolate years, I felt the same creeping chill when Fury began to talk with alarming vulnerability about his mental state.

'I know I've got nothing to be upset about,' he said. 'I'm British and Commonwealth champion, I'm doing OK. I've got a few quid in the bank. I shouldn't be upset. But I don't feel I've done any good at all. I thought when the children were born, it would be a top thing. And when I became English champion, I thought there'd be a great feeling – but no. I thought it must be because it's not big enough. Let me win the British title. But after I took that off Chisora, there was nothing. What have I done? I've beaten up another man in a fight. What's the point of anything?'

Paris helped by joining in the conversation. We were trying to bring back some light, but Fury brooded and said less and less. I suggested there were always touching, amusing and interesting moments in life. He was young and his perspective might change.

'No,' Fury said firmly. 'I don't think it's ever going to change. I just see it going crazy. One loss in the ring and it's all over.'

Sitting in his armchair, wearing a black vest and shorts, Fury looked at me evenly. 'There is a name for what I have where, one minute I'm happy, and the next minute I'm sad, like commit-suicide-sad. And for no reason – nothing's changed. One minute I'm over the moon and the next minute I feel like getting in my car and running it into a wall at a hundred miles an hour. I don't know what's wrong with me. I'm messed up.'

I suggested he could overcome these feelings. 'No,' Fury said calmly. 'I just live with them. I think I need a psychiatrist because I do believe I'm mentally disturbed in some way. Maybe it was the fact that, when I was a kid, my mother and father were always shouting and screaming and hitting each other. My dad had different women and different kids down the road. My mum had fourteen pregnancies, but only four of us survived. We had a little sister born for a few days and then she died. There had to be a funeral. That would affect you.'

Fourteen pregnancies. Ten little deaths.

I asked about the life he and his family had lived as Travellers. But Fury did not feel like the King of the Gypsies that Wednesday morning.

'Every day,' he said, 'you're on a downward slope.'

'I hear this constantly,' Paris told me before smiling more encouragingly. 'But there are good days. If you'd come on a good day, you'd have been all right.'

Fury leaned forward. 'I just want to get across how I feel.'

'Sometimes I listen,' his wife said, 'but depression runs in his family.'

Fury nodded. 'My three brothers are the same. Everyone is a tough guy. They don't talk like you and me are talking. But we all cry instantly. Look at me: six foot nine and if someone said this to me in my family, I would just cry. All of us would. But nothing's talked about in our family. We just push each other aside, or give each other a punch.'

How would Fury cope if he woke up the following Saturday, on the day of his fight against Pajkić, in a depressed mood? 'I won't. I love boxing. I can't wait for the moment I step into the ring. I feel calm then. It's just me and him and we're going at it, old school. But after that, it's back to the reality and feeling angry with life. But, when I get in the ring, I don't have this feeling I've got now. Right now, I really feel like smashing this place up.'

Fury looked around his home. There was a long silence. Paris and I exchanged uneasy glances. It reminded me of those moments when, while interviewing Mike Tyson, I had sometimes been unsure how our encounter might unfold. I felt the same jeopardy in Morecambe.

I asked Fury how he coped with such turbulent emotions as a boxer. 'I don't feel like that in the ring because, if I do, it's all over,' he said simply. 'An upset fighter is a beaten fighter.'

I tried hard to believe that Fury might find some strange refuge in the ring. For a man who had little formal education, he spoke lucidly about his deepest emotions. Some of the most memorable fighters over the decades have been great talkers – but few of them, bar Mike Tyson, articulated their inner darkness so frankly.

'I feel better in the ring,' Fury said. 'That's when I get some relief.'

I asked Paris how she would feel the following Saturday night when her young husband prepared to fight. 'I don't get nervous until I hear his music and he starts walking out,' she said. 'My stomach turns upside down. That's when you think: "He's going in that ring against someone who wants to hurt him." Before that it's OK because he's happy and excited and telling me he's going to win. It all changes when I hear the music, but I remember to trust him. I always think he's going to be all right in the end.'

Fury seemed calmer. 'I love talking,' he said. 'It's one of my favourite things.'

I reached out to Fury. He took my hand as I thanked him for talking so openly. 'No problem,' he said and his handshake was warmer, if still soft and yielding.

Fury nodded when I said I hoped the depression would soon lift. 'I live with it,' he said. 'Hopefully I will get better at dealing with it. We should talk again.'

Five minutes later, looking out of the window of my taxi, I saw him turn back to his little bungalow. His head was bowed. He looked young and helpless.

Fury fought Pajkić on 12 November 2011, in Manchester, and suffered an early scare. In the second round, he was knocked to the canvas by a right hand to the head. It was the first time Fury had been down in his professional career; but he got up. He survived the round and then, in the third, he dropped Pajkić twice before the fight was waved over. Fury had won a dramatic fight and I was even more interested in him.

I interviewed him again in September 2013, at his training camp in Essen, a town in Belgium. It seemed poignant as Fury spoke about leaving school at the age of ten. 'I'm not an educated person with any proper schooling,' he said. 'I'd like to take a course in writing. It's hard when you're one of them people who don't know where to stop sentences or put commas or exclamation marks. You feel like an illiterate dummy.'

Fury's face creased with emotion. 'I can fight but that's the only thing I can do. When it comes to anything other than fighting, or talking, I'm not very good.'

Yet his intelligence had been obvious while he drifted through subjects as diverse as depression and discipline, addiction and religion.

Fury soon displayed a malevolent side. In a 2013 interview, which was a tangled celebration of his culture as a Traveller, Fury told Keith Duggan of the *Irish Times*: 'We are outsiders. Just like the Muslims have their ways, we have our ways. There are these girls who want to open their legs to every Tom, Dick and Harry. But they are looked upon as rubbish in our community. If I had a sister who did that ... I'd hang her.'

When I next interviewed Fury, on a rainy day in Calais in February 2014, his mood had soured again because his fight against David Haye had been cancelled and he'd lost lots of money. 'I was so fed up, I retired for a few months,' he said. 'I've come back because I need the money. I can't get another job, so it looks like I've got to do this for the rest of my life.'

I asked him about his homophobia. In October 2012, he had threatened David Price, his British heavyweight rival, that he was going to put 'you and your gay lover Tony Bellew' in intensive care. He later blamed his cousins for posting that tweet in his name, but they were not involved a year later when, again on Twitter, he ranted: 'I think @LennoxLewis & wlad@Klitschko r 100% Homosexuals!!'

I had interviewed Mike Tyson again in Las Vegas a month earlier. In our conversation, Tyson celebrated the life of Panama Al Brown who, apart from becoming boxing's first Hispanic world champion in the 1920s, had been consumed by his long affair with the gay French writer and film-maker Jean Cocteau.

'I've never heard of them,' Fury said with a shrug.

He paused when I asked if he believed it was impossible for a gay man to be tough? 'I don't know. If a man likes to mess around with another man, it's his own business. But I'm an old-fashioned married man with kids. I'm not interested in that stuff.'

Then, in October 2015, just before he fought Wladimir Klitschko for his world heavyweight titles, Fury gave an explosive interview to Oliver Holt of the *Mail on Sunday*. Holt referenced my 2011 interview and asked Fury if he sometimes still wanted to kill himself. 'Oh yes,' Fury said. 'I still have those moments, but I have channelled it with God. Every time I stray away from the Lord's word, I find emptiness and darkness . . . We live in an evil world. The devil is very strong at the minute and the bible tells me the end is near.

'There are only three things that need to be accomplished before the devil comes home: one of them is homosexuality being legal, one of them is abortion and the other one's paedophilia. Who would have thought in the 1960s that those first two would be legalised?'

There was justified outrage but, a few weeks later, Fury, as a huge underdog, boxed with sublime skill to outpoint Klitschko and become world heavyweight champion. Yet, within hours of his strategic masterclass, Fury had begun to unravel completely. He would say later that, on the night of his momentous victory, a miserable realisation seeped through him – not even being world heavyweight champion could offer solace.

When the rematch was announced, Fury cared little about boxing or himself. On 27 April 2016, he stripped off his shirt at a press conference to show Klitschko his wobbly belly. He seemed proud – as if this was a powerful 'fuck you' to boxing and life itself.

Two months later, Fury postponed the fight. He had sprained his ankle but UKAD, the UK anti-doping body, had suspended him after he and his cousin, Hughie Fury, tested positive for nandrolone, an anabolic steroid. Both blamed the positive test results on eating uncastrated wild boar. They eventually won their appeals against the ruling, but I no longer cared much about Fury.

The rematch had been rescheduled for late October but, on 23 September 2016, Fury withdrew as he was struggling with his mental health. He retired from boxing on 3 October – only to reverse his decision the following day. That same day, he featured in another provocative interview, with *Rolling Stone*, as he spoke about taking lots of cocaine amid deep depression.

On 12 October 2016, he vacated his world heavyweight titles and, a day later, his licence to box was revoked by the British Boxing Board of Control. Fury seemed determined to drink, eat and snort his way to oblivion. Darkness and silence settled over him.

I told my sister about the resurrection of Tyson Fury as she sat up in her hospital bed on Sunday 10 June 2018. The previous night, Fury had stepped into the ring for the first time in two-and-a-half years. He had made his unexpected comeback in Manchester against a journeyman called Sefer Seferi.

Heather was in King's College Hospital in Camberwell, south London. I did not know it then, but it would be the last time I saw her alive.

She had developed a rare condition six years earlier which meant her bile duct kept closing. The blockage prevented bile from the liver reaching the gallbladder and small intestine. Whenever the duct was sealed shut, her entire body was affected. She had been through many operations so that stents could be inserted in the duct, but none had worked. Surgical complications at a different hospital had torn her oesophagus badly. It made future surgery extremely risky.

The consultants at King's found that Heather's kidneys had deteriorated markedly since the perforation of her oesophagus. She was also on a very high oxygen concentration because her lungs were so full of fluid that she sometimes had trouble breathing. The following morning, she would have X-rays to check for pneumonia, as well as a scan to uncover further information about her kidneys and a barium swallow test to examine the alimentary tract.

Heather was upbeat, despite the acute problems. After we had spoken about the various procedures, and her belief that they might finally help her, she wanted to talk about life beyond illness.

'OK, Small,' I said, as Heather smiled at my old nickname for her.

Heather was just five foot two, but she had been a massive presence in my life. When we were young, she allowed me to tag along on her adventures with the older kids and, whenever I got tired or frightened, Heather made sure I felt better. She also spent hours on the tennis court with me and I started calling her Wilson. I thought it was hilarious. Wilson was the make of a tennis racket, while sounding like an old man who slept on a park bench. Heather didn't mind because she knew I revered her. Even though I cried when she kept beating me on the court, she always told me that, one day, I would find a way to win.

When we were teenagers, and I grew taller than her, I began to call her Small. She loved books and music and she opened up these worlds in a way that changed my life forever. Small seemed impossibly cool for she was listening to David Bowie and reading Simone de Beauvoir when she was sixteen. I was thirteen and stunned by everything she told me. Bowie wore make-up and called himself the Thin White Duke. De Beauvoir was a feminist. These words confused me, but Small explained what they meant. She played me all her favourite records until they became my favourites too, and told me about the books she loved.

Small was the first person in whom I confided my secret ambition to become a writer. It was a crazy plan. I was going to leave Johannesburg and travel to London to become an author. My mother and father were concerned. I knew no one in London. But Heather believed in me. She told me I could do it.

Heather was also the first person to really make me think about apartheid. When I decided I could not go into the army and do my national service, she saved me. The alternatives were limited. I didn't want to go to jail for six years, but I was heartbroken at the thought of leaving my parents and South Africa. My mom and dad tried to dissuade me, but Heather bolstered me. She and her husband Ross drove me to the airport on the Friday afternoon of 3 August 1984 – the day I left home, at twenty-three, forever. I cried but Small gave me courage.

She and Ross followed me later that year and, while we missed my parents terribly, we did our best in London. It was hard and lonely, but my big sister protected me. I stopped calling her Small. She was just Heather – the person I always looked up to when I was struggling.

Heather was so full of life and hope in hospital. We slipped back into our old routine and opened up. I usually avoided talking about boxing to her because it was such a harsh and alien world. But I mentioned that a future book might be set in contemporary boxing. It would be a counterpart, in the 2020s, to *Dark Trade*.

Heather disliked boxing but she liked reading about the fighters I met, so I told her about Tyson Fury. I spared her the precise detail that, after 558 days outside the ring, I had watched him beat Seferi on a fourth-round stoppage.

Heather and I then discussed flying together to visit our parents in South Africa. The altitude in Johannesburg affected her breathing, but she was so bright that anything seemed possible.

Our mother was in the early stages of yet another battle with breast cancer and our dad supported her decision not to undergo chemotherapy. The thought of losing her hung over us. Heather had not been as close to my parents as I was but, on a summer afternoon, I felt her love for them. Finally, I stood up to say goodbye.

'I'll see you soon, Heather,' I said as I kissed her cheek.

'I hope so,' she replied.

As I walked down the empty hospital corridor, the truth hit me again. I might once have called her Small, but my big sister had always been, and will always remain, a giant to me.

On Saturday 15 September 2018, I worked quietly in my office in the garden on an interview I had done earlier that week with the young Scottish boxer Lee McGregor. Over the previous months, McGregor had endured the death of his mother and two grandparents. The bantamweight spoke movingly about loss and grief and how he had howled with anguish. I had written half the piece and, late that morning, I took a coffee break. I went inside and the house was very quiet. My daughters, Bella and Emma, had not been awake for long and I went to see them. Alison had taken Jack to a university open day.

Sunshine flooded my office as my mobile rang. My brother-in-law Ross was already crying when I picked up.

Heather had died that morning. His wife was gone. My sister was gone. We had lost Small.

It took a while to piece everything together but, eventually, Ross explained. Heather had gone to bed early the night before as she was exhausted after treating one of their horses who had cancer. When Ross checked on her at 10 a.m., he was shocked to find her dead in bed.

The paramedics concluded that she had died during the early hours from lung congestion.

I could not howl like Lee McGregor had done. I still had my parents and it was down to me to break the catastrophic news to them. It was just after lunchtime in South Africa and they would be resting. I wanted them to have another hour of peace before I shattered their world.

I went inside to tell the girls and then I called Alison. Everyone was kind to me and full of love. But there was shock too. We knew Heather had been knocked further when test results, the day after I saw her, showed the early stages of heart failure. She was warned that the prognosis was around five years unless they reversed the ailment. They had booked her in for more cardiac tests, but her consultant was worried about a clot on her lung which could cause a heart attack or stroke. There were so many issues, but none of us knew that death was so near.

I looked at my last messages from Heather. Most of our texts and emails since I had seen her had been about her illness – or concern for our parents. Her final message came on Sunday 2 September 2018 at 5.12 p.m. It was a thank you for her birthday gift, a bird sculpture.

'Hi Don,' she texted. *'Thank you for the lovely, lovely birthday present. You know how I have loved birds all my life so it could not have been a better choice. I am really touched by the gift and particularly that it came from Crete. Spoke to Ma and Pa this morning and it became very apparent they were very stressed about me last week. So sad. Am so sorry I have caused this trouble with my ongoing illness. Hope all going well for you and everyone with prep for back to school and uni. Speak soon, I'm sure. Love H xx'*

There had been no answer to my subsequent messages.

Just before three o'clock in South Africa, almost 2 p.m. in England, a beautiful bird, a kite, wheeled high in the blue September sky as I listened to the phone ringing in my parents' study. I knew they would be watching sport on television while waiting for their afternoon tea and biscuits. It took a long time for him to answer but, finally, I heard the familiar voice.

My dad was shaken but calm. After he had asked for as many details as I knew, he said I should talk to my mother. It was one of their rituals that, when handing over the phone, they would tell each other the gist of what I had just said. Sometimes it drove me quietly mad because there were days when I wanted to be the first to tell both of them my news. But, today, I understood.

I heard my mother gasp and then, with a crack in her voice, she said my name. 'Don, I can't believe it.'

My mom was strong. She knew Alison and Jack were away for the day and she asked if the girls were with me. I reassured her that they were close by. My dad was then back on the line. I told him about the kite. The bird of prey was hunting and it drifted slowly across the cloudless sky. It made me think of Heather.

'I know,' my dad said before he echoed her last message to me. 'Heather always loved birds.'

I could no longer see the kite. My eyes were too full of tears.

Eleven weeks later, and the night before Fury fought Wilder in LA, I watched his new documentary. 'I didn't care about nothing,' Fury said on *Road to Redemption*. 'If I had 100 million in the bank or if I bought a Ferrari or a Bentley, it didn't mean anything. Seven billion people in the world and I was the man who became world heavyweight champion. But I was depressed and I really wanted to die. I wanted a date with the death-man.'

My sister and the heavyweight could hardly have been more different. There were no analogies to be drawn between her death and his suicidal depression. But, as I watched his film, I felt the old stirring which I had explained to Heather. I was being pulled back to boxing. After so many days drained of colour, I started thinking about this book again.

Fury stressed that training had saved him. 'If I stay in shape, I'll be depression-free forever. If I can do it, anybody can do it. I'm no one special. I was a fat pig at nearly twenty-eight stone, drinking and taking drugs on a daily basis. Suffering with depression up to the point of suicide, anxiety attacks, everything. You couldn't get any lower than I was and here I am, living proof that anyone can do it, because I'm back, telling my story and inspiring millions around the world.'

Fury said he felt like he had already won, just by coming back from a deadly depression. 'Being a fat lazy bum with millions in the bank, that's no life at all,' he said. 'Being hungry and fit and being a lion in the middle of a jungle? That's life. I don't fear being knocked spark out or even killed. I don't fear nothing.'

Sunday 2 December 2018

At 4.52 a.m. my time, I feel the trepidation Tyson Fury claims to have conquered. Deontay Wilder has his right hand cocked as he waits for an opening in the first round. Fury soon follows a snaking double jab with an even more impudent gesture as he places both hands behind his back. But Fury knows the fight is freighted with danger and he does not tease Wilder for long. He jitters and feints, with intense concentration, as Wilder stalks him.

Fury absorbs a left hook but then makes Wilder miss. He pops his jab into the American's face and closes the round with a sharp combination and a right-hand counter. At the bell, he raises his arms. His nerve is thrilling.

The pattern of the fight becomes obvious in the next five rounds. While his jab peppers Wilder's solemn face, Fury evades most of the champion's frightening punches. It's intriguing to watch a chaotic figure fight with such precision. But I feel a constant hum of dread that, at any moment, Wilder might land a crushing blow.

Blood trickles from Fury's nose. 'You're boxing beautifully,' says Ben Davison, his twenty-six-year-old trainer. 'Just don't get greedy.'

Fury switches to southpaw in the sixth and lands some clubbing combinations. Wilder's face swells beneath and above his left eye. Stepping back, The Gypsy King snaps repeated jabs into Wilder's face.

There is more of the same in the next two rounds as, between showboating, Fury makes the champion miss while spearing him with the jab and clubbing him with heavy hands. Davison is almost purring before round nine. 'What did I tell you when we took this fight? You'll beat him with your left hand. But don't get greedy, don't get complacent.'

Wilder has success a minute into the ninth as two right hands back Fury into a corner. Fury taps his chin as if inviting Wilder to have another crack. The Bronze Bomber does not need an invitation. A scything overhand right crashes against Fury's temple. He tumbles to the canvas.

Fury does not look especially hurt as he lies on his side, placing a glove on top of his head, as if to say 'What an idiot!' He is up by the time Jack Reiss says 'nine'. When asked if he is OK, Fury places both gloves on the referee's shoulders and says a firm 'Yes'.

Reiss tells Fury to walk away and then turn back. Fury does so without difficulty and the referee waves them on. Wilder steams in, throwing hellacious right hands. One minute and thirty-five seconds are left in the round and Fury is in a dark storm.

But this is no ordinary fighter. Fury ties up Wilder in a bear-like clinch and then avoids some swinging right hands. Suddenly, Fury drives Wilder back with powerful punching. With thirty seconds left in the round, he spreads his arms to the side and roars at Wilder. He then puts his hands behind his back and wags his tongue. After the bell, Fury looks intently into the crowd and yells. 'Come on!'

Fury comes out aggressively in the tenth and lands a crisp early combination, which he soon follows with an even harder one-two. Wilder looks unexpectedly fragile on his spindly legs.

The champion tries hard in the penultimate round, but Fury evades most of his desperate punches. Breland, in Wilder's corner, asks: 'You're gonna give me a big finish?'

After forty seconds of the last round, a big left hand from Wilder makes Fury step back. Sensing his chance, Wilder moves in quickly and detonates another right hand against Fury's chin. The big man goes down when a huge left hook smashes against his head. I sink back into my seat as Fury collapses in a heap, his head smacking against the canvas. He looks unconscious.

Wilder makes a throat-slitting gesture as a woman at ringside covers her mouth in horror. His family and his manager, Shelly Finkel, celebrate wildly, while the boxer is lost in a shimmying dance, his lips puckered in a kiss of ecstasy. The fight is all over in his head as his wife screams 'I love you, I love you!'

Fury's arms lie limply at his side, his left leg stretched out while his right knee is bent. The referee has reached 'five' in his count over the prone figure.

I can see that Fury has opened his eyes and, as the ref yells 'six', he starts to move. He is on his side at 'seven'. At 'eight', he has one foot on the canvas as he uses his hands to push himself up.

I stand up too, in disbelief at his resurrection.

Fury is on his feet as Reiss barks out 'nine'. The referee sounds almost incredulous as he asks the stricken boxer: 'Can you continue?'

'Yes.'

'Do you wanna go?' Reiss asks. Fury puts his gloves on the referee's shoulders and nods his assent.

'Walk over there,' Reiss says, pointing to his right, 'and come back to me.'

Fury does as he is told, almost jogging to show his superhuman powers.

Wilder stares at him in profound shock. His celebrations had been interrupted when, out of the corner of his eye, he saw the miraculous sight of Fury rising from the dead. Wilder looks as if he has been plunged back in a horror movie where, at the end, the monstrous killer removes an axe from his head and resumes his murderous carnage.

Reiss gestures for them to continue fighting. I stay on my feet as Wilder starts throwing bombs again. A heavy left catches Fury who, against the ropes and covering up, takes it well. Fury clings on in a clinch but one minute, forty-five seconds are still left on the clock.

The referee forces them to break. Fury has the audacity to put his hands behind his back again, but he then nails Wilder with an overhand right. Wilder, this time, is forced to hold on.

With a minute left, Fury takes charge. He throws more punches before Wilder resorts to another exhausted clinch. A right hand from Fury jolts him and then, in a blur, the last bell rings. Fury wheels away as he kisses the inside of his left glove. He then climbs the ropes in the corner and raises both hands. He sticks out his tongue and shakes his head vigorously.

The fighters come together in a long embrace and, with their heads touching gently, Fury speaks warmly. Wilder buries his face in the shoulder of The Gypsy King. He keeps nodding while rubbing Fury's back with his glove.

It's raw and intimate and so different from the ferocity of the fight. Only in boxing does pathos follow violence, and brutality melt into vulnerability.

They kiss each other on the cheek before Fury hollers at the camera. 'That's pay-per-view!'

Ricky Hatton cuts the wraps off Fury's bruised hands. 'What balls,' he says softly. 'How you got up, mate, to come back like you did ...'

Jimmy Lennon Jr takes the microphone. 'Ladies and gentlemen, after twelve rounds of action at the Staples Center, we have a split decision.' I take a deep breath of surprise. Wilder had knocked down Fury twice, once with terrifying force, but I'm still startled that a judge has scored the fight in his favour.

'Alejandro Rochin scores the bout 115 to 111 in favour of Deontay Wilder.'

The familiar old deflation of boxing descends, but Lennon Jr ploughs on. 'Robert Tapper scores the bout 114–112 in favour of Tyson Fury.'

Fury lifts his right arm and jogs on the spot. Wilder raises his left arm in hope.

Lennon then says in a velvety American drawl: 'Phil Edwards scores the bout 113 to 113 even ... A draw, *a split decision draw.*'

Fury shakes his head as the referee lifts his left arm, and Wilder's right.

Fuck. Only in boxing.

Fury is magnanimous. 'That man is a fearsome puncher, but the world knows I won. I hope I did you all proud after nearly three years out of the ring. I fought my heart out and we'll do the rematch. We are two great champions, the two best heavyweights on the planet.'

Wilder echoes him. 'We poured our hearts out tonight. I'm ready to do it again.'

At 6.15 a.m., in the wintry dawn, I switch off the television and walk slowly into the garden. The dank air is full of birdsong. It is as if, after such a war in the ring, and so much loss in my family, a few surviving birds celebrate our survival. I pause, look up and think of Heather as I see another kite, flying high and alone in a winter sky.

2

Loss, Again

On yet another flight back to Johannesburg, in mid-June 2019, memories of more traumatic journeys rose up. When my parents flew to London for the last time, exactly five years earlier, calamity struck. In the hours before landing, my dad could not hold a fork as he tried to eat breakfast on the plane. Even though he said he was just tired, his speech started to slur as I drove them home from Heathrow airport. The dread my mother and I felt, that he had suffered a stroke, was soon confirmed.

His next few weeks in hospital were among the most difficult of my life. There were deep concerns about his health, as well as paying the vast hospital bills as a South African visitor, but my dad lifted us with his capacity for hope. He worked hard with the occupational and speech therapists who taught him how to walk and talk again.

On his first morning out of hospital, I felt heartbroken as I helped my shuffling dad to the shower. He was hunched over, unable to stand on his own, and I could have cried when I saw how much he had been reduced. But as soon as I turned on the taps, and my dad felt the steaming water cascading down, he closed his eyes and let out a blissful sigh.

'Oh, boy,' he said softly, 'that's beautiful …'

Afterwards, as I towelled him down, Dad kept saying, with a slur, 'Beautiful … beautiful …'

Three years after Dad recovered from his stroke, in June 2017, the matron at my parents' care home called me in agitation. I needed to fly urgently to Johannesburg as she was concerned he could die within days.

When I walked into their room around nine o'clock the following morning, it took just one look to realise my mother was even worse. I rushed them to their cardiologist and, within two hours, my parents were both in intensive care at Milpark Hospital. Six days later, they were moved into a ward together. I took photos of them, smiling and sitting up weakly in adjoining beds. After more than sixty years of marriage, they still did everything together. This time, they shared heart failure and pneumonia.

When I returned to Johannesburg in June 2019, my second trip of the year, my mom was a shadow of the remarkable woman we so loved. As cancer took hold of Jess, we were relieved that her pain was dulled by increasing doses of morphine. But the medication robbed us of her wit and vitality. Jess could no longer talk much.

My father, Ian, had been a giant in South Africa and, in his role as the chief executive of Eskom, the state electricity supplier, he had gone against government policy under apartheid. He had slipped into the townships at night to meet with the then still-jailed Nelson Mandela's banned African National Congress to discuss bringing electricity into Black neighbourhoods. After Mandela's release, he had met the world's most famous former prisoner as they decided how best to turn his vision into reality.

Ian spread his 'Electricity for All' ambition into a plan that covered much of Africa. He had done great things and, in his retirement, his name still resounded as his old company had collapsed into chaos with constant power cuts. Eskom, beset by corruption and inefficiency, had become a national joke and a parody of the company he once led.

In the last weeks of my mother's life, all Ian's dwindling energy was used to care for her. When the pain was harsh, Jess would moan and reach out. Ian's hands would envelop hers. Eventually, the morphine worked its dark magic. Her cries would subside and her breathing slowed from a jittery rasp to a peaceful rhythm as sleep reclaimed her.

My dad could not find the same refuge. He lay in the dimly lit room, wondering how much more Jess would have to endure.

By the time I arrived at nine every morning, my dad would be in a terrible state. Yet, as soon as my mother groaned, he stretched out his hands and her pain softened.

He would get distressed if the nurses were delayed by other residents at the care home, which meant that they might be late in helping him shower or preparing Jess for bed. It was a test of my patience but it helped when my mother broke through her fog on the fourth evening – just as my usually calm dad was at his most fraught.

After the nurses had arrived, and he had been taken for his shower, my mother opened her eyes. She sat in her favourite chair in front of the television. Jess wore her blue dressing gown and normally, as the morphine lulled her towards sleep, she was very quiet. But after my fretful day with my dad, she turned to me.

'I feel for you,' she said in a ragged voice.

My lovely old mom was back, at least fleetingly. I smiled and said we would get Ian through this rough patch. She could not talk any more but I felt immensely moved.

Maybe she dug deep within herself that night and managed to soothe my dad. When I returned the following morning, there had been a change. Ian had finally had a decent sleep.

There was tenderness in our parting every night. After I kissed my mom, who had already been helped into bed by the nurse, I turned to my dad. I would remove his slippers and socks and lift his bare feet onto the bed. I would then pull the sheets and heavy winter blankets over him and tuck him up as if he was a huge baby rather than my incredible dad who had done so much in his life, and for me in mine.

'Be careful,' he always instructed me, as if we were back in those days when I used to work as an English teacher in Soweto in my early twenties and they worried endlessly about me.

As I walked away down the echoing corridor, I felt a bitter-sweet pain. Another day was over.

Boxing rescued me during those long winter nights in South Africa. I was back in the fight game. I wanted it to sweep me away from real life, and death.

Mainstream coverage was minimal, but I devoured my weekly copy of *Boxing News* and every day I crawled across fight websites like a punch-drunk social media slug. I used Twitter to keep up with the gossip. I checked *Boxing Scene*, *The Ring*, *Bad Left Hook*, *Boxing Social* and the rest. There were some writers I really liked, but the online coverage was swamped by clickbait and ingratiating videos. Still, I trawled through them.

I opened a 'Boxing Calendar' folder on my laptop. Documents organised by month were filled with daily jottings and links to boxers. I accumulated masses of information, most of it useless, as I decided who to track in the coming years. The best or most popular fighters – including Fury, Wilder, Anthony Joshua, Saúl 'Canelo' Álvarez, Terence Crawford, Naoya Inoue, Gervonta Davis and Oleksandr Usyk – were given separate folders.

I watched the fights on TV every weekend and, when it was a big promotion in the US, I got up in the dead of night. One early Sunday morning in April, I saw Crawford showcase his malicious brilliance as he dismantled Amir Khan in New York. The following month, Canelo Álvarez and Danny Jacobs fought a riveting battle as the Mexican won three of the four world middleweight belts in Las Vegas.

It made getting up at 3 a.m. seem logical rather than crazy, especially as Jacobs's courage shone through. The New York boxer had overcome a terminal illness after, in 2011, he had been diagnosed with osteosarcoma, a rare form of bone cancer. The tumour had wrapped itself around Jacobs's spine but hours of surgery and twenty-five rounds of radiation saved him.

Jacobs was called the Miracle Man; boxing dredged up miraculous stories. I needed its bewitching spell more than ever.

At my B&B near the care home, I kept reading and making fevered notes about boxing, updating my daily calendar religiously. Then, on 25 June 2019, Regis Prograis, the WBA junior-welterweight world champion, emailed me for the first time. He had started reading *Dark Trade* and he began a long email thread which he titled 'Introduction'.

I didn't really need an introduction to Prograis. I thought he was one of the most interesting and intelligent fighters in the US. He would soon get his own folder.

Fourteen years earlier, in August 2005, Prograis's life had changed forever when New Orleans was devastated by Hurricane Katrina. His family lost everything and he had to start a new life in Houston – where boxing became his salvation. As our emails flowed, I came to understand that Prograis reflected on the disaster in a positive way. 'It definitely forced me to grow up early and, looking back, it was the best thing that ever happened to me.'

'When Hurricane Betsy happened [in New Orleans in 1965], my grandma remembers her and her daddy getting round in boats. She said: "If it's going to be like that, we gotta go." We left for Houston the day before Katrina. It was a shock because that life in New Orleans was gone forever. We were seeing the hurricane on the news. Water was drowning the city. Where I lived in New Orleans was right next to a lake and you couldn't tell the difference. I knew we're never going back there again.'

Prograis lived and trained in Los Angeles in 2019, but his New Orleans roots ran deep. 'It's home,' he stressed. 'Where I come from, the people around you determine your success. When I was young, I always looked at rich people and thought: *I wanna have those things*. Katrina took away everything we had, and we did not have much, but as I get older, I realise it's the people that matter. It's the relationships you have, the love you have.

'I once looked at my grandparents as being unsuccessful. They had nothing and were real poor. She was a maid for twenty-five years. My grandpa worked two jobs for forty years. He was a janitor and worked on the garbage truck. At first, you think those are not good careers. But my grandma and grandpa succeeded in life because everybody loves them. My grandma talks to everybody. I'm a fighter but I try to be like that because it's the right way.'

Prograis was a thirty-year-old African American world champion on the rise. I was a fifty-eight-year-old white South African writer reeling in the dark. But I felt a connection. I looked at my parents the way he looked at his grandparents. My mother and father had achieved conventional success, but I felt their greatest achievement was that they were loved by so many people.

Prograis and I shared a mutual love of boxing and books. When his family moved to Houston, these became the cornerstones of his life. 'I was at a disadvantage because I started boxing late,' he explained. 'I had to catch up. And, for me, catching up was reading and studying. Everybody works hard in the gym. But what's the difference? For me, it's your mind.

'Mike Tyson was a student of the game. I thought: *I wanna do that*. So I watched thousands of fights of all the greatest fighters. I was also probably watching five hours of TV a day and I thought: *Damn, imagine if I read that much. Imagine how much I will know.* I started doing that. Of course, I don't read as much as I used to because I got two kids and I'm busy. But when I first started, I was reading six, seven hours a day. I lost myself in books.'

Talks had begun for Prograis to fight Josh Taylor, who came from just outside Edinburgh and was trained by Shane McGuigan and managed by my old friend Barry McGuigan. It promised a thrilling final to the World Boxing Super Series, a tournament set up with the specific goal of identifying the best junior-welterweight in the world. Taylor was the IBF champion and both he and Prograis had won two bouts each to make it to the WBSS final. Prograis was willing to travel to London and he instructed his promoter Lou DiBella to close the deal.

The prospect of being ringside for Taylor and Prograis in late October helped me look beyond death in the care home.

Patrick Day was about to fight again at the end of that week – in California on Friday 28 June 2019. He had only lost twice in twenty bouts and his story would soon consume me. I think, as time passed, I became fascinated with Pat Day because he didn't look or talk like an ordinary boxer. He also didn't have to fight professionally. His father was a doctor and his mother an administrator for the United Nations in New York.

His school grades were so good they called him 'Straight-A Day' and he then obtained an excellent college degree in nutrition. He was eloquent, good-looking and charismatic. Lou DiBella, who also promoted him, told me that Pat Day was the kind of young man you hoped your daughter would be lucky enough to marry one day.

He was also close friends with Danny Jacobs, the Miracle Man, who had overcome cancer to fight Canelo in one of boxing's biggest fights in 2019.

Pat came from a Haitian family in Long Island, New York, and his three brothers worked in accountancy, psychology and nursing. His parents had divorced when he was a kid, but his mom was the lynchpin and he still often saw his dad who drove him and his best friend, Patrick Aristhene, to tennis lessons when they were young. They tried out most games, but Pat did not shine in mainstream sports like basketball. There was no real flair to his play, but he was tenacious – which meant he was suited more to the solitude of boxing where resolve, grit and the ability to withstand pain matter so much.

The Days lived across the street from Joe Higgins, a former marine and firefighter who ran the local boxing gym. Higgins kept his garage doors open and Pat could see the heavy bag dangling from the rafters. When he was a skinny fourteen-year-old, Pat crossed over Buchanan Street and, out of curiosity, began hitting the bag. Higgins chided him – because he was slapping rather than punching. Pat and Patrick A soon joined Higgins at his Freeport PAL gym. The trainer promised Pat's mother, Lyssa, that her son would learn discipline and good habits as a boxer.

Lyssa hated violence, and disliked boxing, but she respected Higgins. He and his brother Tim had been among the first wave of firefighters who went into the burning Twin Towers on 9/11. Tim died, after he had saved many lives. Joe survived, but he carried the darkness of that horrific day in hidden corners of his mind.

At first the boys did not understand that Coach Joe was haunted by loss and grief. They just knew you never cursed or looked like a slob around him. They did not want to give the tough old fireman any cause to reprimand them. It was far better when he grunted 'Good ... real good!'

Every day, as soon as they got off the school bus, they raced home, changed into their boxing gear and ran to Coach Joe's house. The boys would wait for him outside and then the drive to the gym would be filled with boxing talk as they fired questions at Joe.

They revered Seanie Monaghan, a fighter from Long Beach who was eleven years older than them. The son of an Irish immigrant, Monaghan was Higgins's star boxer and chasing a world title shot. He came to boxing late but, as a pro, he racked up twenty-eight straight victories in front of a vociferous following. Seanie was their big brother.

Pat became a Golden Gloves champion, and Patrick A matched him, but there was no thought of following Seanie into the pros. The art of boxing, rather than the big money it promised, capti-vated Pat. He was a successful student and still wrote 'Straight-A Day' into his headgear and boxing boots. But nothing made him feel as alive as boxing. Nothing gave him a deeper sense of self-worth when, pushing through hurt and doubt, he became a national champion. He was named as a substitute in the US team for the 2012 Olympic Games. Although he didn't get to fight at the London Olympics, Pat's ambitions were stirred.

He turned pro and, with Coach Joe in his corner, made his debut in New York in January 2013. Pat stopped his opponent Zachariah Kelley in fifty-nine seconds. Patrick 'All' Day, as he called himself, was on his way. In his first two years as a super-welterweight, he fought ten times, winning nine and drawing once.

Pat knew how much his mother worried about him, but he was smitten with boxing. He wanted to eventually win a world title. Joe Higgins shared this dream for he believed in a kid who had never let him down. Pat had also dragged Joe away from memories of the burning Twin Towers by giving him fresh hope.

DiBella agreed to raise the stakes and, in January 2015, Pat was offered a fight against Alantez Fox, a hot prospect who remained unbeaten after fourteen bouts. Fox was dangerous and a concerned Patrick Aristhene felt the fight had come too soon for Pat – a neat and classy boxer who lacked a devastating punch.

In a gruelling contest over eight rounds in a Californian casino, one judge scored it a draw while the two other officials had Fox winning clearly. It was the unforgiving nature of professional boxing that a first loss usually meant that DiBella terminated his fighter's contract, but the promoter had a special bond with Pat and he considered Fox a world-class operator. He decided to retain Pat.

After winning his next two fights, Pat was given an easy runout against a Puerto Rican journeyman in November 2015; Carlos Garcia Hernandez had won only nine of his twenty-four bouts. Coach Joe instructed Pat to take a good look at Hernandez before he let his hands fly, but Pat was desperate for a stoppage win. He came out fast and, without his usual intelligence, left himself open. He was hurt after barely a minute. In his corner, while Hernandez threw busy flurries, Pat didn't punch back and the referee stopped the fight.

Unlike the loss to Fox, this was a humiliating defeat. DiBella decided to let Pat go. The words were never said out loud, but maybe it was time he used his college degree in the real world.

The boxer refused to believe he was done, even though he had been relegated to the B-side of future bouts. Pat won his next two difficult fights and agreed to take on a fast-rising prospect promoted by DiBella. Eric Walker had a perfect 15–0 record and was expected to win easily. But Pat was as tough as he was smart and he won the decision on all three cards in Uniondale on a sticky July night in 2017. It felt like he was back – and he and DiBella reunited.

He reeled off six consecutive victories, the last had been against another unbeaten fighter, Ismail Iliev, in February 2019. DiBella was not surprised. Pat was better than most fighters below the very highest level and he was tired of making just $15,000 for tough bouts. He wanted to reach contender status where he would be guaranteed at least fifty grand. But that sort of purse demanded he take on someone even more dangerous than Fox.

Pat was in Tokyo, earning decent money as a sparring partner to Ryota Murata, the former world middleweight champion, when the offer came in for a big fight. The only catch was that it was against Carlos Adames, an unbeaten boxer from the Dominican Republic. Adames was a big super-welter who hit extremely hard.

'What do you think, Joe?' DiBella asked when he spoke to Higgins.

'Pat can beat this guy,' the trainer said with his usual intensity.

Patrick Day would fight Carlos Adames at the Pechanga Resort and Casino in Temecula, California, on 28 June 2019.

Ryan Songalia had written on *The Ring* website that 'this kind of assignment against an unbeaten knockout puncher rated in the top ten by all four major sanctioning bodies is usually a dead end for a fighter on the B-side ... but the fight will be Day's third against an undefeated fighter over the past two years, as he tries to pull himself out of boxing's version of purgatory'.

Day sounded defiant. 'I used to dream of easy fights and an easy road to the top. But boxing is like life, and life is not supposed to be easy, whether you're a millionaire or just a middle-class or poor guy. You're gonna have adversity. I started out a prospect, then suffered two losses in a year and moved to the B-side. Now I'm ranked in the top fifteen of three of the organisations ... I love humbling these undefeated guys with the big egos who think they're invincible.'

He paused, and smiled. 'In life, nobody is invincible.'

When he was introduced in the ring, Patrick 'All' Day' rolled his shoulders, cupped both ears and raised a fist. Joe Higgins applauded him and removed Day's fluffy black tunic.

Across the ring, and supported by his celebrated trainer Robert Garcia and the former world lightweight champion Mikey Garcia, Adames was introduced as 'Caballo Bronco' – 'The Wild Horse'. He had won all seventeen of his fights; fourteen by knockout. A day earlier, Adames, who grew up in poverty in the Dominican Republic as one of thirty-five children sired by his father, had said that he was 'going to destroy Patrick Day. I am going to chop him up into little pieces.'

Day boxed beautifully in the opening round, winning it clearly behind his crisp jab and fast combinations. Adames, who started slowly, remained impassive. Day's craft and movement edged a few rounds, but The Wild Horse carried much more power. 'You've got to stay safe, Patrick Day,' the ESPN commentator Joe Tessitore warned.

The fight was delicately poised as they moved into the fifth round. Higgins encouraged Day to maintain his speed because Adames was intent on landing one crushing punch to end the fight. Robert Garcia told Adames he could not afford to give rounds away. He was so much stronger than Day and needed to use that power effectively.

'It's an interesting dynamic between Higgins and Patrick Day,' the journalist Mark Kriegel suggested on the ESPN broadcast. 'Day's dad works as an obstetrician and his mom at the United

Nations. Higgins said: "I had to tell his mother that everything is going to be fine. She was grilling me and making me nervous and I had to show that her son's going to learn from the sweet science.""

Day landed another precise combination to the body. He was still on course – as long as he could evade the hardest blows Adames threw with malevolent intent. Day was slick again in the sixth but, halfway through the round, Adames caught him with an overhand right. He backed away as the bigger fighter stalked him. Adames landed heavy punches. Day blocked some of them with his arms but he looked weary.

The ninth was a bad round for Day. Thudding right hands from Adames connected with damaging regularity and Day looked hurt on the ropes.

A minute into the tenth and last round, Day showed his courage and skill as he dug a left hook to the body. Tim Bradley, the former world champion on colour commentary duty with Kriegel, admired Day's tenacity. 'I love the will.'

Day swallowed successive overhand rights which rocked him. Forty seconds were left as one brutal punch after another sent Day reeling backwards. It seemed as if only the ropes were holding him up. In the last seconds of the fight, Adames kept punching ferociously and, at the bell, one final sickening blow almost dropped Day.

'Patrick Day survives and goes the distance, but Day nearly turned to night,' Tessitore yelped.

DiBella climbed into the ring to comfort Day before congratulating Adames, who won the fight 97–93 on two cards, with the third judge scoring it as a more lopsided 99–91.

'After the fight, Pat was very positive,' DiBella told me months later. 'He was disappointed he didn't win, but he knew he had put on a good performance against a top guy. Sometimes you lose and it's very solitary, but this was different. People wanted to take pictures of him and tell him how well he fought. Pat was clear-eyed and he didn't look beaten up. We hung out a while and I told him I wasn't going to release him. I told him I believed he would be able to get another opportunity at the top of the division, and still fulfil his dream of winning a world title.'

Two nights later, I flew back from Johannesburg to London. I hoped that, when I returned to South Africa in ten weeks, my mother would still be alive. My dad lifted me by reminding me that my mom had always loved the amaryllis plant which grew on the patio outside their sitting room. When the amaryllis burst open into a gorgeous red flower in early October 2018, a few weeks after Heather died, Jess called Ian to the window.

'No man could ever make something so beautiful,' my mom said as she pointed to the wonder of the amaryllis. She hoped she would see it flower again – a year later.

On 30 June 2019, my final evening of that long trip, Jess surprised me. My dad was being showered by the nurses and I always talked to her even though she could not respond easily. But this time, breaking her silence, she told me she loved me.

I knew it had taken a deep will for her to say those simple words. I told my mother that I loved her too. I reminded her that I would be back in time for Ian's ninetieth birthday on 24 September and that we would see the amaryllis bloom together.

Jess nodded, a faint smile crossing her lips, and then she closed her eyes to rest.

Many other fighters chased the same dream which drove Patrick Day. On Friday 19 July, two unbeaten boxers, Maxim Dadashev and Subriel Matias, fought each other on the outskirts of Washington DC.

Max Dadashev had been a successful boxer in Russia. He now wanted to become a world champion and gain US citizenship. He would then be able to bring his wife, Elizaveta, and their two-year-old son, Daniel, from St Petersburg to California. Dadashev would do anything, even risk his life, to fulfil that dream.

Matias was another dreamer. He saw boxing as a way out of pain and poverty. Before he fought Dadashev, Matias had spoken of how, as a boy, he had suffered in Maternillo, Puerto Rico. He had been bullied because he was darker than every other kid in their neighbourhood. He had also been in trouble in 2012 after he was shot in the back and the legs in a drug bust. Matias did time in jail on drug conspiracy charges. He could have avoided prison by divulging some names, but Matias wouldn't snitch on anyone.

He had turned his life around and only Dadashev blocked his path to a world title shot.

Matias always looked like he was winning a one-sided bout, but Dadashev kept trying to fight back bravely. By the end of the eleventh round, the Russian had taken 319 blows. The computer stats indicated that 260 were power punches. But the referee, Kenny Chevalier, made no move to end the slow beating.

It needed Buddy McGirt, the vastly experienced trainer in Dadashev's corner, to make a stand. 'I'm gonna stop it, Max,' McGirt said.

The fighter made a moan of dissent. A Russian cornerman pressed a sodden sponge against Dadashev's head.

'Please Max, please,' McGirt urged. 'Let me do this.'

Dadashev shook his head. McGirt turned to the ringside doctor. 'I'm gonna stop it, doc.'

He then turned to Chevalier and said 'That's it.'

Matias sank to the canvas. He was on his knees, his head raised in joy as he mouthed silent words of thanks.

Dadashev wanted to walk back to the dressing room. McGirt reached out a hand to steady his fighter. He helped Dadashev sit on the edge of the ring to rest. A minute later, with the trainer and the doctor supporting him, Dadashev tried again. It was no good.

The doctor called for a stretcher. They laid the fighter on it, but he began to vomit. McGirt used a white towel to catch the sick. When the towel sagged, they used a red bucket into which Dadashev vomited some more.

They moved quickly then. Within five minutes, the stricken fighter was in the back of an ambulance. Its siren screamed as it tore through the streets.

Dadashev slipped away into unconsciousness as the subdural haematoma swelled in his skull. His brain was bleeding.

The operation lasted two hours as surgeons cut away a portion of Dadashev's skull to relieve the pressure of the haematoma. The fighter remained in a coma for four days and then, on 23 July 2019, Maxim Dadashev slid away into death. He was just twenty-eight.

A second boxer died two days later. On 25 July, Hugo Santillán passed away in hospital after fighting Eduardo Abreu to a draw the previous night in Buenos Aires. Santillán, from Argentina, and Uruguay's Abreu had been fighting for a meaningless trinket called the WBC's Latino silver lightweight title. Santillán was just twenty-three.

Lou DiBella, who promoted both Regis Prograis and Patrick Day, tweeted that Santillán's demise was 'unacceptable, HAUNTING, and sickening to watch. This has been a terrible week. As a sport/industry, we have to look in the mirror . . . I have to look in the mirror.'

Maxim Dadashev and Hugo Santillán were dead but, rather than looking in the mirror, I prepared myself for a far more personal loss.

Exactly two weeks later, I was asleep on a Greek island when my phone rang at 6 a.m. on Thursday 8 August 2019. I was on holiday with Alison and the kids. My dad had insisted we take our vacation, but I called him every day and the news was not good. He had to stop me flying back to Johannesburg three nights earlier because he was not even sure Jess would know me. My dad said he would need me more when we arranged the funeral.

I got out of bed quickly to answer the phone. I heard my cousin Brian's voice in Johannesburg. I knew my mother had gone as soon as he said my name.

There was sadness, and grief, but my mother had died at ninety-one. She had lived a long and wonderful life. And so that evening, as the sun set in Lefkada, we celebrated an unforgettable and generous mother, mother-in-law and grand-mother. We had a barbecue and played some of our favourite songs. We laughed, and cried a little too, as we remembered the mighty Jess.

My dad was also free of bitterness and regret. When I arrived in Johannesburg, he told me that, the day after we lost Jess, he had been visited by Mildred Mngoma, one of the nursing sisters. Mildred explained that, a week earlier, she had brought my mother's morphine. She was startled by Jess's voice. It was frayed but quite loud.

'Thank you for looking after me so well,' my mother said.

When I asked Mildred about it, the striking word she used was 'fervour'. She said my mother had expressed her gratitude with such fervour.

I remembered how other Black nurses called my mother 'Queen' or, even more intimately, 'my sister'. This is how Jess made people feel. She carried that love and fervour inside her.

Those feelings helped me on the Friday morning of 16 August as I got up very early to write the eulogy that would be read at my mother's funeral that afternoon. I wrote about a photograph of her I have always loved. It is a black-and-white snapshot of the young Jess singing at the piano. She is surrounded by many male admirers. My dad is among them and he got lucky because my mom had already chosen him.

I also wrote about my mother as a feisty rebel. I explained how she had done great work in the dangerous township of Alexandra in the 1980s and '90s. She had such heart and years before, when apartheid was enshrined, she had stood up at a conservative power station in the Afrikaans heartlands where she and my dad gave out prizes at an Eskom function. Many of the power station staff were uncomfortable with Ian's policy of instigating multiracial evenings. The two racial groups sat apart, but Jess liked seeing the sea of Black and white faces.

A wave of white managers and engineers appeared on stage, beaming as Jess handed out their prizes. Near the end, the names of two women were announced. The first, a young Afrikaans woman, swapped handshakes with my mother, who pecked her on the cheek.

A middle-aged Black woman was then called to the stage. Jess smiled at the woman and stretched out her hand. The Black lady accepted her handshake and bowed her head. Jess had not planned anything, but instinct took over. As she had done with the Afrikaans lady, Jess leaned closer.

The silence thickened as people watched Jess McRae, the wife of Eskom's future chief executive, do something unthinkable.

She kissed a Black woman. Gasps echoed around the hall.

Later, Jess was cornered by an Eskom executive. 'Hell, Jess,' he said, 'why do you have to kiss that girl?'

'I think we should treat everyone the same,' my mother replied.

Decades later, my dad and I sat together at the funeral in a packed church that sunlit winter afternoon. We helped each other stay strong.

A couple of weeks before Jess died, Ian had heard that the lesion on his arm was cancerous. It was obvious to the oncologist that the cancer was spreading. But they could not know how far or how fast it had moved without surgery.

Ian was emphatic. Jess had only weeks to live and so he would not consider any form of treatment. My dad, at his age, also saw no need to cut out his cancer and delay the inevitable.

As we sat together after the funeral, my dad told me he would savour every day he had left. He already missed Jess terribly, but he could keep her alive in his head by remembering everything they had shared. It was easy for him to summon the memories whether they were from just weeks before, when she would call out his name and reach for his hand, or from six decades earlier when they had loved to dance on Saturday nights.

My dad looked over at me and smiled. It was hard, but we would go on.

A third boxing fatality in less than three months occurred in Albania. On 21 September 2019, a Bulgarian boxer, Boris Stanchov, died after fighting Ardit Murja the night before. Stanchov had been knocked down in the fifth round and then suffered a heart attack.

Amid such catastrophe, boxing was no longer a distraction from life or death.

'Hello, everybody,' Patrick Day said as he stood at the dais in Chicago on Thursday 10 October 2019. He wore a short-sleeved dark blue and green shirt with the lower half covered in thin white and blue hoops. He looked exactly like the man he had become – a charming and thoughtful twenty-seven-year-old college graduate with a ready smile. 'It's an honour to be here, in Chicago, the Windy City. You know, it's my first time here and it's beautiful. It looks a lot like New York, just less crowded. That caught me off guard.'

Day turned around to look at the fighters who shared the stage with him at their final press conference before they went to work that Saturday night at the Wintrust Arena in downtown Chicago. The bill was headed by Dmitry Bivol, the WBA world light-heavyweight champion, who would defend his title against Lenin Castillo. Bivol, a highly skilled Russian fighter, had been close to Max Dadashev. He was still reeling from the death of his friend.

Egis Klimas was also at the top table. Apart from managing Dadashev, Klimas also looked after Ukraine's Oleksandr Usyk, one of the best pound-for-pound fighters in the world. Usyk had made his name as the undisputed world cruiserweight champion when he became only the fourth man in modern boxing history to hold all four major titles – the IBF, WBA, WBC and WBO belts – at the same time. Only Bernard Hopkins, Jermain Taylor and Terence Crawford had done this before him. Usyk was about to make his heavyweight debut against Chazz Witherspoon. He dreamed of fighting Anthony Joshua and Tyson Fury.

Day nodded respectfully to Bivol and Usyk, as well as their opponents and the other fighters. There were eighteen of them, including Day. Sixteen were men and two, Jessica McCaskill and Erica Farias, were female boxers. 'Everybody here looks great,' Day said. 'I'm excited for this card. A lot of talent, so thank God we're all here, healthy, and God willing everyone makes weight tomorrow and we get to the arena safely and in one piece on Saturday.'

There was a slight pause as if Day might have been thinking of Max Dadashev, Hugo Santillán and Boris Stanchov. His family worried about the dangers of boxing and he and his eldest brother, Jean, had even stopped talking for a while after they argued about the threat of brain damage. But Pat was close to Jean and all his family; he understood their concern. He looked happy as he switched his attention back to boxing.

'I'm excited. I'm ready, physically, mentally, spiritually, emotionally, for my fight on Saturday against the undefeated Charles Conwell. It's going to be a great fight. I know he's ready, he's undefeated, he's an Olympian. He has a lot to prove. And so do I, at every fight. People look at me, and my demeanour, and they're like: "Oh, you're such a nice guy, well spoken, why do you choose to box?" But it's about what's in your heart eternally.' He touched the left side of his chest. 'I have a fighter's soul, a fighter's spirit, and I love this sport. Boxing makes me happy and that's why I choose to do it.'

Even the hard-bitten fighters were listening. Day spoke with a depth and sincerity which showed he had thought carefully about why he kept fighting, despite the jeopardy of the ring. So many people who heard him talk that day were spellbound. He looked and sounded different to everyone else. Day smiled again.

'We're going to go out there and have fun, box and do what we love to do. Hopefully you guys will enjoy the show that me and Charles are going to put on. It's going to be an entertaining fight. You don't want to miss it. And after that, you have all these great fighters here that are just gonna seal the deal. So God bless every-body. I'm looking forward to Saturday night. So see you then.'

Charles Conwell occupied a darker space. He spoke and smiled less while concentrating on everything he needed to do to beat Patrick Day. On his hotel room wall, he had pinned a piece of paper which said:

I WILL KO MY NEXT OPPONENT AND DOMINATE.

Conwell stuck that message above his bed before most fights and it served him well. He had won all ten of his pro bouts, seven of them by stoppage, and at twenty-one he was a rising force in the super-welterweight division. Conwell was the fifth of six sons and the first to show the aptitude needed to fulfil a father's dream.

Charles Conwell Sr, or Chuck as he was known, was a brickma-son in Cleveland Heights, Ohio, and he yearned to make his mark in boxing. He failed as a fighter but was determined to succeed as a coach. Chuck hung a heavy bag in the family living room, and another in the basement, so that his sons and other boys from the neighbourhood could learn to punch. A third bag dangled from a tree in the yard.

Charles Jr and his younger brother, Isiah, would sometimes be woken by their father before four in the morning and taken to a graveyard to run laps. The headlights of their dad's truck cut through the darkness of the cemetery.

Charles didn't like being pushed so hard, but he had talent and power. He began to win youth tournaments and climb the national rankings. He started to love boxing. Year after year, Charles kept improving and, eventually, he fought for the USA at the 2016 Olympic Games.

He made his professional debut in April 2017, aged nineteen, and his dad soon changed his nickname from 'The Body-Snatcher'. Charles 'Bad News' Conwell still had a hellhound on his trail. Even when Charles moved to Toledo to train with Otha Jones Jr, Chuck came to every fight.

The Atlantic reported that, after a bout which Charles had won without lighting up the ring, Chuck said to Jones: 'You gotta cattle-prod him, man. You gotta light a fire under this motherfucker's ass!'

Seeing his sombre son, Chuck turned back to Jones. He started laughing as he told the trainer: 'He's mad at you now. But if he wins, he'll love you later.'

In Chicago, Charles Conwell knew what he had to do to generate that love. He needed to beat Patrick Day – and knock him out. And so he said little when it was his turn to talk at the press conference. He would make his statement between the ropes.

The brooding menace of Conwell made a stark contrast with the sunshine of Day. They would meet in the ring in a little more than fifty-four hours. Time slowed for both young men.

Patrick Aristhene had a terrible dream the night before the fight. At home on Meister Square in Freeport, Long Island, in the house where he had lived almost all his life, the twenty-seven-year-old dreamed of his best friend, Pat Day, whose home was still on Buchanan Street, just around the corner. When they were boys, he could run to Pat D's house in seven seconds.

Their families had been close ever since the two Patricks were born in 1992. Pat D was an August baby, Patrick A was born in October. Both families came from Haiti and Patrick could not remember a day when Pat had not been at the heart of his life. The only time they had not lived four houses away from each other had been during college when Patrick spent just under three years in Philly. Pat stayed in Long Island and went to Nassau Community College before completing his degree online. But the two friends matched each other as they both studied public health, majoring in nutrition.

Patrick A always said, 'We're two peas in a pod.' But it was obvious to everyone else that Pat D was the optimist and Patrick A the realist. Patrick described Pat as 'pure-hearted' because he was always open and positive. When Patrick expressed scepticism about another person's attitude, Pat would invariably urge his friend to take another look. Sometimes Pat was right and Patrick would change his mind and agree that the person he had dismissed was not so bad.

It worked both ways. There were times when Patrick said, 'Pat, you gotta be careful. This guy is taking advantage of you.' Pat would step back and look at the situation and there were plenty of occasions when he said: 'You're right. I can't allow this to go on.'

They were proud that, in twenty-seven years, they had never had a serious argument. The closest they came to a scrap was when they squabbled over a seat on the bus to a kids' camp when they were seven years old. They hung out together, played and watched sport together, discovered boxing and became Golden Gloves champions together.

They were serious young African American men, proud of their Haitian heritage and families, and they were not shy in expressing their love for each other. Most weeks, whether they were saying goodbye in person, texting each other or talking on the phone, Pat and Patrick would say the same meaningful words. 'Appreciate you, man ... love you, bro.'

Pat was the smaller boxer, a welterweight compared to a light-heavyweight back when they were amateurs, but he took everything Patrick threw at him in sparring. And when he turned pro, the real grit of Pat Day became evident.

Protecting your zero, your undefeated record, was the best way to build you into a money-making prospect. But a loss turned you into damaged goods. It was different in other combat sports. In mixed martial arts, and especially the UFC (the lucrative Ultimate Fighting Championship), the aim was always to make the best fights. Some of the best UFC fighters had four or five losses. Such records were not seen as a weakness or lack of marketability.

That strategy was different to boxing where records were padded and the very best seldom fought each other. They held onto their meaningless titles given to them by rival sanctioning bodies because that's how everyone made money. Television bouts featured countless undefeated champions who were 15 and 0, or even 25 and 0, without being really tested.

It was tough for the defeated. Patrick saw how gruelling it became for Pat once a second loss sealed his place as 'an opponent' and he struggled to fight his way back onto the A-side. He became the boxer in the away locker room, the B-side guy who was meant to roll over when he stepped into the ring with some hot new talent backed by a big promoter.

After the heavy beating Pat suffered against Carlos Adames three-and-a-half months earlier, Patrick wished his friend could take a long break and come back again with a couple of easier opponents. But Pat and Coach Joe accepted the harsh business of boxing. If he was going to resume his climb up the rankings, Pat had to take the hard route.

There had been some respite at least, earlier that year, when Pat felt rejuvenated by the time he spent in Tokyo, working with a world champion in Ryota Murata. Pat fell for Japan. He loved the culture and the cuisine. He felt at peace.

Patrick remembered Pat glowing with health and happiness before the Adames fight. The only problem was that Coach Joe kept urging Pat to get back into the ring. Patrick and Sean Monaghan both felt that Joe was jealous and worried that he might lose Pat if he spent any more time out in Tokyo. There was pressure to take a big fight back in the US – even against a monster like Adames.

Pat was still full of hope. One night that summer, between the Adames and Conwell bouts, Patrick and Pat hung out in Freeport. 'Man, I wanna dance,' Pat said.

They headed to a bar in Rockville Centre, another town in Long Island. In Parlay, one of their favourite haunts, they soon met two beautiful girls and danced with them for hours. It was the last time they went out together before Pat headed into deep training for Charles Conwell.

Patrick was worried. 'This guy is real tough,' he warned Pat. 'Conwell looks a beast.'

'I know,' Pat said. 'But I can beat him.'

They were bolstered by the fact that Conwell had not looked great in his last fight against Courtney Pennington four months earlier. Pennington had survived the ten rounds and, while he won unanimously on points, Conwell had been less ferocious than normal.

In the week before the fight, they saw each other briefly. Pat was driving home and, as he turned onto Buchanan, he spotted Patrick on his lunch break from his job as a schoolteacher. 'Wass'up, man?' Pat shouted out as his car slowed to a stop. Patrick ran over and shook hands with the usual warmth. Pat was eating a prego wrap and Patrick laughed as he knew how much his friend loved Dominican food.

'Your weight must be good,' he said to Pat.

'The weight is great,' Pat said with his wide smile. 'I'm all set to put on a show in Chicago.'

Patrick reached out a hand to his friend. 'You look good, Pat,' he said.

'Love you, man,' Pat replied.

It was the last time that Patrick saw Pat before he fought Conwell on Saturday 12 October 2019. The fight must have been on his mind, troubling him, because Patrick dreamed of it that Friday night. It was a deeply unsettling nightmare.

In his dream, Patrick was at the back of the arena and the fight between Pat and Conwell had begun. Patrick could sense that someone was badly hurt. But he could not find a way through the heaving throng to reach ringside. He was blocked at every turn and then, suddenly, the awful end came in the third round. The horror of the crowd made him understand it was over.

Patrick cried out. 'Who won? Who won?'

Strange faces turned to him, grotesque and leering. 'Yo, he's knocked out cold!'

'*Who's knocked out?*' Patrick asked in his fevered dream. '*Who?*'

He felt a hand on his shoulder. Patrick spun around and a man with a blurred face said, 'Someone got knocked out bad. Real bad.'

'*Who did?*' Patrick pleaded. '*Who?*'

Patrick woke up then, sweating and agitated. He looked at his phone. It was after three in the morning. He sank back into his bed, full of dread for fight night.

Patrick A texted Pat D the next morning. He did not mention his dream. 'Hey man,' he typed. 'Would love to be in Chicago. I know you're gonna look great.'

The reply from Pat was fast. 'Appreciate you. Tonight I'm going to do my thing up there. Love you man.'

3

Night and Day

Patrick Aristhene felt a pain in his gut as the two fighters faced each other in Chicago. He was at home in Freeport when, on his television screen, the referee called Patrick Day and Charles Conwell together. Conwell was dressed in black while Pat's bright blue trunks were given another burst of colour by the band of red around the waist and down the sides. PAT was stitched in red, with DAY in gleaming white.

The previous night's bad dream fuelled Patrick's anxiety even though, at the start, Pat used his jab and looked calm. Conwell was the aggressor and it didn't take long for some of his punches to thud into Pat. They were hard blows, but he absorbed them without flinching.

Pat scored with combinations, but they made no visible impact on Conwell who stalked him implacably. The ache in Patrick A's stomach was at its most intense in the third, for this was the distressing round which haunted his dream.

Pat seemed unscathed as the round ended. Patrick breathed more easily. Nightmares were not real.

Towards the end of the fourth, there was a jolt when Conwell dropped Pat. But Patrick was reassured when his friend rose quickly from a flash knockdown. Pat stayed out of trouble the rest of the round. He just needed to get through the last six rounds. Patrick had given up all thoughts of Pat snatching the win to revive his career. Safety was everything.

The rounds passed slowly. Conwell was dominant but Pat kept moving and punching back.

Round eight began and Conwell closed the distance with suffocating intent. They stood toe to toe in the centre of the ring and Pat followed a left jab with a right cross that caught Conwell.

The time-keeper rapped the wooden clappers against each other to let the fighters know that ten seconds were left in the round. Conwell threw a sharp left followed by a straight right which landed flush on Pat's jaw. His head swivelled, his face distorted.

'Down goes Day!' the DAZN commentator Brian Kenny cried. It had been a heavy knockdown, but Pat looked alert while the referee counted. *'Six ... seven ...'*

'Are you good?' the ref asked after he had reached 'eight'.

'Yes,' Pat said.

'You want to continue?'

Pat nodded before, just when he needed it, the bell rang.

As Joe Higgins worked to revive Pat in the corner, Patrick A felt sick. 'It will be very hard for Patrick Day to recover from that,' Kenny suggested as the disturbing footage showed the full force of the blow. Pat's arms spread wide as he fell.

The ring card girl held up the placard for round nine. Joe told him to keep his guard tight and to give Conwell as many angles as he could.

Pat climbed wearily to his feet. As soon as Conwell moved with malice towards him, Pat's fighting guile kicked in again. He boxed steadily for the next three minutes.

Just before the last round, Joe put his hand on the back of Pat's damp neck. 'You good?'

'Yeah.'

Joe touched Pat's cheek, and then they parted.

Ninety seconds of the fight were left when Conwell let his fists fly. To stem the tide, Pat wrapped his arms around his opponent. Conwell wrestled with him, relying on his superior strength, and landed some cuffing overhand rights while they clinched like two drunken men at the end of a bad night.

They broke and Conwell threw a ferocious right uppercut on the inside which caught Pat flush on the chin. He was dazed, blinking and squinting as if trying to focus on Conwell. The referee Celestino Ruiz was poorly positioned and he could not move quickly enough to prevent Conwell landing a looping overhand right that hurt Pat badly. He staggered back in retreat. There was still time to stop the fight. But neither the referee nor the corner intervened.

Conwell came after him again, but missed with a straight right. But then, with Pat helpless and wide open, a devastating left hook smashed against his chin.

Pat's head smacked hard against the canvas and his arms floated down slowly. He looked as if he had been crucified as his eyes rolled back in a white glaze.

'There he goes down again,' Kenny shouted into his microphone. 'This time for good.'

Ruiz hunched over Pat's stricken body, opening his arms wide in a familiar gesture which meant *no more. Stop punching. Stop watching.*

Patrick A stared at the screen in horror. Pat's breathing looked ragged. His eyes were open, as was his mouth, but Pat was stretched on his back.

Conwell pummelled his chest in delight but an official sensed the gravity. 'Get away,' he shouted at Conwell. 'Get away from him.'

Patrick A felt frightened as he watched a medic try to remove the gumshield. Pat's right arm moved towards his mouth in an involuntary gesture of distress.

As the final punches played again in slow motion, Kenny said, 'Pray Patrick Day is OK as he is tended in the ring following this nasty knockout from Charles Conwell.'

'The paramedics have gone to get the gurney,' the former boxer Sergio Mora added ominously.

The camera cut away to a woman covering her mouth in shock. 'Obviously everyone in this crowd is concerned right now for Patrick Day,' said Kenny.

Four medics lifted Pat onto the stretcher. Patrick tried to calm himself by remembering how Curtis Stevens had been knocked out terribly by David Lemieux in 2017. He too had been put on a stretcher. But Stevens had regained consciousness on the gurney.

Patrick remembered how even Manny Pacquiao, one of boxing's greatest fighters, had been knocked cold by Juan Manuel Marquez in their fourth fight in December 2012. That punch was so ruinous that Manny fell face forward onto the canvas and didn't move for a very long time. But Manny fought eleven more times after that night. There was still hope.

Patrick tried to call Jean, Pat's eldest brother, but the line was busy. He phoned Coach Joe, but the call switched to voicemail. Patrick called Jean again but he was still engaged.

He could do little else but wait. He turned on a local TV channel. Twenty minutes passed and Patrick could not reach Jean or Joe.

Suddenly, the woman reading the news transfixed Patrick. She said Pat had been taken to hospital in Chicago. There were grave concerns following reports of a seizure.

Patrick thought of Adonis Stevenson who, in December 2018, had been knocked out savagely by Oleksandr Gvozdyk. Stevenson was nothing like Pat. He had been sentenced to four years of prison in Canada after being convicted of working as a violent pimp. Stevenson became a world champion who stopped many of his opponents. But the Gvozdyk fight left him with severe bleeding on the brain. Stevenson ended up in a coma for six months, in a critical condition and needing mechanical assistance to keep breathing. Eventually, Stevenson had begun to speak again and he was learning how to walk. His boxing career was obviously finished but, ten months on, he was still alive.

Stevenson was Haitian too. 'There's something in Haitian people that helps us pull through,' Patrick told himself. He picked up his phone again and, this time, he heard Jean's voice. 'It's bad, real bad,' Jean said with terrifying simplicity. 'We're going to Chicago.'

The next morning, after little sleep, Patrick flew to Chicago. By late afternoon, when he walked into the Northwestern Memorial Hospital room, an immense sadness swept over him.

Pat lay very still in his bed. A ventilator helped him breathe but his eyes were closed and a tube ran into his mouth. His skull was bandaged.

Patrick turned to Pat's parents. He held them and tried to find the right words. Coach Joe was next. His eyes were red with exhaustion and grief. Patrick heard later how, as Joe cried and said sorry to Pat's mother when she arrived at the hospital on Sunday morning, she had comforted him. Lyssa Day told Joe not to blame himself.

Patrick reached out to touch his friend. Pat's arm and chest still felt hard and muscled, but life had drained out of him. Brain death had already taken Pat away.

Conwell's punches had burst a blood vessel inside Pat's head. Blood filled the meninges, the three layers of filmy membrane which protect the brain and the spinal cord. As blood entered the brain, pressure had begun to build. The flow of oxygen weakened and Pat moved into the danger zone. The doctors in the ring had strapped an oxygen mask over his face, but the paramedics hit trouble as they carried him to the ambulance.

A seizure gripped Pat. As Joe watched helplessly, they had struggled to intubate him. The breathing tube would not fit into his twitching mouth. They kept trying even as the ambulance screamed its way towards the hospital. But they could not oxygenate Pat's brain and nearly thirty minutes passed before the doctors took over in hospital.

The surgeons operated with little hope. Even five minutes without a flow of oxygen to the brain can be catastrophic. They cut away a chunk of Pat's skull to lessen the pressure bearing down on his injured brain. But it was too late.

Joe Higgins had been through the trauma of 9/11, losing his brother Tim in one of the Twin Towers. They were both Brooklyn firefighters: Tim for Company 252 in Bushwick and Joe for Ladder 111 in Bedford-Stuyvesant. When the first plane hit Tower One, Tim had been among the initial wave of emergency responders at the World Trade Center. Joe's crew arrived soon afterwards, but the brothers never saw each other again. It would take many months before the charred remains of Tim's body were found. Other firefighters, and survivors, told Joe how Tim had saved up to twenty people that day.

'My brother was found on top of a civilian woman and we think he had been trying to save her,' Joe told the boxing writer Kevin Iole. Joe spent weeks at the smouldering wreckage, digging out bodies even as they buried the final hopes of families who had been praying that people they loved would, somehow, survive. 'You could see the metallic dust in the lights at night,' Higgins said. 'It was going right through our masks. You could taste it. It was killing me but I kept digging. Nothing could drag us out of that hole. We stayed to the very last day.'

The smoke and ash inhalation were so bad that Joe had two throat surgeries while struggling with various afflictions in his oesophagus. Friends and comrades died of cancer, while post-traumatic stress tore up the survivors' lives. Joe was in a very dark place when the teenage Pat Day crossed the street to hit the heavy bag in his garage.

Joe reacted gruffly at first to Pat and Patrick, but their enthusiasm and sincerity gradually softened him. Their devotion to boxing brought him peace.

'That kid from across the street,' Joe's wife, Jesse, told him, 'makes you feel better.'

Before Pat fought Carlos Adames earlier that summer, he had been interviewed on ESPN. The broadcast team, led by Mark

Kriegel, were fascinated by his background. Pat explained that his mother, who was fluent in French and Spanish, worked at the United Nations. His father had his own obstetrician and gynaecological practice in Brooklyn.

'I'm not the stereotypical boxer story,' Pat told ESPN. 'But I love to fight. What's in your heart doesn't depend on your socio-economic status. I need to be great at something. I cannot die and accomplish nothing.'

Kriegel asked Pat about his mother's views on boxing. 'She doesn't condone it,' he conceded.

Pat lay lifeless on his back as a machine helped him to breathe. Joe answered a text of condolence sent to him by Kriegel. 'I'm dying,' he wrote. 'I feel like I'm responsible, like I let him down. My special kid.'

Joe also told Kriegel that, 'Boxing sucks. It's a bloodsucker sport.'

He had asked his son Joe Jr and his assistant Sal Giovanniello, who helped him run the Freeport gym, to fly home from Chicago. He wanted Joe Jr and Sal to change the locks on the gym door. 'In honor of Patrick Day, no one's going to hit the last bag he hit, or spar in the last ring he sparred in,' Joe told Kriegel on Monday afternoon. 'I'm not even donating it. I'm never training another kid. I'm never going to put another kid in danger of a punch. Ever.'

Kriegel reminded him that boxing had saved so many young lives. 'Pat saved my life,' Joe said. 'Now I'm praying God saves his.'

There were no miracles left. On Wednesday 16 October, everyone who mattered – Pat's parents, his three brothers, his aunts, uncles, cousins and close friends – said goodbye to him.

Patrick Aristhene was among the very last. He was in pain, but he also felt grateful to have known Pat for twenty-seven years. As he sat at the bedside, his hands cupped Pat's left hand and he told his friend he appreciated and loved him.

'You hold it down on the other side and watch over everybody,' he said gently, 'and I'll hold it down this side 'til I see you again.'

They would soon switch off the machine. Pat's hospital room would fall silent. Patrick could see the real Pat so much more clearly in his head and so he did not look back. He closed the door behind him and went to find Pat's family.

Charles Conwell had needed stitches above his right eye after the fight. He felt no pain as the doctor sealed the cut. Charles just felt apprehension and guilt. When he got home to Cleveland the next day, his girlfriend tried to console him. She also tried to be practical and unpacked his belongings. When Charles saw his blood-flecked trunks and boxing gloves, he urged her to dispose of them.

He barely slept and his phone stayed on silent – and he only checked every now and then to see if there had been an update on Pat. He had no idea how to contact Pat's family and so, on Tuesday morning, he sat down to write an open letter:

'Dear Patrick Day, I never meant for this to happen for you. All I ever wanted to do was win. If I could take it all back I would. No one deserves for this to happen to them. I replay the fight over and over in my head thinking what if this never happened and why did it happen to you. I can't stop thinking about it myself. I prayed for you so many times and shedded so many tears because I couldn't even imagine how my family and friends would feel. I see you everywhere I go and all I hear is wonderful things about you. I thought about quitting boxing but I know that's not what you would want. I know that you were a fighter at heart so I decide to fight and win a world title because that's what you wanted and that's what I want so I'll use it as motivation every day and make sure I always leave it all in the ring every time. #ChampPatrickDay With Compassion, Charles Conwell.'

On a cloudy morning in England, I walked up the hill that leads from Canterbury West station to the University of Kent. The long hill felt endless as I thought about Patrick Day. There was little hope in the reports of his hospitalisation. I had never met the boxer, but his fate preoccupied me. I watched his claim to have 'a fighter's soul', from the press conference, again and again.

I knew I would stick to my habit. My excuse was that there were just eleven days left before Josh Taylor and Regis Prograis stepped into the ring for the best fight to be staged in Britain in 2019. The final of the World Boxing Super Series – a tournament featuring eight of the leading junior-welterweights in the world – would be a unification contest as Taylor held the IBF belt while Prograis was the WBA champion.

Death also hung over the Canterbury training camp of Taylor, a twenty-eight-year-old Scot who was managed and trained by Barry and Shane McGuigan. His fiancée Danielle's father, Jimmy Murphy, had died a month earlier. The loss of Danika McGuigan, Barry's daughter and Shane's sister, was still raw after the young actress had died on 23 July. Barry and I were friends and I knew how devastated he was by Danika's death.

Taylor was sharply aware of Day's fate. But he spoke initially of his bout against Prograis.

'It's hard to say this without sounding vicious, but you want to hurt him,' Taylor said when we sat down together at his training camp. 'You want to go in there and hit him as hard and as often as you can. But you hope you don't do any lasting damage.'

When I asked him about Day, Taylor said: 'I'm so sad for Patrick and his family. He's just a year younger than me. It shows how dangerous our sport can be.'

There was no point sanitising the truth. He and Prograis were intent on hurting each other and, if Taylor was to prevail, he would have to win a ferocious battle. Prograis had a perfect 24–0 record. Taylor had won all fifteen of his fights. They had both knocked out 80 per cent of their opponents.

Taylor's face clouded when he reflected on death in his own life. 'Jimmy was a good man and it's hard because I've not been able to grieve for him. It's the same for Shane and Barry because it was a real shock. Danika was a lovely girl. I can't imagine how it has been for Barry and [his wife] Sandra having to bury a child. I am using these memories to drive me on.'

*

On Wednesday 16 October 2019, the day after his social media post about Pat Day, Charles Conwell felt happy for the first time since he climbed the ropes to celebrate his victory. His girlfriend told him she was pregnant and Charles stopped thinking about Pat for a while. They went out that night, to the mall, and it was then that Charles heard the news.

Patrick Day had died earlier that afternoon.

'One more, one more,' Regis Prograis said urgently that same day as his grey T-shirt darkened with sweat. We were tucked away in a back room of the Peacock gym in east London. Prograis's face was hidden beneath the black headguard he wore on his last morning of sparring before, in ten days' time, he fought Josh Taylor.

I sat on a bench with Evins Tobler, a big man who was Prograis's strength and conditioning coach. 'Didn't he just say that two rounds ago?' Tobler asked. 'That's fourteen rounds so far.'

Fifteen rounds seemed an evocative way for an old-school boxing connoisseur like Prograis to end his preparations for a throwback fight. He had sparred against four different fighters who took turns to enter the ring with him for two or three rounds at a time. When he completed his fifteenth round, to sustained applause, his drenched T-shirt stuck to his skin.

But Prograis was on a loop. 'One more,' he repeated.

Bobby Benton, his trainer, looked at him carefully. 'One more?'

The buzzer sounded and Prograis turned back to the centre of the ring. A young featherweight, brought in at the end to sharpen the champion's speed, tore after him. Prograis knew that he couldn't punish a kid who was smaller than him and much less experienced. He concentrated on slipping punches, but his sweat left dark circles on the canvas.

Benton was adamant. 'That's it. Sixteen rounds is enough.'

After peeling off his sodden hand wraps and shirt, Prograis reached into his bag. 'I wanted to show you what I bought after we spoke the other day,' he told me in his New Orleans drawl. He held up a pristine copy of *Unbeaten*, Mike Stanton's biography of Rocky Marciano.

We were back on familiar territory – talking about books and boxing. I reminded Prograis that we were in the very gym where part of the last chapter of *Dark Trade* was set. It was in the Peacock that I saw Michael Watson walk again after he overcame the paralysis, following his bitter second fight with Chris Eubank, which had left him in a wheelchair.

'I've got Pat Day on my mind,' Prograis said. 'It's a tragedy, but I'm in too deep to walk away. I want to win this for Pat. We share a promoter in Lou DiBella – and Lou is in a bad way.'

Prograis was confident. 'Josh Taylor's the best in the world at 140 pounds after me. But it seems to me Taylor is more intimidated than I am. He knows I'm not scared of him.'

Did he feel any animosity towards Taylor? 'No. I don't have to be mad at them. Fighting is just something I love to do. But boxing is so hard. I read most of your books and there's so much death in boxing. You're so aware of it in this week of all weeks.'

They came in vast numbers to pay tribute and say goodbye to Patrick Day in Freeport on the Saturday morning of 26 October 2019. The line of people waiting to get into church snaked around the block. Patrick Aristhene walked past everyone, feeling the love and the grief, to join Pat's family at the front. He was grateful, but unsurprised, that so many people had come to honour Pat at his funeral.

Ten days had passed since Pat's death. Patrick had gone back to work the last few days, even though the temptation to stay in bed, and cry, felt overwhelming. Patrick was a schoolteacher and, had he chosen a different career, he would not have been able to get up. But he knew how much his kids at school needed him, just as he needed their positive energy to help him.

School also gave him a connection to Pat because his oldest friend had visited the kids exactly a year before. Pat brought in the

WBC Continental Americas Super-Welterweight belt he had won when beating Elvin Ayala at Madison Square Garden in October 2018. Patrick knew that the plethora of meaningless titles ruined much of professional boxing. But that morning in Freeport, at a high school full of kids denied the opportunities that he and Pat sometimes took for granted, Patrick saw how much that belt gave all his students who took turns to hold it.

They looked at Pat with big eyes as he told them that one day he would come back and show them a world title belt. Pat made them believe in him and, most of all, believe in themselves. Patrick knew he needed to keep going for their sake and in memory of Pat.

He found the strength to talk beautifully of Pat as he gave one of four eulogies that morning. Pat's three brothers – Jean, Bernard and Mike – all spoke powerfully. Boxing had killed their brother and they addressed the tragic waste of Pat's life.

Lou DiBella sat in church and felt that the anger and bitterness was justified. He knew why some of it was directed towards him. He had been Patrick Day's promoter. He was still Charles Conwell's promoter. Lou beat himself up because he wondered if he could have saved Pat. Maybe he should have refused to make the fight because he knew how hard Conwell punched? Perhaps he could have persuaded Pat to get out of boxing?

Two days earlier, Lou had been in London. Regis was about to face the most difficult fight of his life but, on Thursday afternoon, Lou said: 'I've got to get on a plane to New York tomorrow. I have to be there for Pat at his funeral.'

'Lou,' Regis said, 'I understand. It's important you go back for Pat.'

Lou felt deeply moved as he heard the stories of how Pat was a churchgoing kid who had even sung in the choir as a boy. The Day family would cling to their faith amid the wreckage.

His guts were ripped out as Lou listened. The beautiful yet harsh words felt appropriate. They were at the funeral of a bright and brilliant twenty-seven-year-old because of boxing.

O2 Arena, London, Saturday 26 October 2019

Two hours after the funeral, Michael Buffer stands in the middle of the ring. 'Ladies and gentlemen, this is the moment we've been waiting for,' he booms in his voice of honeyed gravitas. 'It's undefeated champion versus undefeated champion. Somebody's O has got to go, so let's get this party started!'

Apart from the ring, the O2 is dark. 'Coming to the ring first,' Buffer growls, 'he is the Tartan Tornado … *Josh Tayyy-lll-aaa-yyy-rrr*!'

After the roar of a sold-out crowd of 20,000 dies away, the giant video screen above the ring lights up. Images of Taylor smacking the pads held by Shane McGuigan are accompanied by the boxer's eerie cries. We're being sold a slick package of simmering violence and the O2 erupts as Taylor comes skipping down a long walkway to the thunderous sound of 'Step On' by Happy Mondays.

Inside the ring, Taylor fist-bumps Eddie Hearn. Two weeks earlier, Hearn had promoted Patrick Day. Boxing just keeps whirring, week after week, fighter after fighter.

The screen cuts to Regis Prograis. He wears the mask of the Rougarou, a mythical monster from Cajun folklore. The Rougarou is said to have the body of a man and the face of a monstrous wolf. Prograis's paternal grandmother came from a small town near the swamplands of deepest Louisiana where a strong belief in voodoo persists. The ferocious mask is topped by a Native American chief headdress, with red and white feathers, in another reminder of Prograis's heritage. His maternal grandfather, Clay, was Native American.

Prograis's six-year-old son, Ray, wears a replica Rougarou mask and little boxing trunks. A heavy rumble of booing reverberates as Buffer shouts, 'Now making his entrance to the ring … *Regis … Rougarouuu … Prograaaiiiisss!*'

A howling werewolf melts into the sound of Prograis's voice extolling his supremacy, which then fuses with Muhammad Ali proclaiming himself as the greatest of all time. Regis and Ray walk purposefully to the ring, an image of Ali resplendent on Prograis's white trunks.

Buffer is a week away from his seventy-fifth birthday and his battle cry sounds a little worn. But maybe I've just heard it a few hundred times too many. 'For the thousands in attendance and the millions watching around the world,' he croons. 'Ladies and gentlemen . . . *Let's Git Ready To Ruummmbbblllleeeeeeee . . .*'

The crowd still loves it.

Marcus McDonnell, the referee, brings the two fighters together. Holding each man by the wrist, McDonnell speaks in a London rush. 'I spoke to yer both in the dressing room. Yer know what I expect. Defend yerself at all times, obey my instructions, watch yer heads, and keep it clean. Let's go to work.'

They leave their corners, two feinting and weaving southpaws, their faces etched in concentration. Their mutual respect is plain and it takes a couple of minutes before the first serious punches land. A crisp Prograis jab is answered by two hard left hooks from Taylor. But Prograis counters immediately and he ends the round spearing accurate jabs into Taylor's face.

A swelling forms under Prograis's right eye while Taylor deftly uses his gloves to block most of the early shots from the American in round two. He also nails Prograis with his spiteful jab before he takes a jolting uppercut in return. Their shared technical excellence is obvious.

Prograis goes to the body in the third, but Taylor lands with enough force to cause blood to seep from his opponent's nose. In immediate response, Prograis pierces Taylor's defence with another left uppercut which rocks the Scot. As Taylor fires back, Prograis shows slick head movement and glides away. The round, shaded by Prograis, ends with Taylor on the offensive.

I am with Prograis. He is marginally ahead, but Taylor is an outstanding and fiery boxer.

Prograis's jab is a bludgeoning weapon and there is a swagger about his work as he sinks a blow into Taylor's gut. Taylor looks at his corner as if acknowledging he has been thrust into the toughest fight of his life so far. He lands a long left and then a solid body shot, but the fourth ends with Prograis cuffing him for his impudence. A clear Prograis round.

The momentum stays with the American as, in the ascendancy, he backs up Taylor. With less than a minute left in round five, an uppercut and a body shot hurt Taylor, but he fights back. Prograis, bobbing from the waist, evades most of the blows. Taylor still lands a left hook, and then another right, and fires one more punch after the bell rings. Bobby Benton crosses the ring to complain to McDonnell, but it is a sign that Taylor has started a dogfight.

'You've got to be a little more slick, son,' Benton says to Prograis.

An icy compress slows the swelling under Prograis's right eye while, in the opposite corner, Taylor sips from a bottle of water.

There is now more venom to Taylor's punching. He takes advantage of his long reach and, as blood trickles from Prograis's nose, Taylor shoves his shoulder into the American's face. McDonnell warns him, but he follows up with a couple of meaty right hooks. After his best round of the fight, Taylor raises his arm.

Taylor's work is even more intense when they resume and Prograis stands and trades. It makes for riveting viewing, but Prograis is being dragged into trench warfare. His right eye is more swollen and Taylor bangs his chest at the bell.

At the start of the eighth, Prograis is the busier fighter. His jab is again crisp and decisive as he backs up Taylor whose right eye also looks raw and puffy. But back comes Taylor, walking Prograis down with his superior strength. More blood runs from Prograis's nose but then, with sublime speed, he nails Taylor with a short left cross. It is a terrific punch, but Taylor absorbs it well. This is already an unforgettable fight.

Prograis's jab dictates the tempo of the next round until Taylor stops him in his tracks with an uppercut and a hook. The American dabs at the blood weeping from his nose and Taylor, shark-like,

NIGHT AND DAY | 67

attacks Prograis's body. Momentum has shifted and Prograis seems drained of energy.

In round ten, he still snaps out his excellent jab, but Taylor hurts him again. Prograis looks ragged as Taylor pours forward.

'How bad do you want this?' Benton asks Prograis before the eleventh.

Knowing he is now behind, Prograis comes out with renewed purpose, backing up Taylor and punishing him. Taylor's eye begins to close. Prograis's right eye is also a lumpy mess. A beautiful upper-cut snaps back Taylor's head before the Scot lands a left cross. It is the most gripping round of an exceptional fight and Prograis finishes it by pounding Taylor to the body.

McDonnell applauds the fighters as they come out for the final round. The O2 rises while Prograis and Taylor tap gloves and nod admiringly at each other. They go toe to toe again, one body punch following another. Prograis finishes like a train, steaming in with hooks and jabs. Taylor refuses to surrender to this ferocious last charge, even as Prograis clubs his head and body. With a minute left, Taylor tags Prograis with a hard left. It is just the prelude to a furious climax as both boxers leave everything in the ring. It is brutal yet thrilling and everyone is on their feet – including all of us in the normally jaded press row.

Shaking his head, as if refusing to lose, Prograis unleashes a final burst of punching in the last ten seconds. Rather than buckling, Taylor fires back before the bell rings. Taylor is still punching as the referee jumps between them. An epic, moving display of bravery and skill is over.

Shane McGuigan races into the ring to lift Taylor into the air as the Scot raises his right arm. Benton and Prograis do the same. When they are both back on the ground, the fighters embrace. It's a fleeting hug because Taylor and Prograis are too anxious about the result.

I hear the commentator Adam Smith's voice above the surrounding bedlam. 'Regis Prograis tragically lost his stablemate, Patrick

Day, and that's why his promoter Lou DiBella is not here tonight,' Smith explains on television. 'Patrick was laid to rest in America, and our thoughts continue to be with his family, and Regis managed to put on a performance like that. But has Josh Taylor done enough? Anxious wait at ringside. I think Michael Buffer has got the cards . . .'

Referee McDonnell, his shirt soaked with blood, holds both fighters by the wrist. Prograis lifts his right fist high in the air, while Taylor does the same with his left.

'Benoit Roussel scores it 114–114 even,' Buffer says. Prograis drops his arm in disappointment.

'Alfredo Polanco has it 115 to 113 and Matteo Montella scores it 117–112 to the winner by majority decision . . .'

Buffer pauses, dramatically, and Prograis raises his arm expectantly. The next cry decides it.

'The fighting pride of Scotland!' Buffer yells as Taylor slumps to his knees.

Barry McGuigan jumps up and down and punches the air while Buffer hollers *Josh Taylorrrrrrrrr!'* The winner's face is buried in the canvas as he sobs.

A few minutes later, having paid 'all respect to Regis Prograis . . . he's a great fighter,' Taylor tells Andy Clarke, the ringside interviewer, that he wants 'to dedicate this fight to my father-in-law who passed away on the 15th of September'. Taylor looks up, but his right eye is completely shut. 'Jimmy, that's for you, man. I know you were here. I love you.'

Prograis is moving in defeat, and I like him even more. 'It was a close fight and he was at home,' he says. 'But the better man won tonight, so that's cool. He won. I give no excuses. Thank ya all, England. I'll be back. I definitely enjoyed it. I'm pretty sure he enjoyed it too. It was one hell of a fight. Hopefully we come back for Part II and make twenty million dollars.'

Shane McGuigan admits it had been 'very close', but his mind soon turns to grief. 'It was a very emotional camp. I lost my sister in

July. Josh lost his father-in-law in September. We pulled each other through it. And it's moments like this that make it all worthwhile.'

Barry McGuigan is only three months older than me and, at the age of fifty-eight, he looks battle-worn when we embrace outside Taylor's dressing room. We speak more about his daughter Danika than the fight and then Barry asks me a question: 'How's Regis?'

'I'm just going to see him.'

'Send him my best,' Barry replies. 'He's an incredible fighter.'

Raquel Prograis, Regis's wife, and his mother stand in a corner of his dressing room. They are crying. It seems invasive to ask any questions.

I head to the bowels of the arena and wait. The Prograis family soon join me. There is no sign of Regis.

Then, slowly, the ambulance rolls towards us. Its blue lights flash in the dark.

I look at Benton. 'Bobby?' I say, the trainer's name sounding like an anxious question.

'I'll tell Regis you came to see him, Don,' the trainer says quietly. Two more cars, for Prograis's family and his cornermen, follow close behind the ambulance.

I watch the small convoy, led by the ambulance carrying Regis Prograis, as it snakes away into the night. All the earlier drama and exhilaration have gone. I stand alone on the kerb.

The ambulance gathers speed, its blue light blinking and turning. There is no screaming siren – just a haunting silence.

Just after twelve noon the next day, Regis Prograis sent me a message on WhatsApp. 'Hey Don,' he wrote, 'it was a close fight but I felt I had the lead early, then gave up some middle rounds, and then won the championship rounds. But I can't argue with the decision. He won the fight. My main thing was that I messed up and started to fight him in the middle rounds. He couldn't hurt me, so I was just taking his punches and thought he was going to get tired – but that was his fight. When I was being slick and boxing him, he couldn't touch me. And I hurt him a few times. But it's just another fight and learning experience. I'll be back.'

I was impressed all over again by Regis. His composure and intelligence were obvious and, even after being through a twelve-round war, he represented everything I admired most about fighters. Later that day, I saw images of him and Josh Taylor smiling into a phone together. They had bumped into each other in their hotel after Regis had been released from hospital. Big grins, swollen eyes, cuts and bruises, warm words and images of them together were posted on social media. Boxing could still be uplifting.

Fourteen days later, tragedy struck again. On 10 November, Dwight Ritchie, an Australian boxer known as The Fighting Cowboy, ended up in a Melbourne hospital after a sparring session against Michael Zerafa. He died from brain injuries that night.

Ritchie and Patrick Day had each campaigned in the super-welterweight division and both were twenty-seven when they lost their lives. The Australian had a decent record with nineteen wins and only two losses, but Day had fought at a higher level.

Three months earlier, Ritchie had offered a first-person account of how boxing had saved him. Unlike the college-educated Day, Ritchie believed he was nothing without boxing. 'If I wasn't a boxer, I'd be in jail. I only made it to Year Seven of school. I was in trouble growing up. I hated the world and blamed everyone else for my problems. But boxing changed me. If you can't motivate yourself when you're in the trenches in that ring, you've got nothing. I love that about boxing. From the moment I threw that first punch, I knew that's what I wanted to do.'

Dwight Ritchie, like Patrick Day, had loved boxing until it took his life.

4

The Boy from Brixton

I could defend boxing to people who demeaned it. It was easy to recount many examples of men and women whose lives would have been far worse if they had not found the discipline and hope of the sport. I could describe the intelligence and courage of boxers I knew and how they were often the most engaging of all sports people. I could point to how they used boxing to show others a way out of poverty and crime, abandonment and despair.

But, still, it was shocking that five fighters had died between 23 July and 10 November 2019. There had been one boxing death in 2016, two in 2017 and three in 2018. Five fatalities in 110 days averaged one ring death every twenty-two days and made me question myself all over again.

Then, on Thursday 14 November 2019, I met Isaac Chamberlain in Islington and everything changed. Chamberlain had once been an eleven-year-old drug runner in Brixton, ferrying cocaine, crack and heroin, but he was fast asleep when I arrived to interview him. He had flown in from Miami that morning.

Chamberlain was a cruiserweight and, apart from being in the division below the far more glamorous heavyweights, he was in a slump. He had last fought thirteen months before, in October 2018, when he beat a decent opponent in Luke Watkins to improve his record to 10–1. But that solitary loss haunted Chamberlain.

In February 2018, Chamberlain and Lawrence Okolie had head-lined the O2. In contrast to Regis Prograis and Josh Taylor, who were hardened world champions and the two best fighters in their division when they produced their majestic fight twenty months later, Chamberlain and Okolie were raw pros who had no business topping the bill at a formative stage of their careers. Chamberlain had won all nine of his bouts, while Okolie's record was a modest 7–0. The premise for their headlining double act, which Eddie Hearn promoted under the banner of 'British Beef', was that the two young Black London fighters were bitter rivals.

The manufactured drama could not prevent a stinker. Okolie won a wide decision on points, but his performance was not much better than Chamberlain's. A boring bout exposed how much they both needed to learn.

Maligned on social media, Chamberlain had retreated from the glare. Much of his time since then had been spent in obscurity in the US.

After thirty minutes, I thought I should see the snoozing young fighter. Quietly, I opened the door to a room in his sponsor's office in Islington. Chamberlain woke with a sleepy apology for keeping me waiting and, within minutes, he was alert and candid.

Brixton was not even six miles away but, as Chamberlain drew me back into his past, we moved into a totally different world full of uncertainty and strife for a small boy.

In a cramped flat deep inside one of the concrete blocks on the Loughborough Estate, less than a mile from Brixton station, Isaac would hear the key turn in the latch at night. The stumbling and cursing told him his dad was drunk again. He knew what was coming and, soon, the shouting would begin. His mother, who was only twenty-two, would send Isaac to his tiny room.

The five-year-old climbed into bed, pulled the covers over him and switched on his little Game Boy. He reached for the volume button so that he could muffle the sounds of his father hitting his mum. It was one of the formative memories of his childhood, but the repetitive pattern of domestic abuse became normalised.

The violence became even noisier as his mum always fought back. She had fast hands and power in each bunched fist. The heavy hitting sounded, to a tiny boy, like the *pow* and *ka-pow* of cartoon violence.

One day his father left the house and never came back. Isaac didn't see him again for years. His mum met a better man who eventually became Isaac's stepfather. But, for a long time, she struggled to feed the family. There would be many nights when there was nothing to eat and Isaac would think *It's sleep for dinner.*

He didn't complain. Even when he was woken in the middle of the night by his growling stomach, Isaac would just drink another couple of glasses of water. It was one way to try to fill himself up before he got a free school lunch the following day.

But he could not shut out the stress. Every day Isaac heard his mother on the phone as she spoke of her money worries. At least he could escape when he was out of the flat and on the street. From the estate, he would walk down Brixton Road and take a left on Atlantic before he hit Coldharbour Lane. It was hard to miss the dealers and the gangsters, blinged up, sitting on gleaming car bonnets or hanging out on a corner.

Some girls loved them because, with their chains and tattoos, their sharp gear and barely concealed knives, they carried a sense of danger and glamour. The dealers exuded a cool confidence that, to an introvert like Isaac, seemed alluring. They had power and money. It looked an irresistible combination to a shy boy.

Isaac yearned to buy a sparkling new pair of Nike Air Max or white Air Force trainers. He was sick of his run-down shoes that threatened to trip him up whenever he and friends ran from the Woolworths pick 'n' mix where they stole enough sweets to line their pockets.

Isaac eventually found the nerve to approach one of the gang-sters he knew from the estate. Looking like a hard man to Isaac, he was only nineteen or twenty. The young man stared at him with a dubious gaze. But Isaac spoke up. He wanted to work. He wanted to earn some money.

Isaac was asked his age and he added a year to say he was twelve. After he was grilled a little more, he was given a time and a side street where he should ride his bike later that evening. It was important he made sure no one was watching. If it was all clear, then he should ride slowly past the gangster and stretch out his hand as if saying hello. Everything centred on that fleeting touch of hands because it was then, in the moment, that he would be handed the stash.

The gangster gave Isaac the name of another street a five-minute ride away. Someone would be waiting and it was down to him to use the same hand trick and avoid drawing attention to their secret transaction. If all went to plan, they would pay him. But, if he fucked up, there would be hell to pay.

Isaac wanted to run. But he made himself saunter away, as if he was already a little gangster, the excitement rising inside him. He could feel the money in his hands. He could see the pair of white Air Max in his head. He could taste the sweetness of a new life.

The more he walked, the more confident he became. Isaac was being sucked in and he didn't care. He was sick of being hungry and lonely.

On a cool, grey evening Isaac rode his bike through the familiar streets. He turned the pedals with a steady rhythm, his eyes fixed on the road. Isaac's hoodie covered his head.

He came round the corner and the man was waiting. Isaac con-centrated hard and his bicycle only wobbled a little as he took his right hand off the handlebars. He got the timing just right. The gangster's hand briefly touched his own and Isaac closed his fingers around the packet.

There was a rush when he turned down an empty street. Stage one had been a breeze.

A few minutes later, he saw the user. He was tall and twitchy. Isaac cut his speed as the kid raised his hand. It looked like a wave but Isaac's right arm snaked out.

The kid's bony fingers closed around the packet and Isaac's hand felt suddenly empty and free. His legs turned the pedals a little faster and his face cracked open into a beautiful smile. He could do this. Soon, those trainers would be on his flying feet.

A few hours later, the gangster made him wait because he was cackling with his friends. Isaac kept his distance but, eventually, he was beckoned over with a nod. Isaac felt almost proud as the man told him he had done well and led him to a fast-food joint.

A few minutes later, he gave Isaac a greasy bag of fried chicken and chips. He also slipped him a note. Isaac looked down and saw £10. It wasn't much but, with the food, it was better than a pocket full of Woolworths sweets.

Isaac knew that it had started. He was on his way into a very different world.

Sometimes they paid him £20, but usually it was just a tenner with the chicken-and-chips thrown in as a bonus. 'Don't worry, you're going to get the big ones,' various dealers from the gang told him. They let him gaze at their chunky gold necklaces and bracelets and he couldn't stop himself smiling when they promised him: 'You can get this.'

But Isaac didn't trust them and he soon bought a knife. Everyone else working the streets carried far bigger knives. Any of them could come for him and so he kept it in his small bag as he rode from one deal to another. He was still too young to join a gang, but he yearned for the acceptance and the sense of belonging it would offer him.

His cousin, Alex Mulumba, was three years older. Alex's father, Kamondo, had left the Democratic Republic of the Congo for Britain, just like Isaac's parents, and settled in Brixton. Isaac turned twelve in March 2006 and, three months later, Alex completed his GCSE exams. Alex and two of his friends went out to celebrate one warm night that June.

As a member of Man Dem Crew, a gang of boys under the age of sixteen, Alex called himself Tiny Alien. His friends in the crew were Tooth, Smacks, S-Man, Drowzie and Stemz, and they set up a website. They tried to look hard in the photographs they posted because they were caught up in a beef with a crew from Kennington.

At around 11 p.m., Alex texted his dad to say he was about to catch the bus home but then, as they walked down Black Prince Road in Kennington, he and his friends were intercepted by ten kids from the rival gang. There was little they could do when a few of the Kennington kids ran into the adjoining Ethelred Estate to pick up baseball bats and knives.

Abu Sarpong, an eighteen-year-old from the Kennington estate, stabbed Alex with a kitchen knife. As blood ran from Alex's chest, the Kennington crew disappeared back into the estate or zigzagged down side streets to make their escape. It was left to Alex's friends to flag down a passing car and they were driven to St Thomas' Hospital. They managed to call his dad and Kamondo Mulumba arrived twenty minutes later to see his son on a ventilator. A nurse soon told him that Alex's heart had been fatally damaged and they could not save him.

It was a devastating loss and, on social media, Alex's dad posted a photograph taken shortly before his death. Alex had a tube running out of his mouth and his eyes were shut.

The case made national headlines and lurid stories were written in the tabloids. Sarpong was sentenced to life imprisonment, which meant a minimum of fourteen years in prison. The *Daily Mail* warned that 'the killing has raised searching questions about the involvement of ever-younger boys in violent gangs. Often lacking positive role models at home and adrift in a sub-culture built around instant gratification through drugs, sex and crime, it would appear that youngsters are being increasingly manipulated by older, more established criminal gangs.'

Isaac's mum knew she had to save him. Miguel's Boxing Gym, under the Railway Arches on Hardess Street, was less than half a mile from the Loughborough Estate. His mum didn't know much about boxing, except that it was a place for boys and men to pour out their aggression and troubles. Isaac was not an angry boy, but she was terrified that he would slip towards the same fate as Alex. Boxing, she hoped, would take him to a safer place.

When they walked into Miguel's, two men were punching each other in the ring. No one ran to break them apart and, instead, people shouted out encouragement and advice. Isaac couldn't believe it. Miguel's was mayhem but he loved it. He loved the sweaty gym walls and the rank smell of the joint. There were all kinds of characters lurking in the corners.

Isaac nodded when one of the trainers, having spoken to his mum, asked if he wanted to learn how to box. 'OK,' the man said, 'but you got to follow the rules.'

One of those rules meant that Isaac needed to earn the privilege of pulling on the gloves and then hitting the heavy black bag dangling from the rafters. Eventually he would get to spar in the ring but, first, he had to learn how to help out. He was sent across to Delroy Lewis, the Jamaican janitor, who kept the gym running.

Delroy inspected Isaac with military precision and gave him some tasks. Isaac was a keen worker, eager to impress, and he loved helping Delroy. He wiped the mirrors clean, rubbing away the clammy humidity that misted up the glass, and swept the gym and the ring. Isaac didn't mind picking up the damp, discarded hand wraps, while the pungent stench of the boxing gloves made him breathe more deeply as if it might help him absorb the strange essence of boxing.

The old janitor took a shine to him. He saw the goodness in Isaac and so Delroy sometimes paid him £5 for his work. Isaac would use the money to buy a tin of pilchards, a small brown loaf, chickpeas and a bottle of Lucozade. There was usually enough cash left for a KitKat Chunky which would complete the bonus meal he devoured.

Delroy also boosted him in a way no one had ever done before.

When it was Isaac's turn in the ring, he showed a natural athletic ability and resolve. Carly Carew, Isaac's first trainer at Miguel's, shouted a lot, but Delroy could see that Isaac bloomed when he was praised. The novelty of kindness lifted him. His face broke into a proud smile and he tried even harder.

Eventually, Isaac stepped into the ring with a kid who had been at the gym for months. When Isaac was punched, a white flash went off in his head, but it just made him more determined. He started punching back and wouldn't stop until the buzzer reverberated. Of course, he needed to learn how to pace his attacks and, most important of all, defend himself. But Delroy loved his courage and spirit. The janitor had been part of Miguel's a very long time and seen young amateurs like Richard Williams, Keith Long and Danny Williams become successful pros. Delroy thought Isaac had more talent than all of them.

He began to talk more and more to Isaac who revelled in the attention. Delroy would pick him up from school so that they could begin working early at the gym. Some mornings he would take Isaac running in Camberwell. Isaac would hear scornful voices telling Delroy that he was wasting his time. So many people refused to believe Isaac would amount to much in life, but Delroy was different. He saw vast potential in Isaac.

'You have a hard road ahead of you, Isaac,' Delroy said, 'but you can be one of the best if you keep working.'

Isaac looked at Delroy in disbelief. No one had ever said such words to him before. 'You think so, boss?'

'I know so,' Delroy responded and then, because he was a gruff former military man, the janitor gave Isaac another task and shut down any more talk.

Isaac thrived at Miguel's, but he was yet to escape the clutches of the gangsters. His knife was gone because his stepfather had thrown it away, warning him to never bring another weapon into his mum's flat. But the kings of the street still used him. Even though Isaac didn't spend much time riding around Brixton on his bike after he found boxing, they still had his number. They messaged whenever they had a job for him and, while Isaac didn't respond every time, he couldn't always resist. He kept doing the odd run and drop once boxing was over for the day. But he made sure his drug work and boxing stayed separate. Isaac knew Delroy would be furious if he found out.

He kept out of trouble until he was fourteen and he and his friend did a job together. It was on the fringes of Kennington and, after the drop-off, they caught the number 133 bus back to Brixton. Isaac hid the remaining stash inside his trousers and they sat on the top floor of the bus home. But he turned cold when they got off and saw that the police had begun a stop-and-search near his estate in Brixton. They were intent on nailing the Black kids, as always, but Isaac could think only of the prison cell that would be waiting if they found the coke on him.

Isaac's friend whispered that they should walk the other way. But a policeman shouted 'Stop!'

Isaac ran harder and faster than he had ever run before, the street beneath his feet a concrete blur as he hurtled away. People stared at him in shock, but they all made sure to get out of his way. Isaac did not dare look back, but he could imagine a line of burly white policemen coming closer and so he kept running though the estate across the road. He said later that he felt like he ran faster than Usain Bolt but, in his terror, it seemed as if his heart might burst. But he kept going, faster and harder still, his heart hammering in the cage of his chest like a trapped bird.

It was only when he reached the other side of the estate that he looked back. There was pure relief then. He had outrun them. But he still had to get rid of the coke and so Isaac headed to his friend's home, slowing to a walk. It was a struggle to control his jagged breathing as sweat rolled down his face.

Isaac was inside the flat and in his friend's small bedroom when he reached for the coke. 'I'm not doing this no more,' he said as he handed it over.

'C'mon, man,' his friend urged, 'we'll deliver it together.'

'No, bro,' Isaac said angrily. 'I'm done.'

He left quickly and made his way home. The little flat was empty and Isaac closed the bathroom door behind him. He felt like sobbing as he stood under the steaming shower. Tears ran down his face, lost in the cascading water, and it took a while before he looked down at his legs. They were coated in white streaks of powder. Isaac washed himself, slowly and methodically, making sure that every last bit of cocaine disappeared down the swirling plug hole.

Boxing would help him get out of that world. Boxing would become his life.

The gangsters kept calling him. They left texts and voicemails urging Isaac to make contact. He wasn't scared of them, but he feared losing the support of Delroy and everyone at Miguel's. And so, a few days later, Isaac took the sim card out of his mobile phone. He cut the little gold card into miniscule pieces, breaking the hold the gangsters had over him.

Isaac felt a surging freedom as he swept the fragments of the phone card into the bin. He left the flat five minutes later, his gym bag slung over his shoulder, and made the short walk to Miguel's and his new life as a boxer.

Soon after five o'clock on Tuesday morning, 19 November 2019, Isaac Chamberlain sat alone in an apartment in Sutton, on the suburban fringes of London. After another restless night, the distressing thoughts took hold of him again. He was still haunted by the pain of losing to Lawrence Okolie twenty-one months before. Chamberlain had not fought for over a year. The usual complications of boxing dragged him down.

The twenty-five-year-old reached for his phone and opened up WhatsApp. He began typing a long message to me. The first word he wrote was *Hell*.

Chamberlain was working with new trainers, Jorge Rubio in Miami and Angel Fernandez in London, and the powerful if mysterious American promoter Al Haymon was also interested in him. So much was happening – but hardly anyone knew what he was doing.

Until he could get back in the ring, he was locked inside a seemingly endless limbo. Chamberlain's words in his text were dark and heavy but they still flowed.

'Hell is a perception. Or perhaps it's a nightmare. For some people fighting is hell. For me, inactivity has caused me more depression and made me drown in my own perception of hell. I'm not talking about the physical and all you can see. I'm talking about something much more detrimental and lingering. The hell in your mind. I honestly can't stand the quiet whistling sound that I hear, when it's silent in my room and it's pitch black, as I'm writing this at 5.18 a.m. The hell of inactivity has taken its toll and I'm tired of hearing the fake promises from promoters. I get through my days by living a third-person view, as if I'm at the cinema watching myself. I wonder if the demons in my mind have been staring at me this whole time.'

Waking at 6 a.m. and reading his message, I was worried about Isaac. I replied and we agreed that we should meet again.

A couple of days later, the seemingly tormented man who texted me had changed. 'It's better to express the feelings you have in those dark moments, rather than bottling them up,' Chamberlain said calmly in his apartment. 'I feel better when I write everything down.'

At his training camp in Miami, conditions had been so barren that, without any Wi-Fi, he simply worked, read, wrote and slept on a tiny bed, which eventually collapsed and left him with just a mattress. We discussed whether to share his writing in my first article about him.

'Tell everyone the whole story, boss,' Chamberlain urged.

I asked if he recognised the Brixton of his youth whenever he went back home. 'No. It's totally gentrified. Brixton has changed big time. Everyone's in jail.'

His mother was seventeen when she gave birth to him. Life was not easy but now, Chamberlain said, 'I'm always speaking to my mum. No one's going to love you like your mother.'

What about his dad? 'What's dat?' he said with a wry smile. 'There's no dad here. My stepdad is the legal guy.'

Chamberlain made his pro debut in late January 2015, but he had shared serious sparring sessions with Deontay Wilder who was a seasoned 32–0 heavyweight then. It must have been daunting, as a novice cruiserweight, to face the man who would become the WBC world heavyweight champion that month.

'I was ready, bro,' Chamberlain said. 'I saw him knock out lots of guys in the gym before I stepped in. The first time I sparred him, I did so well they changed their plans. The next day they said to the other sparring partners: "We're only using Isaac today."'

Did he taste Wilder's power? Chamberlain winces. 'Bro, that power! I sparred Anthony Joshua too and they have different kinds of power. Joshua is like a sledgehammer hitting you. And jabbing his body was like jabbing the wall. Wilder is more lethal – like a sniper. But I used my speed against Wilder. Going in and out with my footwork, using angles. Before the second session, they'd studied me because they had recorded the first spar. I'm trying to fake down low and go up. He would go down low to get me and I would catch him. The second time he stepped back and then, bam, nailed me with this uppercut.'

Chamberlain smacked his fist into his open hand and threw back his head. His eyes widened. 'I thought I was back in London! I don't know how I stayed up on my feet.'

Chamberlain had already proved his courage. In only his sixth pro fight, in September 2016, he faced the experienced Wadi Camacho, a Spanish-born British cruiserweight. It was a real test for a twenty-two-year-old and his task seemed almost impossible when he dislocated his shoulder in the third round. He refused to quit and, instead, insisted that his trainer, his uncle Ted Bami, should try to work his right arm back into its shoulder socket. Chamberlain's grit helped him win a brutal fight over ten rounds. It was British boxing's fight of the year.

'When I threw that big right hand, I did it with such force. The sweat was flying and it slid off his head and my shoulder popped. The pain was disgusting. He came rushing at me and I couldn't lift my arm. I'm clinching, moving my head, thinking: "Why me? I worked so hard for this big chance." And then midway through the fight I think *I ain't losing. Use the jab. Fucking win this.*

'All the time, in the corner, I'm telling my uncle to work the shoulder back into the socket. I'm telling the officials: "I'm OK." People were screaming: "Pull him out. We'll get a rematch." I said: "Bollocks. You ain't stopping it." I don't know what the hell came over me. He nailed me with some big shots, but you have to accept the consequences. I only forced myself to use my right arm again when they said they would stop it if I kept it down. I just placed my arm, rather than punched with it, and the pain was excruciating. He was looking at me like: "This guy is fucking insane." He had more knockouts than I'd had fights, but you can't measure my heart.'

That fire and resolve were strangely missing from the most important fight of his career against Okolie. 'I had my best sparring session two weeks before,' he remembered. 'I felt amazing. I should have tailed off my training then because I was ready, but my Uncle Ted kept flogging me.'

Ted Bami fled war in the Congo and arrived in London aged twelve. He had eventually become a pro boxer who won the European light-welterweight title in 2006. But he was dogmatic with his nephew, causing Isaac to complain. 'I was running eight miles in the morning and sparring after that. I was telling Ted, "Listen, I'm tired." He was like, "Nah, that's part of the process." I trusted his experience instead of my own body.

'On the day of the fight, I'm looking outside the window and seeing big posters of me headlining the O2. I was like, "I did this. Shit." I hadn't slept much and I didn't feel in control. There were so many people around me and they're all on Snapchat. "Yo, I'm with the champ!" I should've been more selfish and gone: "Fuck off. I'm the one going in there."'

Chamberlain had sent me a selection of photographs. One captured the young boxer sitting alone that night in his dressing room, hood up, hands tucked in his pockets. He added a message: *'This picture affects me the most. The changing room as soon as I arrived to the O2 for the Okolie fight. You could see my head was filled with everyone else's thoughts. A young man that has just turned 23. Such a weird feeling that I'll never want to experience again.'*

He shook his head. 'I was there, but I wasn't there,' he said simply. 'My uncle was bragging to his friends: "Hey, look, my nephew headlining the O2 and I got him here." He had his son playing table tennis in the changing room, bouncing the ball everywhere. How the hell can I focus? When the Sky cameras came in before the fight, everyone's walking behind me so they can get spotted on TV. Warming up, I'm cold and nervous. Then, walking to the ring, there is so much heat, noise and light. All you see is phone lights and I'm preparing for war in front of 12,000 people. It's rocking – and then the fight happened.'

Chamberlain was knocked down in the first round but, most of the time, he and the notoriously awkward Okolie clinched and grappled. The let-down after the massive build-up was painful – with Chamberlain's hurt magnified by defeat. 'I was in shock. Everything I've worked my whole life for and did this really happen? All the people in the changing room before the fight had gone. Fighters like Tony Bellew and Johnny Nelson came to see me afterwards. My uncle said: "That was all on you. I gave you all that training blah-blah-blah." Bellew said: "What the fuck is wrong with this guy? Why the hell would you say anything like that?" He could see I was so hurt. I was fighting back tears.

'The next day I booked a flight to New York. I just wanted to go where I didn't have to see nobody. Ted said he would make sure the money went into his account and he'd pay everyone. He would give my money to my mother. Once I'm in New York, I'm hearing there are arguments and I ask: "Mum, what's going on?" Ted gave her much less money than I was due and so my mum said to Ted:

"Where's the receipt?" He goes: "You should learn to trust me as his uncle." We knew something was up.'

When Chamberlain returned home, he confronted his uncle. After Ted denied any wrongdoing, the boxer and his mother obtained the receipts from Eddie Hearn's office at Matchroom Boxing. Chamberlain said: 'He never gave it back, but he admitted to us he had to pay his mortgage. He's so sorry, blah blah blah. Crocodile tears. But he told the British Boxing Board he never done it. He made up all these expenses.'

Ted declared his innocence and refused to terminate their contract. Chamberlain shrugged. 'It runs out next year. That's one of the reasons why I won't fight at home until the contract ends.'

He had become more vigilant and refused contracts with American promoters because the deals were slanted against him. 'Don King would rob you straight,' Chamberlain said with a bleak laugh. 'He might get five million but at least he will make you a millionaire. I'm tired of the way these promoters use you as their pawn. You end up with no money and brain damage.'

Chamberlain was about to return to Miami for another long training camp the following week. He did not look like a man who had been to hell and back. He looked like a young fighter who was ready to start all over again, in a new country and a new decade.

On the train back into central London, leaving the quiet of Sutton, I scrolled through the photos he had sent me. I paused at the image of Isaac as an eleven-year-old boy and read his words:

'Me as a young kid from Brixton. I had no confidence but I was a big dreamer. I wanted to be someone. The trials and tribulations, and constant failures, built my character. They made me think I can do this and I can do anything – because I've been through the worst.'

As the train clattered down the track on a dark and freezing November night, my concern for Isaac Chamberlain gave way to real hope. The boy in the photo had been dragged down into running drugs. Boxing helped him find a way out. Now, all these years later, he had survived the dark times. I remembered what he had said an hour earlier. 'I'm still that kid but the nightmare's over. I battled doubt and depression. But I faced it down, bro. I looked into my soul and I've come out stronger. I cannot wait to show that belief in the ring in America next year. It's a new start. It's a new me.'

Three weeks later, on 11 December, Chamberlain sent me a photo of a stark room. 'We go again. I'm in Miami, 5,000 miles from home. Away from friends, family and loved ones. Alone. Rottweilers are barking outside. The dawn quickly turns to darkness and reality sets in.'

5

Long Island Blues and Las Vegas Highs

Across the street from Madison Square Garden, in the lonely blur of Penn station's morning rush-hour, memories of Patrick Day returned. In October 2018, Pat had outclassed Elvin Ayala in the small theatre at the Garden. Less than a year later, they switched off the machines keeping him alive.

Perhaps my own grief made me think so often about Pat and those he left behind. I had told my parents how much I loved them but, apart from our final afternoon in hospital, I had not said the same to Heather. Much remained unresolved. Her relationship with our parents had become complex as illness got in the way, and she found it difficult to stay in regular contact with them on the phone. She had not been well enough to travel and so I was the one who flew three times a year to South Africa. I got the chance to say a long goodbye to my mother and my father – but not to my sister.

I yearned to go back, just for a day, to the life Heather and I had once shared in South Africa, when we were so close. It was a futile longing because Heather was gone. And so I clung even more tightly to boxing, with its primal force and tragic consequences.

I wanted to meet some of the people who had loved Pat. I also wanted to hear why Pat loved boxing as a way of helping me understand why I remained locked inside the business which had killed him.

I travelled first to Sea Cliff to interview Lou DiBella, his promoter. A Harvard Law School graduate, DiBella had been in boxing for thirty years. But ten weeks since the tragic fight between Pat and Charles Conwell, whom he also promoted, DiBella looked shaken. We spoke for two hours as DiBella raged against boxing.

'Patrick was not your usual prize fighter,' he recalled. 'He was a good-looking, eloquent kid with a big smile. He was always thoughtful and you could talk to Pat about anything. He had a tremendous sense of humour and a fertile mind. He could have done anything.'

Pat's tragedy was that he fell for boxing. 'He loved boxing and that's how he touched people. Pat was one of those guys that, between fights, he was in the ring a lot, sparring. I'm sure the sparring was controlled but you're still jolting your head around and getting hit.'

DiBella paused. 'Sometimes,' he eventually added, 'what we love isn't good for us.'

The promoter's ambivalent relationship with boxing tormented him. 'Many more people have been saved by boxing than ruined by it,' he said. 'But boxing is unforgiving. You play other sports, but you don't play boxing. You can have a terrible year on the football pitch, and the next year still come back a multimillionaire and revive your career. You could have ten bad seconds in the ring and your life can be ruined.'

DiBella explained that, 'in my contracts, if my fighter loses I can release him. It sounds cold but that's actually for the good of the fighter. You go from being a prospect to an opponent very quickly. People are hitting you in the head so you're not getting healthier fighting.'

He and Pat parted ways after the fighter's second loss. Pat's family and friends believed that, without the protection of a promoter, he was condemned to the B-side of every bill and forced to fight repeatedly against A-side prospects. He won a string of grinding contests. but there was little respite even when DiBella re-signed him.

'I liked the kid,' DiBella said, 'and it was clear he would fight whether I wanted him to or not. He had won some fights in a row and I thought I could get him another opportunity. The money wasn't very good and I was putting him in fights that were tough but not like King Kong fights. We were continuing his assessment.

'Pat came to see me. His mother didn't want him to fight and he said: "I'm making $10,000 a fight. You've got to get me bigger fights." I believed in him so I got him the Carlos Adames fight. Adames is a big puncher, very physically strong, but Pat and Joe Higgins were very confident. I never wanted Pat to become a perennial B-side. There's no money or future in that. Only risk.'

Adames proved to be a damaging opponent but, five-and-a-half months later, DiBella insisted that, 'two thirds of the way through, it was still anybody's fight. In the last few rounds, Adames wore Pat down and his strength took over. Pat lost, but the fight had lots of positive attention and it was nationally televised on ESPN. I told Pat I wasn't going to release him. Almost immediately, the pressure was on from Pat and Joe to get him another big fight.'

DiBella arranged for Pat to fight Conwell at Madison Square Garden on the undercard of a Gennadiy Golovkin bill. But promotional rivalries broke out and, according to DiBella, 'they tried to bully me. I made a deal and the kid was supposed to be on the New York card – fighting in his own backyard. But they were mean-spirited toward me and Pat's fight with Conwell got moved to Chicago, where it didn't belong.

'Conwell was a huge prospect, an Olympian, but I didn't anticipate a one-sided fight. I thought I was doing a good turn for Pat and that's weighed on my mind because he died in the match I made.

I don't feel responsible for his death but, on a human level, I still feel guilty.'

DiBella watched the fight on television, in the very room where we sat. 'By round nine, it was clear he'd lost the fight. I still thought: *The fight's going ten rounds, and Pat's going to lose 7–3. I wonder what's next for Pat?* This is one of the ironies of boxing. You'd think tragedies happen in mismatched fights, the ones where the B-side guy has no chance. But most of the fights where someone is hurt are the see-sawing battles, or the fight where the guy that gets beaten is still a top professional, able to defend himself and take punishment. It's the battles of attrition that are so punishing. When the tenth round started, I didn't fear for Pat. But then the punch landed and my stomach got sick almost immediately.'

As Pat was taken away on a stretcher, DiBella 'prayed for a miracle. But my gut instinct told me that this was so bad. By the time the first CAT scan came back, it was clear that the injury to his brain was devastating.'

At Patrick Day's funeral, DiBella knew people were angry. 'Listening to his friends and his brothers speak about Pat captured how remarkable he had been, but I also heard the hurt and bitterness which I fully understood. I had my guts ripped out.'

Boxing seemed darker than ever to DiBella. But I knew that he would keep promoting boxing, just as I would keep writing about it. He tried to find meaning in an otherwise senseless death. 'It doesn't bring Pat back, but his last couple of fights were on bigger platforms fighting top level fighters, doing what he wanted to do. That means something.

'It's a bad analogy, but was it *Death of a Salesman* where they say "Attention must be paid" when Willy Loman died? Pat Day's life deserved attention, Pat's career deserved attention, Pat's death deserved attention. Everything that Pat stood for deserves attention.'

*

Sean Monaghan picked me up from Freeport station on a cold afternoon in Long Island. His warmth filled the car and, despite his grief for Pat, Monaghan made our meeting feel natural. We drove through Pat's old town and our conversation flowed as if we had known each other a long time. Monaghan only paused ten minutes later when he held the keys to Joe Higgins's gym, a small brick building in a Freeport park. 'I've not been inside since we lost Pat,' he said. 'Coach Joe closed it for a few weeks and I've not been able to face coming back.'

Old posters, featuring some of Monaghan's greatest nights in the ring and Pat's past fights, lined the walls. Pat had loved Monaghan, a pro from Long Beach who eventually got out of boxing with a 29–3 record and his reputation as one of New York's most popular fighters intact.

The blue ring was empty as the retired fighter remembered his friend.

'Patrick walked in here around 2005,' Monaghan said. 'I was twenty-five and he was this skinny kid. He always had a smile, very humble, a really pleasant kid. Patrick fought at 154 to 160 [pounds] and I was 175, but we sparred a lot. He was tough. I sparred beasts like Artur Beterbiev [the most ferocious light-heavyweight on the planet], but Patrick was so competitive. In the summer, we opened the steel doors and people watched me and Patrick put on some shows. I sparred more with Patrick than anyone else. He was a wonderful person who had such heart.'

Monaghan's reflections were interrupted by the arrival of Higgins. A strapping man, with a cap covering his bald head, Higgins sounded exactly like the tough former US Marine and New York firefighter he had once been. But, as the man who introduced Pat to boxing and worked the corner in every one of his amateur and professional fights, Higgins was grieving. He explained how, after he reopened the gym, he could not bear the thought of it being associated with boxing. Higgins resolved to turn it into a fitness centre. But, as the weeks passed and young men asked him to help them box, Higgins felt torn. He knew Pat would want him to continue, and he saw how the park looked so dark in the winter afternoons when the gym was closed. He missed seeing the steady glow of the gym as his fighters worked inside.

Did boxing help Higgins deal with the torment of 9/11 when he lost his brother after they both fought the fires raging in the Twin Towers? 'There's no doubt,' Higgins said. 'I was diagnosed with everything. But I was a high-profile fire guy, a marine. You don't admit that stuff and going for help made me feel worse. Coming here every day is what helped me. Sean came here a few months after 9/11 when I was still dazed.

'I wasn't always here, but Seanie kept showing up. He was serious about boxing and that helped me. Then Patrick came and he changed me too because I felt he would look at me differently if I got too angry and cursed. So I don't curse no more. Seanie and Patrick were raised right, and they gave me a healing force.'

Higgins remembered that, from April 2016 to February 2019, Pat won six consecutive fights against supposedly superior rivals. DiBella had re-signed him after he defeated the previously unbeaten Eric Walker in July 2017. 'Lou had just signed Walker,' Higgins remembered, 'but we knew we'd beat him.'

In the gym, with his memories, Higgins looked full of life again. Monaghan was quiet. I also wondered if, as a fighter, Monaghan squirmed at Higgins's casual use of 'we'. Words tumbled from Higgins but Monaghan's silence was a reminder of the outcome.

I liked Monaghan, who spoke without bravado, and so I drew him back into the conversation. When Pat fought Adames, Beverly Monaghan, Sean's wife, was worried. 'I was walking around town with Beverly that Saturday,' Monaghan recalled, 'and we saw the wife of Joe Quiambao who used to be DiBella's matchmaker. She and my wife have a bond, and they loved Patrick. They were like: "Oh no, Pat's fighting another fricken beast."'

His crumpled face brightened as he remembered the last time he had seen Pat – dancing in a Long Beach bar. 'He was dressed so nice, dancing with this white girl. He turns round and gives me the biggest smile and sweatiest hug. He was a sweetheart.'

Monaghan still could not quite believe his friend was gone. 'Coach called me from hospital. He said: "It's not good, man. He won't wake up." It was horrible.'

The thirty-eight-year-old former fighter looked up. 'DiBella called me at midnight. He was freaking out: "Sean, the doctors say he might not make it." I told my wife and she gasped. Every time I spoke to Joe, there was no good news. It makes me sick thinking about it.'

On a beautiful December morning in Rockville Centre, close to Freeport, Patrick Aristhene and I met in a diner where he and Pat often went for breakfast. He told me how close they had been since they were little boys. 'Pat was the golden child, but I'd get into fights at school,' Aristhene recalled. 'I'd get suspended and Pat said: "You should think about boxing." Pat was better than me, but he lost his first three amateur fights. I'll never forget we were in his kitchen making pancakes. He said, "Man, if I lose the next fight, I'm done." But he won, and won again. When Pat won the Golden Gloves I was like: "I got to get mine." I did. How many Golden Gloves champions live on the same block like Pat and me? That's testament to Coach Joe.'

Pat loved boxing because it's the ultimate test physically, emotionally and psychologically. 'In other sports you can shove the responsibility onto a team-mate,' Aristhene said. 'With boxing, it's all on you. You can't be with your lady friends the way you want. You can't eat the food you want. Early to bed. Wake up at dawn to run. That discipline is addictive. Pat had no intention of going pro, but the longer he stayed in the game, and kept winning, the competitor in him said: "I need to face the best in the world."'

Aristhene added that, 'when the time came to say goodbye, I told Pat I loved him and appreciated him. It helped that he didn't waste a moment and did everything with good intentions.'

Christmas would be hard, and New Year even worse. He and Pat always spent New Year's Eve together. 'I'm going to be with his brothers,' Aristhene said softly. 'We'll remember Pat.'

Walking through the park to the gym, Aristhene explained that Pat's mother, 'who is like a second mom to me, is such a good person. But it's so hard for her. There have also been days when I could hardly get up. If I was not a schoolteacher, I would have quit my job. But knowing I had kids to help got me up.'

Inside the gym, we saw Pat's fight robe and his locker with his name scrawled above it. We saw the ring where he and Monaghan sparred a thousand rounds.

'I have very mixed feelings about boxing,' Aristhene said. 'Boxing changed me for the better – it gave me discipline and clarity – and winning the Golden Gloves is one of my highest honours. Boxing also did a lot for Pat, but it took his life. He died doing something he loved. When I'm shadow-boxing, I feel close to Pat. But then I have waves of frustration, anger, sadness at the gravity of it. Sometimes I throw punches and watch myself in the mirror. These are the movements that took his life, but I know he submitted his soul to boxing.

'I had another dream about Pat the other night. I shave my head now. So when people touch my head, it feels different. I felt Pat touch my head. In the dream I said: "What is [death] like?" He said: "It's nice. It's chill with an all-knowing feeling." I found peace in that.'

As we left the gym, Aristhene reached out and touched Pat's locker. It was his way of saying goodbye again.

At Freeport station, we embraced in a heartfelt way. 'We'll make sure his name and his legacy live on,' Aristhene said with certainty. 'Patrick Day will never be forgotten.'

On 6 January 2020, my mother would have turned ninety-two. It felt important that I went back to South Africa to be with my dad. His cancer had begun to spread and the palliative care doctor, Nosisa Matsiliza, warned me that it could move into his brain and change his character. It was possible that my kind old dad might become unrecognisably aggressive and angry. I resolved to treasure every good moment left with him.

We missed my mom deeply but, five months after her death, it helped that the same nurses who had looked after her so tenderly still helped my dad. I had spent so much time at the care home that I became friendly with the staff. The nurses who were around my age had seen their children detained, tortured and killed under apartheid – and yet they were full of forgiveness.

My dad was especially close to Tryphinia Kelitlilwe, the senior night sister, who always chatted to him about the state of the country, and the world, before he went to bed. Tryphinia had suffered under apartheid, but intelligence and generosity poured out of her – and younger nurses like Thandeka Dlamini.

When he was showered one evening by Thandeka, he told the thirty-year-old nurse he felt grateful to have had Jess as his wife for sixty-four years. Thandeka made my dad smile when she said she would instruct her boyfriend that this was the example she expected him to follow. She soaped my dad's crinkly skin and washed his thin grey hair while she shared her hopes and troubles with him. Thandeka also checked my dad's body with great care because Tryphinia always reminded her to examine him for new lumps or lesions.

The painful divisions of South Africa remained obvious. Almost all the residents were white. Apart from the white matron, all the nurses and carers were Black and they lived in the townships. I suggested to Thandeka that it must seem as if she was caring for people who had once oppressed her own family. She shook her head.

Thandeka told me she felt at peace caring for the elderly and the dying. She had learned how to lift the fragile residents in a way that did not bruise their skin which was as delicate as old parchment. Thandeka said it did not matter if we were Black or white. We were all bruised on the inside.

The day before my mother's birthday, I told my dad about an

interview I had done with a thirty-year-old female athlete paralysed from the waist down after she had been hit by a tractor. I praised her courage and resolve. He listened, with typical interest, but as soon as I finished talking, he tried desperately hard to get to the toilet in time. My dad could not move his walker fast enough and he felt mortified.

Ian McRae was still revered by some people in South Africa. In the depths of apartheid, his plans to bring electricity into every Black location and rural area were daring. He could have lost his job as the chief executive of Eskom and gone to jail if the security police had found out what he was doing in Soweto at night.

Yet there he was, in January 2020, frail and full of cancer, apologising for his soiled nappy.

I tried to reassure him that it didn't matter. Thandeka was even more emphatic. 'It's nothing,' she told me. 'I have changed all my babies' nappies. I can change a nappy for an old person. We will be lucky if we live so long as your dad.'

Las Vegas, glinting in the desert, was quiet in mid-February 2020. The big fight was ten days away and I liked the hush in the brittle winter sunshine. But something more ominous loomed.

In a taxi to the gym, I asked the driver if he felt any concern about the strange new virus which had appeared in Wuhan, in China. Could this be a reason why Vegas seemed so empty?

'Nah,' the driver, who was called Hank, reassured me. 'It's got nuthin' to do with us.'

The rest of our journey passed slowly as Hank praised Donald Trump and bitched about his backache after too many hours of driving tourists along the Strip.

At the Top Rank gym, down a little side street called Business Lane, the door was sealed shut by a trashcan that stopped it blowing open to the world outside. Tyson Fury was inside and I knew a different kind of virus had taken hold of both the heavyweight and boxing itself. I shifted the garbage bin to one side so that I could slip through the doorway.

Fury, who would soon step into the ring to fight Deontay Wilder for the second time, noticed me as soon as I walked in.

'Here he is,' he shouted. 'The first man to see the darkness in Tyson Fury!'

I walked across to shake his hand which, as always, was soft and pliable. He said we would talk once he finished his workout. Incredibly, I had not seen Fury in person for almost six years. Our last interview had been in 2014 and so much had happened since then. It had still been a surprise to hear Fury immediately reference our first interview, in Morecambe more than eight years before, when he'd told me about his suicidal thoughts.

I was uncertain how our latest interview might unfold as I weighed up whether I should quiz him about his friendship with Daniel Kinahan, an Irish gangster who led a drug-running cartel worth more than a billion dollars. Kinahan was in hiding in Dubai with his father, Christy, and his brother, Christopher Jr. Even though the Irish Garda tried to extradite the family, and law enforcement agencies across Europe vowed to bring them to justice, Kinahan had become an insidious force in boxing. He ran through the fight game like the creeping threat of Covid-19.

Kinahan loved the prestige and glamour boxing brought him. He also saw it as a way to whitewash his reputation and he had become an adviser to hundreds of fighters. Kinahan had brokered many major fights, cutting deals on behalf of his boxers with promoters who seemed awed or intimidated when negotiating with such a notorious figure. It was an open, if dirty, secret that Kinahan had become one of the most powerful men in boxing.

He was clearly involved in the resurrection of Fury as one of the biggest stars in world sport. In the process Fury had made me believe again in the redemptive powers of boxing. He had turned me into a sucker once more for those beautiful nights in the ring when glory and joy lit up the darkness and it was possible, at least for a while, to forget the corruption and damage that poisons boxing.

Yet, as a simple timeline revealed, Kinahan's drug-trafficking and money-laundering mitts were all over this story. Almost three years earlier, on 6 March 2017, Fury had announced his return to boxing after 463 days outside the ring owing to mental health problems. He tweeted: 'Breaking news. Return of the MAC, May 13th, working on an opponent. Keep my belts warm guys as they belong to the king. Whoever got my belts I'm coming for you! Big or small.'

Two days later, he posted a now-infamous photo of him smiling alongside a beaming Kinahan. A bearded Fury looked very full in the face, but both he and Kinahan seemed jubilant as they raised their thumbs. Fury chose not to write any words alongside the photograph, but he did add fourteeen 'thinking' face emojis. It looked as if he and Kinahan were cooking up a scheme together.

Ben Davison, the young trainer who helped Fury get back into fighting shape and was in his corner for the first fight against Wilder, suggested that Kinahan had been the heavyweight's saviour at his lowest point. Remembering the legal issues and financial worries that Fury faced in retirement, at a time when he was 'drinking tequila for breakfast', Davison said: 'At that point, Tyson was questioning everything about himself, even his own existence. To have someone come along and say "Don't worry, I believe in you, I've got your back" was a godsend to him. Daniel gave him the footing to start again, a positive outlook and a pathway back to the top. It was huge for Tyson.'

On 10 March 2017, Fury was back on Twitter: 'I've moved on from the dark & scary place I've been living & if I can beat depression then I can beat anything! The hardest fight of my life! I'm letting go of the past & concentrating on the future, got to keep moving forwards, startingfromthebottom.

'Talk about being a fat man,' he added. 'I'm 25st or 350lb, but getting the weight off has never been a problem!'

His proposed return was blocked by the British Boxing Board of Control who had suspended Fury in October 2016 'pending further investigation into anti-doping and medical issues'. The Board had been dismayed by his admission to *Rolling Stone* that he was taking 'lots of cocaine' and, even more pressingly, that he was still subject to a UK anti-doping investigation after testing positive for nandrolone. That excuse of Fury's, that the adverse findings had been caused by eating uncastrated wild boar, made me increasingly queasy.

Fury was only cleared to return to boxing after accepting a backdated two-year doping ban, which meant he was free to fight again from 12 December 2017, having just signed a managerial contract with MTK Global. Kinahan's malign influence was evident again.

Kinahan and Matthew Macklin, who was then still an active fighter, had set up MGM (standing for Macklin's Gym Marbella) in Spain in 2012. It soon expanded into an events and management company rebranded as MTK Global, with the initials coming from Macklin's nickname of Mack the Knife. MTK quickly built a huge roster of fighters because they paid their boxers generously and on time, and promoted them aggressively.

Macklin, a decent man, soon stepped away but MTK continued to be linked to Kinahan. His money reeked as it had been made from drug deals which decimated the lives of addicts across Europe. There were constant reports of the brutal ways the Kinahans controlled their business. Intimidation and killing were part of the strategy.

Many of the people associated with MTK, from the employees to the fighters and YouTube outlets, praised Kinahan as a beacon of hope.

All these thoughts swirled in my head in Las Vegas as I put down my bag in a corner of the gym and walked over to Andy Lee, the former world champion middleweight turned trainer who is also Fury's cousin. Lee was working with Fury as they prepared for Wilder and it was a pleasure to see him again as he is one of my favourite people in boxing.

Born on a Travellers' site in Bow, in the East End of London, and having given up school at fourteen when his family returned to the Irish countryside in Munster, Lee educated himself. He had since emerged as one of the most intelligent men in professional boxing. Lee had once acted in a Chekhov play in Dublin and we spoke about books and his own past which included the seven years he had lived in Emanuel Steward's house in Detroit.

One of modern boxing's greatest trainers, who built up the legendary Kronk gym in Detroit and shaped world champions as diverse as Tommy Hearns and Wladimir Klitschko, Steward said towards the end of his life that, as a man, he rated Lee above all his other fighters.

I had interviewed Lee towards the end of his boxing career and we struck up a rapport. We changed roles in the autumn of 2019 when Lee was involved in the making of a short documentary about my book *In Sunshine or in Shadow*, which focused on the courageous trainer Gerry Storey and four boxers at the height of the Troubles in Northern Ireland. Lee interviewed me and Storey at the Holy Family Gym in New Lodge, Belfast, and told me afterwards that he had agreed to become a boxing trainer and steer a promising young Irish fighter, Paddy Donovan, through the pro ranks.

He had negotiated a lucrative contract for Donovan with Top Rank, but the American company had since announced that MTK would look after their fighters in the UK. Lee was full of doubt because he understood the consequences. There had been no professional boxing in Ireland since warfare between the Kinahan and Hutch gangs had been sparked by a shooting at a fight weigh-in held at Dublin's Regency Hotel in February 2016. After the Hutch gang had mistakenly killed David Byrne, when Kinahan was their target, the cartel feud escalated.

There had been tit-for-tat murders in Ireland and Spain. Kinahan had not been seen in Ireland since he attended Byrne's funeral as criminal bureaus across Europe collaborated in an effort to shut down one of the continent's largest drug consortiums. It had become too dangerous to hold professional boxing in Ireland.

MTK denied it but their association with Kinahan remained an open secret. Every top promoter in Britain, meanwhile, worked with MTK and Kinahan. If you wanted to avoid any association with them you had to get out of boxing in Britain. I trusted Lee implicitly and I worried about him having to cross such difficult terrain.

Fury had less qualms. He seemed to regard Kinahan as a friend and his key adviser.

Rather than making their pro debuts as a trainer and fighter in Dublin or their hometown of Limerick, Lee was in the corner for Donovan for the first time in Belfast on 11 October 2019. I was in the dressing room with them at the Ulster Hall both before and after the fight. It was held the night before the fateful bout that took the life of Patrick Day. So this tangled story hung over my reunion with Fury in Vegas.

In the secluded space of the gym, as Fury continued his warm-up, Lee played a recording of an iconic fight: Roberto Durán's defeat of Sugar Ray Leonard forty years before. Durán and Leonard were both fighters of huge ego, their skill supplemented by ferocious will. A fascinated Fury watched the old bout as he skipped rope.

Despite believing that Fury would win the rematch against Wilder, Lee admitted that the fight was on a knife-edge. 'Both men have huge self-belief, just like Durán and Leonard had,' he said quietly. 'You can analyse all their words and tactics, but you can't see what's inside either man. Emanuel Steward used to say champions were built from the inside. Their mental strength, toughness and resilience is deep inside them. Wilder and Tyson have these qualities.'

Lee paused as the rope whirred and Fury's giant feet danced with light delicacy. 'We can't know for certain who will be the stronger inside,' he said. 'I believe Tyson will win but it's like Durán against Leonard. Who could have predicted what would happen?'

Durán won the first encounter, but in their Vegas rematch five months later, in November 1980, he turned away in humiliating surrender, saying 'No más'. Whenever boxing pits two fighters of immense ego and will against each other, something mysterious rises up. In the 2020 rematch, the Detroit connection between Fury and his new trainers SugarHill Steward and Lee also carried some mystery.

The trio had first hung out together in 2010 at the Kronk, where Steward had helped forty boxers become world champions. One of those was Lee, who won the WBO middleweight title in 2014 after he had flown from Dublin to Detroit on a whim nine years earlier to sample the Kronk's gritty magic.

Fury joined us. He looked thoughtful as he turned a chair around so that, when he sat down, his long arms dangled over its back. His chief trainer SugarHill Steward faced him with a bag of tape, gauze and scissors. 'Emanuel asked my dad if I would go to Detroit and train with him,' Fury remembered as Steward wrapped his massive hands. 'But my wife was pregnant and it wasn't the right time. Then I had another fight and thought: *If I don't go now, I'll never know.* So, aged twenty-one [in 2010], I jumped on a plane. I didn't let anyone know I was coming. I flew into Detroit airport, got a yellow cab and said, "Can you take me to the Kronk gym?"

'I was going in to see if I was welcome. If I wasn't, I was going straight home. I walked in. SugarHill's in the ring and I said, "Is Emanuel around?" Sugar said, "Who are you?" I told him: "I'm Tyson Fury, the next heavyweight champion of the world."'

That brashness surprised Steward. 'I didn't know what to think,' the trainer admitted as he looked up from his task. 'He's this huge guy with a strange English accent. I wanted to watch him box to see if he could live up to everything he said.'

Fury flexed his wrapped left hand, appreciating Steward's work with the tape and gauze. 'I've always been an outspoken, controversial character,' he said. 'I've never been shy. I suppose they weren't used to seeing this because Americans look at the British as reserved. But I was louder than any American in the Kronk.

'Emanuel used to take me, Sugar and Andy to this special place. It was all boarded up on the outside. But when we went in, it was a restaurant and bar full of ex-Motown singers and people who didn't quite make it. Everybody was singing and it was unbelievable. Best singers I've ever heard.

'I said: "I'll sing a song." I took the mic and sang Eric Clapton's *You Look Wonderful Tonight*. Everyone fell in love with me. I was only a young kid, but I was happy getting up in front of this crowd and singing. It felt very natural because I was always very high on me.'

It was easy to understand why Emanuel said Fury was one of the three biggest characters he had met in boxing – alongside Muhammad Ali and Naseem Hamed.

'I only went to Detroit for three weeks,' Fury said nonchalantly, 'but I left a mark. Like a dog pissing on the wall.'

Fury left his biggest mark in the ring. 'Me and Andy tore up the Kronk one day. I sparred every heavyweight and cleaned up. Andy sparred and beat up everyone under that weight. The old fellas at the side who were ex-champions couldn't believe it. They were shouting: "Oh my God, I never thought I'd see the day! White boys taking over the Kronk!"'

Steward's laughter was soon replaced by his more serious point. 'It wasn't just two white boys, it was two Gypsies. We recognised that Black and Gypsy fighters have been discriminated against. They have a chip on their shoulder and that same determination forged in adversity. It's like when Andy moved to Detroit [in 2005]. No one but Manny knew him. He was just this white kid. Then his boxing, and his similarities to the Black community, shone through. That won him approval and made him one of us. Tyson was the same.'

The conversation flowed so easily that I decided not to ruin it by mentioning Kinahan. There were two other factors to consider. I was in the gym because Lee had asked Fury if I could join them and I did not want to place him in a compromised position. I was also just lost in the bewitching boxing talk. I wanted to hear more.

Fury had taken Lee's advice to appoint Steward as his new head trainer, but it seemed odd that he would become aggressive and attacking in the ring after he had bamboozled Wilder so skilfully for long stretches of their first fight. The old Kronk strategy, of seeking the knockout above safety-first tactics, seemed a worrying gamble against a devastating puncher.

Steward had been brought in to instil key technical changes and a routine training session became a lesson in footwork, closing down angles and how to throw a punch with authority. Fury admitted that initially, despite having fought professionally for eleven years, he felt like a novice when he began working with Steward seven weeks earlier.

'But I knew it would come right,' he told me. 'We've practised keeping my hands up tight, and taking his right hand away by hitting the right elbow. Old tricks of the trade. Detroit tricks. Even though they say an old dog can't learn new tricks, I'm going to show you a few new ones.'

Was Fury hitting harder? 'Yes,' Steward said simply. 'Improved balance means greater power. He can definitely knock Wilder out.'

For the first fight, Lee had been ringside in Los Angeles, commentating on BBC radio, and he was 'amazed by everything Tyson did in overcoming the depression. It was remarkable.'

Steward remembered being in hospital that night. I looked at him quizzically and he said: 'Quebec City. Adonis Stevenson against Oleksandr Gvozdyk. Same night as Fury–Wilder I.'

On 1 December 2018, Steward trained Stevenson, who lost his WBC world light-heavyweight title and almost his life when he was knocked out in the eleventh round by Gvozdyk, sliding into that coma after suffering brain damage.

'It wasn't a war,' Steward said. 'He just got hurt in that round. We went back to the dressing room and he complained of being hot. They called the ambulance and put him on a stretcher. I'm as close as you are to me and I'm watching him slip away.'

If they hadn't called the doctor, would it have been too late? 'Yeah. He was in a coma for a month. He's doing better now. Talking. Walking. But it's a long process.'

I told the two trainers that, of all Fury's revelations, the one that had stayed with me longest was his story about how his wife, Paris, sat down on their hotel bed in LA after the first Wilder fight. She took off her make-up and began to sob. She told her husband she could not bear to watch him go through the ordeal again.

The two boxing men nodded in silence. The Gypsy King would soon face the same brutal test.

The following afternoon, at a gym in Henderson, a city just outside of Vegas, Fury undertook a strength-and-conditioning session. He was quieter than the previous morning. 'Tyson's a gentleman,' said Lee. 'People don't see that. A big part of my job is just to talk to Tyson. Our conversations about boxing are relatively small, but the conversations about life, about his past and his future aspirations, are much deeper. Special people come along every now and then, like Elvis Presley, David Bowie or James Brown. Muhammad Ali is the one in boxing. But here, with Tyson, we've got someone special as well. It's a privilege to be here.'

Lee, however, was measured in assessing the bout. 'Tyson and Wilder have both improved since the first fight,' he said. 'We've got one aim – to win the fight. But in boxing, as in life, you never know.'

Before leaving, I walked across to see Fury. We spoke for a few minutes and he was amiable and amusing. I would ask him some awkward questions about Daniel Kinahan the next time we did a formal interview but, in that moment, it felt right just to wish him good luck.

'I'll be all right,' the big man said with a little smile. 'It's going to be some night – unless I'm a total idiot and run into one of those massive bombs again.'

Another taxi driver picked me up in Henderson. She was more considerate than Hank, the driver from the previous day. We chit-chatted easily on the journey back to the Vegas Strip and then, as the traffic thickened and we slowed, she paused.

'Have you heard about this Chinese virus?' she asked. 'It scares me.'

The middle-aged driver began to tell me how she had moved to Vegas after her life had been shattered eighteen months before in Illinois. Her husband of thirty years had died after a sudden heart attack. I could see her eyes glistening with tears in the rear-view mirror.

'I really don't know what I'm doing,' she said as we crawled along the Strip. 'Life seems so fragile . . .'

Before he fought Tyson Fury for a second time, Deontay Wilder's most troubling words rose up again. 'I want a body on my record,' Wilder had said in 2019. 'I don't have no feelings towards the man I'm fighting . . . I thought I had one [body] one time, with [Artur] Szpilka, because he wasn't breathing when he hit the canvas. He was dead three to five seconds.'

There was a terrible photograph of Wilder punching Szpilka, a Polish heavyweight who was knocked out in the ninth round of their bout in January 2016. The punch landed just below the Pole's temple, shutting his right eye, squashing his nose and the left side of his face as if his features were being smeared by a drunken painter across a bloody canvas.

'I always think about this when they ask about my best knock-out,' Wilder said. 'I thought I took his life.'

Szpilka had been out cold but, eventually, he regained consciousness. The Pole even boxed again, but he was never the same. Fury had been punched just as hard when he and Wilder fought in December 2018 and yet, somehow, he got up from seeming obliteration.

Perhaps Wilder had absorbed a different perspective since that humbling night, when the draw with Fury meant it was the first time he had failed to win, because he showed another side to his character in Las Vegas. He was still unbeaten after forty-three fights, but he insisted that being the father of eight children in Alabama mattered far more than his destructive punching.

'They say you don't know what love is until you have a child,' the thirty-four-year-old Wilder said, 'and that's true. Every time I step into the ring, I am fighting for my children.'

He had turned to boxing late and after a deep depression. At the age of twenty, he was the father of a one-year-old daughter who suffered from spina bifida. The trauma of his little girl's condition and the accompanying financial burden wore him down and, feeling helpless, Wilder considered taking his own life.

'In 2005, I reached the lowest point. I'd lost my family and I had a gun in my lap. I was ready to commit suicide. It felt like this was the only way to get out. I was close to ending it all.'

Wilder found a way out. 'It's a dark and heavy business, but boxing saved me. I put the gun away and here I am today . . . heavy-weight champion of the world.'

He still carried a grave view of the business which had been his salvation. 'I risk my life for your entertainment and, as a boxer, you must have the mentality of a killer. No one outside boxing can understand the intensity and danger.'

Wilder was convinced he would knock out Fury in the rematch. 'The first fight was like a baptism. He got dipped and he rose up. This fight is going to be clear-cut. Tyson Fury will not rise up this time. He will end up stretched out on the floor, still and unconscious.'

All the odds seemed to favour Wilder. The American had won his two subsequent fights with chilling knockouts. Wilder was called the most destructive puncher in the history of heavyweight boxing and his knockout-to-win percentage was a staggering 97.67 per cent. It seemed crazier than ever that Fury planned to climb through the ropes and, rather than box Wilder at distance, seek to knock out the American on 22 February 2020 at the MGM Grand Garden Arena.

It looked surreal when Tyson Fury was carried to the ring on a golden throne as he sang along to 'Crazy' by Patsy Cline. Only Fury could choose such a song by a great country singer. Deontay Wilder, in contrast, wore a Black History Month metal mask and costume which weighed forty pounds. He looked frazzled when he stepped out of his clanking paraphernalia.

Wilder never recovered. From the opening bell, Fury did exactly what Lee and Steward had predicted. Rather than dance his way out of danger and try to steal a win on points, Fury beat up Wilder with methodical precision.

I was incredulous because the fight unfolded the way in which the three friends had told me it would. I watched spellbound as a work of fistic art revealed itself. Fury dropped Wilder in the third round, as a heavy right hand sent the intimidating champion to the canvas for the first time in ten years. Wilder got up and fired back. He was ragged, but I still worried that one of his shattering right hooks would change the fight. The American could look terrible in the ring and then, out of nowhere, end a bout with one vicious punch.

Fury made Wilder sag when he knocked him down with a body punch in round five. Blood poured from Wilder's ear and he looked vanquished long before the referee Kenny Bayless ended the contest midway through the seventh. The stoppage was instigated by Wilder's trainer, Mark Breland, a former fighter who understood the damage.

Wilder would protest later. 'I'm upset with Mark because we've talked about this many times ... I want to go out on my shield. If I'm talking about going in and killing a man, I respect the fact that the same can happen to me. I am ready to die in the ring.'

Fury, the King of the Gypsies, took the microphone in the ring. 'I said I'd sing a song tonight ...'

Bob Arum, his eighty-eight-year-old American promoter, smiled quizzically as Fury crooned through the first three verses of Don McLean's 'American Pie' before shouting, 'All together now ...'

Fifteen thousand voices joined in to roar 'Bye, bye, Miss American Pie' and how they would be singing this song on 'the day that I die'. As soon as Fury sung that fateful word 'die', he shouted

'What?', as if in rebuke of Wilder wanting a body on his record. The new heavyweight champion of the world sang to his wife, Paris, and then shouted, 'Thank you Las Vegas!'

As Fury left the arena, he was joined by a smiling Andy Lee. They yakked away to each other about a night like no other. Only boxing could make them feel this alive.

6

Death in Lockdown

Illness and death swept across the world. On 11 February 2020, the World Health Organization had given a new name to the disease which would change our lives forever. The 2019 novel coronavirus outbreak became Covid-19. Exactly a month later, on 11 March, after more than 118,000 cases in 114 countries, and 4,291 deaths, the WHO declared that Covid-19 was officially a global pandemic.

In my house, the pandemic began to feel personal the following night when, around 10 p.m., my son Jack came hurtling down the stairs to tell me that Mikel Arteta, the manager of Arsenal, our football club, had tested positive for Covid and been forced to self-isolate. This showed how, to an absurd extent, sport gripped us. We had no idea how our lives were about to change, but certain phrases in the language of the virus – from 'self-isolation' to 'social distancing' – were already familiar.

A few hours earlier, we had watched Boris Johnson's television address as he warned that 'this is the worst public health crisis for a generation. Many more families are going to lose loved ones before their time.'

Cancer made my dad far more vulnerable to Covid. As the virus continued its insidious spread, Cyril Ramaphosa, South Africa's president, declared a national state of emergency. I would no longer be able to fly to South Africa, even if my dad fell seriously ill.

The world was shutting down, but my dad, as always, stayed positive. We would keep in touch on the phone every day and ride out the Covid storm.

Boxing, a staple of my life, was also about to disappear. On 17 March, the British Boxing Board of Control cancelled all contests under its jurisdiction in the wake of government advice for people to avoid all 'non-essential contact'. They would review the situation in April.

In the United States, Top Rank had already cancelled seven shows in three different countries between 14 March and 2 May, which included bouts featuring fighters of the calibre of Shakur Stevenson, Artur Beterbiev, Naoya Inoue, Josh Taylor and Michael Conlan. There was confusion and uncertainty as to when boxing might resume.

Two-and-half-months before, on New Year's Eve, Isaac Chamberlain had messaged me just before midnight Miami time. 'I've been through hell in 2019. I've suffered countless setbacks and failures that would make anyone quit ... Even when everything around me was crumbling, I wiped my tears and had faith. Now I'm at the end of this dreadful year, with seventeen minutes to go into a new year, a new decade, a new life. This year will be mine, this decade will be mine.'

Such hope had already been tested. Chamberlain's attempts to resume his career had been blocked by his American promoter being jailed, while a new trainer in Miami let him down. Chamberlain had still managed to turn his life around when he phoned Mick Hennessy, who was most famous for guiding Tyson Fury to the world title in 2015. Hennessy agreed to become Chamberlain's new promoter, offering him a five-year contract and arranging for him to fight in England on 28 March and 25 April. Those bouts had since been cancelled.

Our plan for me to interview Chamberlain in person was also

affected. We spoke remotely and I heard his breath catch when I asked how he felt after he received the news about boxing shutting down. 'I was fighting back tears on the train, trying not to show anyone I was so upset,' Chamberlain said. 'But almost straightaway I told myself: "Let's not be selfish. Coronavirus is affecting everyone. Other people are suffering more than me."'

The twenty-six-year-old was more philosophical than I had expected. 'How can I stop when I've got this far? It's also been better because Mick Hennessy and his team are so great. They really appreciate me. I never had that relationship with [Eddie Hearn's] Matchroom when I was going through so much shit on my own. Now I have these people around me, consoling me, supporting me.'

Chamberlain seemed better equipped than most in adjusting to lockdown. 'Everyone is talking about isolation and how they're struggling. I've been isolated in Miami for months. I was isolated from people – and also from hope or guarantee. But I dealt with it. Even if all my money went, it wouldn't be the end of the world. I've been very poor before.'

Despite the unsettling times, Chamberlain sounded strong. I pointed out that he had not been writing. 'That's because I'm not depressed. I only write when things are getting on top of me. I still feel I will become a world champion.'

On Chamberlain's latest Twitter masthead, it said 'The Path To Paradise Is Through Hell'.

'I know I can go through hell,' he said calmly. 'I've sacrificed so much it's got to the point that it's become normal to me to go through these trials and tribulations. The world is in a very tough spot right now but I just think: *I've been here before, in a very dark place.*'

As was his way, Chamberlain found fresh hope. 'Whatever you're going through, you can get past it. If you feel you're in hell right now, why would you stay there? That's why it's very important to keep going, no matter what life throws at you. Keep working, keep believing, and you will come through it. We can all get through this time.'

My father's world had shrunk still further as he would no longer be taken to the shops or to church on Sunday mornings. Those rare outings were forbidden, as were visits from any of his friends or family following the announcement of a national lockdown in South Africa on 23 March. I wondered how long it would be before I saw my dad again.

That Monday evening, Boris Johnson confirmed that Britain would enter a stringent lockdown.

'I must give the British people a very simple instruction,' he said in his shambling impression of a Churchillian speech. 'You must stay at home. We must stop the disease spreading between households.'

Our isolation was sealed – yet it was a curiosity of the first lockdown that one beautiful blue-skied day followed another. In my house, all five of us were back home again as schools and universities shut down and we spent time on the new Covid platform of Zoom. My days began early and, soon after 7 a.m., I would walk to the local supermarket to buy groceries and try to find elusive items like toilet paper. The great loo paper wars, as panic-buying emptied the shops, became more urgent than the next world heavyweight title fight – whenever that might happen. On my return home, I scrubbed my hands for a very long time while ignoring Johnson's advice to sing 'Happy Birthday' twice during the virus-cleansing process.

I wrote, went running, marvelled at the way the air seemed so clean, and called my dad every day. He was lonely but he insisted he was well.

'You remember what your mother would always say,' he told me. 'This, too, will pass.'

I was close to Alison's mum, Pat Musgrave, whom my dad sometimes phoned to say hello. Pat knew what it felt like to be alone because her husband, John, had died twelve years earlier. Ian and Pat had known each other since 1993, when Alison and I first met, and there was a bond between them. Twenty-seven years later, he listened closely when I said that we were concerned. Pat was unwell and she had fallen numerous times.

We spoke to her on Mother's Day, on FaceTime, as she was too ill to visit us. Her deterioration was marked. All the usual spark of Pat had gone as a urinary tract infection debilitated her.

Early on Thursday 26 March, Alison was called by her sister, Anna. Their mother had become incontinent and her confusion had escalated. I went to our local pharmacy to buy some adult nappies. It felt as if our world was tilting as our parents became as vulnerable as infants.

Later that morning, Alison and Anna watched helplessly while the paramedics tended to their mum. The medics wore full protective clothing, with white masks covering their heads and faces, as if they had stepped straight out of a science fiction movie.

Alison and Anna saw their mum carried down the stairs towards a waiting ambulance. A man and his young son stared out of their car window as they watched the ghostly scene. Horror spread across their faces as they saw the PPE-clad paramedics wheel Pat into an ambulance.

That night, Alison and I sat with our kids – Bella, Jack and Emma – while we absorbed a terrible day. Italy, Spain and the UK had recorded the most deaths they had experienced in a single day of the pandemic. The new British record tally of 115 deaths would be surpassed the next day, but the Department of Health confirmed that 759 people in Britain had died from Covid since the start of the pandemic. The rate of infection doubled every three days.

At 8 p.m., that evening, as darkness settled over our small corner of the world, we stepped outside. It was the first Thursday night where millions of people in Britain came out of their homes to clap for the NHS and everyone else on the Covid front line.

The applause started slowly but, within thirty seconds, it rolled up and down our street, growing in volume and appreciation as more and more people opened their doors to join us. The scene was replicated across the country, and at different times and in different cities all over the world, as the clapping was joined by whistles and cries, beeping horns and even a drum. One of our neighbours lit sparklers and sent a firework soaring into the night sky.

Slowly, reluctantly almost, the clapping subsided. People waved to each other and then stepped back inside the safety of their cocoons.

Pat had been diagnosed with pneumonia and then, on Saturday 28 March, she tested positive for Covid. A routine test had been taken on her admission to hospital on the Thursday. Back then, even a hospital needed forty-eight hours to obtain a test result and so Pat was moved from a normal ward to a Covid ward. Her isolation from us, and the world beyond, intensified.

Alison also had to self-isolate. We had no idea if she had the virus as, then, there were no home testing kits for Covid. It was down to me to occasionally step outside our incubated home to buy food and provisions. The days seemed long and hushed, but the sun outside still shone and the blue skies were gloriously empty of planes. Birdsong replaced the lost hum of traffic.

There was little we could do but keep phoning the hospital for attempted updates, stay inside, keep in touch with my dad and try to live.

Regis Prograis and I kept emailing each other. On 30 March, he wrote: 'Hey what's up, Don. We're doing the best we can over here. Everything is in lockdown so we can't do anything except be in the house all the time. At first it didn't hit me but now it's starting to get to me. I can't be in the house all day. I've been going to the gym at night when no one is there so that makes it a little better. But staying inside all day is driving me crazy. Hopefully this all gets sorted out soon. I'm disappointed my fight with Maurice Hooker is off. I was going into my third week of training camp when they pulled the plug on the fight. But, hey, shit happens.'

In his next email, he admitted that he still felt haunted by losing to Josh Taylor. 'I can't wait to get the rematch one day. I definitely fought the wrong fight. I could've stopped him, but I didn't step on the gas. I think about it all the time. It will only make me better in the future. But, right now, these are scary times.'

Four days after her admission, Pat finally answered her mobile phone and spoke to Alison. She was weak, but she said there was 'a good crowd' on her ward and that she was next to 'someone quite famous'. She lowered her voice mysteriously and, while it seemed unlikely that there would be anyone famous in Pat's ward at Luton and Dunstable Hospital, we couldn't be sure. At least Pat, at that stage, seemed to almost enjoy the surreal novelty of her confinement.

In the world outside, socially distanced queues stretched for so long that it took almost an hour to get into the supermarket. The blue skies seemed crisper than ever.

I called my dad each day and we always spoke about Pat's condition. Of course, we often talked of my mother too. On the last day I had been with him, in early January, we had buried a small casket of her ashes in a special place which my dad had reserved for her in the grounds of St James, their church just down the road from the care home.

I had taken a photograph of my dad sitting on a bench next to the hole in the ground where we had placed my mom's ashes. His head was bowed in prayer. When I missed him badly, I looked at that photograph and tried, without always succeeding, to feel grateful.

Life became more fragmentary. For a week we had no contact at all with Pat as her phone switched to voicemail every time we called. The nurses on her ward were exhausted and working to the limits of their endurance. When they answered our calls, they confirmed that Pat was stable but her confusion had escalated. She was still testing positive for Covid and struggling to sleep on the noisy ward. They explained that they aimed to move her to an assisted care facility once she was clear of the virus.

The Coronavirus Resource Center run by Johns Hopkins University in Baltimore tracked the devastation. They updated a Covid-19 map every hour as the number of infections and fatalities clicked over at a remorseless march. When I checked the latest global data on Sunday 26 April, nearly three million people had been infected and more than 200,000 deaths recorded. In the UK, there had been 150,000 confirmed cases and more than 20,000 deaths.

My father, dealing with cancer on his own, was in quarantine in South Africa where there had been 4,300 cases and eighty-six deaths.

Pat was moved to a community hospital and rehabilitation centre closer to our home. I sometimes joined Alison when she visited and, even though we were not allowed to enter Pat's room, we could talk to her through an open window. Pat looked so thin and so ill as she sat in a chair. At least she seemed serene as she told us about all the parties she was attending upstairs at the White House.

Of course, there was no upstairs, no party and no White House – except in Pat's hazy mind.

When Alison was about to leave the centre after her usual daily visit, she promised her mum, as cheerfully as she could, that she would see her in the morning.

'You will,' Pat said with a cheeky little laugh, 'if you can catch me ...'

On 29 April, I visited Pat on my own at the rehab centre. We had always got on well and spoken easily to each other. We did the same again as we chatted about her seven grandchildren and how well my dad was doing in isolation. But I admitted that I was still worried about him and I had no idea when I might see him again.

'Oh, I wouldn't worry,' Pat said with a smile. 'Ian's coming to the White House tonight.'

A new pressure bore down on us. The community hospital needed to free up bed space and so we were told that Pat was 'medically fit to leave', even though it was clear that she could not look after herself. We had to either find full-time carers to look after Pat in her flat or begin paying for her to live in a care home.

Our only concern was for Pat's well-being and so we found her a care home. Her situation deteriorated rapidly soon after she arrived. She fell out of bed and onto the bare floor. When we came to visit her, we were shown a place to stand in the bushes outside so that we could talk to Pat through an open window.

She was propped up in a chair and looked terrible. Aside from a black eye, which looked like it came from a punch she might have taken in a boxing ring, Pat leaned badly to the right. We feared that she might have had a stroke as she also could not talk. She looked old and crumpled.

A doctor decided that Pat needed to be hospitalised and given numerous tests in an effort to ascertain why she could no longer sit in an upright position. It was a sad afternoon when the ambulance arrived to return her to hospital for our window visits would not be allowed.

A week later, after multiple delays in assessing the test results because of the pressure of Covid, Alison finally heard the shattering diagnosis from Anna on the phone. Their gorgeous old mum had an aggressive brain tumour. There was little time left.

On Wednesday 26 May 2020, the video footage played on a loop online and across news channels around the world. It captured the horror of Monday night in Minneapolis.

I sat and watched, in silent disbelief, as George Floyd, a forty-six-year-old African American man, slowly suffocated to death on the street. He was held on the ground by four policemen who had been called to the scene after it was alleged by a store owner that Floyd had tried to use a fake $20 bill when buying a packet of cigarettes.

One of the policemen, Derek Chauvin, pressed his knee against Floyd's throat as a way of pinning him down. This lasted for more than nine minutes.

Floyd became increasingly agitated and his last words before he died were a desperate refrain of 'I can't breathe . . . I can't breathe.'

The US had since been engulfed in riots. Isaac and I spoke the next morning.

'How could they do that to a human being, bro?' he asked helplessly. 'The world is fucked.'

Deep in lockdown, with Covid decimating the country, communication from the hospital was sketchy. Days passed and we kept phoning and hearing the same automated message about the restrictions blocking visitors. It was only later that week when, while calling a special family line, Alison heard a different automated message which said that visitors were allowed on palliative care wards.

Five days had slipped away and Pat had been on her own. But at last, on Wednesday 3 June, Alison and I visited her mother on Blossom Ward. We wore full PPE outfits, which the hospital supplied, before we entered Pat's room. Alison went in on her own, initially, for a moving reunion with her mum. It was the first time they had been able to touch each other in months.

Pat, in a sudden burst of lucidity, understood the severity of her diagnosis. 'It's terminal,' she said simply.

We took our three kids to see their beloved mama the following day and, again all dressed in PPE clothing, shared time with Pat. She sat up in bed and, briefly, she was less confused as she relished the chance to see her youngest daughter and three grandchildren. We spent an hour with her and, as we left, Jack gave Pat a last wave.

'See you later, alligator,' Pat called out.

On 5 June, we were with Pat when the ambulance staff arrived to take her to the nursing home where she would spend the final weeks of her life. The driver asked Alison if she would like to be with her mum in the ambulance and so, as I drove ahead, they travelled slowly to their old town of Harpenden. Alison attempted a cheery monologue as they passed her dad's favourite pub, The Fox, and other places which had always meant so much to them as a family. Her mum, who used to fill a car journey with her constant chatter, was now mute.

The following day, there was noise and a large crowd just five miles from where we lived. That Saturday afternoon, Anthony Joshua led a peaceful Black Lives Matter march from Watford High Street to Cassiobury Park, a tranquil setting which was very different to the grittier town centre. Joshua, like everyone else, wore black.

Once the protesters had formed a huge circle around him, he began to read a speech which had been written by his friend Reece Campbell. Joshua urged the protesters to boycott white business-owners. 'Show them where it hurts. Abstain from spending your money in their shops and economies, and invest in Black-owned businesses.'

Joshua then acknowledged his own troubled past in Watford, having been on remand for criminal activity, and promised that he would invest in the development of Black businesses in the local community. 'I've taken my street knowledge and put it into the corporate world and I've gained a lot of respect in that sense. And, anyway, gang culture is done. We have to engage with the youth and put an end to Black youth gang culture. This postcode war? How many houses do we own on that postcode that we're fighting for? Let's inject the vaccine.'

'Every life matters,' the world heavyweight champion added. '100 per cent I agree with that. But that does include Black lives and that's why we're here today. George Floyd was the catalyst in a list that is already way, way, way too long.'

It was a restrained protest, but a small furore broke out when

Joshua posted his speech on Instagram. There was immediate controversy as the march had contravened Covid regulations. 'I understand the concerns in regards to social distancing,' Joshua responded. 'However, I hope those who are complaining about social distancing have the same energy about those gathering for a day at the beach and those going to the park for a picnic.'

He was accused far more vehemently of being a racist by an army of trolls, but Joshua replied bluntly. 'If you think I'm a racist, go fuck yourself. If you watch the full video, the speech was passed around for someone to read and I took the lead. I personally spoke from the heart about the Watford community, ideas of us personally investing seven figures to create unity and opportunities and adding change to the African/Caribbean community. Shops aren't the issue here. Before you talk shit, you better boycott racism.'

Tyson Fury claimed later that 'if it had been me who said don't shop in any Black-owned stores or any Asian-owned stores, then I'd have been crucified like Jesus Christ'.

'I've suffered racism all my life,' Fury said. 'I'm thirty-two years old in August, and I come from a travelling background. Gypsies [are] hated by racist people. It's the only race that it's acceptable to be racist towards these days. Even the TV companies are allowed to be racist towards Travellers. It's terrible. But I'm not a person who gives a damn about what colour somebody is or what background they're from, because to me everyone is the same.'

On Wednesday 10 June 2020, at 4.10 p.m., Fury's head was shaved and his chest was bare when he made a startling post on Twitter. Filming himself in close-up, the heavyweight began with a ridiculously upbeat 'Hello there!' He was in a chipper mood as he unleashed a bombshell.

'I'm just here after getting off the phone with Daniel Kinahan,' Fury continued. 'He's informed me that the biggest fight in British boxing history has just been agreed.'

Fury shattered the code of silence which was meant to hide the influence Kinahan wielded over professional boxing. The heavy-weight shouted out his glee instead. 'Get in there, my boy!'

I wondered how his boy, who was trying to sanitise his notoriety by becoming the most powerful man in boxing while hiding in Dubai, felt about Fury's disclosure. But I also imagined that Kinahan, who seemed as vain as he was dangerous, would relish the adulation heaped on him by the WBC heavyweight champion of the world.

'Big shout out to Dan,' Fury said. 'He got this done, literally over the line, two-fight deal. Tyson Fury versus Anthony Joshua next year. One problem. I've just got to smash Deontay Wilder's face right in in the next fight and then we go into the Joshua fight next year. The Gypsy King versus AJ is on for next year, but there's a hurdle in the road called the Bronze Bomber, AKA the Knockout King. I will knock him spark out and then we go onto the big fight. A big thank you Dan for getting this deal over the line. All the best and God bless you all.'

Above the video he had tweeted: 'It's official FURY VS JOSUAR AGREED FOR NEXT YEAR, I got to smash @bronzebomber first then I'll annihilate @anthonyfjoshua #WEARESPARTANS MASSIVE THANKS TO DANIEL KINNERHAN FOR MAKING THIS HAPPEN.'

There was such alarm in Ireland that the Taoiseach, Leo Varadkar, was questioned in parliament about Kinahan's involvement in boxing. 'I was taken aback by Tyson Fury and his video and dropping in that name you mentioned,' Varadkar said. 'While I cannot comment on any particular garda operation, I can assure you there has been contact between the Department of Foreign Affairs and the authorities in the United Arab Emirates about that matter.'

Fury was emboldened by the support of Bob Arum, whose company Top Rank promoted him in the US. A few weeks earlier, Arum had brushed aside Kinahan's criminal activities. 'Dan is like the captain when it comes to the practicalities of doing a fight in the Middle East. He's one of my favourite guys. I like to deal with no-nonsense people whose word is their bond.'

The old Vegas hustler suggested a heavyweight world title unification showdown would have to be held in the Middle East to satisfy everyone's greed. Having spent a number of days in Dubai with Kinahan, Arum said, 'Tyson and I have great confidence in Kinahan. We think he's very, very, very honest, very astute, he has great connections and, when that fight happens, the Middle East is coming up with a very, very large number. That's what Dan is looking into because everybody trusts Kinahan.'

When John Hand of the *Irish Sun* contacted Arum to point out Kinahan's links to organised crime, the promoter bristled. 'I'm not naïve. I was a federal prosecutor.'

Arum – who had once said that 'Yesterday I was lying, today I'm telling the truth' – regurgitated boxing's stock retort to the Kinahan allegations. 'I can disregard all that stuff. It doesn't affect me. I have absolutely no involvement with the Irish authorities. My philosophy is: "Stick to your business, son, and don't be distracted by the background noise." Anything that allegedly went before? That's none of my business.'

It felt like my business. In December 2018, Tyson Fury had dragged me deep back into boxing again on the night he fought Wilder for the first time. But it seemed like I had been duped because Kinahan had been at the heart of Fury's return. Kinahan also negotiated Fury's bouts against Tom Schwarz, Otto Wallin and the rematch with Wilder. But his involvement only emerged after Fury boasted of Kinahan's key role in clinching the Joshua deal.

I have always been interested in fighters and trainers, rather than promoters, managers and advisers. The corruption of boxing deflated me and so I often skimmed the latest grim rumour of wrongdoing. I preferred to concentrate on the actual boxers in a sometimes romantic attempt to capture their courage and determination. I professed to care about them, and I do, but not enough to turn my attention until now on those that sought to control their business.

Kinahan was so shameless in his desire to be photographed with fighters who visited him in Dubai that his presence became impossible to ignore. Fury, Billy Joe Saunders, Sunny Edwards and others signed to MTK Global were eager to tell the world that Dan was 'a great guy'.

For six years, MTK, as a company, had tried to hide the presence of Kinahan amid their operations. But during lockdown they became more brazen. In May 2020, MTK, with a roster of more than 300 fighters, celebrated a new partnership with KHK, the Prince of Bahrain's combat sports organisation, who had hired Kinahan as their special adviser. On social media, Kinahan praised their 'fantastic ambitions to grow into a global powerhouse', while Mohammed Shahid, the CEO of KHK Sports, said, 'Daniel has the same vision for sports as us; changing lives, equal opportunities, making dreams come true and uniting the world through sports.'

It went beyond parody – as did Sandra Vaughan, the former CEO of MTK. She celebrated Kinahan's rise and seemed mystified by repeated questions about drug-dealing and murder. 'All of these big fights will happen because of Daniel Kinahan. That is fact. The other part is fiction. I don't know whether it's the Irish mentality, but would you not be proud that someone from inner-city Dublin is actually sitting at the table with that level of organisation – with the Prince of Bahrain or Bob Arum, making history?'

Just four days after Kinahan had been confirmed as a special adviser to KHK, Dublin's Special Criminal Court accepted further incriminating evidence. It declared that Kinahan's cartel carried out 'execution-type murders', as well as drugs and firearm trafficking on a global scale.

The constant drip of pressure on Kinahan finally forced him back into the shadows. On 24 June 2020, Arum stressed that Kinahan would no longer negotiate fights for Fury. 'I've had a lot of conversations with Tyson and we decided that myself, Top Rank and Tyson will do all negotiations for fights in the future,' Arum told the *Daily Telegraph*. 'We've talked with Dan, who Tyson and I both love and admire and respect, and he understands it's best the negotiations on Tyson's side be handled that way.'

Bob Yalen, MTK's new CEO, added a few days later that Kinahan would no longer advise any of their fighters. 'Daniel's going to be taking time away from the sport to focus on other interests and hopefully this will put a stop to the negative press from Ireland. No court has ever found this man guilty of anything. He has never been charged or convicted of a crime. The only basis for these allegations is the hearsay testimony of biased parties. It's unfortunate for his fighters that he's taking this step back. But he wants to do what's right for the sport.'

On 27 June, Billy Joe Saunders, a two-weight world champion, gave an exclusive interview to iFL TV, the YouTube channel sponsored by MTK. 'I took a lot of advice from a very good personal friend of mine, Daniel,' Saunders said. 'I know that he's walking away from boxing, which is a big, big, big loss in my eyes. I don't know if I want to be a part of it moving forward.'

No one believed Yalen or Saunders. It was almost certain that Kinahan would continue talking to fighters and arranging their bouts despite the dark hum of controversy.

There was a worrying change in my dad. On the Monday morning of 6 July 2020, he told me that he felt very tired and even a little depressed. All this was so unlike him and he could hear my concern. He tried to reassure me that it was just a cold.

Early the next day, the matron, Lesley Gubler, emailed me. 'Dr McRae has flu-like symptoms and a slightly elevated temperature. We are keeping him in bed and in isolation. All care centre patients are being tested tomorrow as a precautionary measure after one of our patients was diagnosed with the virus.'

He was not well enough to take a call from me that day but,

on Wednesday, Ian told Jack he was slowly improving. We spoke briefly the next two days and he insisted he was recovering.

Early on Saturday 11 July, I read an email from the matron. 'Your dad is deteriorating. Despite having a negative Covid result, he needs to be in hospital as we cannot keep him oxygenated in the care centre. The doctor has told us to send him to hospital but your dad refuses. Please contact the care centre urgently to give a directive.'

Sister Rebecca Mkhonto was in charge of the day shift. She had lived a hard life in the townships, but I knew she took great care in her work. I could tell from her voice that my dad's condition was serious and I asked her to arrange for him to be taken to hospital.

Just after 10 a.m. UK time, I spoke to the doctor on duty at Linksfield Hospital where my dad had been admitted. I explained that he did not want to be resuscitated if he was close to death, but they should oxygenate him when necessary. We had prepared for this moment, but I had always imagined I'd be at my dad's bedside.

That evening, I spoke to another doctor who confirmed that my dad had a lung infection. They had also tested him for Covid, but the doctor sounded hopeful. 'Try to get some rest tonight,' he said. 'We should have better news tomorrow.'

I was woken just after six that Sunday morning. As soon as I heard the jangle of the landline, I knew what to expect. My cousin, Brian, who had also broken the news of my mother's death to me eleven months earlier, hesitated after his initial hello: 'Don, I'm so sorry. Your dad passed away twenty minutes ago.'

Death still felt surprising and I wondered how my dad had been in his last moments. Had he felt lonely or frightened?

I persuaded Alison to go back to bed. She needed all her strength as we did not have long left before we faced the same news about her mum.

I went downstairs and called my dad's hospital ward. The sister on duty answered immediately. 'Your father was very calm,' she said. 'I think he was peaceful when he went.'

There was little else she could say, but I liked believing her. I only took in a sharp breath when she said that he had tested positive for Covid. It would be listed as the likely cause of his death, reducing my dad to another statistic on Covid's roll-call.

I felt no anger towards fate, or the pandemic. It seemed as if, in his final week of life, my father just ran out of fight.

The red button on the Sky box no longer shone as it had done when I first came downstairs. For once, it was not a boxing recording from the US. Instead, I had recorded a UFC promotion featuring my favourite mixed martial arts fighter. Rose Namajunas looked fragile, but she fought with fire. Her nickname was Thug Rose, but she was the least thuggish young woman imaginable. Her shaved head made her look like a young Sinéad O'Connor singing 'Nothing Compares 2 U', but Rose was an American of Lithuanian descent.

I guessed that my dad would understand as, forty minutes after hearing I had lost him, I turned on the recording of Rose Namajunas fighting Jéssica Andrade for the UFC straw-weight title. He would have expected boxing but, in its absence, I turned to Thug Rose who was trying to win back her belt on Fight Island – as the UFC called their Covid-secure hub on Yas Island in Abu Dhabi. There were no spectators and the lockdown made the sight of Namajunas and Andrade in the steel cage look starker than usual.

Andrade had won their first fight, in May 2019, on a second-round stoppage and I yearned for Thug Rose to win the rematch. 'Do it for my dad,' I said under my breath, despite knowing my gentle old father and a brutal MMA battle did not belong together.

After three ferocious five-minute rounds, they went to the scorecards. Andrade wore a blue and yellow American Native headdress, while Rose's nose was cut and there was a purple swelling under her left eye. They were both barefoot and looked vulnerable and worried. They each received a 29–28 score in their favour before Bruce Buffer paused.

'C'mon, Rose, do it for my dad,' I whispered.

'29–28 for the winner, by split decision …' Buffer cried. *'Thuggg Roseee Namajunasss!'*

It was not boxing, but it still felt profound. 'She won, Dad,' I said, knowing that my father had never even heard of Rose Namajunas. *'She won.'*

Rose dabbed her bleeding and broken nose, and seemed only slightly bemused when the post-fight interviewer suggested she had been having fun in the cage. 'Mostly,' she said dryly. The interview went through the usual routine of discussing the fight and when she would challenge for the world title again. But, as it ended, Rose remembered Susy Friton, the UFC make-up artist who would die from breast cancer in September 2021.

'Oh wait, can I say one thing?' Rose asked as she held up her gloved right hand. 'I'm auctioning my fight kit for Suzy. She is battling cancer. We love you Suzy!'

Life and death mingled together in the soft light of that Sunday morning. I sank back into my chair and cried.

I still couldn't fly to South Africa, but Alison and I planned my father's funeral. We chose the songs and hymns, selected the forty photographs that would be screened on a loop and informed those closest to my dad in South Africa that they would be among the eighteen people permitted to attend on Friday 31 July 2020 at 2.30 p.m. We would follow it on a livestream.

Our concern was that we would lose Pat that same day because, on the morning of Thursday the 30th, Alison was called by the nursing home. She and Anna were asked to come and say a possible final goodbye. Their brother, Tim, would soon drive from Cardiff to say his own farewell. We were told that it could be days, or just hours, before Pat slipped away. She was no longer eating, her eyes were closed and her breathing had changed. Death was coming.

I drove Alison to Harpenden and watched her and Anna disappear into the care home. It was a quiet lunchtime as I sat outside and waited. In just over twenty-four hours, we would be remote guests at my dad's funeral. We were locked down in a time like no other – just days away from the global number of Covid cases passing the twenty million mark.

On our way home, Alison told me how she and Anna had shared stories of their past at their mum's bedside. Pat seemed to be asleep but, occasionally, she would open just one eye. That deep brown eye stared unseeingly at them before, eventually, it closed again. Then, just before it was time to go, Alison felt her mum's finger gently scratch the inside of her hand. It was as if her mother had found a way to say she had heard every word that had been said.

On the morning of my father's funeral, the sky was the deepest blue while sunshine flooded our garden. My phone beeped with a WhatsApp message from Brian. 'It is a lovely balmy winter's day in Johannesburg. 22C, cloudless and not a breath of wind. I believe it is also hot and sunny in London.'

'Just as my dad would like it,' I replied.

A minute before we joined the livestream, Brian sent me an image. A photograph of my dad, placed at the front of the church, was surrounded by a beautiful display of lamps. 'An abundance of electricity,' Brian texted. It looked even more powerful when we logged on.

Gavin Lock, the minister, welcomed us to the service, making special mention of those joining the funeral remotely. He turned back to his congregation. 'I know it's awkward to be sitting here with masks on your faces,' he said, 'to be exercising social distance, not even able to give a hug to a loved one who is grieving.'

He paused and it felt as if we were there, rather than 6,000 miles away. 'I don't know what it seems like for you but, for me, this world is going to be less without Ian McRae. He was a big, imposing man, but without him, the world is going to be a little less kind, a little less wise, a little less gentle. That's the thing about death. It just seems to take away, to rob us ... but if Ian meant nothing to us, we would have no tears. The point is that when we feel the pain of loss, that hurt is sacred. It reminds us of the magnitude of love we have for the person we have lost.

'You see the man who shook the hands of presidents and the heads of liberation movements. If anyone had the right to throw his light around it was Dr Ian McRae. But he had the knack of making sure other people's light shone. When I was in his presence, he made me feel like a king. And so this is the reason we wanted these lamps around Ian's picture. They don't represent Ian's light. They represent the many people whose light Ian uncovered.'

Gavin turned to my eulogy and began to read. 'Ian McRae, my dad, was often called South Africa's Mr Electricity. He had so much energy and clarity of vision that a newspaper headline once extolled him as 'The Man with Volts in His Veins'. He was also, simply, my dad. He was the dad who sang 'Hello Dolly' to me, doing his best Louis Armstrong impression, when I was very small and capable of laughing hysterically after he swapped Dolly's name for mine.

'He would infuriate me in later years when, while I wanted to nurse my hangover after a teenage party, he would burst in, fling open the curtains and break out into song again – either 'When You're Smiling' or 'Donald, Where's Your Troosers?'

'After I left South Africa, my dad never missed a Saturday morning when he wrote a long letter telling me about his week while offering so much support and love for all I was trying to do, alone, in a strange and teeming city like London. I remember being so moved every time I opened a letter from my dad and his spidery scrawl burst into life. He didn't use flashy words. He just wrote as he spoke, calmly, and made me feel that I was doing well even when, in truth, I was floundering.

'His capacity to find beauty and even joy amid seeming catastrophe made me admire and love him even more. Ian was diagnosed with cancer himself the same week we lost Jess. He said he would just make the most of however long he had left. I was with him last

August, and again this January, when I came home to be with him. My last visit was full of happiness and peace.'

Gavin choked up, briefly, over that little word of 'happiness'. And then the flow returned to his reading. 'During those last days together, we also watched a lot of sport on TV – and almost as much news. My dad's worldly nature meant that we would move from local channels to CNN, the BBC and Al Jazeera. Rather than becoming inward and decrepit, Ian continued to look outward with interest and optimism.

'Mr Electricity did not have volts in his veins, but he lit up the world. And so I can put my sadness to one side. Rather than gloom or darkness, I still feel the warmth and see the light of the man I was lucky enough to call my dad.'

Gavin smiled as he told us that, after his final prayer, we would hear one last song as the funeral came to an end. 'It's another song that emulates Ian's hopefulness so beautifully. It's a testament to that twinkle in Ian's eyes when he was mischievous with his children. We are going to be serenaded out by Louis Armstrong as a testimony to Ian's singing . . .'

Rather than 'Hello Dolly', which my dad massacred for my amusement, we had chosen 'What a Wonderful World', recorded in 1967 when I was six years old.

As a teenager, and in my twenties, I derided that old ditty as a cheesy dollop of schmaltz. It was different on the final day of July 2020. I was a fifty-nine-year-old orphan. I was the last remaining member of my original family of four. So I smiled, rather than cried, as the gravelly voice of Louis Armstrong sang of how 'I see trees of green' and 'skies of blue', 'I see the bright blessed day' and 'the dark sacred night'. As he sang, I remembered my dad singing to me, and of my mom telling me how they had danced to Satchmo on Saturday nights.

After he had crooned 'what a wonderful world' one last time, Armstrong finished the song with a breathy *'Oh yeah . . . !'*

We went out into the garden with the kids. I cracked open a

bottle of champagne, in honour of my dancing and singing parents, and Alison brought out a beautiful lunch. We sat in the sunshine and talked and even laughed. It was a sweet mystery how such a day could carry so much light and love.

Pat had been so fond of Ian and so, while she could not rally, she allowed us to honour him. She lived for one more week, without saying another word. Early the following Saturday morning, Alison took the call from Anna which told us their mum had died.

Alison cried. But, then, she just looked at me in surprise, and even wonder. It was 8 August 2020 – a year to the very day that I had lost my mother. There was a perfect symmetry, amid the grief, in losing our mothers on the exact same date.

7

In the Bubble

Isaac Chamberlain's sweat fell like drops of rain on the wooden floor of a gym near Clapham Junction. It glistened in little pools alongside blue-and-white stickers of a large arrow which told the fighter to stick to the 'One Way System'. Other signs of social distancing were pasted on the walls. Chamberlain, who understood isolation, kept working hard.

He would return to the ring on Saturday 22 August 2020, in an empty Channel 5 studio in Redditch, near Birmingham. His opponent, Antony Woolery, had a modest record of two wins and two losses. Chamberlain's own record was 10–1 and it seemed sensible that his promoter Mick Hennessy had chosen an easy challenge for his first fight in nearly twenty-two months.

Boxing had begun to make its tentative way back in bizarre settings. On 1 August, Eddie Hearn had staged the first of four Fight Camp promotions in the back garden of his family home, spread across fifteen acres in Brentwood, Essex. A limited number of spectators were allowed at Hearn's outdoor venue on successive Saturday nights. It would be different in Redditch when Chamberlain and Woolery climbed into the ring in a studio devoid of fans.

On another searing day in Clapham, temperatures rose to 37°C, I settled into the sounds and sights of the gym, of buzzers and cries, of rope being skipped and pads being hit. It felt soothing to be back inside this hermetically sealed world.

Towards the end of his ninety-minute training routine, Chamberlain kicked off his trainers and knelt on a mat. He looked as if he might bow his head to pray as his breathing slowed. Chamberlain kept kneeling while looking at the deserted ring for nearly five minutes.

'I was just concentrating,' he said with his familiar grin once we sat two metres apart on the apron of the ring. 'I'm going to make sure I don't fight with too much emotion. If I was a brain surgeon facing a difficult operation next Saturday, I couldn't allow any emotion or doubt to take over. The patient would take one look at me and think: *What the heck is going on?* If I act clinically, then I am going to operate properly. But it's difficult because I'm from Brixton, man. I have so much emotion after all the frustration and pain.'

Chamberlain was no longer working with the Cuban trainer Jorge Rubio in Miami. He was far happier to have teamed up with another Cuban in Rasel Hechavarria, and with Bobby Mills, his old friend from his first gym in Brixton. 'Rasel is a former national coach in Cuba,' Chamberlain said. 'He has taught me a lot and helped me relax in the ring.'

Neither Hechavarria nor Mills held a professional British training licence. They had applied to the British Boxing Board of Control, and submitted their credentials in amateur boxing, but Covid had slowed the processing of such requests. It would be a few more months before they could work Chamberlain's corner during a fight.

'Mick will sort out a replacement [trainer] for next Saturday,' Chamberlain said calmly.

It had not been easy working with Rubio in Miami. 'Five thousand miles from home, I had no Christmas, no New Year, no birthday,' Chamberlain recalled. 'Miami was like a jail. It cost $15 a night and I shared a dorm with nine other people. I'm lucky I'm a big guy and I'm Black so nobody wanted to touch me.'

He shrugged when I asked what his room-mates were doing in such a desolate place. 'I didn't ask. I was just trying to get by. Wake up early, go run. Come back, shower, read my books. It was like a prison cell. Every time I went to the gym, I'd spend excessive hours there. Train extra hard, spar more rounds. Do anything to avoid going back to prison.'

Chamberlain would have become a chemical or an electrical engineer if he had not fallen for this unforgiving business. But he carried renewed purpose and, as we left the gym, he revealed that he had started writing again.

'I'll send it to you, boss,' he said.

A few hours later, my phone pinged and the words of boxing's secret writer lit up my screen.

'I'm not the same person I was when I entered this game. It's turned me darker, it's turned me into a bit of a monster. When I'm relentless they crumble because they have not been where I've been. They haven't swam in deep waters. I was underwater for eighteen months, trying to swim to the shore. I thought I drowned a few times ... but I was born to be a champion.'

'We're in the bubble, bro,' Chamberlain exclaimed as, rather than bumping elbows, he gave me a bear hug in a Covid testing room at a Holiday Inn on the outskirts of Redditch on Thursday 20 August. It was easy to understand the boxer's readiness to demolish social distancing measures because his previous four bouts had all been cancelled and he was just sixty hours away from fighting again.

His mask was blue, and mine was black, but the crinkly folds around his eyes told me Chamberlain was smiling. A Covid test was one of the final barriers he had to clear.

Chamberlain moved to the designated spot, where the nurse waited, and slipped off his mask. He opened his mouth so a swab could be taken. A nasal swab followed and both were sealed in sterilised containers. I completed the same procedure. There was nothing more we could do but wait for the results.

The fighters, Hennessy's promotional team, Boxing Board officials and I disappeared to our respective rooms of strict quarantine. Meals came and went, delivered and left outside our hotel room doors. I worked, swapped messages with Chamberlain and looked out of the third-floor window. NO EXIT was painted on the road outside.

At 10 p.m., I heard voices in the corridor. A gentle knock on the door and a cheery voice confirmed I had tested negative for coronavirus. I opened the door and accepted a black band, to be worn on my wrist, which carried the message: *Testing Passed*. Everyone in our bubble was clear. Saturday night was on.

None of us were allowed to leave the hotel for the next forty-four hours – and no one else could come in. But just before lunchtime on Friday, the familiar televised weigh-in unfolded in the same room we had been tested in. Paul Booth, the shaven-headed and bow-tied MC, called each fighter to the scales.

Chamberlain ambled over in white socks and sliders. He wore his mask, tracksuit bottoms and a black T-shirt. The sculpted fighter stood barefoot and bare-chested on the scales and Booth confirmed he had made the cruiserweight limit. Chamberlain's squat opponent, Antony Woolery, looked as if he was trying to hide his little paunch as they did their masked face-off.

As always, the night before the fight dragged. Michael Hennessy, the promoter's son who was a baby-faced twenty-year-old middleweight, broke the unsettling monotony. He and his trainer Junior Saba stepped into the corridor on the third floor where most of us were in our isolated rooms. The *whappity-whap* of gloves smacking into pads echoed outside the elevator as Hennessy Jr and Saba killed time.

Fight day was slow. In the deserted hotel lounge, Chamberlain and I watched videos on his phone of his favourite boxer. Joan Guzman, a former world champion super-bantamweight, was a slick stylist from the Dominican Republic who carried enough power to have earned himself the name of 'Little Tyson' in the late 1990s.

Chamberlain loved his fluid technique and he also showed me how Guzman used to leave his corner after the first bell and leap and twirl in the air before throwing a punch.

'I'm gonna do that tonight,' Chamberlain cackled.

There was less frivolity at 6 p.m. as Chamberlain and I sat on two wooden chairs in the Channel 5 studio. A ring was lit up by the surrounding red screens which all carried the number 5. It was dark in our corner at ringside. Instead of thousands of people drinking and singing 'Sweet Caroline', the studio was hushed and empty. 'This is surreal,' Chamberlain said softly. 'It's making me have deep thoughts and powerful emotions. I can't believe I'm fighting again.'

It was exactly six months to the night since Tyson Fury knocked out Deontay Wilder in Las Vegas. So much had changed. I watched the Covid cleaning team chatting at ringside. Later, I learned that the four temporary cleaners, who sanitised the ring after every fight, were actually doctors. Sultan Hassan, who worked that night as a medic and a cleaner dressed in full PPE, sent me a tweet: 'This would be the most qualified cleaning team comprising a consultant plastic surgeon, anaesthetist and two emergency/GP doctors.'

By the time Michael Hennessy stepped into the ring, for the second bout of the night and the fifth of his career, we had almost forgotten Covid. Chamberlain's voice echoed above the fighters' gasps and grunts and the disconcerting thud of fists smacking into flesh and bone. Boxing seemed very raw without any crowd noise to disguise the hurt.

'Good shot, bro,' Chamberlain shouted to Hennessy. 'Use your feet. Hunt him down. That's great ... Feint to the body. Double jab, right hook, beautiful boxing, bro.'

Between rounds, Chamberlain turned to me. 'This is nerve-wracking, man!'

Hennessy Jr won on points and, with an hour left until he stepped into the ring, it was time for Chamberlain to retreat to the curtained area of his makeshift dressing room. His hands were wrapped in silence before, in an eerie blue light, Chamberlain lay on the floor and stretched.

Later, he stood patiently while Vaseline was applied to his eyebrows. His gloves were pulled on and then, with twenty minutes left, Chamberlain began to hit the pads held up by Junior Saba, his trainer for the night.

The next call came. 'Ten minutes ...'

Chamberlain was concentrated and gleaming as he crashed punches into the shuddering mitts.

'Five minutes, gents,' a Channel 5 production man said as sweat flew across the tented room.

Chamberlain offered his glove so we could bump fists. 'Ready, lads?' a voice shouted. Chamberlain wore a shimmering black singlet with two words stitched in white on the back: *End Racism*. It was a timely reminder, from Chamberlain, that Black lives matter and that he had not forgotten the murder of George Floyd. I walked behind the fighter, but there was a long pause when, close to where we had sat, Chamberlain watched Woolery enter the ring.

Without any fans it was like nothing I had seen in boxing. It was a fight for our Covid times.

Chamberlain kept his promise and, after the opening bell, he leapt and twirled in his corner, in honour of Guzman.

The gulf in class was obvious, even if it took two rounds for Chamberlain to shake off his ring rust against an aggressive Woolery. After a minute of round three, having repeatedly snapped his jab into Woolery's face, Chamberlain speared heavy hooks into his rival's sagging frame. A savage left to the body dropped Woolery. The referee stopped counting at seven.

'It felt like a fight,' Chamberlain said in his dressing room. 'I was zoned in and didn't notice anything outside the ring. As soon as he stepped in, I hit him with the jab. I then went *bap*, *bap*, *bap* to the head, to bring his hands up, and then, boom, back to the body!'

After Woolery visited Chamberlain's dressing room to pay his respects and ask for a photo, it felt tranquil but strange. This was how boxing, and life, had to be for the foreseeable future.

On 27 August, there was another funeral when we said goodbye to Pat. There were just thirteen of us, apart from the celebrant and the undertakers, at the service. We then spent the afternoon in our garden and, as we ate and drank, we remembered Pat with warmth and love.

The following day, the *New York Times* ran an obituary of my dad under the headline of 'Ian McRae, Who Brought Electricity to Black South Africa, Dies at 90.' I sat in the shade of a tree and read. 'During South Africa's struggle against apartheid, demonstrators with clenched fists would proclaim *"Amandla Ngawethu, Matla kea Rona!"*, loosely translated as "Power to the People". Ian McRae interpreted the phrase in a more practical sense. As head of the state-owned electrical utility, Mr McRae, a white South African, flouted the country's racial laws to deliver kilowatts of power to the woefully underserved Black townships.'

The newspaper confirmed that, 'the cause [of death] was complications of the novel coronavirus', before adding that 'a decade before the election [of Nelson Mandela], Mr McRae and Eskom flouted apartheid and in so doing contributed to the country's social transformation. They prepared to provide electrical power to the segregated urban areas reserved for non-whites; upgraded the utility distribution systems in Angola, Lesotho and Mozambique with the intention of integrating them into a sub-continental power grid; and hired and trained Black workers to manage and maintain new power plants as demand for electricity grew.'

The obituary also detailed how my dad had worked at Eskom for forty-seven years, starting as an apprentice fitter-and-turner, which was the exact same job his own father, my grandad George, had done for years at the company. I read on, thinking how far my dad had travelled from a blue-collar job to an obituary in the *New York Times*.

The finality hit me, too, when I reached the last short paragraph: 'His son is his only immediate survivor. A daughter, Heather, died in 2018. His wife, Jessie (Scott) McRae, died last year.'

Regis Prograis drove through the darkness of Texas on Halloween night, 31 October 2020. One hundred and seventy miles separate San Antonio from Katy, on the outskirts of Houston. He had two-and-a-half hours to think as his car sped through the quiet of that Saturday night. Prograis had been out of the ring for a year and five days, but his return saw him defeat the previously unbeaten Juan Heraldez in a third-round stoppage at the Alamodome in San Antonio. He had to curb his desire to get home even faster. His wife Raquel was due to give birth to their third child, and second daughter, that night.

The following morning, he sent me a message on WhatsApp. 'Raquel is having contractions now. Baby is probably gonna come today.'

Later that day, their little girl Khalanni arrived safely in a home birth. 'It was so good, man,' Prograis said on Zoom. 'When I was in the bubble in San Antonio, I was nervous she was going to have the baby while I was fighting. But when I had left home to go into the bubble, my wife was all business. Raquel said she's going to handle it and that's what she did. She and the baby also waited for me to get back and so it was perfect.

'But it was so weird being in the bubble. On Tuesday, we couldn't leave our rooms at all. Usually Tuesday is the big day where I lose three or four pounds by running with a sauna suit on. The bubble messed me up. It felt like jail. But once fight night came, I was good. I'd been in training camp for nearly a year, so I almost felt sorry for [Heraldez] that I took it out on him.'

While 9,000 fans were allowed into an arena which can hold 72,000 people, in US boxing's first major card with spectators since the start of the pandemic, social distancing made it feel odd. 'They had to space people out and so it wasn't a regular fight where the place is packed,' Prograis said. 'I also couldn't understand why there were these guys in sci-fi movie suits [sanitising the ring between fights]. We knew we didn't have corona because we came from the bubble and wore masks all week. It was strange.'

There had been a more beautiful strangeness when, after his hand was raised in victory, Prograis was joined by his seven-year-old son, Ray. 'It's crazy how he snuck in the ring. He was with my mom, but ran off and said: "I want to be with my daddy."'

Prograis paused when I asked if little Ray had been upset the previous October as, at ringside, he saw his dad endure a ferocious night against Josh Taylor. 'I remember right after the fight he got in the ring and said: "Why didn't you duck?" I laughed and said: "I ducked a little bit."'

Would he steer Ray away from becoming a boxer? 'It's crazy because my son is in the gym right now, boxing my nephew. The things we go through are so brutal I wouldn't want my kid to feel it. But he might have it in his blood, so if he wants to do it then, yeah, I'd let him.'

Prograis looked at me and smiled, almost helplessly. 'What can we do, man? It's boxing.'

MTK Global had moved into American boxing and clinched management deals with eight promising fighters including Vergil Ortiz Jr and Joshua Franco. But in December 2020, they hit a roadblock. JoJo Diaz, their first American signing, was still under contract to Heredia Boxing Management. Moses Heredia and his company were minnows, but the American promoter and manager was defiant. Five days before Christmas, he filed four counts of racketeering in the US District Court in California.

The significance of the allegations centred on Heredia's claim that Kinahan and MTK were in breach of the RICO Act. RICO stands for Racketeer Influenced and Corrupt Organizations and Heredia brought serious charges to court. He said Kinahan had founded MTK Global as a front to launder illicit proceeds from drug trafficking.

It had been obvious for a long time that no one in boxing had the desire or power to stop Kinahan and MTK. The Irish government and their Criminal Assets Bureau had also failed to bring him to justice. But contravening the RICO Act meant that the Irishman would be brought to the attention of the US Federal Bureau of Investigation. Maybe the Feds would concentrate their gaze on Kinahan. Such hope offered a chink of light in the gloom of boxing.

On 1 February 2021, the Kinahan story gained traction when the BBC's *Panorama* investigation into his work in boxing aired. *Boxing and the Mob* did not break fresh ground, but there was a seismic shift as almost a million British viewers with little previous knowledge of Kinahan watched an hour-long documentary which presented clear evidence that the leader of a violent drug-running operation was working in the highest echelons of boxing.

Rather than boxing's indifference, or trepidation, there was outrage that a sport had become involved with the Kinahan Organised Crime Group, described by the BBC as 'one of Europe's most brutal drug cartels' and which the Irish courts 'have accepted is involved in drug trafficking, money laundering and gangland executions'.

In explaining the silence surrounding Kinahan's involvement in boxing, Barry McGuigan told *Panorama* that 'there is no doubt there is an intimidation effect. There is no question about that. Someone has got to look out for this sport. They really need to look at this situation very carefully, because it's bloody dangerous.'

Those four short but brave sentences gave outsiders a glimpse of the hard truth. Boxing was in the grip of gangsterism. McGuigan remained a household name, a fighter who had won his world featherweight title in front of twenty million viewers on BBC One in 1985, and a man who had appeared on reality television shows while retaining his boxing identity. National newspapers, radio and television stations and social media lit up with furious attention. The Kinahan story had gone mainstream.

Kinahan's lawyers told the BBC he had no criminal convictions and dismissed the 'wild' and 'false' allegations. They said of Kinahan: 'He is proud of his record in boxing to date. He has operated on the basis of honesty and with a commitment to putting fighters' needs first. Mr Kinahan is a successful and independent adviser in the boxing industry.'

I called Robert Smith, the general secretary for the British Boxing Board of Control, and he said there was nothing his governing body could do to curb Kinahan. 'It was disappointing for the sport, obviously,' Smith said of the BBC evidence, 'but the gentleman is not licensed by the Board in any capacity. We don't license MTK as a promoter. We license individuals, so the named promoter is Lee Eaton [of MTK] and he is the only person we deal with.'

Promoters, managers, trainers and fighters all needed a professional boxing licence, but advisers, of whom Kinahan was the most notorious, did not answer to the Board.

The UK's leading boxing administrator paused when I asked if he felt ashamed that the issue had not been addressed properly in Britain. 'I am not going to argue with you,' Smith said. 'However, wrongly or rightly, he has not been convicted of any offence. That makes things very difficult and we have to let the authorities take the upper hand.'

The governing body also had no power over Fury. 'Tyson Fury is not licensed with the British Boxing Board,' Smith said. 'After his first world title fight with Deontay Wilder, when he was licensed with us, Fury decided that he would relinquish his British licence and box under a Nevada licence. So we have no jurisdiction over him.'

Boxing remained a lawless and unregulated mess.

Billy Joe Saunders was boxing's most vocal supporter of Daniel Kinahan. He led the onslaught against Barry McGuigan for talking openly about Kinahan. Saunders also mocked the death of Barry's daughter, Danika, from cancer in June 2019.

I remembered the only time I had interviewed Saunders. Before his pro debut in February 2009, I met the fighter and his father in a gym tucked away in a derelict warehouse in Canning Town. The nineteen-year-old fighter worked hard in the ring while his dad told me about their Romany Gypsy heritage. Tom Saunders described the persecution of the Roma under the Nazis and explained how draconian legislation shackled their misunderstood tradition in Britain. I listened sympathetically, as I did when Tom said he hoped Billy Joe could change perceptions of their community.

'I'd like to do that,' the fighter himself said an hour later. 'When most people hear we're Travellers they think *Gypsy! Trouble!* It ain't nice. Look at my dad, or my great-grandad. They're proud and decent men.'

Absolom Beeney, Saunders' great-grandfather, had been a bare-knuckle fighter at fairgrounds run by the Romany Gypsies more than seventy years before. 'He was a champion, my old great-grandad,' Saunders said, 'and you can still see that today. We never had birth certificates in them days, so no one's sure of his exact age. He says he's ninety-six, but he might be a year or two older. He still goes drinking in different pubs around Hertfordshire and they all know him.'

We had not spoken since that interview. My interest in Saunders had been eroded by a suspicion of doping, a stream of cruel online videos and his subsequent support of Kinahan. In September 2018, Saunders had tested positive for oxilofrine, a banned substance which helps cut weight. The boxer blamed an inhaler, but he was forced to give up his WBO middleweight title. That same month he released a video online of him taunting a female addict by making her do various demeaning acts with the promise he would give her £150 worth of crack. He was fined £100,000 by the British Boxing Board of Control for bringing the sport into disrepute.

That punishment did not stop Saunders from posting another

video in March 2020 when he offered men advice on how to hit their female partners if 'your old woman is giving you mouth' and 'she's coming at you, spitting a bit of venom in your face' during lockdown. As he pounded a heavy bag, Saunders showed how to 'hit her on the chin' and then 'finish her off'.

The video caused justified outrage. Saunders was forced to make an apology as crass as it was cloying. 'I would never condone domestic violence and if I saw a man touch a woman, I would smash him to pieces myself. Apologies if I offended any women, stay blessed.'

Eight months later, in November 2020, he was cruel towards Daniel Dubois after the heavyweight sank down on a knee and allowed himself to be counted out after his swollen eye was pummelled by Joe Joyce. Dubois had suffered an orbital bone fracture but Saunders called him a coward and a quitter, insisting that 'before I go on one knee, I'd go out on my back with my pulse stopped'.

He was close to Fury and they trained together while Saunders prepared for his fight against Saúl 'Canelo' Álvarez. Canelo was rated the world's best boxer in the pound-for-pound rankings, but Fury seemed convinced that his mouthy friend would prevail when they stepped into the ring in May 2021. 'I think Billy Joe gives him a boxing lesson,' Fury suggested. 'Everyone raves about Canelo, but Billy Joe came out of the womb fighting like myself. We are cut from the same cloth. Canelo has never fought a Fighting Gypsy. We are a different breed and Canelo will be under a curse. There will be Gypsy magic in the air.'

The fight gripped my attention. Saunders represented everything I disliked about contemporary boxing, while Canelo forged a link with the fight game's more magisterial traditions. I never want a fighter to be hurt, but I hoped Saunders would be exposed by a great champion in Canelo.

'I love this,' Canelo Álvarez said as he gazed at the scattered debris of his gym in San Diego. He scanned the heavy bags and speed balls, the hand wraps and water bottles, the gloves and head guards, with an empty ring at its heart. It was just after ten in the morning and the familiar clatter of his training camp had begun for the day in mid-April 2021. Canelo switched to Spanish to capture the surprising ardour he felt as a thirty-year-old boxer who had been fighting professionally for more than half his life.

'I love it,' he said in Spanish. 'I'm always motivated because I love boxing.'

After months of boxing gangsterism, it felt moving as, in a rare one-to-one interview, Canelo switched back to English. 'This is the reality of my life. No boxing, no life.'

I was far from the first person to whom Canelo had said these words. 'No boxing, no life' had become his promotional mantra. T-shirts and caps, coasters and mugs, carried those words. They could look glib in print but, when Canelo said them, they sounded resonant. He had lost only once, to Floyd Mayweather in 2013, in fifty-eight bouts. Canelo was now on a roll of fights, preparing for his third in five months, as he set about bringing order to a murky business.

From the 1920s to the 1970s, when the fight game remained a mainstream sport, it was not uncommon for world champions to defend their titles three or four times a year. It was very different in the 21st century when the best boxers rarely faced each other and many seemed content to fight just once a year.

Canelo occupied more traditional terrain as he fought more than he talked. After defeating Danny Jacobs, the Miracle Man and Pat Day's friend, in a middleweight world title bout in the summer of 2019, Canelo had ended the year as a world light-heavyweight champion when he moved up two divisions to knock out Sergey Kovalev in the eleventh round. It meant that he had become a world champion in four different weight categories from light-middleweight (147 pounds) to light-heavyweight (175 pounds).

His new mission was to become the first undisputed super-middleweight champion of the world. Canelo already held the WBA belt and, in December 2020, he dominated a good fighter in Callum Smith, from Liverpool, to become the WBC champion.

Two months later, he defended his WBA and WBC titles by stopping Avni Yildirim in three rounds. When we met, he was preparing to head to Texas to fight Saunders, the WBO champion, on 8 May with the aim of then facing Caleb Plant, the IBF title-holder, in September in a world super-middleweight unification contest. I liked the way Canelo swept aside all promotional squabbles and sanctioning body obstacles in his quest to bring clarity to boxing.

Even the gym was devoid of frippery. A seriousness of purpose meant it looked anonymous on the outside. Tucked away in a utilitarian business park in a modest quarter of San Diego, the windows were shut and the door usually remained locked. Even the most zealous of Canelo's Mexican fans did not seem to know he did most of his work here.

Token gestures of colour made it look a little less sparse. A huge mural of Canelo, his right fist raised as he was carried on the shoulders of his trainer, Eddy Reynoso, dominated the entrance, while one wall was covered in a collection of flags from boxing countries around the world. The largest of these, by some distance, was the huge green, white and red flag of Mexico.

I had met so many fighters over so many years, but this interview felt more intense than most. It reminded me of the feelings I'd experienced just before interviewing Mike Tyson for the first time – or those occasions when I had sat down with great old champions from the past in Sugar Ray Leonard and Roberto Durán. Canelo belonged with them in the pantheon.

Yet Canelo was not stainless, for he had tested positive for clenbuterol in February 2018. There had been a wave of positive test results for Mexican athletes; their defence usually rested on the claim that contaminated meat was so prevalent in their country. Canelo argued that Daniel Eichner, the highly regarded scientist at the Salt Lake City lab which carried out the VADA (Voluntary Anti-Doping Association) tests, concluded that the trace amounts of clenbuterol 'are all within the range of what is expected from meat contamination'.

Canelo also agreed to take additional tests of his hair, which offer a more rigorous analysis than blood and urine samples, and produced restaurant receipts which apparently proved he had unwittingly eaten contaminated beef. It was still impossible to know with certainty whether he was innocent, but Canelo received a mere six-month suspension.

We returned to the roots of his story, and his childhood in Juanacatlán, not far from the much bigger city of Guadalajara. Canelo, who was just called Saúl then, was the youngest of eight children, seven of whom were boys. He had been a small, shy boy who felt 'very different to everyone else. I didn't look like an ordinary Mexican kid. My hair was red and my skin was very pale with lots of freckles. It was not easy.'

When Saúl was six years old, his father, Santos, sent him to sell ice-creams in downtown Guadalajara. 'There was a big bus station there,' Canelo said in Spanish, 'and I had to take all these *paletas* [ice pops] because we needed the money. I was quiet, but it wasn't necessarily a sense of being timid when I got onto the buses. It was more a real embarrassment. I could see how they looked at me and what they said because I was a redhead. They would also pinch me when I walked past. There were lots of tears and melted *paletas*.'

The teasing and the bullying continued close to home as little Saúl was pushed around in the streets of Juanacatlán. 'My brothers all became boxers and Rigoberto [his oldest sibling] told me to fight back when I was about ten. But it took another year before I decided. This big kid was teasing and pushing me and I thought: *No. Enough.*'

Saúl bunched his fists and, from nowhere, he let them fly. He was as stunned as everyone else when he saw blood spurt from the nose of the other kid who immediately ran away. Almost twenty years later, Canelo grinned at the memory. 'I liked it too much. I knew everything would change from that moment.'

He followed his brothers back to Guadalajara and the rickety Julián Magdaleno gym run by 'Chepo' Reynoso and his son Eddy, who is Canelo's trainer today. There was no holding back his prodigious talent as he stormed through the tough Mexican amateur ranks. In October 2005, just three months after he turned fifteen, Saúl climbed into the professional ring for the first time.

His decision to fight for money had been hastened by the fact that his girlfriend was pregnant. Saúl faced eighteen-year-old Abraham Gonzalez, who had fought once before.

'I remember it very clearly,' Canelo said. 'I did well and they stopped it in the fourth round because my opponent had a cut over his eye.'

He acquired the evocative nickname of Canelo, which meant 'cinnamon' in Spanish. Chepo Reynoso, who understood how much the teenager had suffered, chose the name as he wanted it to be 'something softer, nicer, because he was being called such harsh things'.

Life had since become much more tangled. Canelo's celebrity meant that his family was now targeted and, in December 2018, before he fought Rocky Fielding, one of his brothers was kidnapped. In the week of the bout, Canelo had to negotiate his brother's release without involving the police. It was not surprising when Canelo said, 'nothing is easy in this life'. Deep into his sixteenth year as a pro, Canelo insisted that he would not be derailed by fame. 'People come out of the woodwork offering you drugs and money and trying to align themselves with you. And when you have fame, there is this sense you're untouchable. That is even more dangerous because once you start thinking this way, you won't put in the work that got you to that position. I never believe what fame tells me. I believe only in hard work.'

Amid the bluster and sleaze of boxing, Canelo's words sounded refreshing. He had retained his thirst for work after signing a mammoth $385 million, eleven-fight contract that his former promoters, Golden Boy, brokered with the streaming service DAZN in 2018.

Even when that contract hit an impasse, Canelo seemed like no one else in modern boxing. His ties to Golden Boy and DAZN were severed and he had become the biggest force in the fight game and a free agent. But did he feel concern that boxing gets every fighter in the end?

He nodded. 'It does worry me. I know what boxing does to fighters. But this is another reason why I train so hard. This is my life. And this is boxing. The two are the same for me.'

He smiled. 'Now, my friend, it's time for me to work again. It's time for me to do what I love.'

On Saturday 8 May 2021, as the lights dim at the AT&T Stadium in Arlington, Texas, Winston Churchill's 'We will fight them on the beaches' speech merges into a honeyed R'n'B track that has Billy Joe Saunders dancing and singing on his walk to the ring. Booing rains down on him from most of the 73,126 people crammed into the home of the Dallas Cowboys, making this the largest indoor crowd in boxing history to watch a fight in the United States.

There are still reminders of Covid at ringside. One of the three judges wears a PPE visor and a ghostly group in full PPE uniforms have just sanitised the ring.

Meanwhile, Tyson Fury, wearing a floral top and white trousers, grins in the Saunders corner. But not even the world heavyweight champion can compete with the roar as Canelo emerges at the darkened mouth of a tunnel in a silken white and gold-trimmed Dolce & Gabbana robe.

A Mexican band strikes up a jaunty ditty as scores of women twirl their colourful dresses around Canelo like giant fans. He smiles and beats his chest.

Canelo starts the fight slowly and Saunders, a tricky southpaw, shades some of the early rounds with his clever movement. At the start of the sixth, Saunders comes out with his arms raised, but Canelo simply walks towards the fray with methodical intent. Halfway through the round, Canelo hurts Saunders to the body, but the Traveller responds with a sharp left. Saunders is doing well but, with thirty seconds remaining, Canelo jolts him. The outsider waggles his tongue in defiance of Canelo.

Saunders still looks full of self-belief and he is narrowly ahead on some scorecards.

Canelo bides his time. He even allows Saunders to throw all the punches in the opening thirty seconds of round seven. And then, after a minute, Canelo whacks Saunders with a right to the body, just below the ribs. Saunders retreats and Canelo hits him with a thudding left. Two more body punches from Canelo show how the tide is turning. But Saunders fires back and, at the bell, he raises his right fist after another competitive round.

Eddy Reynoso, in the corner, urges Canelo to use the uppercut. The Mexican nods quietly.

Round eight initially replicates the pattern of the fight with the busy jab of Saunders looking to rack up points while a withering body punch from Canelo is followed by a left. Saunders holds on desperately. Canelo clubs him again to the body and then lands an uppercut.

Canelo knows the momentum has shifted dramatically. He waves his fists in the air to urge his roaring supporters to create even more of a din. Sickening body punches make Saunders reel and Canelo's right glove dances skywards again. Saunders misses with a wild punch and leaves himself wide open for a crunching right uppercut which Canelo throws from below waist level. As soon as it cracks into his face, Saunders winces and staggers. The impact is so shuddering that even Canelo takes a step back as the force of the blow runs up his arm.

The bell rings in mercy.

A forlorn Saunders walks slowly to his corner. His right eye is suddenly swollen, with a small cut in the middle of the raised lump. One of his cornermen presses a metal enswell against the wound in an attempt to flatten the puffiness. As his trainer Mark Tibbs talks urgently, Saunders shakes his head.

Canelo, in the opposite corner, stands for the duration of the break. He knows the fight is over. Before anyone else understands what has happened, he lifts his right hand and walks to a neutral corner. It is suddenly clear that Tibbs has waved the fight over.

Canelo climbs the ropes before being lifted on Reynoso's shoulders for a tour of the ring. A doctor, meanwhile, examines Saunders' broken eye socket. The crowd shows no compassion and booing rolls down from the bleachers as Saunders' bulging face fills the giant screen.

While the belts are draped around Canelo's shoulders, a white towel covers Saunders' bowed head. The shattered fighter is booed again as he leaves the ring.

Canelo confirms that he knew it was over as soon as round eight ended. 'I think I broke his cheek and he wasn't going to come out,' he says bluntly before turning his attention to the only other super-middleweight champion who holds a world title.

'Caleb Plant,' Canelo says as he names the IBF belt-holder. 'I'm coming for you, my friend.'

The same white towel still covers Saunders' bruised face and broken orbital bone as he walks to a waiting ambulance.

I have no desire to gloat, even if Daniel Kinahan's most obnoxious cheerleader has suffered a horrible defeat. Billy Joe Saunders is in that lonely and unforgiving place boxing reserves for those who have had all their big talk beaten out of them.

8

Heavy Business

Every time I spoke to Regis Prograis, we went somewhere new and surprising. This time we discussed death and the visions he sometimes saw. They could be serene or terrifying figures, or the face of a murdered friend who wanted to pass on a message to him.

A kid he knew at school, a boy called Shaddy Boo, had been murdered a few years earlier in New Orleans. When Shaddy Boo visited Prograis in his dreams, it felt as if 'he is trying to get a message to me. I always wonder what it means. It's strange he comes to me because Shaddy was not a close friend. He would pick on me when we were younger at the same high school and he was a big-time football player. One day, all the football players were in the classroom making noise. I knocked on the door and went in with a few of my friends.'

Prograis was amazed all over again. 'Man, they were boxing in the classroom. I was a soft boy at the time and he was like the cool kid, the older kid, with all the cool football players. Shaddy Boo says: "You can't come in unless you fight somebody." All of my friends were scared, but I said OK and I ended up beating someone up. That gave me something different and Shaddy Boo liked it because he ran boxing at school.

'Years later he got murdered at his house in New Orleans. I think my dream is also me saying, "Hey, Shaddy Boo. Look who I became." But, more than that, I feel him trying to tell me something. Maybe one day I will understand.'

Prograis sometimes saw spirits. He talked so calmly that his words sounded credible. 'I've not really spoken about this, but my grandmother said I was born with a veil over my eyes. The first time I described what I saw my grandma said: "You have something about you." People won't believe me, but I've been seeing things for a long time.

'The first one was a really, really tall lady. I was in my bed and I rolled over and she was standing there. She was taller even than the doorway. She stared at me. I turned away to the other side because I was scared. Then I was like: "All right, maybe I'm tripping after watching too much TV." So I rolled back over and she was still there. I kept looking at her for quite a while and then I turned away. When I rolled back a little later, she was gone.

'The second time I seen something was in my room in New Orleans. It was two little kids sitting on the top shelf. They were watching me. It's like I'm hallucinating, but I don't take drugs or drink. So what is it? Sometimes it's peaceful and sometimes it's like a demon. One of the worst things I ever seen happened about four years ago. I turned over and it was a black thing right here [over his head] looking deep in my face. I screamed to my wife: *"Raquel! Raquel!"* She was fucking scared because I never did that before. That was one of the worst.'

Did he regard these visons as an eerie gift? 'Yeah, being from New Orleans, I'm into this stuff. I know other people won't believe it, but I've had this since I was eleven years old. I do so much dangerous stuff and I could have died a bunch of times. But I feel something's protecting me.

'It helps me in the ring. We know how dangerous boxing is, but I'm very resilient. Every sparring session and every fight, I'm willing to put everything on the line. I'm not wanting to die, but I'm going to bust my ass every day until I almost pass out. I know the human body is capable of so much more than we think. There are extraordinary people who can pick up thousands of pounds or run hundreds of miles or swim under the ice.

'I look up to those people – like guys who can be underwater for ten minutes at a time [without an oxygen tank]. Our bodies are capable of so much more than we think. I can hold my breath for almost four minutes underwater. I can do that if I'm static. When you dive, it's different because you're moving and so I can only do maybe two minutes.'

Prograis loved catching alligators in a lake near his house in Rosenberg, Texas. He liked to wrestle them and clamp their jaws shut before releasing them open-mouthed into the water.

'It's crazy,' he said, 'but I'm not scared to die. That's how I felt even when I was skydiving and the parachute got tangled. I was strapped to an instructor and he was panicking and screaming. *"Kick! Kick! Kick!"* But you're going down so fast, it's hard to hear. When we got to the ground, he told me he'd had to cut it [to open the emergency parachute] or we would have died. I was cool. I'll know when it's time to go, so I'm going to live every day to the full.'

Our talk of death was sparked by the loss of his favourite fighter, Marvin Hagler, who had died at the age of sixty-six just weeks earlier, in March 2021. Hagler had been a blue-collar marvel who gained late recognition for his ferocious talent after years of disappointment and being ignored.

Prograis had lost only one fight, that agonisingly narrow defeat to Josh Taylor. He had won his twenty-five other bouts and remained in the top three of the world in the 140-pound division. Taylor, the IBF and WBA champion, and José Ramírez, the WBC and WBO title-holder, were about to meet in a unification contest on 22 May in Las Vegas – with Prograis hoping he would fight the winner. But, as had happened so often in his career, he was on the outside looking in while Taylor and Ramírez battled for all the belts and glory.

He was preparing to fight Ivan Redkach in Atlanta on the

undercard to a headline bout featuring Jake Paul, the YouTuber trying to become a boxer. It seemed insulting, but Prograis, who was without a promoter, pointed out how well he was being paid by a new outfit called Triller.

Redkach had a credible 23–5–1 record. He had lost to Danny Garcia in his last fight but, in the bout before that, he beat Devon Alexander. 'He's definitely a real opponent,' Prograis said. 'He does have sneaky power, but I should beat him easy.'

It hurt that it was not a landmark fight and it made Prograis feel deep affinity with Hagler, a boxing great who only fought for a world title in his fiftieth bout. 'I love Hagler,' Prograis said. 'He was so determined because he had a chip on his shoulder. I've also got a little chip and I'm out to prove people wrong. I had a real good amateur career. I was ranked number four in the country, I went to the [2012] Olympic trials. But when I came out of the amateurs, I didn't get signed. Nobody wanted me. It took Hagler even longer but we both became world champions.'

I had seen a photograph of Hagler and Prograis together. 'It was taken in Verona in New York [State]. I normally don't get starstruck, but I did with Hagler. You felt his aura. People ask how it feels to be in my position now and I always say I believe in stuff way deeper than wealth or material stuff. I'm not religious, but I thank God every day. I have my family, my health and boxing. I love what I do every single day. Most people cannot say that. They've got to work somewhere they don't want to be or come home to someone they don't like. But I love everything about my life.'

Prograis, a visionary and a fighter, smiled. 'Yeah, man,' he said softly, 'happiness is a choice.'

Ten days later, channelling his inner Hagler, he stopped Redkach in the sixth round. His victory did not cause much of a stir, but I believed in him. Prograis's next world title night would come.

When boxing went into hibernation in 2020, there had been a vague hope that Covid might bang heads together and the best fighters would eventually meet in the ring. But that outcome was blocked by opposing sanctioning bodies and warring promoters. The IBF, WBA, WBC and WBO anointed their own 'world champion' in each division and drew up ratings which ignored challengers associated with rival organisations. It was difficult for unification contests to happen because each respective champion had to defend his or her 'world' title against mandatory challengers favoured by their sanctioning body which took a chunky cut from every championship contest.

The promoters had the power to ignore the alphabet boys, because most fans had no idea which belt belonged to whom, but they mostly refused to work with each other.

It was the equivalent of Real Madrid never facing Manchester City, Bayern Munich, Paris Saint-Germain or Juventus in the Champions League because rival leagues in Spain, England, Germany, France and Italy refused to allow their best clubs to play each other. In an absurd scenario, each club would claim to have won their version of the Champions League against mediocre opposition.

The idea, therefore, that Tyson Fury, the WBC champion, would actually fight Anthony Joshua, who held the IBF, WBA and WBO titles, transfixed many boxing fans. Their willingness to ignore Kinahan's involvement and Saudi sportswashing stemmed partly from the fact that there had not been a title fight for the undisputed heavyweight championship since November 1999. More than twenty years later, I also bought into the longing for Joshua and Fury to restore some kind of clarity to boxing and its flagship division.

'Hi there, it's Tyson Fury, The Gypsy King,' our old friend said amiably on 16 May 2021. On his Instagram post, Fury's head was shaved completely and he wore a white T-shirt and gold chain. 'I've got some massive news. I have just got off the phone with Prince Khalid of Saudi Arabia and he told me this fight is 100 per cent on. August 14, 2021, summertime. All eyes of the world will be on the

Kingdom of Saudi Arabia. I cannot wait to smash Anthony Joshua on the biggest stage of all time. This is going to be the biggest sporting event ever to grace the planet Earth. Do not miss it. All eyes on us. Peace out. God Bless. See you all in Saudiiiiiiii!'

Less than eleven months had passed since the previous occasion Fury had announced a showdown between him and Joshua. Back in June 2020, while giving a 'big shout-out to Dan' Kinahan, Fury had described their proposed bout as the biggest fight in British boxing history. Presumably with the help of Kinahan, he had moved on to the repressive Saudi royal family and upgraded the fight with Joshua to the biggest sporting event in history.

The grimy fight business, and its usually disillusioned fans, rejoiced. Fury vs Joshua was on. An undisputed heavyweight king would soon be crowned.

But this is boxing. Chaos and disruption always lurk just below the surface.

Twenty-eight hours later, a judge in a US court of arbitration ruled that Deontay Wilder was entitled to exercise his option for a third fight with Fury. And so the Saudi extravaganza was off unless Wilder could be persuaded by a hefty financial inducement to step aside.

On 18 May, Fury posted a picture of Wilder on his Instagram story and said: 'What a joke @bronzebomber has become. Asked for 20 million to move over. Looks like I have to crack his skull again.'

By 23 May, the prospect of Fury vs Joshua was dead and two different fights had been confirmed. The WBO insisted that Joshua had to defend his title against his mandatory challenger, Oleksandr Usyk, while Fury released another crass video about Wilder to prove he had accepted their third fight. 'Shall we do it and put him out of his misery?' he asked of Wilder. 'Crack the other side of his skull? Wilder, contract's signed. You're getting smashed. One round. I've got your soul, your mojo, everything. I own you.'

Whether yelling at the 'dossers' he promised to crush, praising Daniel Kinahan and the Saudi royal family or boasting of fights that failed to materialise in his constant search for attention, Fury seemed much like modern boxing – often lamentable and occasionally riveting.

His third fight with Deontay Wilder was scheduled for 24 July 2021. Five weeks earlier, on 17 June, he turned up at the Los Angeles press conference in an extraordinary white suit covered in images of his own face. His chest was bare and he wore a white baseball cap turned backwards. Wilder wore a black T-shirt and grey jeans. Beneath his sunglasses and headphones, the American gave fleeting thanks to Jesus and his lawyer, announcing that it was 'time to cut off his head and, come July 24, there will be bloodshed'.

Three months earlier, and certain he would face Fury again, Wilder had said: 'We built a whole facility to commit a legal homicide and that's just what it is. My mind is very violent.' Those bleak words echoed March 2018 when Wilder said he wanted 'a body' on his record because 'boxing is the only sport where you can kill a man and get paid for it at the same time'.

But, at the LA press conference in 2021, he preferred silence as a way of trying to unsettle Fury. When they came together for the face-off, Fury was naked from the waist up, having removed his jacket, while Wilder remained in his bubble of shades and headphones.

After twenty-one seconds, and settling into the stillness, Wilder took off his sunglasses. The two heavyweights stared at each other searchingly, as if burrowing into each other's psyche.

Thirty seconds passed when, at last, Fury said, 'Boo! Bogeyman here, to get you again.'

Wilder stared back impassively. Another minute slid past.

Bob Arum, who was eighty-nine, rose wearily to his feet while PR people suggested that the photographers needed Fury and Wilder 'facing the front'. The boxers ignored them. After two minutes of unbroken staring, some of Wilder's corner began to shout 'Two-Time … Two-Time!' while Shane Fury, Tyson's brother, yelled 'Dosser … dosser!'

Two minutes and twenty-five seconds into the standstill, the broadcaster Cynthia Conte spoke politely to the frozen heavyweights. 'Can you guys turn and face forward, to the cameras? Please? Pretty please?'

There was no response.

At the three-minute-twenty-second mark, Fury began nodding, in seeming amusement. Wilder stared at him.

Kelly Swanson, the formidable publicist I had known for years when she represented Bernard Hopkins and Floyd Mayweather Jr, clapped sharply. 'Thanks guys. We've got media to do.'

Malik Scott, Wilder's new trainer, spoke firmly while the fighters kept facing each other in silence. 'Kelly,' Scott said, 'they'll be doing this for a long time.'

'Twenty minutes?' Swanson asked.

'Longer.'

'OK, Malik,' Swanson said in resignation. 'You tell me when they're ready to break it up.'

Five minutes had passed when some beefy security men moved towards Fury and Wilder in an attempt to end the face-off. The two camps followed and stood behind their respective fighters.

'Two-time . . . two-time . . .' the Wilder entourage hollered while, amid lots of swearing, the Fury clan yelled back: 'No time . . . retire this time.'

Shane Fury pointed at one of Wilder's men. 'Me and you,' he said with husky belligerence, 'no bother.'

After five minutes and thirty-nine seconds, Wilder turned away to whoops from the Fury crowd. It had been the longest and most intense face-off in the history of heavyweight championship boxing – and one of the most extended periods of public silence from the usually chattering Fury.

A sickly silence enveloped the heavyweight champion when, in early July, he fell ill with Covid. A week passed and then, on 15 July, Fury announced that their trilogy fight would be delayed until October. 'I want nothing more than to smash the Big Dosser on 24 July, but I guess the beating will have to wait. We will fight 9 October and I will knock him spark out.'

The carnage of boxing negotiations had, somehow, produced two intriguing heavyweight title fights. The first, between Joshua and Usyk, was hard to predict. Usyk had only fought twice as a heavyweight, his divisional debut coming on the same bill where Patrick Day lost consciousness forever.

Usyk was one of the most accomplished and unconventional boxers in the world. The Ukrainian had dominated the cruiserweight division, becoming a rare undisputed world champion, and he boxed with a skilful assurance which Joshua would never possess. Both men had become Olympic champions at London 2012, but Usyk had 350 fights in the unpaid ranks. Joshua, in contrast, boxed just thirty-five bouts as an amateur. The difference was obvious in the way they fought. Joshua relied on his power, but he could be predictable against resilient opposition, while Usyk used artistry and versatility.

Usyk offered a litmus test for Joshua – even if the British fighter was still much the bigger and taller man who had won twenty-four of his twenty-five professional bouts, all but two victories by knockout. The consensus was that Joshua had been exposed by the roly-poly Andy Ruiz Jr, who had knocked him out in a shock result in June 2019. But it seemed to me that a very different bout had changed the world champion forever.

Joshua's greatest victory had come in April 2017 when, in a thrilling and savage contest, he stopped Wladimir Klitschko in front of 90,000 fans at Wembley Stadium. After he knocked down the formidable Ukrainian in round five, Joshua was sent crashing to the canvas in the sixth. He hauled himself up and, even though he was tested repeatedly, dropped Klitschko twice more in the eleventh round before the referee rescued the older man. Joshua retained his world titles, but he had never been the same fighter again. It was almost as if Joshua had decided he wanted to avoid the hell he had been through against Klitschko.

He then looked confused and outgunned when Ruiz stopped him in New York. Joshua won the rematch by adopting a cautious approach against Ruiz, who had spent the preceding six months partying wildly. It was an easy victory, but Joshua had looked gun-shy.

While he was often dismissed as a corporate heavyweight, shaped by glittering marketing contracts rather than pure fistic glory, Joshua yearned for respect. But he was surrounded by a small coterie of men who wanted to protect him as a money-making asset above all else. They tried to control Joshua and restrict access to him.

They were wrong to do so because Joshua was at his most likeable when he opened up. When I first interviewed him, in May 2015, Joshua was 12–0 as a pro. We spent a memorable afternoon talking about great old heavyweights. Joshua understood that even seemingly impregnable champions ended up in chaos, debt and drug addiction. He told me he had taken their bitter lessons to heart.

Joshua was at his most candid when he remembered how, while still a Watford teenager, he had been on remand and preparing for a ten-year prison term. 'It was a turning point,' he said as he explained how close he had come to a long stretch in jail. 'I was in trouble for fighting and other crazy stuff. There are idiots inside and you realise what you are dealing with in prison. I was on remand in Reading for two weeks. Once you're there, it's 50/50 because you've been found guilty, so I was preparing myself for the worst. It could have been ten years.'

Joshua shook his head at his narrow escape. 'My guardian angel decided I didn't need to be punished with a jail sentence. But I was on tag for over a year and that helped. I became so disciplined and changed the way I lived. I would be at home by eight o'clock and, because I had boxing, I lived the disciplined life. I started reading because I learned that so many champions educated themselves.

Joe Louis, Mike Tyson, Bernard Hopkins. The discipline and reading changed me.'

In the build-up to their fight in September 2021, the thirty-one-year-old Joshua nodded when I asked if Usyk offered a psychological test. Despite his distinct disadvantages in size and heavyweight experience, Usyk clearly believed he could win. 'Definitely,' Joshua said. 'But you have to beat that confidence out of your opponent. Usyk has fought just two heavyweights, so he's jumping in deep. He must believe in himself so good luck to him.'

On the Saturday evening of 17 September, I spoke to Usyk on a Zoom call to his home in Ukraine. I could imagine the scene exactly a week from then. Usyk would be on his way to a vast dressing room at the Tottenham Hotspur Stadium. He would be three hours from hearing the call for him to begin his long walk to the ring. And so I asked him about nerves at such a fraught time.

Usyk, an amusing thirty-four-year-old who liked playing pranks almost as much as he enjoyed fighting, insisted through a translator that he would feel relaxed. 'I am not going to be nervous. Why would I be? It would not change anything. I will not get stronger, only weaker.'

Most fighters acknowledge that the most unsettling time for them is usually in the last hours before the first bell. Time drags and doubts can crowd the mind. But Usyk smiled. 'I will be calm and confident and probably read a book or watch a film. I am not doing nerves at all.'

Asked what he might watch and read in his dressing room, Usyk made his contrasting choices. 'I am watching *Peaky Blinders*. Everything looks realistic and my favourite character is the boss, Tommy Shelby [played by Cillian Murphy]. It's a cool and emotional drama and it feels real to me. It is the way a family should function, protecting and standing up for each other. And he looks very cool in the way he dresses. The book will be the Bible.'

Peaky Blinders is full of rage, retribution and violence – as is the Bible – but Usyk cut a composed figure. The seriousness of his task against Joshua had also instilled a deep concentration. 'It is the biggest fight of my career. My opponent is the biggest [challenge], an Olympic champion and he has three [world] titles. But it will be more difficult for him because he is defending his titles at home.'

Usyk's face split into a big gap-toothed grin as he pointed to his head which was shaven apart from a limp Mohican which looked more like a strange comb-over. 'A bald guy will come to his home country and look for a big fight. I love London and the UK is my lucky place. But there is a saying in Russian that, if you rush, you make people laugh. So I would prefer to be calm. I don't have any dreams how it will happen, but I am looking forward to the victory.'

Tumultuous times would soon engulf Usyk and Ukraine. But, on a warm and sultry September evening, a week away from his defining battle, Usyk looked serene. He looked like a man who could find comfort and meaning in both *Peaky Blinders* and the Bible.

On the Thursday of fight week, after a low-key press conference, even the ritual stare-down was muted. There was mutual respect and it needed Usyk to produce some colour.

Joshua looked utilitarian in a black tracksuit, while Usyk wore a red suit, black shirt, gold polka-dot tie and a mustard waistcoat. He said his suit was 'inspired by the Joker – but he is not a positive hero. I am a positive hero. My look, the hair, moustache, earring are all inspired by my ancestors who were 17th-century Cossack warriors. I used to do the Cossack dance after some of my amateur wins. I might do it again if I win on Saturday. I am very unpredictable.'

Usyk explained that his impressive moustache was a homage to his name. He revealed that 'usyk' is the Ukrainian word for moustache, which led to frantic checks to confirm he was telling the truth. The Joker was not joking.

He was more interested in talking about life outside boxing. 'After school, I wanted to study theatre and the arts at university. But, when I won the junior Ukraine championships, I decided to enter the Physical Education Institute. But I like theatre, I write poems and play the guitar.'

One last question was put to Usyk. If Hollywood made a film of his life, who would play him? His eyes twinkled and his moustache bristled as he named himself: 'Oleksandr.'

Tottenham Hotspur Stadium, London, Saturday 25 September 2021

It's the day after my father's birthday. He would have turned ninety-two. I think of him as the gleaming stadium turns dark. Only a steady blue glow remains as the crowd's growl of anticipation turns to a fierce roar. I draw in a deep breath and say a belated happy birthday to my old dad.

The deep blue backdrop is lit up by thousands of mobile phones as Usyk walks to the ring. He slips a Perspex visor over his face and, beneath the white hood covering his head, looks eerie and purposeful as he strides through the crowd. Inside the ropes, Usyk kisses a Ukrainian flag and then retreats to his corner to pray.

The entrance of the heavily favoured Joshua is more leisurely. Strolling out to some slinky British-Nigerian Afrobeat, as Maulo croons about 'Ambition', he waves and bounces his glove against the raised hands of his fans. He looks as if he is on his way to pick up an award for being a cheerful celebrity. Joshua eventually breaks into a little trot and then stops at a platform where a giant A and J are burning. He begins to shadow-box, as Maulo's song segues into a terrible power rock ballad from *Rocky IV* and fireworks shoot from the stadium roof.

It's extravagant and indulgent. When he finally resumes his ring walk, almost five minutes after it began, Joshua keeps stopping to greet individual people. It makes me long for the days when Mike Tyson, sockless and bare-chested, marched to the ring in just black trunks. Iron Mike had nothing but menace and bad intentions for company.

They are finally alone, Usyk and Joshua, waiting for the bell.

When it rings, they move swiftly towards each other, Usyk boxing as a southpaw and Joshua in his orthodox stance. Usyk is the first to land a left jab that smacks Joshua straight in the noggin as if to offer the champion a blunt welcome to a new level of skill. Halfway through the round, a heavy right hand from Joshua connects but Usyk absorbs its impact without difficulty. The challenger then throws a couple of sharp backhands which nail Joshua. Holding his ground, and using his fast feet and lateral movement to stay out of danger, Usyk again finds Joshua's head with his laser-like left. It's Usyk's round, clearly, and he gives a little nod.

In round two, with Usyk staying clear of the ropes and any damaging punches, a bizarre call comes from Joshua's corner. One of his assistant trainers, Joby Clayton, praises him for being 'really in control'. As if affronted by such a notion, Usyk leaps forward, cat-like, to catch Joshua with yet another clean straight left.

I am immersed in the fight, and the nerve and skill of Usyk. I love the way the Ukrainian underdog sets Joshua so many little puzzles with his movement.

Usyk, again, lands the first meaningful blows in the third with a left and then a hard right down the pipe. He moves and feints, denying Joshua the chance to close the distance, and then Usyk unleashes another searing straight left. He follows it with a bludgeoning punch which wobbles Joshua. The champion's head swivels on the giant base of his neck and his legs buckle briefly. At the bell, the Ukrainian cracks a grin.

Joshua finally makes Usyk reel back from a heavy right in round four. A small swelling forms beneath Usyk's right eye and Joshua switches to the body with thudding success as he wins the fifth. Stalking Usyk and pushing him back, Joshua looks to be gaining parity as they approach the halfway stage. A big right from Joshua has the crowd of 60,000 roaring and Usyk blinking. Joshua catches him again before the bell. It's three-all in rounds.

Joshua can't sustain his momentum. In the seventh round, a right cross and then a left hook clip him, which the Ukrainian follows up with still more precise punching. Usyk is in the ascendancy as, suddenly, he uncorks a big left which makes Joshua stagger. He lets rip with another flurry of punches as the champion retreats.

Joshua is much more compact in round eight. He sinks solid shots to the body, and Usyk replies with a similar punch to the gut, before they return to their feinting and jitterbugging. A battle for the heavyweight championship of the world has become an absorbing fight.

Usyk picks off Joshua for most of the ninth, cuffing him in a steady rhythm. A left hand then stuns Joshua who, valiantly, fires back. Usyk, looking weary in the end game of a brutal chess match, ties him up and accepts some respite.

Blood seeps from Joshua's nose early in the tenth round and a lump under his right eye matches the swelling on Usyk's face. A hard right from Joshua adds to the markings and a cut is now visible above Usyk's right eye.

The crowd sings *'Ooohhhhhh, Anthony Joshuaaaaa . . .'* as it tries to rouse him down the stretch, but Usyk shifts gears and lands at will. He is dangerously accurate.

In Joshua's corner, they try to contain the bulge under his right eye while the cheerleaders in his team attempt to convince him he is winning. Rob McCracken, his more pragmatic head trainer, reminds him that only two rounds remain and he needs to keep his left hand high.

Joshua looks depleted as he rises from his tiny stool for the penultimate round. He is peppered by the right jab before, abruptly, Usyk doubles up the combinations and Joshua resembles a giant oak threatening to crack and fall when lightning strikes. He teeters amid the electrical storm of Usyk's power punching.

Yet the courage I've always admired in Joshua emerges again as he responds with a strong right hand that forces a rampaging Usyk to back away. Joshua now stalks his previously dominant challenger, landing punch after punch. Usyk takes them and stays calm, looking for the chance to counter.

The cut around Usyk's eye oozes blood. But his head movement is as slick as ever and, before the round ends, he unfurls a series of combinations to the head and body. It is a masterly display and a drained Joshua struggles to see the punches flying at him.

As they come out for the twelfth, Joshua needs a stoppage, but Usyk remains the more destructive puncher. His left hand stiffens Joshua's legs, but the outgoing champion rallies once more. Such determination is met by a pair of scything overhand lefts as Usyk shows his audacious skills. And then, in the last ten seconds, Usyk goes in search of the knockout. Joshua sags beneath the assault, supported only by the ropes, before the last bell rescues him.

Usyk crosses himself and sinks to his knees. He knows he has won and looks to the heavens.

Across the ring, while a doctor examines him, Joshua's face scrunches up in pain and frustration.

He only rises from his stool after Michael Buffer reads out the first scorecard of 117–112. The referee holds his left wrist, and Usyk's right wrist, when the next score of 116–112 and a far less accurate 115–113 are called out in favour of, as Buffer yells, 'the *new* heavyweight champion of the world and the fighting pride of Ukraine ... *Oleksandr Usyyyyyykkkkkkk*!'

Tears roll down Usyk's face before all the belts are draped around his shoulders in tribute to his magnificent performance. Joshua offers dejected congratulations and then slowly, with none of the grandeur with which he had entered the ring an hour earlier, he ducks through the ropes. Bare-chested, and stripped of his titles, he begins the solitary walk of a fallen champion.

The new world champion ambles in first, just after one in the morning, his face bearing the brutal realities of heavyweight boxing. A jagged cut runs above Usyk's right brow while his bruised skin has turned violet below that same eye. The swollen mouse beneath his left eye is even more prominent and a reminder that Usyk fought twelve rounds against a world champion who weighed nineteen pounds more than him.

Usyk is not a small man, but he gave away four inches in reach and three inches in height to the six-feet, six-inch Joshua. He sits down nonchalantly to address his stunning rise as the new IBF, WBA and WBO world champion. 'I tried a few times [for the stoppage] but my trainer said: "Throw your jab because if you concentrate on knocking him out, you'll lose rhythm."'

I like Usyk most of all when, speaking with soft urgency, he confirms his desire to live normally – at least until the next time he steps back into boxing's dark world. 'I wanted to take all the belts, but I also wanted to take my kids to school. I wanted to plant trees. I wanted to water the apple trees. I wanted to see my wife more often. I spent three months in camp. I want to live.'

He seems just an ordinary man now, tired and emotional after a testing night, and the unusual applause from the media is warm.

I am even more moved by Joshua's arrival. Two hours earlier, there had been rumours that he had suffered a broken orbital bone. We were told he would be taken to hospital. But Joshua walks in, as ready to talk after a crushing defeat as when anticipating another multimillion-pound victory.

It would be understandable if Joshua had slunk home instead to nurse his wounds. His face is less marked up than Usyk's, despite the outcome, but the swelling above and under his right eye show some of the damage he endured.

'I couldn't see in the ninth round because my eye was shut,' Joshua says. 'It's the first time that's happened. But it was good experience because in adversity you learn to control yourself.'

Defeat against Usyk, the second loss of his career, has ruined his hopes of a unification contest with Fury, which had been spoken of as a £200m showdown. Such staggering money, and a fondness for platitudes, have sparked resentment among his more strident critics. But Joshua is a generous and decent man. He is also, at his core, a fighter. This explains his desire for an immediate rematch – despite

Usyk being markedly superior. 'When I was walking back to the dressing room, I said to myself: "I'm ready to get back to the gym and improve, so when I fight these good guys and see that they are hurt I can capitalise on the opportunity." I've already been watching the fight and thinking, *I could've done that better.*'

It feels appropriate, after the final question, to walk over to Joshua. He is alone, briefly, and I thank him for talking to us. 'No problem,' he says with a little smile as his hand curls in an invitation to bump fists gently at 1.45 a.m.

I step out into the chaotic streets of Tottenham. Thousands of people are still milling around as there are no trains, taxis or Ubers to be found in the early-morning madness. I settle down to wait and to think of Oleksandr Usyk. I imagine him a few days from now, watering one of his beloved apple trees on a tranquil autumn afternoon near Kyiv.

9

The Kings of Vegas and Crystal Palace

An ominous hush filled the Alder Hey Children's Hospital in Liverpool. Tyson Fury looked at the incubator where his baby daughter Athena lay silent and still. Tubes and wires were fed into her tiny body as the giant heavyweight champion stared helplessly at the baby whom he and his wife, Paris, had named after the goddess of warfare and wisdom. Athena was their sixth child and she had been born prematurely.

Tyson himself had been a premature baby who had nearly died on the night of his birth. But he had grown into a six-feet, nine-inch monster who, in prime condition, weighed 270 pounds. Paris had also given birth prematurely to most of their other children, so there had been no immediate concern when Athena arrived early. But, soon after her birth in a Manchester hospital, the baby's heart rate had rocketed to 300 beats per minute when it should have been around 120. The doctors used medication to reduce it to 140bpm, but that relief did not last. When Athena's heart rate spiked dangerously again, she was rushed to Alder Hey's specialist unit. The baby's condition remained critical.

Fury moved into accommodation, for the parents of seriously ill children, attached to the hospital. He spent his days and evenings inside the hospital ward with Paris and Athena, and slept at night at Ronald McDonald House. Fewer than two months were left before he fought Wilder and so one morning, he and his father, John, went for a run around the hospital grounds. He said later that his lungs felt like sheets of sandpaper rubbing against each other when Paris called his mobile phone. She was crying and screaming. 'The baby's dead! She's dead . . .'

Athena had become unresponsive when Paris held her. Doctors were trying desperately to bring her back to life as Fury sprinted to the ward. He arrived after they had resuscitated her, but there was still deep concern as they returned Athena to the safety of the incubator. She remained there for much of the next fortnight while Paris and Tyson slept on the floor of the ward. As she improved, they felt confident enough to rest in the hospital accommodation. After another week, Athena was sufficiently strong to be released from hospital. They took her home, feeling drained but grateful she had survived.

Fury had just weeks left to prepare for one of the most difficult fights of his life – against a determined and ferocious Wilder. A combination of Covid, little training and the near death of his daughter left him more vulnerable than he had been for years.

Tyson Fury and Deontay Wilder are flawed and often troubled but, when they step inside the ring, they are gripping dance partners. I am ready for one last tumultuous ride through their wild rivalry in Las Vegas on Saturday 9 October 2021.

When he is introduced at the T-Mobile Arena, Wilder makes repeated chopping motions, like an axe-wielding executioner. A bearded Fury bounces up and down as he fixes Wilder with a goggle-eyed stare and snarls 'Bitch . . . bitch-ass.' More hospitably, the referee Russell Mora brings them together and, after his instructions, says 'God bless you both'.

Wilder begins the first round with a new tactic, sinking heavy jabs into Fury's body. The champion is forced to retreat as blow after blow to the belly land with percussive force. Fury's excess flesh jiggles over the top of his trunks as he tries to adjust to Wilder's different strategy.

Both men land some meaty blows in the second, but there is also plenty of clinching which makes Mora bark 'Stop, gentlemen, stop!'

Midway through the third, after Fury is warned for putting Wilder in a headlock, they both throw dangerous punches. With thirty-five seconds left, Fury unleashes a barrage of blows, including a hard right cross. Wilder begins to pitch face-first towards the champion. He falls into a right uppercut from Fury which lands squarely on his jaw. Wilder crashes to the canvas.

He rolls over and hauls himself up at the count of four. Wilder looks befuddled as he walks away from the referee. He turns back to Mora at the count of seven.

After he has shouted 'eight!', with each number being matched by a new finger snapping into Wilder's face, Mora asks: 'You OK?'

Wilder nods. 'Put your hands up!' Mora shouts. 'You wanna fight?'

'Yeah,' Wilder says. 'Let's go.'

In the remaining fifteen seconds, Fury lands five more right hands as Wilder sags against the ropes. The bell saves him.

Wilder looks unsteady for the first two minutes of round four, but he clinches often enough to help clear his head of the numbing fog. And then, out of nowhere, Wilder throws a hellacious right hand which catches Fury flush on his shaven skull. It is such an explosive punch that its impact seems to detonate from deep inside the stricken Fury. As the blast spreads through him, Fury collapses and hits the canvas with a mighty thud.

Fury lies on his back, his arms supporting him as he blows hard, trying to drag air down into his scorched lungs. The arena is full of seething disbelief as Wilder celebrates.

Mora has counted to seven by the time Fury is back on his feet. The referee repeats the ritual from the previous round. He asks

Fury if he is OK, tells him to lift his hands, wipes his gloves and then waves the glazed champion back into the fray.

Fury ducks away from a couple of roundhouse swings, but he can't evade a right hand which sends him tumbling down again. He looks hurt as he gets up slowly.

After the count reaches eight, he has to be told twice to put his hands up. He is fortunate that the bell rings just as Mora signals a resumption. Fury takes in a deep gulp as he trudges back to his corner. They pour water over his head, apply ice packs to his swollen face and his trainer SugarHill Steward tries to rouse him.

Fury lands a few decent jabs early in round five. He then cracks Wilder with a classic combination, proving yet again that he has startling powers of recovery. Wilder is forced to clinch. When they're separated, Fury's jab is as precise as his brain had been scrambled a few minutes before. Wilder looks uncomfortable under pressure but he fights back, driving Fury towards the ropes with bludgeoning blows. He raises his arm in triumph at the bell.

We're in the grip of one of the great heavyweight fights. I am lost in the bout, cut adrift from the rest of life.

In the sixth, Fury and Wilder administer and absorb thunderous punches, taking turns to look imperious and vulnerable in equal measure. Chunks are taken out of both heavyweights in a brutal contest which threatens to damage them as men while offering glory to them as fighters.

Malik Scott cuts through the siren call luring Wilder to the rocks. 'Look at me,' the trainer says as he smacks Wilder gently. 'Wake the fuck up. You're getting a little lackadaisical off the break. That's all you gotta do, stay alert, and you can control this dude. Get back to the body.'

Halfway through round seven, after bearing down on a tiring Wilder with his full weight, Fury catches him with a trademark right. They fight at close quarters, their heads almost touching, as they dig to the body or try to land sneaky uppercuts and cuffing overhand rights. And, when distance opens up between them, Wilder connects with a big right hand, a stiff jab, and another right. It spurs on Fury. He unleashes a right cross which almost freezes Wilder and leaves him wide open for an uppercut. Wilder is badly hurt, but he clings on for the last thirty seconds of another epic round. He still has the temerity to raise his right hand as he retreats to his corner.

Wilder is the first to land a hurtful blow in the eighth, but Fury answers him with three single shots of shuddering power. The challenger backs away and Fury keeps powering home the right hand. But Wilder, his will undimmed, refuses to buckle. He keeps punching back with enough force to make the sweat fly from Fury's head.

In the corner, Wilder takes a slug of water. He spits most of it back, in a blood-flecked stream, into a black bucket.

The doctor talks quietly to Wilder to check on his ability to keep fighting. Wilder says a few words and the doc slips away. Fury is merciless. He skips across the canvas and pops a couple of jabs into Wilder's solemn face. A minute into the round, Wilder fires another heavy fusillade of punches. They are hard enough to make Fury drop his hands involuntarily as he blinks at Wilder's enduring power. But Fury gathers himself and, with a pawing jab, takes control again as Wilder back-pedals on spindly legs.

Fury opens up and, for a moment, it seems as if Wilder must go down again. His mouth is wide open, but he ends the round by bouncing punches off Fury.

Wilder retains the ability to change everything with a devastating blow and Scott reminds him of this truth. 'You was blessed with something that can end this right now, but it has to come behind the surgical ways. We have to keep thinking . . .'

Scott wheels round to his assistant trainers. 'What round we in?'

'Ten.'

'We're in ten,' Scott tells Wilder, 'and you're still hurting him. Hold it together, bro. You're going to be so proud of yourself tomorrow.'

Steward, in the opposite corner, keeps his advice simple. 'Just jab the motherfucker and keep the goddamn left hand up.'

Another goddamn right hand rocks Wilder and Fury follows it with a combination which makes it hard to believe the challenger is still standing. With one minute and twenty seconds remaining in the round, Wilder misses with a crude left, leaving him wide open for the precise powerhouse right that almost lifts him off his feet before dropping him in a heap.

Somehow, Wilder gets up. He confirms to Mora that he can continue. His bravery and spirit is remarkable, but I want it to be over now. Wilder looks finished.

Fury comes in for the kill and Wilder clings on in an effort to stop more blows raining down on him. After Mora forces them apart, Wilder lands a solid punch, but takes a jolting uppercut in return. The round ends with Wilder, incredibly, clubbing Fury with one punch after another.

People at ringside cover their mouths in disbelief, bury their heads in their hands or simply stand and scream at the mayhem and courage. Telli Swift, Wilder's fiancée, taps her heart as if trying to slow it down. Paris Fury, meanwhile, looks ill with the tension.

Wilder has been extraordinary all night but, in the eleventh, he is finally unable to stem the sickening rush of right hands. A minute into the round, he is pinned in the corner as Fury lands an uppercut, followed by another right. Wilder clinches but, then, darkness settles over him. One more uppercut and a left cross set up a monstrous right hand.

The knockout is so concussive, and conclusive, that referee Mora does not even need to count. He waves the fight over and bends down to attend to a motionless Wilder. Fury climbs the ropes and stands on the bottom rung as he spreads his arms wide in celebration and relief.

One of the greatest heavyweight fights in history is over. Fury has been hurt and dropped, twice, but he has won. He is still the WBC heavyweight champion of the world.

Wilder is helped to his stool. Blood coats his lower lip, smearing it crimson, while a swelling has risen beneath his right eye. He gazes at the masked doctor while more blood seeps from his left ear. His fiancée blinks back tears and nods again and again. Each nod seems a search for consolation that, at least, the battle is over.

Wilder stands up. A sad look of fresh disappointment steals across his face and he closes his left eye as if he can feel an unsettling pressure in his head. He is persuaded, gently, to sit down again on the small wooden stool. After such a savage contest, the thirty-five-year-old Wilder accepts that he has to be taken to hospital.

Fury is exhausted as his team pour water over his gleaming head. He looks like a magnificent racehorse who needs to be cooled down, as steam rises from him, by bucket after bucket of water following a gruelling Grand National.

Fury leans on the ropes and says a silent prayer. His gloves are off, but his hands are covered in sweat-sodden wraps. He laces his fingers together and, as he prays, Fury also cries. His brother Shane covers the world champion's bald dome with his hand. It is a tender gesture that confirms his big brother has come through a dark ordeal. The prayer continues amid the falling tears.

Fury eventually turns back to the ring. He finds Paris and kisses her before he is engulfed by demands for his post-fight reaction. Fury, in a worrying moment, touches the back of his throbbing skull. At its base, he can feel a lump.

He wonders if his brain has begun to swell. Fury waits until the ring empties and then he seeks out the doctor and asks to be examined. The doctor takes him through a series of tests before giving him his verdict. Fury has a swelling on the head but no signs of lasting damage can be detected. He should be fine.

Only an MRI scan can confirm that upbeat assessment, but Fury is relieved. He knows these moments are reminders of how much boxing takes from even its greatest champions.

I sink back into my chair, amazed and even dazed by the ferocity and vulnerability of these momentous men. There is nothing else like boxing.

*

As if reminding Tyson Fury that he was still the king of boxing, Canelo Álvarez flew into Las Vegas on a private jet on Monday 1 November 2021. He stepped onto the tarmac in a blue silk Dolce & Gabbana pyjama suit. Canelo then posted a photograph on Twitter of him in his pjs next to the jet with a raised right index finger to confirm he was still the world's leading boxer. His caption said: 'You ready Vegas? #CaneloPlant #LETS60.'

The second hashtag indicated that his world title unification contest against Caleb Plant that Saturday night would be the sixtieth fight of Canelo's professional career.

Canelo, in terms of his fame and wealth, still dominated boxing. He also remained the number-one fighter on most pound-for-pound lists that try to rank boxers across the weight divisions. On that basis, he seemed entitled to swan into Vegas in silky pyjamas.

I flew back into Vegas the same evening, catching a shuttle bus to the Strip, rather than the limo which took Canelo to the MGM Grand. I felt more hopeful about boxing because, following the heroic battle between Fury and Wilder, Canelo and Plant were about to fight a rare unification contest. The Mexican would defend his WBA, WBC and WBO titles, while the American brought his IBF belt into the ring. The winner would be the first undisputed world champion in the relatively short history of the super-middleweight division.

During the 1920s, boxing had been the most popular sport in the United States. It helped then that only eight boxers at a time could call themselves world champions. There were no rival sanctioning bodies and only eight weight divisions, compared to seventeen today, and each was ruled by one champion. Such select purity made boxing compelling and easy to follow.

Canelo, a throwback to boxing's illustrious past, was about to contest his fourth title fight in eleven months and he suggested that beating Plant would be the most significant moment of his career. 'Only five [male] fighters in the history of boxing have accomplished being undisputed,' Canelo said, 'and I will be the sixth. This fight is going to be [historic].'

That claim to history came with a heavy asterisk. Boxing's 'four-belt era' came into existence in the 1990s. It took a while for the WBO, which was formed in 1988, to be accepted alongside the WBA, WBC and IBF as one of the four main sanctioning bodies, so Canelo's version of history did not run deep.

The 168-pound super-middleweight division was only recognised officially at world championship level in 1984. It bridges the gap between middleweights, who weigh a maximum of 160 pounds, and light-heavyweights, who scale up to 175 pounds. Adding nine weight classes to the original eight divisions had clear merit. Most of all, it saved smaller fighters from challenging men who could naturally weigh fifteen pounds more than them. The rise of the four sanctioning bodies also offered many more boxers opportunities to fight for money-making world titles. But the accompanying chaos and devalued meaning of a 'world champion' was damaging.

Canelo remained emphatic. 'Being the undisputed champion is huge for my legacy and it will be an honour to be the first Latin American fighter to do it.'

Plant, the IBF champion, had won all twenty-one of his fights. He was still an obscure figure outside the boxing hardcore and, having grown up dirt-poor near Nashville, Plant's life would be transformed if he could beat Canelo.

There had been tension when they came together for a press conference to announce the fight in Los Angeles in September. When Plant made a comment about Canelo's mother, the Mexican shoved him violently. Blows were exchanged and a cut opened up under Plant's eye.

'You can say whatever you want to me, but not about my mother,' Canelo snarled. I interviewed Canelo again a month later. 'You can see in his body language Plant is insecure,' he said, 'and that's why he tried to do something different and land that hook.'

Yet Canelo nodded when I asked if he thought that, deep down, Plant believed he could win. 'Of course. Plant is a good fighter, a skilled fighter, a smart fighter. But I am always switched on when

guys like Saunders and Plant make it personal. It's really bad
for them.'

That statement was supported by the experience of Saunders,
whom Canelo had stopped so violently. It was uncertain if
Saunders, having suffered a broken orbital bone, would ever box
again. I asked Canelo if he felt haunted by the prospect of causing
permanent damage to an opponent. 'I always remember how dangerous boxing is,' he replied. 'Your opponent is coming to hurt you,
but it's even more difficult for a fighter if something happens to the
other guy. But I can never think how boxing can kill somebody. It
would be too sad.'

I sat down again with Canelo on the Wednesday of fight week
and, after we chatted about his arrival in Vegas, I mentioned one of
Marvin Hagler's trademark insights: 'It's tough to get out of bed to
do roadwork at 5 a.m. when you've been sleeping in silk pyjamas.'

How could Canelo do so in his Dolce & Gabbana pyjamas? 'The
desire comes out of my love for boxing. I want to always get better
and make history. That's what matters.'

Canelo smiled. 'There's nothing wrong with the pyjamas by the
way. But Hagler is a legend.'

Hagler had retired in 1987 at the age of thirty-two, after sixteen
years and sixty-seven fights as a pro. Canelo was the only contemporary world champion who approached Hagler's numbers. He was
thirty-one and, after sixteen years, he was about to have his sixtieth
fight. The symmetry between them was striking, but Canelo's aura,
with or without his silk pyjamas, could not last forever.

Caleb Plant explained to me how he grew up in a poor white
family, living in a trailer in Ashland City, a small settlement outside
Nashville. His mother had a bad drug and alcohol problem and
Plant lived mostly with his father and his sister Madeline. Their
mobile home was freezing in the winter and stinking hot in the
summer. Sometimes he had to plead for money at school to get a
slice of pizza for him and Madeline.

His father had little direction for years, but Plant believed he and his dad were 'saved by boxing'. Once his dad managed to scrape together enough cash to take over a kickboxing gym, life at last found a purpose and Caleb eventually became a successful amateur.

Plant made his pro debut in May 2014 and, by then, had become a father himself. The previous May, when he was only twenty, his daughter Alia had been born with brain damage, which prevented her from being able to eat normally, develop the motor skills necessary to sit up on her own, walk and talk. Her rare medical condition also caused multiple seizures which Plant said could exceed a hundred a day. She had to be on life support on five separate occasions before he and Alia's mother, Carman Jean Briscoe-Lee, decided it would be merciful for the hospital to turn off the machine in January 2015.

He now fought to keep her memory alive. Plant was also driven to remember his mother who was shot dead by the police in March 2019 when she had become violent and pulled out a knife. Beth Plant died knowing that her son had, two months earlier, become the IBF super-middleweight champion after he beat José Uzcátegui in Los Angeles.

'Boxing is an imitation of life,' Plant told me. 'You get knocked down and you get back up. You don't quit no matter how dark it gets. My life has prepared me for Canelo.'

I ran slowly away from the Strip towards the giant billboard of Canelo Álvarez. As I neared the image of Canelo glinting in the Vegas sunrise, I remembered that, on the night of Heather's death on 15 September 2018, he had fought his bitter rival Gennadiy Golovkin for the second time. Canelo won that night, but I had lost a part of my life.

I kept running and Canelo's red hair gleamed in the low sun. He was fourteen hours away from stepping into the fire of fight night.

Eight hours earlier, on the Friday night, I had watched a women's world title bout between Mikaela Mayer of the US and France's

Maïva Hamadouche at the Virgin Hotel. I had arrived with reasonable expectations because I knew Mayer was a fine boxer and Hamadouche a determined slugger. But Mayer's points victory turned out to be one of the greatest fights I'd ever seen live. It was a battle of remarkable courage and will, and relentless punching, and I felt fortunate to have been there. The prospect of seeing the world's leading female fighters – Katie Taylor, Amanda Serrano, Claressa Shields and Savannah Marshall – in 2022 gave me fresh belief and energy.

Just after dawn that Saturday morning, I reached a mostly Hispanic neighbourhood where the streets were empty. Suddenly, from nowhere, an old Black man appeared as he carried his trash to the garbage container.

He paused as he watched me run. 'Morning,' he said.

'Morning,' I replied, puffing slightly.

'How old are you, man?' he called out.

I ran on, feeling almost insulted. Did I really look so old that my age would be the first thing to enter his mind? As much as I don't fear growing old, or dying, there have been other reminders that time is running out. On a crammed Tube earlier this year when, with most of us wearing our Covid masks, a young woman saw the colour of my hair and the wrinkles around my eyes, she offered me her seat. It was an act of kindness but I shook my head, gruffly, when declining her generosity. I should have thanked her properly and smiled.

It happened too when I was told that I no longer have to pay for my NHS prescriptions or if I was offered a deduction on a ticket at the movies. Alison and our three kids tell me I did the right thing in never dying my hair. I am less sure. Sometimes I reckon that a cinnamon wash, in homage to Canelo, would disguise the fact my hair has turned white in startled surprise that I have been alive and doing this for so long.

In Vegas, the man's question hung in the air before, looking over my shoulder, I shouted out the truth about my age. 'Sixty.'

'Same age as me!' the man yelped. 'You're looking good, baby! You're flowing!'

It was pretty ridiculous but I felt happy. I shouted a breathless reply. 'You too, baby.'

He lifted his free hand in a stately wave and I headed back to the Strip, feeling lighter again.

Life and death had marked me, but they'd also left a certainty that boxing holds a cracked mirror up to both. And so, if the man carrying his garbage had asked me what I was doing in Vegas, I would have told him I was working on a new book. A book about life, death and boxing, baby.

MGM Grand Garden Arena, Las Vegas, Saturday 6 November 2021

While most of the crowd in the sold-out arena chant his name, Canelo is quiet in his corner. Down on his right knee, he makes the sign of the cross and bows his head in a short prayer. Caleb Plant does a series of exercises in his own corner like a park runner preparing for a leisurely jog. He looks less intense than Canelo but, at six feet one, he has a five-and-a-half-inch advantage in height and the greater reach by three-and-a-half inches.

Plant starts confidently, working behind a jab as smooth as it is fast. Halfway through round four, Canelo backs Plant against the ropes and sinks a shuddering hook to the body. Then, exerting his customary suffocating pressure, Canelo goes to the head and back to the body. Plant is skilful, though, and pops off a triple jab followed by a right hand. They have each won two of the first four rounds.

The next four follow a pattern. Canelo throws the more venomous punches, but Plant deflects or evades them while peppering the favourite with his smart jab. Canelo is still winning an absorbing contest through his constant pressure, ringcraft and more powerful punching. At the end of the eighth, Canelo's face is flushed, his red hair damp with sweat. A small cut and swelling, meanwhile, are visible beneath Plant's right eye.

Plant's swift movement and ring IQ make it difficult for Canelo to unleash the full force of his arsenal. The American also punches with crisp precision and then, in a sudden display of virtuosity, Plant unfurls a blurring combination. Four hard punches smack into Canelo's face and, with each one, Plant lets slip a grunt as if showing off in a gym session. He raises his arms at the end of an excellent ninth round.

Plant comes out fast for the tenth, trying to maintain his rhythm, but he soon runs out of steam as Canelo's clubbing punches take their toll. A jolting left uppercut makes Plant sag and then Canelo throws a double left hook to the body.

Thirty-two seconds into round eleven, Canelo shatters Plant with another huge left hook. The power of the punch makes Plant's right ear visibly flap with the force of the blow. He totters forward, but Canelo pushes him back to find the space to land a clinical right uppercut and short left. Plant tumbles to the canvas and gets tangled up with the ropes. He manages to rise quickly and even breaks into a trot as he pretends not to be badly hurt. But he is so disorientated that he runs into the opposite set of ropes.

Referee Mora asks if he wants to continue. Plant nods his assent.

It is almost over and Canelo comes after Plant like a heat-seeking missile. He tags him with another left hook and Plant veers away, trying to stay out of trouble. But Canelo's blows come in a dark and unstoppable train. Six punches crash into Plant, including a crushing right hand which leaves the American sprawled on the canvas.

The new undisputed super-middleweight champion of the world pummels his chest while Plant is examined by the doctor.

They soon find each other and embrace. The two fighters talk intently for seventy seconds before they hug again. It is a moving end to another brutally involving fight.

Isaac Chamberlain, the boxer who was often a writer, was brave. He wrote to me openly about his doubts and fears. 'I've been through so much trauma that it's a constant battle to convince myself I deserve the smallest success. I'm just a little peanut-head boy from Brixton who was never meant to be anything. Bullied at school, no father figure, no real direction. I endured a lot. But when dark times come, I smile and think, *I've lived here many times*.'

There were times when I couldn't get Isaac's words out of my head. 'I've tried to run away from my problems mentally by taking trips to Dubai and paying for all my friends,' he wrote. 'So when they're happy, I'm happy. At least, when they smile, I rent some of their happiness.'

Isaac's record in the ring was 13–1 and his next fight, against a decent opponent in Dilan Prašovic, would headline a bill live on Channel 5 on 10 December 2021. So it was surprising to read his admission of trying to buy happiness.

The way in which boxing provided him with structure was a recurring theme in Isaac's reflections. His dedication was admirable, but I worried because he sometimes felt compelled to isolate himself. In a different message, he told me that 'family friends I haven't seen in ages were at my mum's house celebrating my sister getting engaged. It's been a while since I took part in any family social gathering. It felt weird but I warmed to it. Some hours pass by until the voices in the back of my head start speaking louder, telling me to go home. So I snap back into this introverted self and say my goodbyes. I pass through Rotherhithe Tunnel and imagine it's the tunnel of my secluded mind.'

Isaac was inspired by the idea of sacrifice and he pushed himself to match the romantic notion of the solitary fighter who gave everything in the ring. 'The Russians and Mexicans have something UK fighters don't have,' he wrote. 'They know if they don't win, they have nothing and they will return to poverty. They train in insufferable conditions and all they have to their name is a dream. That has to be my mentality. I have to work in the trenches and live there. I try to be normal. But I don't want to be. I want to sit alone. I want to do damage. I've suffered too much. I've endured too much.'

It was lonely being a fighter and Isaac craved validation. His life was documented in minute detail by the photographs, videos and stories he posted every day on Instagram. He also longed to find 'a feeling of being at ease with the family you love and protect. I didn't know what it was like to sit together as a family discussing the day and making jokes. I never experienced such love and togetherness growing up. My mum would channel her troubles to me through her aggression and stress. I don't expect her to have known better. She came to this country when she was sixteen and had me at seventeen. Coming to the UK because of war in the Congo, raising a child on her own must have been difficult. But I know that love is the healer of all things.'

Isaac was back with Zalia, his first girlfriend. They had been together from 2014 to 2018 but, after they broke up, he became more introverted and fixated with boxing.

They began communicating again when Isaac was trying to rent happiness in December 2020. 'I messaged her while I was in Dubai and we met up on Christmas Day,' he wrote. 'Explaining everything that happened between us from each other's point of view, I sensed her maturity. We spent New Year's together and it felt like my heart was at peace.'

I felt happy for Isaac when, in the spring of 2021, he called to tell me Zalia was pregnant. He asked me what it felt like to be a father and spoke of his own dreams and hopes for the baby.

There were still difficulties as he underwent eye surgery. He had been out of the ring for a year and five days. Even when he made his return in September 2021, his opponent was ruled out just before the weigh-in. Twenty-four hours later, after a desperate search, a replacement was found but that late substitute, Ben Thomas, was knocked out by Isaac in the first round.

I visited Isaac often at the Afewee Gym in the basement of the Brixton Recreation Centre. The gym was run by Bobby Mills, Isaac's new trainer. I liked Bobby and he brought great care to his work. They had first met in 2016 when Isaac had just become the

Southern Area cruiserweight champion, despite dislocating his shoulder in the third round.

'I remember Isaac coming to my gym after he won that title,' Bobby said. 'He gave a great speech to the kids and he was so inspirational. We began working together when he came back from America [in 2020] and it made a lot of sense. I was local and he wanted to be home in Brixton and around his family and friends again. My gym is round the corner from Miguel's, where he started boxing. I had been an amateur coach for eight years and built a club up from scratch with Afewee. I had an amateur team and kids boxing for national titles. So Isaac saw something in me and I decided to get my pro licence.'

A thoughtful and intelligent trainer aged thirty, Bobby had brought in Conor Ward as an assistant. Conor was twenty-seven, the same age as Isaac, and the three of them would prepare for the bout against Prašović, a fighter from Montenegro who had won his first fifteen bouts. Prašović's solitary loss had come a few months before when he was stopped in three rounds by Lawrence Okolie, the only man to have beaten Isaac.

Conor's pro inexperience was made obvious by the fact that he had been a spectator for Prašović's defeat. 'Funnily enough,' he said, 'I was sitting in the top row of the Tottenham Hotspur Stadium when Prašović fought Okolie [two-and-a-half months earlier]. I was there as a fan to watch Usyk–Joshua, so it's pretty strange to think that, in a couple of months, I'll have gone from the back row at Tottenham Stadium to looking Prašović dead in the eye with Isaac.'

Conor couldn't be in the corner as he had not yet obtained his pro licence, but he was absorbed by boxing. 'I was always a serious boxing student and I worked for five years as a coach to very good amateurs. But I also had to earn a living and so I sold car insurance over the phone. I also worked in a shop measuring kids for school uniforms. My last job before joining Isaac and Bobby was stacking shelves at night for two years at Sainsbury's.'

The lack of experience in Isaac's team was compensated for by Jon Pegg, who would be in the corner as the cutman. He was also Sam Eggington's trainer and the forty-seven-year-old had worked 'a couple of thousand pro fights'. Jon was also a prolific film-maker. Since 2009, he had made eight short films and two full-length features which he had written and directed. They had won awards at independent film festivals and Jon loved talking about them. He worked at speed, and to ludicrously tight budgets, and yet his films were intriguing.

Isaac's new corner – a novice pro coach, a former supermarket shelf-stacker and a grizzled trainer who doubled as a film-maker – was the most unlikely team I had met in all my decades in boxing. But Isaac blossomed with their support. 'They make me feel like we're family, bro. I've not had this kind of attention before.'

On 22 November, two-and-a-half weeks before he fought Prašović, Isaac became a father. He and Zalia called their son Zion. 'He's perfect,' Isaac said breathlessly down the phone. 'I can't believe it. How did something this good happen to me?'

National Sports Centre, Crystal Palace, London, Friday
10 December 2021

The homespun feel of the indoor arena is accentuated by the blue plastic seats and wooden benches which accommodate a thousand people. Isaac is the headline fighter, but he shares the dressing room with four other boxers promoted by Mick Hennessy. On a sheet of white paper, the words HOME FIGHTERS are printed in black capital letters on the door outside.

Dilan Prašović has his own locker room. A red stop sign stands at an oblique angle on the brown vinyl floor in the corridor outside. Below the word STOP, it says 'the spread of virus'.

Another Covid wave is on its way and a long winter lies ahead. But it is warm inside the dressing room and Isaac sits quietly on a bench when I arrive. He wears white trainers, blue tracksuit bottoms, a white top and a white headband. I know Isaac is better than Prašović, but anything can happen in boxing.

It helps that Jon Pegg is with us. Jon buttonholes me and talks about screenplays and movies. I forget about boxing as Jon draws me into his other world. I am only jolted back into the present when the call comes for him to accompany Stephen McKenna to the ring. Jon grabs his bag and winks. 'Back to the day job,' he says.

McKenna's fight is on a TV in a corner of the dressing room. He calls himself The Hitman and, having stopped all but one of his previous ten opponents, he drops Jack Ewbank twice in the opening minute. The bout is over after sixty-eight seconds.

Two more fights follow and then it's the turn of Aaron McKenna in the main preliminary bout. He is called The Silencer, but Aaron does not hit quite as hard as his younger brother. He wins an eight-rounder on points against a tough Mexican, Carlos Jesús Gallego Montijo, who is Canelo's cousin. Montijo has reddish hair, but he does not carry the menace of Canelo.

Even Jon says little when he returns to the fraught dressing room. Isaac has not had a proper fight since he beat Luke Watkins on points in October 2018. Three years and two months have passed. He has had just three bouts since then against journeymen. They lasted a combined total of five rounds. He now has to face Prašović, whose last fight had been a world title challenge in front of 60,000 people.

The two-minute call comes and Isaac's team gather in a circle. They are joined by Mick Hennessy, the promoter who has done so much to help Isaac, and bow their heads. It is moving to hear Isaac pray aloud for courage and strength, for victory and for everyone to be safe.

Isaac stretches out his glove to touch my hand. I wish him good luck and the door opens.

At a discreet distance, I follow the team of five as Isaac leads them down an echoing corridor. His red hood is pulled over his head and his boots squeak softly.

Michael Hennessy joins me at the back. He has had nine pro fights and become familiar with these grave moments. 'It's like walking to the hangman,' he says.

The introductions are much more understated than for the big fights, but tension runs just as deep in the home corner.

Chamberlain is the first to land a blow when he rams a stiff jab into Prašović's moustached face. He follows with a looping left, but Prašović catches him with a hard hook on the counter.

Prašović also resorts to grappling, illegally pinning Chamberlain's right arm to his side while pummelling the back of his head. The referee Bob Williams sounds irate as he orders them to break. Prašović misses with a wild hook, while Chamberlain switches to the body and lands heavy blows. Prašović backpedals away. I want to stand up and shout encouragement, but I remain quiet, clenching my hands tightly.

Then, with fifteen seconds left in round one, Chamberlain throws a right cross followed by a sickening left hook to the body. It catches Prašović in the kidney area and he drops to one knee. Prašović is in deep trouble. He looks as if he is battling to breathe while the referee counts. When he hears 'seven', Prašović puts both gloves on the canvas. He tries to rise at 'nine', but the fight has been knocked out of him.

Chamberlain spits out his gumshield so he can smile properly.

He has won a bauble called the IBF International Cruiserweight title, but he also stopped Prašović in one round, two rounds less than his old rival Okolie needed.

'He caught me with a left hook and I thought, *I need to take this guy out because this is a fight*', Chamberlain says in the ring. 'He's been at world level, so I had to be switched on and I'm glad I got it done in emphatic fashion. I spent so long away from home. Now, my baby is two weeks old and it feels so good that I can bring home something for him.'

10

Going to War

At 7 a.m. on Thursday 24 February 2022, a thick blue line on the testing kit confirmed I had Covid. It was the first time I had contracted the virus and I quarantined myself in a room downstairs. I had begun to shiver and burn up simultaneously, so I switched on the television for an attempted distraction. It was then that I heard the far more serious news.

A few hours earlier, around 5 a.m. in Ukraine, Russian bombs had rained down on Kyiv, Kharkiv, Mariupol and Dnipro as Vladimir Putin announced the start of 'a special military operation'. War had been declared and, lying ill on a makeshift bed, I watched the distressing footage from Ukraine as cruise and ballistic missiles exploded.

By early evening, Ukraine claimed that 203 Russian attacks had been launched across the country. Ukrainian forces had killed fifty Russian soldiers, shot down six planes and four helicopters, and destroyed four Russian tanks. There had already been civilian casualties and eighteen people were killed in a missile attack on Odesa, six more died near Kyiv and another four were killed after a shell hit a Donetsk hospital.

As my temperature climbed, I switched to Twitter updates and saw a clip posted by the *Washington Post*'s Whitney Leaming who wrote: 'A young boy plays the piano in a Kharkiv hotel lobby as unconfirmed reports come in that Russian troops are advancing on the city.'

In the accompanying video, an overhead camera locked on a white piano in the middle of a swirly carpet. The distant figure of the boy could be seen as his hands moved across the keys with gentle delicacy as he played Philip Glass's 'Tales from the Loop'. I watched the clip again and again.

All the Ukrainians I knew were boxers – Vitali and Wladimir Klitschko, Vasiliy Lomachenko and Oleksandr Usyk. I could not stop thinking of them as the piano played in Kharkiv. Vitali Klitschko had been the mayor of Kyiv since 2014 and I knew that he and his three fellow boxers did not back down from a fight. It seemed as if the boy at the piano carried the same spirit.

I felt worse a day later, but Vitali Klitschko appeared on television to say he would join his brother as Wladimir had already enlisted in Ukraine's reserve army. 'I don't have another choice. I'll be fighting,' Vitali said. 'I believe in Ukraine and in my people.'

Vitali was fifty years old. I had been impressed by his intelligence and decency whenever I interviewed him. I felt the same when interviewing Wladimir. They might have both been mechanical and methodical, but they had dominated heavyweight boxing for a long time.

The Klitschko brothers were soon joined by the great Lomachenko and Usyk. On 27 February, Lomachenko posted confirmation that he had joined a territorial defence battalion. In the accompanying photograph, he wore military fatigues with a gun strapped across his chest.

Usyk had been in London when war broke out and he immediately flew to Warsaw and then drove 500 miles to Kyiv so he could be with his family and enlist in the Ukrainian army. In a television interview with CNN, Usyk spoke from a basement in Kyiv as he addressed the possibility of killing Russian soldiers. 'If they want to take my life, or the lives of my close ones, I will have to do it. But I don't want to shoot. I don't want to kill anybody.'

Usyk said that being a boxer had 'helped me to be calm and mentally prepared. And it helps me to help others who are panicking and nervous. [The Russians] just bombed Mariupol and one of my friends got a rocket in his roof.'

My fever raged and, in my sick bed, I watched a video of a captured Russian soldier. He had been told that they had to rescue Ukraine from a fascist regime. The soldier said he had only learned the truth when he heard Lomachenko and Usyk speak out. They were his favourite boxers – 'back home I loved watching them'. The two fighters had made him question everything he had been told in Russia. 'They said, "We didn't call you here." And so I feel shame that we came [to Ukraine].'

On 2 March 2022, Russian paratroopers landed in Kharkiv. Kyiv was also under siege and President Zelenskiy, after announcing that nearly 6,000 Russian soldiers had been killed in the first six days of the war, warned that Putin wanted to 'erase our history, erase our country, erase us all'.

The blue line on my Covid tests remained unwaveringly clear. I would test positive for twelve successive days while, in quarantine, I kept following the war with feverish attention. In one corner, I saw the squat and demonic figure of Putin. Across the ring, Zelenskiy wore a military uniform with the bearing of Ukraine's leading boxers. Zelenskiy's task was grim and terrifying but his past, before he became president, was rooted in comedy and acting. He had even been the voice of Paddington Bear in Ukraine during a simpler time of peace. The war intensified, but the difference between right and wrong had never been clearer.

At an extraordinary press conference in Dublin, on 12 April 2022, the United States government stressed that it had become a priority for President Biden and his law enforcement departments, in conjunction with their counterparts in Ireland and Europe, to bring the Kinahans to justice. The cartel would be hunted down by US agencies in the same way they had pursued the Italian Camorra, the Yakuza of Japan and the Russian Izmaylovskaya.

Claire Cronin, the US ambassador to Ireland, also announced the US Department of the Treasury's reward of $5m for information that would lead to the 'financial destruction' of the Kinahan gang and the arrest of Daniel Kinahan, his father, his brother and their four closest associates.

Drew Harris, the Irish police commissioner, said anyone in boxing who dealt with Kinahan should understand that they were working with a wanted criminal who led a drug cartel worth more than €1bn [£830m]. 'What was implicit before, and what some individuals could choose to ignore, is now absolutely explicit,' Harris stressed. 'If you deal with the individuals who are sanctioned as part of the Kinahan Organised Crime Gang, you are dealing with criminals engaged in drug trafficking. They will resort to vicious actions, including murder.'

Harris also warned broadcasters – including BT Sport, Sky, the BBC and talkSPORT – to think carefully about their involvement with fighters known to have had links to Kinahan. 'I'd ask them to look at the probity of their own business. They should ask themselves if this is something they want to be involved with in terms of their legitimate business. I think the answer is a resounding no.'

Tyson Fury had been in Dubai in February and a photograph had been posted of him and Kinahan together. It was just one of hundreds which showed Kinahan in the company of his fighters. Beyond the Fury collection, the most infamous photo featured Sunny Edwards and Kinahan. They smiled while Kinahan pointed cheerfully at the 'No Drugs' logo on Edwards' T-shirt. A gifted but sometimes obnoxious world champion flyweight, Edwards wrote of Kinahan on his social media post that it was 'always good to see an old friend'.

All the usual Kinahan apologists, even Edwards and Fury, were silent in the aftermath of the crackdown. They did not defend Kinahan or bleat about a fake news agenda. I felt relieved that Kinahan, apparently, was gone from the fight game.

In a curious coincidence, a long-planned press conference took place the following day to publicise Fury's fight against Dillian Whyte on 23 April. But even a world heavyweight title extravaganza appeared redundant when set against the US government's determination to crack down on 'a murderous organisation', international money laundering and 'deadly narcotics'.

The next afternoon, I joined the Zoom media conference call with more than a hundred journalists from the US, Britain and Ireland. I soon realised why the Fury camp had proceeded. It was engineered so that the only reporters invited to put any questions to Fury were those asking him about his golf swing, his faith or how it would feel to fight on St George's Day. The rest of us were placed on mute and, despite our raised-hand emojis, were ignored. Kinahan's name was not mentioned once in more than fifty minutes.

It was my birthday that Tuesday morning. On 19 April 2022, I turned sixty-one. My boxing obsession was more suited to a young man, but I no longer even tried to kick my habit.

I pushed hard to interview Fury that day. I wanted to ask him about Kinahan and I knew Fury would not react well. But I still had the hunger and so I managed to get the only one-to-one interview he would do alongside his obligatory television chores at the Wembley Hilton.

While I waited to be taken to him, I was advised that Fury would not talk about Kinahan. I pointed out that there could not be an interview without such questions. My fixer nodded, but a clear stipulation followed. I could ask one question about the subject near the end.

When the signal came, I walked to the far side of the room where Fury occupied a giant presence alongside the windows. He was relatively friendly but restrained. As I had been given just fifteen minutes with him, we moved swiftly into our old routine. I asked Fury how he was and, as usual, he spoke with bristling immediacy. He told me how he still struggled with depression and that he would retire after fighting Whyte that Saturday night.

'I am suffering all the time,' Fury said quietly as he looked out of the window rather than facing me. Two floors below us, people gawped up at him. They could see his huge frame from street level and men and women, young and old, waved enthusiastically. It looked as if they were shouting his name but, behind the thick sheet of glazing, we couldn't hear them.

Fury waved back as he said of his bleak moments: 'I've learnt to manage it a bit better now. Before I didn't really understand it. Now I know how to manage the problem.'

I had read a few days before that one in ten deaths in the Irish travelling community were caused by suicide. Fury shook his head. 'I don't think it's just Ireland. It's the whole world. It's the biggest killer of men under thirty-five.'

A group of boys jumped up and down in excitement on the street outside. 'All right, boys?' Fury said gently.

He turned to me. 'It's a massive, massive problem. It's like a pandemic. Lots of people are taking their lives today because they don't know where to go or what to do.'

I had interviewed Fury often and we always seemed to end up back where we started – on that day in November 2011 when I went to see him in his modest bungalow in Morecambe and the young heavyweight had said: 'One minute I'm happy, and the next minute I'm sad, like commit-suicide-sad.'

Fury was twenty-three then. Now, in 2022, he was thirty-four and a father of six. He told me how vividly he remembered that first interview. 'I was even depressed back then,' he said.

The small crowd outside continued to grow as word spread that Fury had arrived in Wembley. He nodded when I said he must tire of the attention. 'It's difficult because your life is not your own. I'll be glad when it's all over, after this fight. No more Mr Celebrity Boxer.'

Whenever a great fighter tells me he is about to have his last bout, I always offer a sceptical look and ask, 'Do you mean that?'

'Oh, it's definitely the last one,' Fury said. 'I've earned plenty of money, won plenty of titles, done everything I ever wanted to do. Sounds like a good one to go out with.'

I knew how much Fury loved being in the ring. How would he replace the intensity of Saturday night as he and Whyte walked towards each other?

'It's not the competing that drives me. It's the training. As long as I stay fit and active and mentally well, I'll always train. My dad's nearly sixty and he trains every day.'

Surely he would want to win the undisputed championship against Usyk? 'For what reason?' Fury asked. 'Money or belts? It's got to be one or the other, hasn't it?'

It was a meaningless word in a murky business, but I said the 'belts'.

'But I've won all the belts, haven't I?' Fury countered. 'Belts don't mean much to me.'

We spoke about his savage trilogy against Deontay Wilder, but Fury denied that thoughts of retirement were sparked by the punishment he has already absorbed. 'It's got nothing to do with taking blows or my age. Just enough is enough. I've got a wife and six kids I've got to look after. I'm not really interested in anything else.'

Fury paused and then sounded grandly philosophical. 'As Julius Caesar said, there'll always be somebody else to fight. Another battle. There'll always be somebody.'

He smiled when I said his wife must be relieved, if she believed him, that his boxing career was almost over. 'Yeah, I promised Paris that the last Wilder fight would be the final one. We made a deal and that was it. But I've come back one last time. She accepted it because I wanted the last fight to be at Wembley.'

I asked him about Kinahan and how he felt when the US

government announced their sanctions against his friend. 'You know what?' Fury said, looking up at the brooding clouds outside. 'Rule number one for me is I don't get involved in other people's businesses. Therefore, I've got nothing to say about any of it. Because it's not my business, I don't get involved. I stay in my own lane, because I'm just a boxer. That's all I can say about that matter.'

I tried again, but Fury was emphatic. 'It's got nowt to do with me, has it? I've got my own troubles with six kids and a wife nagging me to death for not being at home to help. I've got a man [Whyte] who wants to punch my face in. Anything else is out of my control.'

We would return to Kinahan, but Fury shook his head when I asked if he enjoyed it most when his rivals were swaggering figures such as Wilder. 'I enjoy them all. I don't look at boxing like a sport or my way of earning a living. Boxing is my life. It's been my life since I was twelve. There is nothing else. Boxing is everything to me.'

Fury did not sound like a man about to leave this vicious old business. As we gazed down at the waving people, he noted that 'it's been an amazing trip with so many highs and lows. So much darkness and so many good, learning episodes. I wouldn't change it for the world.'

Fury and I soon sat down with Frank Warren, his British promoter, and a few other journalists. When it was pointed out that Bob Arum had admitted paying Kinahan more than $4m for four fights featuring Fury between 2019 and 2021, the big man shrugged. 'That's Bob Arum's business. He can spend it all on gummy bears if he wants to. It's out of my control.'

'Let me make a couple of things very clear,' said Warren. 'One, Daniel Kinahan has nothing to do with this show and, two, as Tyson said, he was unaware of any payments made by Top Rank.'

Warren and Fury were asked if they felt concern about the implications for boxing. 'I am concerned,' said the veteran British promoter, 'but I'm also concerned about some of the misinformation that's going around. We're not stupid people. All of us understand what has happened from the US Treasury. It's been going on now for three years and we all know what we have to do and we will not be breaking the law. We've never broken the law. Is it a bad image for boxing? Well, we sold 94,000 tickets for this fight in two days. Are we going to do good business on pay-per-view? Yes, we are. We are very conscious about what we have to do as the guardians of the sport, but we are not policemen.'

Pressed to admit that it was a significant story, Fury said, 'I don't really take any notice of the media. I know what the media can do and I was the victim of a witch-hunt in 2015 and 2016. It's got nowt to do with me. I've got my own troubles.'

A few hours earlier, Bob Yalen had resigned as chief executive of MTK Global amid mounting pressure. Fury insisted that he had 'never been sponsored by MTK'.

Reminded that he had worn the MTK logo before, Fury's mood darkened. 'That was from 2017 until 2020. Three years and that was it. Any more probing questions you can think of to trip me up? Because you can't. There is nothing I have to hide.'

He was asked about the photograph taken of him and Kinahan smiling together in Dubai two months earlier. 'A picture doesn't mean I'm a criminal. There could be a criminal in this building now. It doesn't mean I am involved in his criminal activity, does it?'

MTK Global was in such trouble that, a day later, a company statement confirmed its demise. 'Since leading promoters have now informed us that they will be severing all ties with MTK and will no longer work with our fighters, we have taken the difficult decision to cease operations at the end of this month ... We have faced unprecedented levels of unfair scrutiny and criticism since the sanctioning by the US government of Daniel Joseph Kinahan.'

The sky had fallen in on MTK and Kinahan. It seemed as if a long and terrible war had, at last, been won by the forces of good.

Wembley Stadium, London, Saturday 23 April 2022

'I ain't no world champion,' Tyson Fury said as he began a roaring eulogy at the post-fight press conference. 'I'm a legend. I'm the best heavyweight there's ever been. I have a six-foot-nine frame, 270 pounds of weight, can move like a middleweight, hit like a thunderstorm, take a punch … I've got balls like King Kong, the heart of a lion and the mindset of the Wizard of Oz.'

He nodded. 'It was a very special night. What a way to top it all off.'

The end to a messy bout, which Fury controlled even though he and Dillian Whyte were both warned for roughhouse brawling, came in round six. Fury snapped out a jab and then threw a vicious right uppercut which detonated against Whyte's chin. The challenger was left splayed across the canvas with his arms raised in helpless surrender.

An hour later, having visited Whyte in his dressing room to give him 'a kiss and a cuddle', Fury sauntered into a plush conference room. He ripped off his shirt, placed his WBC world heavyweight champion belt on the table, sat down, smiled and began talking in a near unbroken stream of words for the next thirty minutes.

'I feel at home in that ring, like a dolphin in water. It's what I was born to do because I was always meant to be heavyweight champion of the world. I'm now going to become the second heavyweight in history after Rocky Marciano to retire undefeated. I've done everything asked of me. I've had me brains knocked out. I've been put down, rocked and cut. I've had tough fights and boxed all over the world. How much blood can you get out of a stone?'

Professional boxing is about blood-money and, in beating Whyte, Fury had made a staggering $33,640,500 (£26,192,306). He would earn far more if he fought the winner of the rematch between Joshua and Usyk, who held the IBF, WBA and WBO belts, in a unification showdown.

'I come from fuck-all,' Fury said, 'but it's never been about money. I know lots of people with big money, but none of them are happy. It's not even been about belts or legacies. It's not been about anything but punching a face right in on the night. That's all it's ever been about.'

A Ukrainian journalist, sharing the widespread disbelief that The Gypsy King was about to abdicate, asked Fury if he would prefer to fight Usyk or Joshua. Fury rocked back in his chair. 'Like Clark Gable would say, "I don't give a damn …"'

He thanked Frank Warren who 'brought me back from the brink of death and believed in me and gave me a big contract to box again [in 2018] … I've proved that anything's possible. It doesn't matter where you are, how dark the place you're in. It doesn't get any darker than when you're committing suicide and I was there. To lose all that weight, ten stone, and to get mentally well again, to regain the crown jewels … It's been a fantastic career. But this might be the final curtain for The Gypsy King.'

11

The Lonely Passion of Katie Taylor

On Monday 25 April 2022, I boarded a plane to New York City. Katie Taylor against Amanda Serrano that coming weekend, in the first women's boxing match to headline Madison Square Garden, seemed poignant. Taylor, the world's leading female boxer, had been a professional since October 2016, but the murderous feud between the Kinahan and Hutch gangs meant she had been unable to fight at home in Ireland.

Apart from a few isolated small-hall shows, professional boxing in Ireland had ground to a halt after the Regency Hotel shooting in early 2015. The police considered it too dangerous because of Kinahan's involvement in boxing and so all twenty of Taylor's pro bouts had been held in the UK or the US. But for a decade she had remained the most popular sports personality in Ireland, winning countless awards ahead of Johnny Sexton and Rory McIlroy.

The Irish appreciated Taylor's humility in a business as bombastic as boxing. They also loved her because she was a trailblazer. Taylor's cultural impact in a country which, for centuries, had showed particular prejudice against women, was profound. It was still written in the Irish constitution that a woman's place was in the home, while the struggle for female rights to contraception, abortion and divorce had been long and arduous.

Taylor described herself as a Christian and a fighter, rather than a feminist, but she had changed perceptions and created opportunities for women. Her mother Bridget said that, when Katie was a girl, she had worried about her youngest daughter's shyness. But Bridget and her husband, Peter, knew that a fire burned inside Katie. Rather than asking for a Barbie doll, Katie wanted boxing gloves and football boots. She and her brother, Lee, would pretend to be Rocky Marciano and Jack Dempsey. Her parents encouraged Katie because Peter was a boxing coach while Bridget officiated at amateur shows as a ringside judge.

Aged six, Katie would stand on a kitchen chair, close her eyes and spread her arms wide as if an Olympic medal had just been draped around her neck. Yet female boxing did not exist as an Olympic sport and girls and women were banned from competing in the ring in both Ireland and the UK. Katie still dreamed of becoming a boxer.

'It was not easy,' Taylor told me. 'Boxing runs in my family's blood, but there were no opportunities for girls. I followed my brothers to the gym [at St Fergal's in her hometown of Bray in County Wicklow], but I had to pretend I was a boy to get fights. We had to put my name down as K Taylor. I would pull the headgear on, tuck my hair inside so no one could see it and get into the ring. When I won and took the headgear off, there would be uproar when everyone saw I was a girl.'

Her father began a crusade for her to take part in the first officially sanctioned female boxing contest in Ireland. Pete Taylor was an influential and persuasive coach and, finally, on 31 October 2001, Katie demonstrated her vast potential against Belfast's Alanna Audley in front of a passionate crowd at Dublin's National Stadium. Andy Lee was high up on the bill that night, but Katie stole the show. Her game opponent was five kilos heavier but, with her dad in the corner, Katie won a wide decision on points.

'It seemed like a huge deal,' Taylor said. 'Alanna gave me a good fight, but the hardest part was the media interest. I was very shy and hated it. It was a bit much for a girl of fifteen.'

Katie was such a skilful boxer that she sparred exclusively against boys in the national squad and did well against future pro world and European champions in Carl Frampton and Eric Donovan. She was the only girl in the squad and her gym wars against Paddy Barnes, who would go on to win two Olympic medals, became the stuff of legend in Irish amateur boxing as Katie's determination matched her technical brilliance.

But Taylor still recalled the day when a middle-aged man asked her a question at an awards ceremony: 'What do you do with your breasts when you're in the ring?'

Pioneers are always required to overcome stupidity and, in November 2007, Taylor and Canada's Katie Dunn were invited to fight an exhibition bout at the University of Illinois to decide whether women's boxing was worthy of an Olympic slot. One official told Taylor that the future of women's boxing rested on the quality of her performance. It was enough to make an ordinary person crumble, but Taylor displayed such skill and toughness that even the doubters agreed that women could be great boxers.

But at the 2010 World Championships, the organisers announced that female boxers would be required to wear skirts. Taylor refused to comply and, faced with the unyielding will of the best woman boxer in the world, the male administrators withdrew their demand. By the time she had won six European titles and five world championships, Taylor successfully led the lobbying of the IOC to allow women fighters to make their Olympic debut at London 2012.

Her friend and former team-mate Eric Donovan sparred with Taylor to help her prepare for those Olympics and the threat of the Russian southpaw Sofya Ochigava, whom she would meet in the final.

'Katie was under immense pressure,' Donovan told me. 'A huge banner of her covered the side of a building in Dublin. It said: "Only the strongest shoulders can carry the hopes of a nation." I had to remind myself that Katie Taylor is a global superstar. In Ireland, she is godly. But she's just Katie to me, my friend and great old sparring partner who gave me a few digs.'

Taylor defeated Ochigava in a testing final to become the Olympic champion. Ireland was besotted. As Donovan said, 'Katie is such a gentle soul, almost saint-like, but when the bell goes, she transforms into this absolute machine and becomes a bad ass. It's a beautiful, extraordinary thing.'

So much of Taylor's confidence depended on her close relationship with her father. Pete had given up work as an electrician to help his daughter full-time and, together, they aimed for a second gold medal at the Rio Olympics in 2016. But absolute trust in her dad shattered when he fell for another woman. Pete's marriage to Bridget became unsustainable and Katie was devastated. She felt broken when she decided that, as integrity mattered more to her than success, she could no longer work with her father.

'I felt like I was missing my right arm because I hadn't boxed without my dad in the corner,' Taylor told me in 2021. She recalled how she had cried the first time she went to train in a new gym, without her dad.

Taylor was still a prohibitive favourite to win gold in Rio but, in the quarter-finals, she was shocked when losing a controversial decision to Mira Potkonen. Footage of Taylor looking stricken in the aftermath, unable to voice her distress, was difficult to watch. 'When I remember that moment, I still get emotional,' she told me. 'But, despite the heartbreak, I came back a better fighter.'

Taylor disliked talking about herself and publicising her fights, but I discovered that she was a friendly and likeable woman. She was also different to most male boxers I interviewed. 'I love the fact that God chooses the lowly ones,' Taylor said. She was in the midst of describing her maternal grandmother and how she and her family overcame impoverishment in Bray, a coastal town not far from Dublin. 'My granny had a tough life, but there's not a bitter bone in her body. She grew up in poverty and we were the same. We were very poor and living in the roughest area, but God chose our family. I have two brothers and one sister and we all became successful. But nobody would have looked at our family and thought success will come to them.'

Her brother Peter, obtained a first-class degree in mathematical science at University College Dublin before completing his master's in theoretical physics at Cambridge. He had become a professor of mathematics at Trinity but, as Taylor explained, 'he's a lecturer at DCU [Dublin City University] now. My sister [Sarah] has a managerial job and my other brother, Lee, is working in business.'

Taylor won a place to study at UCD, but she was never going to do anything other than box. After the devastation of Rio, she flew to Vernon, a small town in Connecticut, to work with Ross Enamait. He was not particularly well-known as a trainer, but Taylor had read some of his strength-and-conditioning books, including *Infinite Intensity*. She decided Enamait was the man to guide her pro career in the ring while she made a clean break from her past.

Taylor lived a lonely life in Vernon. When she was not in the gym, running through the snow or going to church on Sunday mornings, she stayed in modest accommodation. She watched movies on her phone and read the Bible. Taylor outlined the importance of her faith when she described how she and her mum always prayed together. 'She prays over me before every fight. I don't know how people get through difficult moments without God in their life. That's my anchor, my rock and there are definitely times I cling onto the word of God.'

When she beat Anahi Sanchez to win her first world title as a pro in October 2017, Taylor had been ill with flu for ten days before the fight. Tears rolled down her face as her mother prayed for her. That night, as she waited to walk to the ring in Cardiff, Taylor wore a red T-shirt which said: *HE TRAINS MY HANDS FOR BATTLE. PSALM 18.*

She dropped Sanchez with a body punch in the second round

and became world champion after all three judges scored the fight 99–90 in her favour.

Taylor had since been in two gruelling bouts with Delfine Persoon, whom she was lucky to beat the first time in New York in June 2019. She insisted that she recovered swiftly. 'I obviously had lumps and bumps on my head both times, but after a few days I felt fine again. I'm a quick healer.'

She was thirty-five and, in November 2021, she conceded to me that 'you can't do this forever. At the same time, I don't feel like I'm slowing down. I also have a group of honest people around me who would tell me when it's time to hang up the gloves. But my desire hasn't diminished at all. I still love boxing. I still love getting up in the cold mornings and training. Those days are the difference between winning and losing.'

Taylor was fortunate to have been managed so astutely by Brian Peters, a friendly and knowledgeable man steeped in boxing. The way they worked together was refreshing in the back-stabbing business of boxing. Taylor had been managed by Peters since 2016 but they had never signed a contract to cement their working relationship. Each considered their word to be their bond and so there was no need to involve any lawyers or financial advisers.

That unusual arrangement stemmed from the trust forged in each other – despite the fact that Peters had twice resisted requests from Bridget Taylor to manage her daughter. Peters explained to Bridget that he had left the boxing business and, having also made money out of the various pubs, restaurants and nightclubs he'd previously owned, he was happy in retirement. He loved fishing in Connemara, in the beautiful wilds of County Galway, and he was disenchanted with the changing landscape in Irish boxing.

But Bridget and Katie Taylor knew how much Peters understood the fight game. He was such a boxing insider that he and the much heftier American trainer Lou Duva used to have ice-cream eating competitions which the British promoter Mickey Duff would judge. Duva was a huge man and he had sharpened his appetite years earlier during similar eating competitions with the unbeaten world heavyweight champion Rocky Marciano – whom Katie often pretended to be when she was a little girl. Peters usually lost to Duva although he did beat him on one memorable occasion when Don King judged the amount of ice-cream each man had consumed.

Peters cared about her as a person while helping Taylor break remarkable new ground as a fighter. She agreed when I suggested that her and Serrano receiving around two million dollars each would be a milestone for women's boxing.

'Absolutely. Money isn't my main priority, but it's obviously important because boxing is a limited career. When I first turned pro, women fighters were making pennies compared to their male counterparts. So the money is huge for women's boxing. This fight deserves it.'

Serrano, who had lost only one of her forty-four fights, would provide an exacting challenge. 'She's obviously a fantastic fighter and a seven-division world champion. She's been very consistent and she's very experienced. That's why this fight will be fantastic. It's a genuine 50/50 contest.'

I thought Serrano was exceptional, but her becoming a seven-weight world champion needed to be set in an appropriate context. A few years earlier, John Sheppard, who runs BoxRec, the definitive public record of professional boxing, had discovered that the four main sanctioning bodies had created more world titles for women than there were actual fighters.

By 2023, the number of women boxers had increased markedly, but Sheppard pointed out that the IBF, WBA, WBC and WBO had still created 1,380 different female titles in fifteen weight divisions. Since there were 1,909 active women boxers, and two are needed to make a fight, it translated to the equivalent of 1.4 titles being available for each pro female bout.

But, finally, we had two women who could match each other at elite level.

Taylor's ambition echoed Tyson Fury's recent claim. She wanted to retire, like Rocky Marciano, as an unbeaten world champion. Her fame continued to grow, but she seemed determined to remain the same. 'I'm always such a quiet person anyway,' she said with a wry smile. 'It's actually very easy to live a quiet life regardless of the spotlight.'

Christy Martin and Deirdre Gogarty were the first female boxers I ever met. In March 1996, while in Las Vegas to watch Frank Bruno try to defend his WBC world heavyweight title against a rampaging Mike Tyson, my attention was snared early in the week by the presence of Martin and Gogarty on the undercard.

Martin came from West Virginia and called herself 'The Coal Miner's Daughter'. She was married to her manager, Jim, who was twenty-five years older than her. Jim Martin wore a terrible toupee and ran the show. No one, apart from Christy herself, knew then that he was a violent and controlling husband who subjected his wife to sustained emotional and physical abuse.

In 1996, we were oblivious to the truth of Christy Martin's life. Don King was determined to make Martin a star and she became the first woman boxer to feature on the cover of *Sports Illustrated*. All the while she carried the terrible secret of her marriage.

Deirdre Gogarty was from Drogheda, thirty-five miles north of Dublin. Women's boxing was banned in Ireland, so Gogarty based herself in Louisiana and fought in various cities across the US. Her record was a modest 8–4–2, but Gogarty's nickname was 'Dangerous'. I liked Dangerous Deirdre as she was kind and soft-spoken and proud to be a boxer.

I saw Gogarty and Martin as fighters rather than novelty acts because there was an admirable seriousness about them. I also wanted them to succeed because boxing usually believed that women in the sport could only be ring card girls wearing revealing costumes between rounds.

Martin and Gogarty were uplifting, even if their skill level was nowhere near the quality that would be displayed by Taylor, Serrano, Claressa Shields and Savannah Marshall in a different generation. Martin and Gogarty also lacked their supreme conditioning. But they were brave and tried hard – as their sweat-streaked faces confirmed. Gogarty was knocked down in the second round, but she got up and went the distance. Their fight marked a start, but it would take women's boxing another twenty-five years to blossom.

One of its hidden benefits came in the form of a letter from an eleven-year-old girl. Katie Taylor wrote to Deirdre Gogarty to say how much she also wanted to become a boxer. She wrote about her Olympic dream and how she loved to fight.

Of course, I knew nothing about this exchange. Instead, in 1997, I went to the West Country to interview one of the most courageous people I have ever met in boxing. Jane Couch and I forged a bond that was rekindled when I interviewed her again twenty-two years later.

'I just think I'm damaged, like really damaged,' Couch said softly in September 2019 as her tears fell. Couch was a world champion who had been barred from fighting in her own country because the British Boxing Board of Control insisted for so long that women were too emotionally unstable to box.

Couch had to win a court case against the sport's governing body to make British sporting history in August 1998. Bernard Buckley, the Board's solicitor, built his case around the claim that 'many women suffer from premenstrual tension which makes them more emotional and more labile and accident-prone. They are too fragile to box and they bruise easily.'

Buckley ignored everything Couch had been through to win her first world title in only her fifth fight in 1996. She had flown to Denmark to face Sandra Geiger, the French world champion who came from a kickboxing background. Couch suffered a broken jaw, shattered cheekbone, fractured eye socket, cracked ribs and a missing tooth, but she still won a unanimous decision over ten rounds. She and Geiger both ended up in hospital.

Yet not a single line about her becoming world champion was written in the national press or mentioned on radio or television. 'I thought I was going to get mobbed at the airport, but no one was there,' Couch told me. 'I got *Boxing News* that next Friday. I was all excited, but there was nothing. My manager shrugged and said: "They don't do women's boxing."'

Even her landmark legal victory was of little benefit to Couch. She still struggled to get fights and there were many times when she travelled abroad and was not even paid. 'I wish I hadn't been the first,' she told me. 'If I had known what it would cost me, I probably wouldn't have done it. I gave up everything. I didn't even get into a proper relationship until I was forty-one. It hurts my pride to talk this openly, but I don't think people realise the damage they did when they'd call me a lesbian or a freak because I wanted to be a boxer.'

We relived the legal battle Couch waged against the Boxing Board. 'All credit goes to them two women [who represented her],' Couch said. 'Sarah Leslie, the solicitor, and Dinah Rose the top sex-discrimination barrister in the country by a mile. Dinah fucked 'em up because they thought she was going only on sex discrimination. She used that, but focused on restraint of trade. I was already a double world champion and the Board was stopping me making a living in this country. We won and, when I got the licence, I thought: *It will be all right now.* But the abuse got worse. I'd be on TV shows like *Richard and Judy* and they would have phone-ins for people to vote. "Is she a freak? Should she be allowed to box?" When people keep calling you a freak, you think, *Maybe I am.* I would just sit on my own, crying.'

A year after she retired, in 2008, Couch had a breakdown. 'I was very down. I didn't want to go out. I had pains in my chest like I was having a heart attack.'

In hospital, Couch recalled, 'This amazing lady doctor told me I was having a panic attack. I was like, "How can I have a panic attack? I'm not scared of anything." I told her what I did and she said, "You've got to bury boxing, otherwise this will always haunt you."'

After all the pain she suffered, did Couch feel any envy when hearing about Taylor's headlining show? 'Not a bit because I've buried it now. What Katie's done for boxing and women in Ireland is massive. I know because my fella's Irish. She's a superstar and that's how it should be. It just wasn't like that for me – or most women boxers today.'

I landed at JFK and, from the airport, took a cab to the exclusive New York Athletic Club in Central Park South. Having rolled straight off the plane, I was still in my creased old jeans, which broke the club's strict and swanky dress code. Urgent talks had to be held in the lobby and, after fifteen minutes of haggling, a compromise was finally struck with the concierge. I was granted entry into the club via a service elevator at the back of the building.

Katie Taylor was amused and we agreed it felt a long way from St Fergal's gym in Bray, where she had been banned from boxing as a girl. Taylor moved through her strange new surroundings with a light touch, smiling and chatting as we meandered down the corridors in search of a suite where she could consider the fight of her life that Saturday night against Amanda Serrano.

Against the backdrop of their historic multimillion-dollar bout, the lavish surroundings made sense. 'It's just so special headlining a huge fight at Madison Square Garden,' Taylor said. 'It's the most iconic venue in boxing and I think of Muhammad Ali against Joe Frazier [in 1971] and those nights when history was made in the Garden. It's a dream to be in a fight like this against a great champion in Amanda Serrano. It tells people how far we have come.

'I've always wanted to fight the best. That's exactly what I'm getting because Serrano has a really good engine and she is very aggressive and hits hard. But she is polite and respectful out of the ring because we both know this fight sells itself. It's the biggest fight in the whole sport.'

Taylor was used to fighting in stadiums in front of 80,000 people on Anthony Joshua undercards. She had also fought at two Olympic Games. In contrast, Serrano had sometimes earned as little as $5,000 or $10,000 for sparsely attended bouts while winning world titles in a staggering seven weight categories – which reflected the shallow pool of elite performers in the undeveloped world of women's boxing.

The arrival of Jake Paul, the YouTube influencer who had become Serrano's promoter, shifted the landscape because he brought a vast new audience with him. The fact that Taylor–Serrano was also being promoted so enthusiastically by Madison Square Garden had helped turn it into the richest fight in the history of women's boxing.

But the shadow of Daniel Kinahan still stretched over us. 'It's been really disappointing,' Taylor said of the block on her fighting at home. 'I would love to fight in Ireland.'

It seemed highly symbolic that MTK Global would cease trading that Saturday – the very day of Taylor's showdown with Serrano. 'I am a little more hopeful, but it's probably too early to tell,' Taylor said of boxing's future without Kinahan. 'But my dream is to fight in Ireland.'

As she looked around the plush club, Taylor added, 'This is such a tough sport. You have to beat your body into submission in training and be ready for anything and everything mentally. It's a real test, but when you have a fight between the best, and that is me and Amanda Serrano, it makes for an incredible night.'

As we spoke of how she and her mum would pray together just before she stepped into the perilous ring, Taylor smiled. 'I can't wait,' she said softly. 'I'm ready.'

Madison Square Garden, New York, Saturday 30 April 2022

The famous old arena darkens and, above the chanting Irish fans, Alicia Keys sings resoundingly of New York, her voice echoing around the Garden. Footage of Amanda Serrano bludgeoning her opponents fills the giant screen as the Keys vocal segues into a more upbeat track – 'Puerto Rico' by Frankie Ruiz.

A previously solemn Serrano dances as she enters the arena. Dressed in a shimmering robe trimmed with red, blue and white, the colours of Puerto Rico, she looks joyous, skipping across the canvas as if she has found freedom at last.

Claressa Shields, the most ferocious female boxer in the world, who campaigns four divisions higher at middleweight, stands behind me. She is already screaming her support for Serrano.

There is a deeper rumble as the crowd sees images of Katie Taylor walking from her locker room. She looks calm. A highlight reel of fight stoppages cuts away to a religious song called 'Awake My Soul'.

In the dark, broken only by the light of mobile phones, the song sounds haunting as Taylor walks slowly and sings softly. Eventually standing on the apron of the ring, Taylor gazes around the seething venue as if telling us that, even if she comes from Bray and Serrano from Brooklyn, the Garden belongs to her.

'This is it, the time has come!' David Diamante shouts into his microphone in the middle of the ring. Diamante, modern boxing's alternative to Michael Buffer, wears a white suit, a black bow-tie and black headband. He is a fifty-year-old white guy with dreadlocks, but Diamante whips himself into a small fury as, with eyes popping, he screams: *'I said ... the time has come!'*

Diamante punctuates each word by pumping his right arm and pointing a finger skywards. It ends with a fist clench of jubilation as if biblical redemption has truly arrived.

There is a pause before Diamante roars his trademark saying. *'THE FIGHT STARTS NOW!'*

This, of course, is not strictly true. Everyone around us is going gaga, hollering, hugging each other or taking photos on their phone, while Serrano and Taylor wait in their corners. But Diamante, a boisterous hype-merchant, is not interested in trifles of linguistic accuracy. 'Introducing first, the challenger,' he continues. 'She fights out of the red corner in white with blue and orange trim. She scaled 133.6 pounds. She has been a professional fighter since 2009, amassing a record of forty-two victories, with one defeat, one draw, with thirty big wins coming by way of knockout. In 2011, she won her first world title and has gone on to become the world-record-setting, nine-time, seven-division world champion. From Carolina, Puerto Rico, and raised in the beautiful borough of Brooklyn, here is the talented southpaw sensation and the reigning and unified featherweight champion of the world. *AMANDA 'THE REAL DEAL' SERRANO . . . SERRANO!!!'*

Serrano bangs her gloves together. A warm and friendly woman outside the ring, she looks ferocious now.

Diamante turns to Taylor. 'And her opponent across the ring,' he shouts. 'Fighting out of the blue corner, she is the defending, undisputed world champion. She wears black with gold trim. She scaled 134.6 pounds. As an amateur, she won five consecutive world championship gold medals, six European championship gold medals and in 2012 in London she captured Olympic gold. Now, as a professional, her record stands at twenty fights, twenty victories, six of them coming by way of knockout. Fighting out of Bray, County Wicklow, here is the acclaimed, celebrated and game-changing two-division and reigning, defending, undefeated and undisputed lightweight champion of the world. *KATIEEE TAYLORRR . . . TAYLORRR!'*

An impassive Taylor lifts her arm to greet the cacophony of noise.

The two fighters come together and, when in earshot of each other, a grinning Serrano shouts to Taylor. 'This is crazy, this is crazy!'

Taylor nods in acknowledgement. The atmosphere is electrifying, matching any other iconic fight I have attended over the past thirty years.

'All right,' the referee Michael Griffin says, his voice booming around the arena. 'You two champions received my instructions in the dressing room. You know what you have to do. Protect yourselves at all times. I want you to touch gloves now. You're boxing in the Garden. God bless you both.'

The two women both draw in a big gulp of breath, almost in unison, in the last moments before the bell rings for the first of ten two-minute rounds.

The Irish fans are already singing 'Olé, olé, olé, olé, olé' as Taylor shows great hand speed, clipping Serrano with lefts and rights. The Puerto Rican responds aggressively, backing Taylor into a corner while her hands fly. Taylor ghosts away, but Serrano tracks her down again, landing a clubbing left hook. The Puerto Ricans in the crowd swamp the Irish songs as they roar on their challenger.

After that blistering opening round, Taylor stands in her corner, not bothering with a stool, while Ross Enamait says, approvingly, 'Use the whole ring and box like that all night.'

But the fact that an ice pack is immediately pressed against her right eye offers clear proof that Taylor is already in an inferno.

Serrano sits in her corner as she also receives an ice pack for a swelling around her right eye. 'I've got it one-nothing,' her trainer and brother-in-law Jordan Maldonado barks.

They fall into a clinch early in round two but, rather than grappling and holding, Serrano and Taylor keep fighting. Even when Taylor backs away, with Serrano immediately trying to close her down, the tension bites hard. Suddenly, Taylor fires a straight right which makes Serrano buckle briefly at the knees. But the southpaw recovers and, with fifty seconds left in the round, Serrano answers with a jolting straight right of her own. She forces Taylor into a corner, but the Irishwoman regains the distance at which she prefers to box.

'She's feelin' it, baby,' Maldonado croons in the corner. 'How ya feelin'?'

Serrano swallows a slug of water and nods. 'Good,' she replies while, incongruously, 'Wonderwall' by Oasis blares around the arena.

'You've got to put pressure on her, baby,' Maldonado urges. 'Hit that body harder. Bombs, baby. Be brave. A little more pressure and you got her.'

Liam Gallagher's voice rolls on as he wonders if, maybe, you might be the one to save him.

Serrano closes her eyes while Vaseline is smeared across her face.

Throughout the minute-long break, Taylor stands in her corner. It could be a silent statement of her resolve – or it might be the fact that, at the age of thirty-six, she wants to avoid cramping.

Serrano is thirty-three and she has had many more pro fights. But Taylor's long and storied amateur career means that she has taken more punishment over the years. This is not the time, however, for ruminations from the past.

They are both intent on forging an opening in the third and, when they come together, Taylor uses her strength to push Serrano away. She picks her shots well and catches Serrano with a couple of meaty blows. But Serrano throws a beautiful left which jolts Taylor. The action escalates in the last twenty seconds of the round. Taylor digs to the body but Serrano steps forward and throws leather. They fire punches at each other for the last ten seconds as the crowd rises in acclaim, making such a din that referee Griffin doesn't hear the bell at first. Something remarkable is building.

'Take a deep breath,' Enamait advises the standing Taylor. It's not easy for her to do so with ice pressed against her eye and a cotton bud rammed up her right nostril.

'Listen,' Enamait continues, 'we're gonna walk her in and when she gets close, we spin and we go with the left hook. You stay there and let two or three go. Then you get back and stay on the jab. If you box in the centre of the ring, you can do this all night and you're never gonna miss. That was a lot better round.'

'Pick it up, baby,' Maldonado says in his contrasting way in the opposite corner. 'She's being hit harder than ever before. You look fantastic.'

A sharp right jab from Serrano starts the fourth and she spends the first minute of the round pressuring Taylor, who stands her ground. They swap hooks to the head and then Taylor launches her heavy artillery as an alternative to backing away. Serrano responds by going to the body and then peppering Taylor with the jab. A small cut above Taylor's right eye begins to weep as they reach the end of another close and absorbing round.

Serrano carries fiery intent and, in the fifth, she forces Taylor to retreat to a corner. The Puerto Rican is a whirlwind, her fists pumping relentlessly. Serrano batters Taylor to the body but the champion, rather than trying to spin away, doles out some spiteful punches of her own. They are fighting in a space no bigger than an old-school phone box. This is war.

For forty unbroken seconds, they throw bombs at each other. Taylor ships more than Serrano and eventually she is forced into a clinch. But Serrano soon clips her with a right hand which hurts Taylor. She takes an unsteady step backwards. A remorseless Serrano follows with a hard combination.

Taylor's body stiffens and then totters beneath the barrage of blows. She tries desperately to hold Serrano. Taylor looks close to being stopped, but she has just enough strength to wrap up Serrano and push her towards the ropes which, suddenly, look like a refuge.

Serrano is in control now and Taylor takes one punch after another in a dark train of pain. An overhand right is followed by a left and then a right cross, which leave Taylor dazed and wobbly. Serrano looks merciless. Taylor's face is smeared with blood at the bell.

Claressa Shields screams with joy behind me. Taylor appears close to defeat.

This time she accepts the stool in the break. Enamait pleads with her to stay off the ropes. 'She wants to fight you like you're a heavy bag,' he shouts. 'Get back to the centre of the ring.'

For the first minute of round six, Taylor looks like she is fighting on sheer willpower and memory alone as they swap heavy punches. Taylor sinks a left hook to the body, but is too woozy to land an accompanying right to her opponent's braided head. Serrano clips her with a couple of decent shots but Taylor, biting down on her gumshield, fires back. She unleashes a flurry of punches, only for Serrano to take advantage of the opening and smack Taylor's already reddened face. Neither fighter hears the bell as they continue to trade.

'You've got to take a little wind out of her sails,' Enamait urges. 'Every time you can, go to the body as it's slowing her down. They're trying to make this into a dogfight and we're going to sit inside with her.'

Taylor listens attentively, her eyes looking clearer than a round before. Enamait taps the side of his head. 'But we've got to do it intelligently. Our hands go back to our face and then we're burying shots to the body. Boom. Coming back to the body and, every now and then, tie her up ... We don't wanna just go rock and sock to the head.'

In the seventh, Taylor looks steadier on her feet. The intensity of battle also lessens as she uses the round to gather herself. The champion is not willing to surrender quite yet.

In the corner, she refuses the stool and listens to Enamait's advice to use the jab and then switch downstairs. 'She took that round off,' he says encouragingly. 'She's getting tired.'

Taylor comes out fast, throwing punches in the opening seconds of round eight. Serrano becomes busy herself as they crank up the ferocity. They both land combinations and the Irish half of the Garden is back in full voice, trying to lift the quiet woman from Bray. Taylor nails Serrano with a left cross before ghosting away and then, taking a sudden step forward, catching the challenger with a straight right. Taylor, having almost crumbled, is back in the groove. 'You had this mother and now you're letting her get over it,' Maldonado warns Serrano in the corner. 'Keep your hands up and start letting your punches go to the body.'

Maldonado turns to his assistant. 'What round is this coming up?'

'Nine', the second confirms. 'Six minutes ...'

The assistant is confused. Rather than watching a men's

championship fight, this is a masterclass of women's boxing. There are just two rounds of two minutes each left.

Maldonado sticks to the basics. 'Believe in yourself,' he implores Serrano. 'You got this.'

The fighters look lost in a storm of their own making. The bell rings and they plunge back into the dark.

'*Kay-tee, Kay-tee, Kay-tee, Kay-tee,*' the Irish fans chant and, lifted by her people so far from home, Taylor lands successive combinations.

Blood streams from her face, but she's having another good round. When they clinch, Serrano bangs her to the body before Griffin makes them break. Taylor clubs her with a right hand, twice, in rebuke. She moves away from Serrano with alacrity, all the befuddlement now gone, and connects with more combinations.

The crowd roars at the bell and Serrano raises her arms as if to suggest that she is just one round away from defeating the unbeaten champion.

After they've wiped down Serrano's face, attended to the swelling around her eye and given her some water, Maldonado is pithy. 'Jump on her. Let's go. You got this.'

In the middle of the ring, Taylor and Serrano touch gloves in a sign of deep mutual respect.

Almost 17,500 people are screaming, shouting and cheering, roaring on their favourite for one last push through the exhaustion and pain. Serrano is on the hunt, stalking Taylor, looking to seal the victory to which she had come so close earlier in the fight. Taylor ties her up and Griffin forces them to break.

Taylor lands an overhand right, and Serrano responds with a stinging left. But the Taylor punch has opened a cut over Serrano's right eye. Blood trickles down her cheek as, with less than a minute left, she comes after Taylor. The champion opens up and catches Serrano with a violent assortment of punches. Serrano fights back.

I am on my feet now, along with the entire row of ringside

reporters, suddenly oblivious to the march of our urgent deadlines and the etiquette of remaining above such raw human emotion. The courage and determination of both women has swept us away in one of the greatest fights ever staged at Madison Square Garden.

Taylor throws another barrage and Serrano, her face bloodied, holds on. They back away and here comes Taylor, throwing punch after punch, only for Serrano, rising up, to match her blow for blow. They trade in the centre of the ring, with Taylor's nose bleeding as she takes the heavier punishment. But she lets her hands go in a dazzling fury while Serrano punches back fiercely. Taylor's effort almost makes her stumble. But she launches one last attack which Serrano replicates. They are still at war, in a far corner of the ring, when the last bell rings.

Taylor breaks into a half-smile, a blend of pride and relief, awe and incomprehension of what she and Serrano have just shared. Griffin steps between the two fighters, wrapping an arm around each of them in appreciation. Taylor and Serrano embrace.

Enamait races across the ring and finds Serrano first. They exchange high fives, the trainer's hand slapping the opposition fighter's raised glove. Maldonado congratulates Taylor and then both boxers are taken to their corners. Their swollen and bleeding faces are rubbed down, with a rough kind of tenderness, and neither can speak as words of praise rain down on them.

Maldonado returns to Taylor's corner. 'Katie, you did it, baby,' the tough New Yorker says to the woman he had tried to break. 'You tore the house down.' He kisses her respectfully on her bloodied cheek.

A beaming Enamait hugs Serrano. Both trainers know how fortunate they are to have been involved in an epic battle that will become part of boxing folklore.

Taylor's pale and drained face is wiped clean of blood. A cut above her right eye, and one around her right ear, are clearly visible. Across the ring, an enswell is pressed against Serrano's right eye. She still smiles helplessly.

'Ladies and gentlemen,' Diamante shouts, 'let's show our appreciation for these two incredible fighters.'

A fresh wave of joy rolls across the Garden as the Irish and the Puerto Ricans stomp their approval. Serrano and Taylor, arm in arm, smile dazedly.

Discriminated against for years, they are now giants of the ring.

'After ten incredible rounds at Madison Square Garden, we go to the judges' score totals,' Diamante says. 'Benoit Roussel, 96–94, Amanda Serrano.'

Serrano's right arm is raised in the air. She just needs one more verdict in her favour.

'Glenn Feldman, 97–93, Katie Taylor.'

Taylor remains calm, looking down as we wait for Diamante.

'And judge Guido Cavalleri scores it 96–93 for your winner by split decision . . .'

Taylor's left hand rests helplessly on the top of her head while Serrano's right arm still shoots skywards. Diamante extends the pause before, finally, confirmation comes.

'And *still* the undisputed lightweight champion of the world . . . *Katie Taylorrrr!*' At the simple but glorious sound of that one word, 'still', Taylor turns away in quiet exultation, and relief, while Enamait and her manager Brian Peters leap up in unison. They soon lift her into the clammy Garden air and Taylor, who is usually undemonstrative, beats her chest with abandon. She then climbs the ropes so that she can take the acclaim, and thank her Irish fans.

She finally settles into the ecstatic embrace of her mother, Bridget, with whom she had prayed so intently before the fight.

Taylor then goes to find Serrano who, fighting back the tears, opens her arms wide. The two women hug, knowing how much they have achieved together on an unforgettable night.

At 1 a.m., after my work is done, I walk back to my hotel. I remember how I felt when, in the basement of the Garden, I told Katie Taylor how moved we had been watching her and Amanda Serrano in the ring. She smiled and said thank you, her face etched with fatigued pride. Taylor and Serrano both spoke well, full of humility and respect for each other.

After a beautiful night, I asked myself a simple question: 'Why couldn't boxing always be this way?'

12

The Stretcher

The clatter and daze of casino life, with its incessant slot machines and constant churn of dead-eyed people hoping to strike it lucky, felt empty. But it suited Dmitry Bivol, the unbeaten world light-heavyweight champion and a ghostly figure slipping through the MGM Grand hotel in Las Vegas.

Anonymity helped Bivol in a crucial week. He usually lived in St Petersburg and his official nationality was Russian. His personal story was much more layered, but war did not cater for nuance. Russian ground forces were locked in bitter conflict in eastern Ukraine. The United Nations confirmed early in May 2022 that nearly sixteen million people were in need of humanitarian assistance inside Ukraine. A further five-and-a-half million Ukrainian refugees had fled to neighbouring countries.

Even boxing, an amoral sporting business, took note. Three of the four major sanctioning bodies – the IBF, WBC and WBO – would no longer allow world title fights involving boxers from Russia or Belarus. But the WBA limited its ban to title bouts taking place in Russia or Belarus. This more lenient policy meant the WBA would allow Bivol to defend his world light-heavyweight championship against Canelo Álvarez in Vegas that Saturday night. But Bivol was not permitted to enter the ring with a Russian flag or hear the Russian national anthem.

Bivol had made it plain that he did not support the invasion of Ukraine and that he hoped peace would soon follow. But he was still seen as the bad guy against Canelo.

He was an accomplished boxing technician who did everything well without producing any outrageous flourishes. Bivol had a deep amateur pedigree and a flawless 19–0 professional record, which included being the WBA champion for four-and-a-half years. He was tagged as mechanical and boring but, in reality, Bivol was controlled and remorseless.

Canelo carried a brilliance and charisma that was very different to Bivol. He had begun boxing professionally as a junior-welterweight, which was five divisions lower than light-heavyweight where Bivol operated throughout his career. The Mexican had won a world light-heavyweight title, but that victory, in November 2019, came against a faded Russian, Sergey Kovalev. Bivol was close to his peak and, at six feet, he was four inches taller, and with a longer reach, than Canelo.

'I like challenges,' Canelo said. 'It makes me feel alive. I chose Bivol because he's a great fighter. But I'm in my prime and I want to make history.'

Bivol waited in the shadows. But I wanted to talk to him properly and, in a long conversation, his real story unfolded. 'My mother and father were born in the big country, the USSR,' he said, cocking a wry eyebrow. 'But my father was really born in Moldova and he spoke only Moldovan until he was ten. My mother [who is of Korean descent] was born in Kazakhstan. Then her family moved to Kyrgyzstan. One day, when they graduated, they met each other in Russia. They got married and moved to my mother's home in Kyrgyzstan. I was born in Kyrgyzstan and lived there eleven years.'

Bivol told me his family spoke Russian but he felt most affinity with Kyrgyzstan. 'It's not a rich country, but it has great people. It's my motherland. A lot of my life afterwards was in Russia but

I love Kyrgyzstan. I love the culture and it's different to Russia. Kyrgyzstan is a Muslim country and I have many Muslim friends.'

Bivol fell for boxing in Kyrgyzstan after his interest in combat sports had been sparked by, he said with a grin, 'Jackie Chan movies. He never killed anyone. He was just funny.'

There was no room for amusement when we turned to the subject of Russia. I asked Bivol what he had felt as a Russian citizen when, ten weeks earlier, Putin launched his assault. 'We have to make a better world for all of us, so of course it's sad,' he said. 'I understand why I am without a flag here. No problem. I am focused on the fight.'

Bivol shifted uneasily when I asked a few more questions about the war. 'I don't know about politics. I'm a sportsman, so I don't know about coronavirus or politics. Most boxing fans just want to see the light-heavyweight champion against the pound-for-pound king.'

Wladimir Klitschko had called for his fight against Canelo to be cancelled, but Bivol shrugged. 'He's political. He doesn't have to watch.'

Bivol admitted that he had 'met Putin once – when he invited athletes at the World Combat Games in 2013'.

Did he talk to Putin? 'No, no. There were a lot of us there.'

Bivol explained that his father would normally have flown from St Petersburg to support him in Vegas, but he had been unable to obtain a visa from the US authorities. Thinking of his parents and his wife, Bivol explained that 'every time they worry about me and this is a real dangerous fight. But they understand I love boxing.'

A stilted exchange softened when I asked Bivol about Maxim Dadashev, the Russian light-welterweight who had lost his life in July 2019 after fighting Subriel Matias. 'Maxim was my friend,' Bivol said. 'I knew him since 2003. We boxed and trained together and spent a lot of time at competitions because we were on the same St Petersburg team. He was a funny guy who always fought so hard. As a professional, we see each other sometimes when I came to Los

Angeles. I knew his family and his wife is now living next to me [in St Petersburg]. We invite his wife and son to our house – like when my kids have a birthday.'

Bivol's sons were aged five and seven while Dadashev's son, Daniel, was also five. The fighter shook his head when I asked how Elizaveta, Maxim's wife, was coping. 'For one year after his tragedy, she was crying every day. It's hard.'

Did his friend's death change his attitude to boxing? 'Of course. In training, I thought so much about defence. All my coaches said, "It's better if you take zero punches."'

In a gambling city like Vegas, where the house always won, there was concern whether Bivol would receive a fair shake. He shook his head. 'I never think about judges. I don't say "Oh, I'm in Vegas, against Canelo, everything against me." No.'

Bivol was a decent man and a very good fighter. 'I just need to be my best version to win,' he said before, with a smile and a hand-shake, he slipped out of sight again.

'It's crazy,' Canelo Álvarez said as he considered the money he had made by signing a new two-fight deal with DAZN in bouts pro-moted by Eddie Hearn. The rumoured figure was a combined $120 million to face Bivol and then, in September, Gennadiy Golovkin in defence of Canelo's undisputed world super-middleweight championship.

Canelo was convinced that no one else in boxing could match him and so a little smile danced across his freckled face when, on the Wednesday of fight week, he recalled how much he had earned for his professional debut as a fifteen-year-old in Tonalá, on the outskirts of Guadalajara. In October 2005, that first fight purse of 800 pesos was the equivalent of just under $40.

'They actually only paid me half of that,' Canelo said. 'The other half was in tickets. I gave all the tickets to my family. I've got an absolutely massive family, so in the end I came home with 400 pesos. But I didn't do it for the money because I was working with my dad [selling ice-creams]. I didn't know any other way of living, so 400 pesos seemed a lot.'

When I asked him how much longer he wanted to keep boxing, Canelo looked serious. 'I am fighting for legacy now. The money's already there. So maybe I will fight six, seven years more.'

It was easy to imagine the publicity that Putin, a boxing fan, would try to extract from a Bivol victory for Russia in Las Vegas. Did Canelo feel added pressure against the backdrop of war? 'No. I always come to win.'

At his final press conference with Bivol, Canelo took his five-year-old daughter, Maria, on stage with him. He spent more time looking at her drawings than trying to appear imposing. Maria stuck her tongue out at Bivol, but Canelo made no attempt to demean the Russian. They exchanged warm handshakes and engaged in a civilised face-off.

'Bivol is really good,' Canelo said. 'He has everything – skill, strength and power. I know it's going to be difficult. But I beat all the champions at 168 [pounds], so I needed to take another challenge, not just for my history, but for myself. To have an opportunity to win another title at 175 is amazing.'

Canelo said his memory of that first 800-peso purse framed everything he had done and might yet do in the ring. 'I remember what I've been through and that's why I'm grateful for everything I've got now. More than anything this [800-peso memory] keeps my feet on the ground because I remember that feeling of being powerless.'

T-Mobile Arena, Las Vegas, Saturday 6 May 2022

Dmitry Bivol, the champion, is made to walk first as the '*Ca-ne-lo . . . Ca-ne-lo . . . Ca-ne-lo*' chant reverberates. It is an insult to Bivol, but a smile plays across his hooded features. He is just as unfazed when Canelo is lifted on a regal plinth before his own ring walk. Bivol simply bangs his brown gloves together.

Once the frivolities and introductions are over, Bivol looks lithe and strong as he uncorks his slick jab and precise combinations. Canelo, in contrast, is squat and muscled as he fights behind a tight guard. It is obvious, as early as round two, that Bivol has the strength to push Canelo back. This gives him enough distance to nail the smaller challenger with his crisp punching.

The gingery Mexican's forehead is soon reddened by the percussive blows. Canelo throws big power shots, but they come alone, while Bivol responds with bunches of punches.

In the fifth round, Bivol's intensity drops and Canelo tries to bully him while producing heavy shots which the champion deflects or absorbs. Then, as if flicking a switch, Bivol flies through the gears. He bruises Canelo with fast combinations. More than twenty unanswered punches from Bivol hammer down on the great Mexican in a stunning display of dominance.

Bivol opens a cut under Canelo's left eye in the seventh. Fatigue has begun to spread across the Mexican's flushed face.

The old chant of '*Ca-ne-lo* ... *Ca-ne-lo* ... *Ca-ne-lo*' resumes in round eight as the crowd try to lift their god from Guadalajara. But Bivol stays busy and cool. Some rounds are close, and Canelo is briefly commanding in the ninth, but the fight slides away inexorably.

In the eleventh, Canelo returns to the body, but Bivol is strong and resilient. And then, with deceptive speed, he sinks two straight lefts into Canelo's face. It is too much for Canelo. He barrels forward, lifts Bivol off the ground and hoists him onto his left shoulder. As the Russian clings on, Canelo carries him around the ring for a few seconds in a bizarre sign of frustration.

In the last minute of the fight, Bivol is the aggressor, his jab tattooing Canelo with relentless accuracy. Canelo launches another big uppercut, but the bout ends with Bivol on the offensive.

Even the Vegas judges cannot rescue Canelo. The only surprise when Bivol is awarded the unanimous decision is that all three judges have settled on a scandalously narrow margin of 115–113. Canelo's bruised and cut face, and his dejected demeanour, tell the real story. Bivol is too big, too fast, too skilful and too concentrated for Canelo who has suffered only his second loss in sixty-one pro bouts.

An hour later, deep in the basement of the arena, Bivol remains admirably restrained. When asked if he had replaced Canelo as the new world number one in the pound-for-pound rankings, he smiles. 'No. In my mind I just beat the guy who wanted my belt. He was a super-middleweight, so I don't feel like I am the king. I'm just better than Canelo today.'

On Monday morning, I took my last run through Las Vegas. I reached the little Hispanic neighbourhood just before seven. It was already warm on a beautiful day. The street was deserted, apart from a group of pigeons pecking around a trash container. They scattered and flew up towards the blue sky to escape my heavy footsteps.

As I turned the corner, I heard the sound of a lawnmower from the gated community adjoining the street. That familiar sound, and the smell of freshly cut grass, made me think of a time when I was still a boy in South Africa. All these decades later, I could imagine my dad, having removed his shirt to make the most of the sunshine, cutting the lawn.

In the distance, I saw a homeless man. His weather-beaten skin had turned a crinkly nut-brown colour. His grubby red T-shirt was less eye-catching than the raggedy Mohican on his head. He sifted through the garbage. As I ran closer to him, I could see that he had found a chunk of pineapple. It looked very dry as he bit into it while ignoring me.

I turned the corner and ran to the top of the road, hoping I might spot the sixty-year-old man who had whooped on this street when hearing we were the same age. But I'd not seen him since.

On the loop back, the lawnmower was still humming and I saw two men walking towards me. It felt like South Africa again. They were dark-skinned men at work. One carried a ladder, while

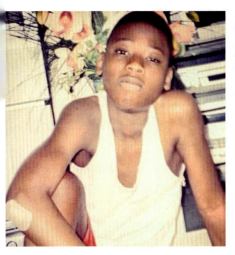

Isaac Chamberlain, in Brixton at
the age of 11, was scared and insecure
as he delivered drugs while looking
for a way out. Boxing rescued him.

I first interviewed Tyson Fury in 2011.
He was twenty-three. 'There is a name for
what I have,' he said, 'where, one minute I'm
happy, and the next minute I'm sad,
like commit-suicide sad.'

Patrick Day, aged five,
at a summer camp.

Patrick Day's finest night, where he out-boxed
the unbeaten Eric Walker in 2017. From left
to right, here he is with his brother Jean, his
then girlfriend MaryEllen, and his two other
brothers Michael and Bernard.

Isaac Chamberlain and his son, Zion, at the Afewee gym in Brixton in the summer of 2023. Later that year, Isaac would beat Mikael Lawal to become the British and Commonwealth cruiserweight champion.

Isaac prepared for his European cruiserweight title fight against Chris Billam-Smith with real intensity in July 2022.

Isaac fought bravely but lost on points to Billam-Smith.

In September 2021 I was in Las Vegas to watch Canelo Álvarez as he knocked out Caleb Plant in their super-middleweight title unification fight. Canelo was regarded, then, as the best fighter in the world.

I felt privileged to be at Madison Square Garden on 30 April 2022 for the incredible first fight between Katie Taylor and Amanda Serrano. They displayed the best of boxing.

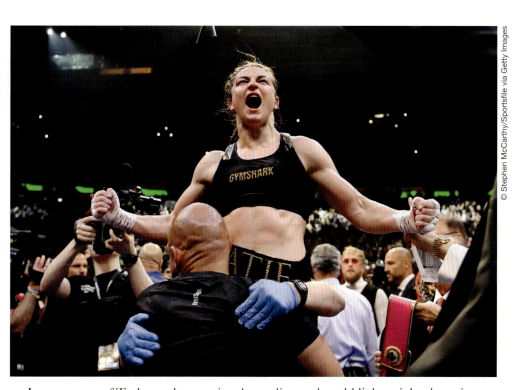

Joy pours out of Taylor as she remains the undisputed world lightweight champion. She won a split-decision after being pushed to the brink of defeat.

© Al Bello/Getty Images

The heavyweight trilogy of world title fights between Deontay Wilder and Tyson Fury were epic battles which saw both men knocked down multiple times. After drawing their first bout, Fury won the next two by stoppage. These were brutal, exhilarating but damaging fights.

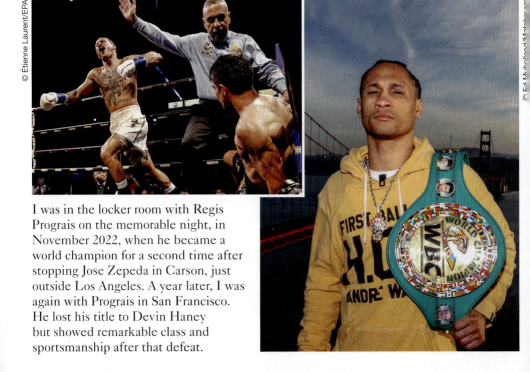

© Étienne Laurent/EPA

© Ed Mulholland/Matchroom

I was in the locker room with Regis Prograis on the memorable night, in November 2022, when he became a world champion for a second time after stopping Jose Zepeda in Carson, just outside Los Angeles. A year later, I was again with Prograis in San Francisco. He lost his title to Devin Haney but showed remarkable class and sportsmanship after that defeat.

Days before Tyson Fury defeated Dillian Whyte in April 2022 he faced intense media scrutiny about his past links with Daniel Kinahan. The US government had just stressed its determination to bring the Kinahan cartel to justice.

After Oleskandr Usyk beat Anthony Joshua in August 2022 he brought out his daughter's favourite toy. In May 2024, Usyk introduced Eeyore personally to me after he defeated Fury and became the undisputed world heavyweight champion.

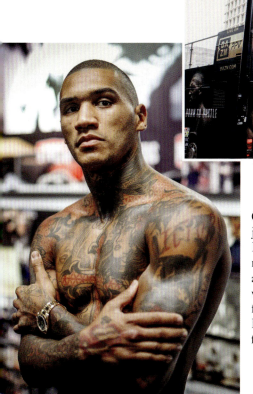

Conor Benn cried when I interviewed him just before he was meant to fight Chris Eubank Jr in October 2022. He spoke movingly of the trauma he had suffered as a child. The day after our interview it was reported that Benn has tested positive for clomifene. As Benn and his promoter Eddie Hearn tried to proceed with the fight, my attitude towards boxing darkened.

It was also hard to love boxing as it embraced the riches of Saudi Arabia. Anthony Joshua, Eddie Hearn, Frank Warren and Francis Ngannou look delighted to be in Riyadh.

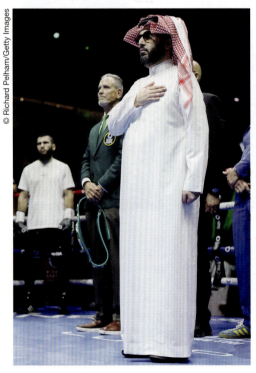

Turki Alalshikh, the chairman of the General Entertainment Authority, has used vast resources to bankroll Saudi Arabia's takeover of boxing.

Manahel al-Otaibi was charged after she expressed support of women's rights on social media and posted photos of herself shopping while wearing dungarees. In 2023 she was sentenced to eleven years in prison in Riyadh.

Tyson Fury makes his grand entrance at fight week before his first bout against Usyk.

Usyk was more typically understated.

They fought one of the great heavyweight title fights in Riyadh. Fury lost a split-decision and suffered his first defeat as a professional. Usyk was tested like never before but then, despite being the much smaller man, he almost stopped Fury. Usyk shed tears after the fight, as he spoke of war in Ukraine and remembered his late father.

In March 2018 Patrick Day defeated Kyrone Davis at the Barclays Center in Brooklyn, NY. Tragically, he lost his life the following year, after he fought Charles Conwell.

Two months after Pat's death I visited his home town of Freeport for the first of many times. I met his best friend Patrick Aristhene who took me to Pat's old gym.

Thanksgiving 2019. Six weeks after they lost Pat, the grieving family are together in Freeport as they hold up a photograph of their twenty-seven-year old brother and son. Left to right: Pat's brothers Michael and Jean, his father Philippe, and his brother Bernard.

the other man held three tins of paint in his hands. I am short-sighted and it was only as I ran closer that I realised they were young Hispanic men. We said hello and I wondered if they had supported Canelo.

I ran towards the homeless man. He stood inside another garbage container and ate another piece of fruit. It looked like a peach. It must have been juicy because his bearded face was wet. He held it up as I jogged slowly past.

'It's a good one!' he shouted.

'It looks it,' I replied, panting.

I kept running, slowly, and this time the pigeons didn't stir. They were also busy breakfasting.

I turned to look back at the homeless guy. He had climbed out of the bin and leaned against a wall, eating his peach. Seeing me, he raised the peach high. 'So good,' he shouted.

It was a moment, after all the fighting, to savour.

Before Oleksandr Usyk considered his rematch with Anthony Joshua, he described the fear he had felt as a soldier in the Ukrainian army. When he patrolled the streets in besieged Kyiv a few months before, carrying a machine gun rather than boxing gloves, dread gripped him.

'Every day I was there,' he said in the contrasting space of a London hotel room in late June, 'I was praying and asking, "Please, God, don't let anybody try to kill me. Please don't let anybody shoot me. And please don't make me shoot any other person."'

Usyk had left the war in late March to begin training in Poland. President Zelenskiy and others had stressed that he could do more for the war effort outside Ukraine, but Usyk initially resisted. 'I really didn't want to leave. At one point I went to the hospital where soldiers were wounded and getting rehabilitation and they asked me to go, to fight [Joshua], to fight for the country. They said if you go there, you're going to help us even more instead of fighting inside Ukraine.'

Footage on social media had shown how Usyk's house had been ransacked by Russian soldiers. 'It's my house in Vorzel [a village outside of Kyiv] and, yes, Russian soldiers broke in,' Usyk explained. 'They broke things and stayed there for a while. My family is not in Ukraine, but a lot of my close friends are still in the country. I'm in touch with them every day. I want to live there and right after the fight I'm going back to Ukraine.'

Would he return as a soldier? Usyk shook his head. His place as one of the most famous men in Ukraine meant 'nobody will let me go to the front line. But many close friends are there. I'm supporting them and, with this fight, I want to bring them some kind of joy.'

Usyk's anger towards Russia was obvious. 'Two days ago in Kyiv, a bomb landed on a house where civilians lived. That same day, a rocket landed on a shopping mall in Kremenchuk full of normal people. But Russian soldiers are saying on their TV that [Ukrainians] are shooting each other. So I don't trust them.'

It felt prosaic to ask Usyk about Joshua. But retaining his titles would mean so much to people in Ukraine and that responsibility lent an edge to his assessment of the man he had beaten so comprehensively nine months earlier. He insisted that Joshua didn't hurt him and he welcomed the idea that the British fighter would box much more aggressively in their rematch.

'Let him think about that,' Usyk said of speculation that Joshua was intent on knocking him out. 'Let him desire that. I watched the first fight many times. We look at the mistakes I made and we will make sure we don't make them again. I don't care whether he has a new tactic or a new trainer. I'm just thinking about me. We are working very hard and, with the Lord's help, we will be better.'

He was once an exuberant joker, full of laughter, but war had changed him. 'Sometimes I force myself to smile,' Usyk said sadly. 'Sometimes I force myself to sing.'

The world heavyweight champion looked briefly helpless. 'My

children are asking, "Dad, why do they want to kill us?",' he said of the Russian invaders. Usyk looked desolate as, after a pause, he finally said, 'And I don't know what to tell them.'

War brings perspective to sport. But boxing is not really a sport. There is such danger and damage, and even death, that it is wrong to compare boxing to sports where games are played. But it is also a mistake to describe it as war. The destruction and the fatalities in Ukraine were definitions of war.

In June 2022, the Ukrainian presidential adviser, Oleksiy Arestovych, said the country had lost more than 10,000 soldiers, with a further 30,000 having been injured during the first four months of conflict. He said more than 30,000 Russian soldiers had been killed, although British intelligence suggested the true figure was probably half that amount.

So boxing is not a war zone. But fighters are capable of doing great harm inside a ring. They can take away consciousness and even life. The families of Maxim Dadashev and Patrick Day lived with the deadly consequences of boxing. I thought of them every day because, if you follow boxing, it would be insulting not to reflect on those who have been lost.

Isaac Chamberlain rested his gloves on the ropes and, after Bobby Mills wiped his face with a towel, he tilted his head as Conor Ward poured water into his mouth. The gritty old Eastside Boxing Gym on the Whitworth Industrial Estate in Birmingham seemed an unlikely dream factory, but Isaac and his small team had spent the previous six weeks there. It belonged to Jon Pegg, the trainer and cutman who doubled as a film director, and they felt comfortable.

The faded boxing posters and yellowing photographs evoked different times and different dreams, but the peeling walls glowed in the midday heat and humidity in July 2022.

As he took a break, Isaac reflected on very different training camps from the past. Early in his professional career, he had

234 | THE LAST BELL

travelled twice to Kyiv to help Oleksandr Usyk. He loved the experience of being in Ukraine, if not the food, and he enjoyed the way in which 'Usyk was always making jokes in the gym. We got on really well because I was his best sparring partner. I would always ask: "What do you think I can do better?" He would give me advice in the beginning and then, once I started getting really competitive, I would ask again how I could improve. He would smile and say: "Nothing. You're good."'

It was soon time to return to work as Isaac drove himself in pursuit of a new ambition. 'I want to be great,' he said quietly before continuing preparations for the hardest fight of his life.

I worried about Isaac. He was locked so deep in his dream of becoming a world champion that he was willing to risk his life. On 30 July, Isaac would take a huge step up in quality against Chris Billam-Smith, the European and Commonwealth cruiserweight champion. Shane McGuigan, his trainer, had helped Billam-Smith grow as a fighter who had once been dismissed as a limited prospect. Billam-Smith worked harder than anyone in their gym and the bond between him and the entire McGuigan family accelerated his progress. He was on track to a world championship.

Isaac was twenty-eight and in his prime, but the unsettled nature of his career meant that he had lost so much time. His 14–1 record also did not tell us enough about his readiness for such a difficult test. He looked a more naturally gifted boxer than Billam-Smith, but Isaac's team did not have the same experience. Shane McGuigan was still young but he had been a trainer of the year and the vast knowledge of his father, Barry, elevated him further. Bobby and Conor, meanwhile, had just three professional bouts between them.

The fight would be held in Billam-Smith's backyard, in Bournemouth, where he had a passionate following. All the odds were against Isaac, but he had jumped at the chance. I was happy for him, but I knew he faced a dangerous ordeal.

After training we went to the rented house, not far from Villa

Park, where Isaac and his team were based. Furniture was sparse and so, in Isaac's room, we sat on his bed, our backs supported by the wall. 'It's strange that we're here now, close to such a big fight,' Isaac said, 'because we have spoken about all this happening these last few years.'

How did it make him feel? 'Excited,' he said with a familiar smile. 'My hardest fights have been out of the ring and I remember what it was like to be alone in America – being let down again and again. I now have a special team around me and I've been waiting for this a very long time. I'm not going to let them down.'

Isaac paused as if to make those words linger. 'My body is a bit tattered from all the training and hard sparring. Four tough fighters, doing two rounds each with me at a time, and Bobby whispering that he will pay a grand to anyone who drops me. They're coming at me and I'm thinking: "Yo, you're welcome. C'mon, I've got more for you." That's the mentality you need.

'I finish 100 sit-ups and I think of Chris Billam-Smith doing the same. So I make it 150. I finish six drills and, even though it's enough, I make myself do another. It can mess with my head because I go to sleep, thinking, "Did I do enough?" So I work harder the next day.'

I was concerned about Isaac becoming consumed by boxing. 'No,' he insisted. 'I definitely have a switch. How long until the fight? Fifteen days? I can't get into that full switch mode now. It turns completely to fight mode three days before the fight. That's when you see me become colder, more emotionless, because there's violent work to be done. I've got to be more sinister, more vicious, more dark. You've got to go to the darkest place you can imagine. I don't care how much it costs me.'

Isaac looked up. It was quiet in the house. 'I need that mentality against Billam-Smith because he's a great fighter, a great athlete. He seems a really nice, respectful guy outside the ring, but it's going to be a battle of will as much as skill. He has a very high work rate and he's really tough and determined. He's going to be desperate to do well in front of his home crowd. But I am going to give everything to win this fight.'

He gazed out of the window. The humidity was a reminder that we were in high summer, but the sky reflected a grey, sludgy Friday afternoon in Birmingham. Isaac curled his hands into fists and spoke softly. 'Even speaking to you about the fight makes it so real. I'm pissed off with how much work I've had to put in for this fight. So how dare he think he's going to beat me when I've been suffering all these years? I've got a chance to become European champion and he is coming to take this away from me? No, he's not. I am going to fight like I've never fought before.'

Bournemouth International Centre, Bournemouth, Saturday 30 July 2022

Just after 7 p.m., at the rear entrance to the arena, I see three ambulances ready to take any stricken fighter to hospital. They are reminders of boxing's gravity.

Mick Hennessy is also nervous. 'It's a 50/50 fight,' the promoter says. 'The first six rounds are vital. Isaac needs to use his superior skills, but he has to be very careful. Chris is dangerous.'

Chris Billam-Smith arrives at 7.15 p.m. His nickname is The Gentleman and he stops to say hello. He shakes our hands and smiles. Five minutes later, Isaac lifts his hand in sombre greeting. This is not a time for words.

Billam-Smith is in dressing room A. Behind its blue door, Shane and Barry McGuigan will bring fresh intensity to his last few hours of preparation. Six years ago to this very night, on 30 July 2016, I had been with Shane and Barry in their Brooklyn locker room as they helped Carl Frampton beat Léo Santa Cruz and become, after an epic battle, a two-weight world champion.

I am still good friends with Barry, but I belong in the opposite camp now. I tap gently on the green door to dressing room B and open it to see Isaac stretched out on a grey sofa. He smiles and says, 'It's good you're here, bro.'

When Barry arrives to observe Isaac's hands being wrapped, he does not offer his usual warmth or a long conversation about life, family and boxing. We say hello briefly.

Bobby begins a familiar ritual. He massages Isaac's right hand while Barry watches with an inscrutable expression. Bobby works carefully and I suspect he is very nervous. Apart from this being his first title fight as a trainer, he has to deal with the presence of Barry, a great figure in British and Irish boxing and a former world champion.

Isaac's right hand is wrapped first and the silence deepens as Bobby methodically covers the knuckles and works his way down past the wrist. He uses a small pair of scissors to cut the gauzy material and then tape it down.

Barry asks him how many pieces of tape he plans to use on the back of Isaac's hands. It already looks to him as if there are enough. 'That's the last one,' Bobby says softly.

The young trainer looks at Isaac to check that the wrap is not too tight. Isaac flexes his fingers and bunches a fist that he hopes will knock Billam-Smith into oblivion. He is happy.

Barry looks carefully and then nods his assent.

Bobby repeats the procedure with the left hand and, this time, Barry accepts it without comment. Isaac opens and shuts his fists again as Barry returns to the Billam-Smith dressing room where Jon Pegg has monitored the wrapping of the champion's hands.

While Isaac stretches and exercises, I go for a short walk. It's a gorgeous evening on the Bournemouth seafront. But, once I am back inside, the arena is uncomfortably hot and crammed. Young men and women are dressed up, drinking and jabbering excitedly. An occasional roar erupts when a decent punch lands in the ring. My seat at ringside is empty. It's in the press row, but I won't be working. This is too personal.

It is very quiet in the dressing room when, just before the fight, they pray in a circle. Andy Knuth, Isaac's great friend, asks God to bless everyone in the room. Then, speaking softly, big Andy says, 'Thank you God and make sure that Isaac leaves with the victory tonight. Amen.'

They all say 'Amen' and break into applause.

Silence returns while we wait for the knock on the door. Ten seconds pass and the hush feels almost suffocating. It needs Jon, the most experienced boxing man in the room, to take charge.

'This is what you've worked for all these years,' he says in his Brummie burr. 'It's time to soak it all up.'

The smothering quiet returns. 'Nice, deep breaths now, Isaac,' Jon says. 'I want you breathing deep, nice and slow, ten of 'em. In total control, like you'll be in the fight.'

Isaac begins to breathe in, deep and slow.

'Total control,' Jon says. 'Even deeper now. And let it out slower.'

The room begins to calm, as Isaac's breathing finds a stately rhythm.

The knock comes and the Sky production man tells us it's time.

'Four more deep breaths,' Jon insists.

Isaac wears a sleeveless white tunic with his hood up. He breathes in and exhales.

'Be smart,' Mick says. 'Show your class.'

Andy shouts out encouragement. 'And the *new* . . .' he whoops, swapping his respectful prayer to mimic the MC at the end of the fight. 'Let's go champ!'

We head down the long passageway. No one talks, but the walk is brisk and purposeful and the crowd sounds increasingly loud.

Isaac waits behind a heavy black curtain and then, when he is given the signal, he walks out into the noise and clouds of smoke to 'Odogwu' by Burna Boy. Boos roll down from the top of the arena while the acrid smoke thickens. I stop at this point, allowing Isaac and his team to complete their walk as I don't want to be seen on TV, pretending I am part of the entourage. I wait in the dark while people yell insults at Isaac. For a minute, my eyes burn from the smoke and then, at last, everything clears and I can see again.

Billam-Smith enters to a tumultuous reception from the sold-out crowd, but The Gentleman makes little fuss. He leaves it to the yelping young MC. 'Fighting out of the blue corner, he stands six feet, two inches tall. He weighed in at fourteen stone, four pounds. He holds a professional record of fourteen wins, one loss, eight of those wins coming by way of knockout and he fights out of Brixton, London, England! Introducing . . . *Isaac 'IC' Chamberlainnnnnn . . .*'

Conor Ward twirls a white towel above his head while Chamberlain ignores the booing.

'And his opponent, fighting out of the red corner, he stands six feet, three inches tall, weighing in at fourteen stone, four pounds. He holds a professional record of fifteen wins, one loss and eleven knockouts, and he fights right here in Bournemouth, England! Introducing the reigning, the defending Commonwealth and European champion, he is The Gentleman . . . *Chris Billaaam-Smithhhhh!*'

It is bedlam in Bournemouth as the trainers leave the ring. There are now just three men inside the ropes. Billam-Smith, Chamberlain and the referee John Latham.

Chamberlain comes out fast, looking sharp behind his jab, landing early, but Billam-Smith ties him up in a clinch. They are both alert, but it's Chamberlain who clips the champion with another series of jabs and a decent left cross. He makes Billam-Smith miss with a swinging right before Chamberlain is bullied back against the ropes. The blueprint for Billam-Smith seems obvious. He wants to use his greater strength to negate Chamberlain's skills. They end the round trading fiercely.

The Chamberlain jab is slick in the second but, a minute into the round, Billam-Smith has the challenger pinned against the ropes. He catches Chamberlain with spiteful combinations, only for the Brixton man to fire back in a blistering exchange.

Billam-Smith rocks him before Chamberlain responds with a peach of a right and then a shuddering left.

'He's hurt him!' Matthew Macklin shouts on the Sky commentary. 'Chamberlain's hurt him.'

Billam-Smith backs away as Chamberlain tears after him.

'The legs are shaking for the hometown hero,' Sky's chief commentator Adam Smith yells as Chamberlain lands again.

Billam-Smith is now on the ropes, but he clubs Chamberlain with two right hands. Chamberlain reels backwards.

'This is an absolute classic already,' Smith yelps on the mic. 'What a start!'

Chamberlain nails Billam-Smith, only to be punished by an immediate hook to the body and a right hand. 'What a round,' Smith screams. 'Chamberlain is hurt!'

They keep firing punches at each other on the ropes as the bell finally rings. 'One of the rounds of the year,' Smith confirms.

They work on both fighters in the corner, trying to replenish them after such a gruelling round. Pride and dread, a curious combination, churn through me.

Billam-Smith comes out brawling for the third, but Chamberlain sinks a left hook to his gut. He then tags Billam-Smith with a jolting right uppercut. The champion fights back and rocks him. Chamberlain's left eye begins to swell horribly and yet he matches Billam-Smith as they swap percussive shots to the body.

Soon after the start of round four, Billam-Smith unleashes an overhand right as Chamberlain stands tall and lands some salty combinations. Barry McGuigan jumps to his feet in front of me and implores Billam-Smith to take charge again. Chamberlain keeps peppering Billam-Smith with the jab.

Natasha Jonas, on the Sky commentary, gives each fighter two rounds apiece.

Rounds five to eight see the fight ebb and flow, even if Chamberlain's eye is puffy and weeping blood. It's a draining bout for both men, but Billam-Smith lands the more sustained punishment.

Heavy body punches take their toll, but Chamberlain fights back again and again. He looks good in flourishes, while Billam-Smith displays his seasoned, bludgeoning power. A shuddering right cross from Chamberlain lands near the end of the eighth. Billam-Smith absorbs it well and pummels his opponent again on the ropes.

In the corner, McGuigan tells Billam-Smith to forget about feeling tired. The champion responds and wins the next two rounds.

In the blue corner, Pegg steps into the ring to address Chamberlain face to face while Mills works from outside the ropes. It's a smart switch because Pegg talks bluntly. He tells Chamberlain that, while he can no longer win on points, he can still win by knockout.

It's the right call but, in his first twelve-round fight, there is not much pop left in Chamberlain's punches. Billam-Smith looks too strong, too rugged, as he targets Chamberlain's almost shut eye. After they clinch, red streaks of blood from the wounded eye run down Billam-Smith's back.

At the start of the last round, Billam-Smith raises his arms in triumph while the crowd whoop and roar. Chamberlain, half-blinded, walks across the ring to touch gloves.

During the next two-and-a-half minutes, hooks and uppercuts sink into an exhausted Chamberlain. The crowd are having a party, chanting Billam-Smith's name, but Chamberlain is not done yet. He begins to throw punches from both wings. With twelve seconds on the clock, he hurts Billam-Smith with a big left hand and follows it with a combination. Billam-Smith punches back before Chamberlain catches him again. The champion sags against the ropes as Chamberlain pounds him twice more in the last five seconds. Billam-Smith is reeling at the bell as the referee jumps between them. It has been a brave finish to an outstanding fight.

Each of the three judges has recorded the same 117–111 score. Chamberlain paws at his eye when the key word of 'still' confirms that Billam-Smith has retained his titles.

I stand up and head for the losing dressing room.

*

It is a long wait as, down the passage, the doctors examine Isaac. Bobby, Conor, Jon, Andy and Mick are with him while I sit with Michael Hennessy and his sister Fran in the dressing room. They feel the same sadness, mingled with deep pride in Isaac, as we discuss the fight. Michael is convinced Isaac would have won if he could have boxed at range. He's right, but Billam-Smith is like a tank. Fran, who will eventually turn pro, is still only seventeen, but she can't wait to fight on nights like these. All the punishment and heartache can't dent her excitement about boxing.

Isaac needs stitches. His girlfriend, Zalia, and her two friends arrive and sit forlornly in a corner of the dressing room. I commiserate with them.

After forty minutes, Conor says Isaac will be on his way back soon. He urges us to applaud him when he comes into the room.

Another twenty minutes pass and the heat feels stifling. But I can't leave until I see Isaac.

Conor is back. He looks worried. 'Isaac needs to go to hospital,' he says. 'I've got to pack his bag.' Zalia leaves with him.

I wait outside in the corridor, not sure what to do next.

Then, down the passage, a door opens. Two paramedics wheel a stretcher carrying Isaac. His eyes are shut, with the left one a small dark hill of swollen flesh.

'Isaac,' I say gently. He turns his head painfully in my direction and opens his one good eye.

He looks dazed and lost. 'It's Don,' I say.

'Don, I'm sorry,' he mumbles, lifting his right hand to take mine. 'I tried. I really tried.'

A tear slips from his open eye.

'I'm proud of you, Isaac,' I say. 'You did so well.'

'Walk with me,' he says.

I walk alongside Isaac on his stretcher, his hand holding mine. He closes his working eye and we move down the corridor. Beyond the clatter of the wheels, there is just silence.

Outside, the ambulance doors are open. The stretcher is pushed towards the gangway. Isaac allows my hand to leave his and then he is gone, up and into the ambulance.

Zalia joins him while Bobby and Conor prepare to follow in Mick's car. The young trainers look shattered and Mick, who tells me that Isaac needs an urgent CT scan, promises to message me. 'Isaac's going to be OK,' he says.

I watch the ambulance head towards the main road, its blue lights pulsing steadily. The ambulance disappears into the darkness, carrying my friend, a fighter who had shown such courage and hope. I lift my hand, but I know it doesn't matter now. Isaac can no longer see me.

At 5.09 the following afternoon, Isaac posted a photo on Twitter. It had been taken deep in the fight and it captured him staring intently across the ring. His brow was furrowed and his mouth half-open so that his gumshield could be seen, while the grotesque mound beneath his left eye was made to look even worse by the oozing blood. Another trail of blood, from a gash above the same eye, ran down his cheek and merged with the first red trickle like tributaries of a river.

Isaac wrote these words above the image: 'Broke my orbital bone in round three and fought to the end. Are you really willing to die for this? I'm built for this. I'll be back.'

Mick Hennessy had called me that morning to confirm the fracture of Isaac's orbital bone and the more gratifying news that the CT scan of Isaac's brain had been clear of any irregularities. Mick said that dehydration and depression had been significant factors in Isaac's near collapse the previous night. The reality of defeat bit hard after he had given so much in the ring. His body surrendered and shut down for a while.

'He's really down and disappointed,' Mick admitted, 'but it was the first time he had been twelve rounds. He will be stronger next time.'

I texted Isaac and told him about all the plaudits he had received in the usually bitter world of social media and how the bout was being described as a British Fight of the Year contender. I also told him how Barry McGuigan had messaged me to praise his talent and bravery. 'Thank you so much bro,' Isaac replied.

He faced eye surgery, but his next tweet late at night on Friday 5 August carried more hope. 'Lots of people are quietly fighting their own battles in life and my performance is inspiration that you can continue long past the point you think you might be done.'

Oleksandr Usyk was a long way from home on a ferociously hot Saturday evening in Dubai as we repeated a strange routine. Almost a year earlier, I had spoken to him on the Saturday night before his first fight with Anthony Joshua. Exactly seven nights before their rematch, we were ready to talk again. It's an unusual time for a one-to-one interview before a world heavyweight title bout. Fighters are edgy while they wait to re-enter the storm. But, as Usyk pointed out, he had been in a constant state of conflict since war began.

It had been forty-nine degrees that afternoon in Dubai, on 13 August 2022, but we discussed the war and its impact on his family. 'It was the day she turned twelve and so of course she cried a bit,' Usyk said as he remembered how his daughter Yelizaveta's birthday was overshadowed on the morning that Russia invaded Ukraine. The world heavyweight champion ran his hand through his damp hair, which was still cut in the style of a Cossack warrior, and for a moment it felt as if he was back home on that terrible February morning when the first bombs fell on Kyiv.

'My wife spoke to her, explaining what had happened, and soon my daughter understood very well what we are all facing in Ukraine. It was difficult but the main thing is that she is safe now.'

Almost six months had passed since that abandoned birthday party. Did his children still ask him the question which he had been unable to answer when we last spoke a few months earlier: why did the Russians want to kill them? 'They do, but I have the answer now. I explain to my kids that the Russians are trying to kill us because they are weak people. I also tell them this is the same reason why they are not going to win the war. We are stronger than them.'

Usyk had ensured that all Ukrainians would be able to see the rematch. He was willing to cover any financial costs to remove the pay-per-view restrictions in Ukraine, but an agreement was soon reached to make the fight available for free in his home country. But did Usyk fear that the world was in danger of forgetting the war? 'Lots of people are trying to hide and just wait until the war ends and hope that it will not touch them. But it's not possible because it will touch everybody somehow. All of us should pay attention and do something.'

What had been the lowest moment for him since the war began? 'I don't want anyone to pity me, but the toughest time was at the beginning because I wasn't with my family. But I got through this because I prayed to God and I felt confident again.'

Usyk had spent his arduous training camp bulking up and had packed on more than thirty pounds of muscle in preparation for Joshua. 'In the first month of the war, I lost ten pounds, but when I started preparing for this fight, I quickly gained the weight and I feel incredibly fit and strong. I won't be just as good as any other time I have fought. I will be better.'

My twenty-year-old son Jack and I stayed up late at night to watch the fight. We were on a family holiday in Croatia, staying just outside Dubrovnik. Evidence of the Croatian War of Independence, and the battle with Serbian forces from 1991 to 1995, remained clear. There were bullet holes in the garden walls of our villa and we became friendly with local people who told us of their involvement in the war. The emotion of those harrowing years lingered and Croatia's affinity with Ukraine was plain.

More prosaically, Anthony Joshua had gone to school in Kings Langley, near Watford, close to our family home. We knew people whose kids had been in the same class as him, and Jack and I liked

Joshua. He was a good and decent man, but he now lived in a different world. Despite losing his world title to Usyk, Joshua had just signed a new contract, worth £83 million, with DAZN and his management team spoke glowingly of the 'vision' the streaming giant had for him. But a second straight defeat to Usyk would damage the AJ brand irrevocably.

Joshua was under extreme pressure and he had fired Robert McCracken, his long-time trainer, and hired the feted Robert Garcia in a bid to transform his corner. Garcia was based in California, but he agreed to train Joshua in Loughborough. It seemed an awkward partnership, but Garcia was right in stressing that Joshua needed to be much more aggressive and use his considerable physical advantages against Usyk.

I was glad to have an excuse, in the form of a family holiday, to avoid Saudi Arabia. No amount of sportswashing could obscure the executions and imprisonments that occurred under a brutal regime, but both Usyk and Joshua had evaded my questions as to whether they felt uneasy about making money in Saudi. They insisted they had been encouraged by signs of progress in Saudi and how people seemed 'happy' to Usyk and 'cool' to Joshua.

Eventually, if I kept writing about boxing, I knew a time would come when I would also be compromised and travel to Saudi. But, on 20 August 2022, I was so much happier being near Dubrovnik than in Jeddah for a world title fight that Eddie Hearn marketed as Rage on the Red Sea.

I supported Usyk because he had dealt with so much during the war. He was also an outrageously skilled and brave boxer. The extent of that courage was tested in round nine when he was badly hurt. Usyk had to hang on as, in the last minute of the round, Joshua landed a series of grievous punches which left the Ukrainian reeling.

The cognoscenti talk about the 'championship rounds' for a reason. Rounds ten to twelve often mark the difference between the great and the good. Usyk was in serious trouble but, rather than buckling, he came out for the tenth with speed and a lightness of movement which belied the heavy shellacking he had absorbed. In a magnificent fightback, he speared Joshua with withering combinations.

Usyk also out-boxed and out-fought Joshua in the last two rounds, using angles, and the weight of his punching power, to dominate. It had been a masterful display.

The scoring was closer than it should have been and one judge, Steve Gray from England, even gave a puzzling decision in Joshua's favour. But Usyk won the fight and Joshua flung the champion's belts to the canvas and stomped out of the ring. Then, suddenly, Joshua returned to the ring and grabbed the microphone from a bewildered Usyk. He delivered a rambling speech which was embarrassing for him and insulting to his opponent, who maintained a dignified silence.

Jack and I wanted to look away, but we watched the distressing psychological damage that boxing can cause even its richest champions. It looked as if Joshua might have been suffering from concussion, too, because his mind seemed so scrambled.

Late that night, at the press conference in Jeddah, he began to cry as he admitted that he had let himself down during his rant. 'I'm upset, deep down in my heart,' Joshua said as he pulled his baseball cap over his eyes. 'I was mad at myself. So I thought: *I've got to get out of here, because when you're angry you might do stupid things.* Then I realised this is sport. Let me do the right thing. [After returning to the ring] I spoke from my heart. I'm a hustler, so I try and hold things together. But it comes at a big cost. It takes real strength for it not to break you.'

Joshua looked up. 'There's a little crack in that armour because I took a loss and you saw me upset. I'm a fighter. I'm not a normal person, even though I try to hold it together.'

T-Mobile Arena, Las Vegas, Saturday 17 September 2022

I am back in Vegas for a fight that comes too late in a long and bitter trilogy. Gennadiy Golovkin had been as good, and probably better, than Canelo Álvarez over the course of their first two fights. But he had been unlucky to draw the first bout in 2017 before narrowly losing the second exactly a year later.

Now, on a stark night in a cruel town, Golovkin resembles a ghost of his former self in a horrible and boring fight. He loses a wide decision, and looks utterly shot, while Canelo also resembles a faded version of his usually imperious self. It is a bleak reminder that not even the greatest fighters get out of boxing before losing their shimmering lustre.

Canelo hugs and consoles his defeated old rival, as if reminding him that there is no shame in succumbing to time and the harsh reality of boxing. They have fought 107 professional bouts between them – and this is Canelo's sixty-second fight. But Golovkin, a once great world champion, is now a forty-year-old man in an unforgiving arena. He still clings to a hopeless illusion.

'Look at his face, look at my face,' Golovkin says as if the lack of meaningful action can be celebrated. 'We're like this because it was a high-level fight. It was more tactical, like chess. Today Canelo was better.'

The only real hurt Canelo suffers is to his left hand. 'I've gone through difficult times with my defeat [to Bivol],' he says later, 'but it enables you to come back and show humility. I need surgery on my hand because I can't hold a glass. But I'm a warrior. That's why I'm here.'

Yet we all know that, even for these exceptional warriors, the time to get out of boxing is near.

13

The Taste of Strawberries

It's hard, but I am out on the street at 6.15 a.m. Running in New York City is a challenge until you hit a stretch of park or a path along the river. I run down East 30th Street and it's cluttered and stinky. I keep alert by trying to reach each new block just as the pedestrian sign pops up to say it's clear to cross. I'm excited because, from 7th down to 2nd Avenue, I don't stop once.

I turn right on 2nd and, even at that hour, it's busy, mostly with hospital workers walking to their morning shift. I keep going another four blocks until, on 26th Street, the lights catch me. Instead of stopping, I turn left and it seems calmer, more residential. I run to the bottom of the street and, suddenly, see water. I slip past the roadworks and, in less than a minute, I'm running on the walkway alongside the Hudson River.

It's beautiful as the water has turned salmon pink at dawn. I think of Patrick Day and how, if he had still been alive, he would have lit up at the sight of it. I had spent yesterday with his forty-one-year-old brother, Jean, in Freeport, their hometown on Long Island. Jean wanted to talk honestly about the reasons for his younger brother's death. I will see him again today.

The river shimmers as I pass an old Chinese fisherman who has set up four rods on the bank. He stares intently at the water and I am sure that when I return he will have reeled in a huge silvery fish or at least a stray boot from the bottom of the river. But, when I run back the same way twenty minutes later, he still gazes out at the water and his rods remain untouched. Only the light has changed and the bridges across the Hudson turn from pink to burnt orange to buttery yellow. My grey T-shirt is dark with sweat as I run slowly but, at sixty-one, I feel my good fortune.

Pat would never see New York again. He had been just twenty-seven when he died. My sister, Heather, had been younger than I am now when she died.

So I am not insulted a few hours later when the man at the Long Island Rail Road ticket office in Penn station asks me a familiar question: 'How old are you?' When I tell him, he shakes his head sadly. 'Damn,' he says. 'Senior citizen deductions start at sixty-five.'

I manage to crack a smile. 'That's a happy thought – not being quite there yet.'

'Yeah,' he quips, 'you're still a young man.'

We laugh and I head to the platform. I'm getting better at being grateful for ageing.

I sit in a quiet booth in the Imperial Diner in Freeport. Across the street is the Word of Life Ministries church, the site of Pat Day's funeral on Saturday 26 October 2019. Almost three years on, I listen to Jean Day talking about his little brother and his last tragic bout against Charles Conwell: 'I remember watching the fight and thinking, "I just want it to be over so we can tell Pat it's time to move to the next stage of his life." But then I saw him fall in the last round and my heart broke into a million pieces.'

Jean, a full-time nurse, looks at me steadily, but his voice is thick with emotion. 'Every day I fight to keep my head above water over this loss. My twin Bernard and our other brother Mike moved out to be with their families, but Pat and I were still living with my mom. Pat was my mom's best friend in the house because I have a career and I'm busy. It was different with Pat. When he was not in the gym, he'd be home with my mom. He'd be in the kitchen with her cooking or he would go to the local rec centre with her to work out. She can't go there now because it reminds her too much of Pat.'

The words keep flowing despite the pain. 'Sometimes, I'd be coming home from work and he'd shoot me a text: "Hey, I bought some steaks. How do you want yours done?" That was Patrick. It's a big hole for all of us now that he's gone.'

Jean explains that Pat had followed his parents' wishes by concentrating on his schoolwork and being a straight-A student. 'Our home was not a professional athlete's household. We knew to get our faces in our books, get our grades, get our degrees, get good jobs. Pat did all that really well, but he got side-tracked and became a professional boxer. It was a foreign idea in my parents' house, but I knew how much Pat loved boxing. It was his one true passion, but I carry a lot of regret because I should have told him to steer away from it.'

Would Pat have listened? Jean smiles sadly. 'I don't think so,' he admits, 'but at least I could have tried. I just wanted him to be happy but I had no idea boxing would take him from us.'

Jean's face clouds as he remembers how Pat had fallen for boxing after seeing the heavy bags hanging in the garage of Joe Higgins across the road. 'Pat had a very timid start in boxing,' Jean continues, 'and after his first sparring session he told us how his head was hurting from the shots he took. Pat persevered, but at one of his first amateur fights, he was so passive we were waving him forward to attack the guy. So it was amazing to see his development as he became a [regional] Golden Gloves champion and then a national champion. I was shocked how good he was.

'Of course, our mom was never on board with the boxing. There was a time when she went across the street and talked to Coach Joe. She told him: "I don't like boxing. I want it to end." He was like: "Don't worry. I'll take care of Patrick, everything will be all right." That's why I eventually lost all respect for this guy because he'd looked my mother in the face and told her he would protect her son. Pat deserved that because he was kind and, as much as it made him a good person, if you want to excel in boxing, you need a mean streak. Pat had none of that.'

His professional debut, in January 2013, when Pat was still only twenty, was against Zachariah Kelley at BB King's Blues Club in New York. 'I was there,' Jean exclaims, his face full of light. 'I remember being so nervous because, while Patrick had been in the [amateur] ring with better opposition, I'd never seen him fight without headgear. I didn't know how he was going to react to his first punch without that protection. So I wanted to see if he was really meant for the sport. And he did extraordinarily well. He took the guy out in the first round with a left hook and I was like: "Wow!" I was so happy. Lou DiBella [his promoter] was saying: "I want to make your brother a star." I was like: "OK, we'll see how this goes." I had no idea that, a few years later, the conclusion would be our burying this kid.'

He won nine and drew one of his first ten pro bouts, but their mother was still filled with dread. 'She always told Pat she didn't want him doing it,' Jean recalls. 'Pat would be like: "Mom, come on, it's a little late now. I'm kind of invested." My dad would be more like: "Let's go, Pat! I believe in you!" Sometimes, if Pat wasn't being aggressive enough, my dad would say: "You've got to watch out. Boxing passive like that, you're going to get hurt." So he was pretty involved whereas my mom was always on edge. She would distance herself from the boxing. All she would do is come and get an update if a fight was on. She'd ask: "Is Patrick OK?" That's all she wanted to know.'

After two years as a pro, Pat suffered his first defeat when he lost a majority decision to Alantez Fox. 'It was Patrick's first live national televised bout and guess who Lou DiBella and Coach Joe chose as his opponent?' There's a bitter edge in Jean's voice. 'An undefeated six-foot, five-inch guy who happens to be a southpaw. Patrick always had difficulty with taller fighters, so why would you take that fight?

Is it for a belt? No. And they only negotiated eight grand for the bout on Showtime. This is his first nationally televised bout and, against such a difficult opponent in California, he's getting paid peanuts. Joe had engineered it so that he was also Pat's manager. Was this deal an example of good management? No. It was terrible.

'The kid [Fox] wasn't a big puncher, but I was more concerned with how my brother was going to cope with all these difficulties. Lo and behold, he boxed tight because he needed a less tricky challenge so that he could get comfortable on that platform. Don't give him a nightmare on his television debut. I was in front of the TV, screaming my head off, because Pat was too cautious. I was at Bernard's house and we knew Patrick didn't show his true self. He was the stronger puncher, but he just couldn't get geared up mentally to press home the advantage. That fight came at the totally wrong time.'

Jean looks out of the window and then, turning back, his eyes blaze with anger. 'Patrick had a manager whose priority was to ask: "What's in it for me?" That's why Patrick ended up in a coffin. His career was managed in an absolutely asinine fashion.'

The words are brutal and jolting, just like Pat's devastating fate had been. 'Things were different for Pat after the loss because boxing was his life,' Jean says. 'I should have taken that opportunity to interject and break his relationship with Coach Joe as his manager.'

The family's Haitian heritage helped Pat in some of his bleakest moments as a young boxer. 'Pat took a trip to Haiti, where he stayed with my uncle Ronald,' Jean recalls, 'and it gave him a chance to look inside himself and to get his mind right. It was regenerative and he was surrounded by people who genuinely loved him in Haiti. We all feel that connection to our family's roots in Haiti and the trip helped prepare Pat make another run.

'He needed that warmth and support because boxing is a cold world, man. You lose and they kick you out. Boxing doesn't give a damn about anybody. They just care about who makes them money. Patrick was a loser at that point, but he showed his character and went on a great run.'

Pat had been reduced to being a B-side fighter, but Eric Walker was one of the lauded prospects he defeated in a string of six straight wins. 'I was definitely a little concerned as I had heard about Walker,' Jean says of that 2015 bout. 'It was a big challenge, but Patrick needed to show that he was still good enough to become a respectable contender again. That was the proudest I've ever been of him in his boxing career. Walker took his best shot at him and Pat outmanoeuvred and dropped him on his way to winning a big decision. But it showed how dirty boxing is because they were trying to extend the breaks between rounds to give the other kid a breather. They just don't expect or want the B-side guy to win. But Pat was way too good.

'That was an incredible night. All my brothers and Patrick's girl-friend MaryEllen [Dankenbrink] was there. Pat had told me how special MaryEllen was because they had just started dating before he lost to [Carlos Garcia] Hernandez. The first fight she saw was of him getting stopped by a journeyman – but she stuck by Pat. They were not together at the end of his life, but they were still close friends and she means a lot to us. So it was glorious to see him beat Walker. I remember watching him get interviewed backstage. I felt like he was my son because I was so proud.'

Patrick kept fighting his way out of the swamp, but Jean noticed that the wins came at a cost. 'I remember there were times where Patrick could hit guys and hurt them, and there was a point when he stopped doing that. His career took its toll on him. It was like he was dulled because of the way he was being moved by DiBella and Coach Joe. It was tough challenge after tough challenge. It wore him down.'

Jean was sufficiently concerned to talk to Pat about brain damage in the ring. 'We were at a restaurant, because it was my niece's birthday, and Pat said: "I love the sport and I feel in great shape." I said, "You've got great cardio shape but you keep getting hit in the head." That's why boxing is crazy. Fighters are running ten miles, skipping rope forever, looking ripped. But what kind of shape are you really in if you're getting bludgeoned to your head?

'I made a comment that it just needed one punch to end up in a coma. Pat didn't like that. He took it personally as if this was me doubting him. He was so upset about it that, a few days later, he confronted me in the house. I said, "Look, I wasn't trying to disrespect you. I was just telling the truth." I tried to leave it at that, but Pat wouldn't let me walk away. We had an argument and it got to the point where we weren't speaking for at least a week.

'He then came up against Ismail Iliev in Texas [in February 2019]. Iliev was unbeaten and, while Pat won the fight clearly, I was concerned by how much he was getting hit. It was the only fight where my mom watched some of it with me. It was in the family room, the same room where later that year I would watch him get killed on TV, and my mom just came in for a little while. I was so surprised that I got out my phone and filmed her watching the fight. She watched without comment before leaving after a short while. Pat could not believe it when I showed him the video later.

'Pat won for the sixth time in a row, but afterwards there were lots of marks on his face. He was getting hit too much and Iliev wasn't really a big puncher. I spoke to his best friend, Patrick Aristhene, and said, "They'd better analyse this fight because if he gets in there with a guy who can punch, he's going to get hurt." It was a premonition of what eventually happened.'

Jean wanted Pat to take a long break but, instead, four months later he was back in the ring with Carlos Adames. 'This guy is a serious puncher,' Jean says. 'Instead of correcting the situation, they just moved Pat onto the next challenge and that's indicative of the character of Joe Higgins. He just focused on getting Pat into bigger fights where the real money could be made. Patrick had the potential to accomplish more than he did in boxing. If there had been more patience and care for him, it could have been very different.

But we had people who wanted to get their hands on money right away. It was totally the wrong approach.

'I was on edge because if you throw something and get loosey-goosey with Adames, he's going to make you pay, big time. Patrick had enough skill to be in there with him, but he was taking his share of hard shots. I was sitting there like, holy shit, because I could hear the blows landing on my brother. He kept fighting, but in the last round he was badly hurt. Right at the bell, a big overhand right landed and he couldn't even stand up on his own. He slumped on the referee.'

There are times when Jean, movingly, looks like an older version of Pat. But then, in the grip of that grim memory, his face becomes a mask of pain. 'That was not a springboard performance from Patrick where you say he's ready for the world. It's a performance where you step back and think, *It's time to take stock. Is this really the right game for Patrick?* Even if the answer is yes, you need to give Pat six months to recover before you spend a long time working on improvements. But six weeks later, DiBella offers them a fight with his A-side star, Charles Conwell, and Coach Joe says yes. How does that make sense?

'Conwell was an Olympian pegged as a contender to become world champion. Joe Higgins, a former president of USA Boxing, was fully aware of Conwell's calibre. This kid didn't sneak up on anybody. He's the top prospect in the division, but Joe thinks it's a good idea to put Patrick in with him so quick after Adames. Why? Money. If Patrick somehow beats Conwell, he can ask for 100 grand instead of fifty grand the next fight.

'I didn't say any of this because I knew Pat was just going to take offence. How is this going to help him against a beast like Conwell? So I kept quiet but I was extremely nervous.'

Our diner is hushed. Jean and I have been here two hours and he pauses when I ask about the last time he saw his brother. 'I remember every time Patrick would come say goodbye to me before a fight, I'd get up, grab him, pull him close and say: "Protect the jewel." I was talking about protecting his brain. He'd always say: "I'll do my best."

'But this time he came to see me the night before he flew to Chicago. I had my nursing exam the next morning and I was hard at work. He said: "All right, Jean? I'll see you." I was so caught up in my studies, I just wished him well and said good luck. He turned upstairs and I went back to my studies. The next day, I took my exam and I did great. I was floating on air and I had no idea that my world was about to be fucking destroyed.'

We meet again the following afternoon, at the Imperial Diner, and Jean resumes talking with the same urgency as he remembers his brother's final fight and the terrible moments when Pat was knocked out. 'I stood in front of the TV and all I could say was "No, no". I only thought stuff like that happened in the movies, where people stand and say "No-o-o!" My baby brother is on the floor, his eyes are turning in the back of his head and he looks like he's going to die. That was it. My whole life I'm identified as a Day brother, one of four. Now, holy shit, am I one of three? My whole life changed.'

Jean's eyes are filmy with grief. He leans across to touch my hand as if to help me understand. 'Pat then did something that still gets me. With his boxing glove on, he reached for his mouth. He was trying to take the mouthpiece out. I think he was literally being suffocated. And then he just went unconscious again while his team stood there, watching. Not one of them stuck a toe in the ring to take the mouthpiece out.'

As the horror unfolded, and Jean watched the medics fail to oxygenate Pat, he and his brother Mike stared helplessly at the television. When Pat was finally taken away on a stretcher, Jean called Joey Higgins, Coach Joe's son, who had also been in the corner. Joey was a babbling wreck, but he promised to get back to Jean once he knew more. Jean didn't hear from Joey again that night.

Instead, Jean walked out of the house and into a cold October night. 'I didn't know what to do,' he said, his voice cracking. 'I thought about going to the water because I love to fish. It brings me peace, so I wanted to sit by the water and collect my thoughts. A group of kids were hanging around, looking like they were up to no good. I thought, *If anything happens with these kids I'll fucking kill one of them. I'll get my ass thrown in jail for life. Let me get out of here.* I walked around the neighbourhood and the only thing running through my head was this: *Is my brother going to die?*'

Jean's phone kept ringing. His dad, a doctor, gave him a little hope when he said the fact they didn't intubate Patrick suggested that, perhaps, the injury was not severe brain trauma. A second cousin, Daphney, also a doctor, was in Chicago and had recently been interviewed for a job at the very hospital where the ambulance had taken Patrick. She promised to get updates.

Amid all the family conversations, there was a missed call on Jean's phone. It came from a doctor at the Chicago hospital. 'He tells me that "We've received your brother and he's unresponsive. The first thing we did was intubate him."'

Jean's face crumples briefly as he recalled that crushing news. 'So there goes the hope my dad had. I'm like, "Shit!" He was not intubated from the venue all the way 'til he got to the hospital. That was horrible news. The doctor said Pat was critically ill and they were operating. It was not a good call.

'As I'm walking, my other cousin called me. Stephan and Pat were like brothers and so I tell him what's going on. I can hear Stephan working it all out like the doctor he is and he says: "OK, a subdural haematoma means they're going to have to do a craniotomy." He started crying then. I understood because I had learned at nursing school that whenever there is bleeding on the brain, and they have to excavate, the odds are bad. Your cranium, which is usually your friend protecting you from all threats outside, is now your worst enemy. The inside of your cranium is crowding in on your brain, squishing it. I started crying too.

'Then my mom called me and she's like: "Where are you? Come home." I knew she was right, so I went straight back and she was distraught. What she feared most had just happened. Our house is full of people coming to show their support and so I just shut myself in my room. I didn't get a wink of sleep as I was waiting for updates from Daphney at the hospital.'

Jean shakes his head, gently, as if to soften the trauma that still feels so raw. 'I heard later that when they opened up Pat's head, they were just greeted by dead brain tissue. It only takes four minutes for irreversible damage to happen to the brain. For twenty-five minutes, from when they attended to him in the ring to taking him to hospital in the ambulance, Patrick was not getting oxygenated. They didn't give him a fighting chance.'

Pat's parents and Patrick Aristhene flew to Chicago early on Sunday morning. Jean and his brothers followed a day later and discovered a desolate scene. 'Patrick is lying there, with a tube in his throat breathing for him. My mom is on her knees by the bed. She's touching his hand and she's whimpering. I don't think she could cry no more.'

Jean's gaze hardens as he remembers what he saw next. 'Coach Joe's in the room and he's just sitting there crying, looking real pathetic and saying over and over again: "It's my fault, it's my fault . . ." I'm consoling him because at that stage all that was on my mind was that my brother was lying there brain dead. That was at the forefront of our minds and we weren't thinking of Joe being the coach and the manager who had let Pat down so badly. So I consoled this fucking guy because he was crying and blaming himself.

'I then concentrated on Pat because I've been told that when you lose consciousness, the last thing to go is your hearing. So somebody in a coma can still hear everything and, when they wake up, maybe even recount things that were said around them. I was hoping there was a slim chance Pat's hearing was still intact. I was talking softly in his ear, letting him know what he meant to me and how proud I am of him. I was begging him that, if he had anything left, we'll fight through it together.'

Jean looks up. 'I also let him know that, if he feels like the fight is over, then it's fine too. He can just slip away, safe in the knowledge that we loved him so much. The strange thing is that he looked the same as normal. It's not like he was disfigured. I knew I was going to lose him so I was going to look at him for as long as I could.

'On Wednesday 16 October 2019, we went as a united front to the hospital. We all had time to say one last goodbye. I was looking at Pat and thinking of how he got beaten to death. But I had a special moment, just me and Pat, and I made sure everyone had the same.

'We had lunch at the hospital and then we told them that we were ready to switch off the machines. They alerted respiratory. And then they came, pulled the tube out and that's it. He had no brain function, so as soon as they pulled the tube, he wasn't able to breathe. He still wasn't completely gone, so we had to wait for his heart to stop beating. It took almost half an hour. And it was crazy because Pat actually started to move as his body was being deprived of oxygen. The heart's no longer beating, and a chemical reaction sparks motion and Patrick raised both his arms like this.'

Jean lifts his own arms, stiffly. 'I guess it was because he spent the whole time in a boxing match punching, punching, punching. When the chemical reaction started happening, his arms raised up. Meanwhile he's stone-cold brain dead. Even though I have my medical training I ran out the room and grabbed one of the nurses and said "He's moving!" She came into the room with me and said "Unfortunately, that's normal."

'After it was over, they cleaned him up, put him on the tray and said, "If you want to watch us wheel him to the elevator, you can accompany us." So we watched them take Pat to the elevator and then he went down to the morgue.'

We pause for a long while and then Jean shares a beautiful memory. 'The next day me, Mike and our cousin Patty went to the hotel to pick up all Pat's stuff. That was a really hard thing to do as all his possessions were in the exact place he left them. We packed everything away and then I saw that Pat had a packet of strawberries in the room. I looked at Mike and at Patty.

'I said, "We should have these strawberries because it's almost like Pat's leaving us something." So we went into the bathroom, washed the strawberries and ate them. I remember taking a picture in front of the mirror with Mike and Patty. The three of us are eating Pat's strawberries. They tasted so sweet.'

Jean nods. 'Yeah,' he says, 'even in his passing Pat still managed to give us sustenance.'

Anger courses through Jean when he thinks of the man he blames most of all for the death of Pat. 'When I first met Joe Higgins,' Jean said, 'I thought he's a real cool guy with an engaging sense of humour. But the more I hung around him, the more I picked up on things that rubbed me the wrong way. If he's a good guy, then why does he talk to people like this?

'His true intentions came to the surface once there was the potential to earn. With the amateurs, it seems wholesome. But when you infuse money into the equation, you see what is really driving this guy. There was a bout early in Patrick's career and, in the week of the fight, he had a stomach bug. He was throwing up and having diarrhoea. He could hardly stomach anything. So I'm like, "Pat can hardly keep a drop of fluid in his body and you're telling me he's going to jump in the ring? Coach, what happens if Pat can't fight this weekend?" It was just the two of us in the gym and Joe immediately turned on me. "What do you mean, if he can't fight? You're a worry wart. You get on everybody's nerves with that worrying shit."'

Jean looks at me. 'I hate the fact that we can now see what I was worried about. How come Joe used two relative novice sparring partners to get Pat ready for Conwell? It made no sense. And then, in the aftermath, what happens? Joe starts a fundraiser using Pat's name and image to try to get the gym remodelled? Why does he even feel like he has the right to do that? He's the main reason why

Pat's not here. I never confronted him, because I know that there is no point. This is the guy in hospital who kept saying "It's my fault", but as soon as the HBO cameras turn on in front of him, he's telling them it's not his fault. It's all bullshit.'

Jean also feels bitter towards Lou DiBella, for the way he had promoted much of Pat's career, and towards Charles Conwell and his team. He points out that Conwell had celebrated, standing over Pat and smiling after knocking him to the canvas. One of his cornermen had also said, 'We've seen death before.' Jean dismisses the seemingly heartfelt Instagram post Conwell had written, expressing his regret, and suggests it was a way for him to keep his career on track.

There is so much pain in Jean that I understand his anger. I had met Higgins, DiBella and Conwell and, in conversation with me, all three men appeared genuinely devastated by Pat's death. They were mortified that Jean blamed them for the tragic end of his brother's life. I think they also understood why he could not easily forgive them.

This is especially true of DiBella who spoke numerous times to me about the pain he felt, that Pat's fate had made him question himself and the fact that he had worked for thirty years in a business as damaging, and damaged, as boxing.

My own perspective, meanwhile, is shaped by my new friendship with Jean and the compassion I feel for the entire Day family. I had not met any of the men involved when Pat was still alive. So I am in no position to make a definitive judgement of anyone. I also know that professional boxing has been shadowed by death and grief for more than a hundred years. Pat was yet another victim of the ring.

But it feels important to give Jean a platform to voice his anguished perspective. No one else, he points out, has really taken the time to listen in detail to him and his family. But I tell him how much his view matters to me.

Jean softens as we gaze at the church where he, Bernard and Mike had all delivered eulogies for Pat on the day of his funeral. 'It wasn't really hard to write,' he says of his tribute. 'I wanted it to be like a piece of art which honoured Patrick and moved people. There was a moment where I started choking up when I spoke about how Patrick used to bring breakfast in to me. I had to stop and gather myself. I pushed through and finished. I wanted it to hit home because we lost Patrick, such a special guy, to stupidity and greed.

'Both my brothers wrote powerful stuff that moved people so much. We basically let everyone know what Patrick meant to us. His best attributes had nothing to do with his fighting ability. His best attributes were how smart, charming and caring he was every day of his life. In boxing, all that is neglected. They don't give a shit about any of that.'

I pay the bill and we walk out of the diner to Jean's car. All his warmth and kindness, which have been darkened by the loss of his brother, pour out of Jean in the pale sunshine of a September afternoon in Freeport. We speak about his family and their happier memories of Pat. Jean smiles when I tell him how much I would love to read his eulogy.

'I'll send it to you,' he says as he stretches out his hand to take mine.

I sit in my New York hotel room and read Jean's eulogy. His words flow in a long and beautiful tribute to his young brother. 'Patrick was the type of guy who strived to make people happy,' Jean writes. 'He spread love in various ways. I remember one morning waking up to the aroma of breakfast being prepared in the kitchen. Before I knew it, Patrick was poking his head in my room asking me if I wanted anything to eat. I would be a fool to say no. Still trying to get my bearings, I lay in bed thinking "Man, I've got a nice breakfast waiting for me in the kitchen!" Shortly after thinking this, I was pleasantly surprised for a second time by Patrick making his way into my room with my breakfast on a tray.'

There are other anecdotes which reveal Pat's humour and intelligence before Jean turns towards the contrasting world of boxing.

'Unfortunately, the field in which Patrick chose to make a living valued none of his best traits. The realm of professional boxing would rather document the story of a former felon who made the transition to the fight game, than the kid with a warm heart who came from a great home. Patrick was welcomed to professional boxing with promises of being a superstar, but a few untimely losses condemned him to the uphill battle of the B-side. Promises of superstardom soon turned into "Beat this top prospect and you'll be in the big money", but after a hard-earned victory, he was only rewarded with yet another empty promise.

'Here lies my source of guilt. My baby brother was left to fend for himself in a realm inhabited by individuals who didn't prioritize his well-being over the value of a dollar. I wish that me, or a family member, or a trusted family confidant, could have been present to oversee business dealings with the preservation of his safety in mind.

'Boxing was one of Patrick's true loves, and yet, as faithful as he was, it betrayed him by claiming his life. I've spent many hours wondering why such a pure soul deserved to be dealt such a wicked hand. I came to a conclusion while having a heart-to-heart with my beloved cousin Patty. I honestly feel like Patrick would've had a tough time coming to grips with the fact that his goal of becoming a world champ, which he had put his all into since the age of fourteen, was unachievable. I think God took Patrick to spare him the pain of that reality. I hate that he's gone. I'd forego all the fights and fanfare just to hear him greet me with his standard "Yeah!" when I enter the house. But Patrick couldn't live without boxing.

'While we were in Haiti two years ago for Christmas, my Uncle Ronald asked Patrick if he would stop boxing if he offered him one million dollars. Patrick looked him in the eye and told him that if he offered him twenty mil, he wouldn't stop. Patrick was loyal to the game.

'So now all we can do is look at pictures and videos, and cling to memories. I miss hearing his infectious laugh, watching TV with him in the basement, and watching him and my brother Mike chop it up like men after seeing both of them grow from infancy. I'll miss the look of proud admiration on my brother Bernard's face every time he greeted him and saw the man he had become. I'll also miss watching him help my mom in the kitchen, or how she would regularly assault him with suggestions on what to do with all his hair, and I'll miss watching him and my dad discuss their mutual love for the fairer sex.'

There was so much more and then, on the last page, Jean told the congregation about discovering the strawberries in Pat's hotel room. It moved me all over again.

'We went into the bathroom and each washed a strawberry. After toasting them up like fine champagne, we popped the strawberries into our mouths. They were surprisingly fresh and juicy. We decided to split the rest of them among ourselves. Still in my phase of grief where I was fighting to stomach a square meal, those strawberries were just what the doctor ordered. Even though his time on earth had passed, Patrick was still able to provide me with the nourishment I needed. The Unforgettable One had lived up to his name once again.'

14

The Change

Conor Benn was shattered. He was strung out and exhausted as his blank gaze slid away from me at the Matchroom Boxing Gym in Essex. Just after two o'clock on Thursday 29 September 2022, the day after he'd turned twenty-six, Benn fiddled with his phone and spoke quietly to his wife as if she might be able to rescue him from meeting me. He'd had enough of talking about his looming fight with Chris Eubank Jr. We were ten days away from that money-spinner and Benn wanted to escape the conveyor belt of chat.

He had spent two hours doing one brief YouTube interview after another, answering the same questions over and over again. He had also done a round-table conversation with the national newspapers and countless other short television and radio appearances. I was the last one left.

I had been asked to arrive discreetly and not too early because I'd been given the chance to see Benn on my own for forty-five minutes. The publicity people, knowing how I had written extensively about the fathers of both fighters, Nigel Benn and Chris Eubank Sr, gave me that extra time at the end of his media day.

Benn carried the look of a man who was sick of everything – of the inane queries and even the sound of his own voice. He just wanted to get the hell out of there but, as his contrived contest with Eubank Jr was a pay-per-view event, he had to go through the publicity charade.

The television crews were packing up, and the last YouTubers and reporters had drifted away, but Benn still avoided me for a few more minutes. And then, with a curt nod, he walked over.

I have done this long enough to rely on a routine to make it feel like we are about to share a moment. I shake him warmly by the hand, apologise for making him put up with yet another interview and offer effusive thanks for his time. It usually helps, a little, but Benn still sits down with a weary sigh. He has dressed with the camera in mind. His many tattoos, which cover his neck, chest, arms and torso, are hidden by a fawn polo neck and expensive trousers which are the same colour. He wears a chunky gold Rolex.

The first fifteen minutes are strained and I swallow the desire to say, 'Look, pal, let's call it quits. I've also got other things I could be doing.'

But here's the kicker. I want to be here. I really want Benn to open up.

I have been duped once more. I've bought the hype Eddie Hearn, Benn and Eubank Jr are peddling. They keep banging on about a family feud between the Benns and Eubanks and how this could be the fight that returns boxing to the mainstream. I want this to be true for I can remember how it felt on weekend nights in the 1990s when Nigel Benn, Chris Eubank, Michael Watson and Gerald McClellan showed such courage and raw desire.

Then, even people who cared nothing about boxing could not look away from the huge TV screens in roaring pubs. Briefly, they saw what I saw. They felt what I felt. Boxing looked less like a lonely freak show then. It looked like a singular world filled with remarkable men who confronted their doubts and fears in the most elemental way. The fighters risked more and suffered more than most of us ever do in our own lives. They were extraordinary in crossing the bleakest terrain in pursuit of glory or redemption.

These might be hopelessly romantic ideas, but maybe they are a way of convincing myself that I have not wasted so much of my life on this battered old business.

The enmity between Nigel Benn and Chris Eubank Sr had fed this narrative three decades earlier. Eddie Hearn tells us now that the same dark grandeur will be uncovered by Conor and Chris Jr, as they resume a battle their fathers never resolved. Barry Hearn, Eddie's father, had promoted those bouts in the early 1990s and he also feeds the hype-machine with nostalgia.

The fact that *Match of the Day* will interview Benn is a sign of how this fight has crossed over into football territory. He will be seen on BBC One, a channel which now shuns boxing. Huge posters are plastered across London. They feature a snarling Benn and Eubank Jr facing each other, their heads blown up to gigantic size, beneath the logo of 'Born Rivals' and the date of the fight, 8 October, one day short of the thirtieth anniversary of the drawn rematch between Nigel Benn and Eubank Sr.

People who never think much about boxing have been asking me about the fight. I tell them it shouldn't be happening but, in the next sentence, I admit to being intrigued. To anyone who asks for more detail, I touch on the bout's problematic nature. Benn is a welterweight. On the scales before a fight, he weighs no more than 147 pounds. Eubank Jr has fought often at super-middleweight, where boxers can weigh 168 pounds. Even his contests at middleweight, the 160-pound category, make him thirteen pounds heavier than Benn's natural fighting weight.

They should not share a ring, but the promotion is set to generate £25m, so they have agreed to meet at a catchweight 157 pounds. This is perilous. Benn is jumping ten pounds in weight, but it's more troubling that Eubank is stretching himself further. He already starves himself to make the 160-mark and to shift another three pounds when drained and dehydrated makes him vulnerable to brain damage from blows to the head.

His father has spent much of the build-up demanding the fight's cancellation. A year earlier Eubank Sr's second son, Sebastian, had suffered a massive heart attack and drowned in Dubai. He now fears for the life of his eldest boy.

'This is insane, it can't happen,' Eubank Sr had said a few weeks before. 'I've already lost one son. I cried. I bawled in private. The love I have for Sebastian is the same for Christopher. I am the father and I say this fight cannot happen.'

Eubank Sr had offered £300,000 to ensure that the fight contracts were torn up and, when his urging was ignored, he promised to start a campaign for fans and media outlets to boycott the bout. 'This is life and death,' he said in a joint interview with Nigel Benn. 'Gerald McClellan is real. Nigel, you did that to him. I did that to Michael Watson. You can't do this to my son.'

McClellan and Watson had suffered harrowing, life-changing injuries during their respective bouts against Benn Sr and Eubank Sr. That reminder did not change Nigel. 'We're in the fight business,' he told Eubank Sr. 'Your son made the decision and he's thirty-two years old. You say it's life and death, but it's also a sport and we all chose it to give us a good life. I never went in there to maim, but it's a contact sport. The fight's been made and the contracts signed.'

Eubank Sr turned to his old rival. 'The love I have for you is beyond the measure of your thinking. I have tasted your blood – it tastes like rust – and smelled it on you. I am the warrior, I've proven it. But protect my son, my king. Let him go and have his career.'

I had written in depth about the boxing tragedies that shrouded the Benn and Eubank families but, still, I am suckered back into the madness. Eubank Jr does not match the grandiloquence of his father, but I've interviewed him three times and he is an intelligent speaker. He is a good, rather than a great, fighter. Yet I'm intrigued to see how he will do against an opponent as seemingly driven as Conor Benn.

It's still hard to gauge the calibre of Benn as he has yet to be tested. I had been ringside in Liverpool in December 2021 when, near the end of round four, he forced his experienced American opponent Chris Algieri to retreat to the ropes. A brutal right hand made Algieri crumple, slowly, before falling face-first to the canvas. I was shocked by Benn's power.

Four months later, he was just as clinical when stopping Chris van Heerden, another veteran, in two rounds in Manchester. His 21–0 record would now be set against a much bigger man in Eubank Jr who had lost only two of his thirty-four fights.

So I stick to my task even when Benn gives me so little. We skirt his relationship with his parents and twin sister, and meander down the predictable fight route and his animosity towards the Eubanks.

We are not really getting anywhere, so I ask Benn what the word 'home' means to him. I know he will have to think harder now because, while he had been born in Greenwich, he had spent twelve years of his childhood in Mallorca before his dad moved the family to Australia. Nigel and his wife Carolyne still live in Sydney while Conor, a fluent Spanish speaker as a kid, returned to England to become a boxer. As I had hoped, the idea of 'home' unsettles his poker face.

'I don't know,' Benn eventually says. 'I don't know.'

He hesitates. 'I mean, where my wife and baby are is home, of course. But I also tend to say I'll go back home as in Australia. But I think that's because my family still live over there.'

I sense his guard slipping and so I ask Benn if his wife is English. 'Yeah,' he murmurs and points over my shoulder. 'There she is.'

I turn to see a young woman look up when Benn calls out. 'Hey, Vic, come join us.'

Victoria Benn picks up her bag and, a little shyly, walks across. Normally I don't like having a third person sit in on an interview, but disruption feels welcome today.

Benn pulls up a chair for Victoria while I check that it's OK for her to talk to me. 'Yeah, it's fine,' she says, sweeping her long blonde hair from her face. 'It's not on video so I don't mind.'

We chat about their one-year-old son, Eli, and I then ask Victoria to describe her emotions when Conor is in the ring. 'Before the fight, I'm absolutely fine,' she says, 'because I believe in everything he does. I see what he puts into it so I've got no reason to worry. But, come fight night, nerves take over. In the last fight [against van Heerden], Conor did amazingly, but I was holding my breath, thinking *How am I going to do this?* I can't help it because he's my husband. I just want him to be safe.'

It will be much harder against Eubank Jr. 'Oh yeah, definitely,' she agrees. 'For all his other fights, Conor's been the big favourite. This fight feels different. He has to go up in weight, there's so much attention on it and it's 50/50. Don't get me wrong, he can win. But this one seems much more dangerous.'

Victoria smiles sadly when I say I will be thinking of her a week on Saturday. 'Thank you. I will be sat there – not breathing.'

Boxers usually say that they will crush their opponent, but the mood has shifted. Does Benn feel the fight is on a knife-edge? 'Definitely. It's 50/50 because of his weight advantage. If it was a level playing field in terms of him being my weight, I'd be heavily favoured. But we're doing something I've never done before. So there has to be that uncertainty. I believe I knock him out. But it would be silly for me to say the weight ain't a factor.'

Benn is finally ready to talk properly, so I ask if he had been lonely when he moved to England to become a fighter. 'Yeah, very. I didn't know anyone. I started off in Manchester, and trained with Ricky Hatton for six months, and then I moved to Brentwood to work with Tony Sims [his trainer who had been one of his dad's sparring partners]. I started to feel more settled but I was still lonely.'

Benn looks down. 'My life's been a bit ...' he says, his voice trailing away.

'Mad,' suggests Victoria.

'Yeah, it's been bizarre. Part of me wishes I had a normal life. I see Victoria with her schoolfriends and it's really nice they're so close. I don't speak to no one from the past. And, as a boxer, you question people's motives. I have one close friend, but the rest are just business associates.'

What were his schooldays like? 'Private, privileged,' Benn says quietly.

He twitches when I say it must have been difficult being described as the devil's child. 'Oh my gosh,' he exclaims, 'have you done your research?'

When I last interviewed his father, Nigel Benn had relived the years when he was swamped by wealth and fame. Benn Sr fell into the chaos of drugs and affairs that almost ended his marriage to Carolyne. The couple left England to live in Spain as a way for Benn Sr to escape his past, and they became evangelical Christians. Conor was sent to a fundamentalist Christian school, which ruined his adolescence.

'It was so difficult and so mad and it troubled me for a long time,' the boxer explains. 'My dad needed that firmness and harshness, whereas I was just a kid. It moulded me into how I am now, some things I hate about myself . . .'

What does he hate? 'Just the way I think – which is changing daily. Sometimes, my thoughts are troubled. I forgive my parents now, but in the same breath I had the most privileged, luxury life. People go, "You're contradicting yourself". But, mentally, it was really challenging.'

His mum accepts that the decision to force him into the fire-and-brimstone of fundamentalist Christianity was a mistake. 'Every time it's spoken about, she sobs her eyes out, doesn't she?' he says to Victoria, who adds: 'She was going through a really hard time with your dad.'

It still sounds like he was exposed to a cult? 'Exactly,' Benn replies. 'I was told the world was coming to an end. We were repenting on our hands and knees, asking God to forgive our sins. At Christmas, Santa Claus was blasphemy, an offence to Jesus. Santa Claus was in red and white because when Jesus was pierced there was blood and water. I was like, "Mate, I'm a kid." But I'm worrying about the world ending, and the Antichrist coming. I used to go to bed and be petrified of my nightmares. How is that normal? How can your son need deliverance from the devil? It was traumatic.'

Benn looks up. 'I don't blame Dad. He was just battling his own demons. As I've got older, I understand Dad more. I admire the man.'

But when he looks back to being thirteen? Benn shakes his head. 'It's just pain.'

It's still a surprise when he cracks open. The tears come from a wound deep inside Conor Benn. His eyes swim with hurt and his mouth crumples while he tries to stifle his crying. 'Sorry,' he says, attempting to gather himself. 'I've gone back there.'

There is a long silence. 'I battle things every single day,' Benn says, wiping his eyes.

I touch the twenty-six-year-old fighter's arm in sympathy as Victoria also consoles him. 'It's good for you to open up like this,' she says to her husband, holding him close. She looks at me. 'Lots of people don't understand Conor. He's a very complex person. But I'm very understanding and I think he's unique. That's why we ended up together.'

Benn is still trapped in the past. 'I remember watching *Tom & Jerry*. I know it's just a kids' show, but there is a part where he died and the escalators went up to heaven or down to hell. I had nightmares for a week. I used to wake up, screaming, thinking I was going to hell.

'I had another nightmare over and over, of me standing on an all-white floor, while something spiralled towards me from far away. It got closer and closer and I saw it was a snowball with horns and there was nowhere to run. It was terrifying. So it's taken me many years to get over being stuck in that way. I used to sing in the church choir and play the guitar. I had no tattoos. I looked like a normal kid and I was trying to be a good kid. But I was hurting bad. Then my dad confessed to my mum that his affairs had not stopped when they moved to Mallorca and he went to live with the pastors for a year. When my mum took him back, I was so angry.'

The family moved to Australia and Conor, as a teenager, harboured resentment towards his father. He fell into trouble and was arrested by the Sydney police who took him home to his dad on a night which changed their lives forever.

'How do you know all this?' Conor asks in astonishment. 'I don't remember speaking about this.'

His dad told me and so Conor smiles. 'OK. I was in a lot of trouble at eighteen and expected my dad to think of all them years of hatred I had towards him. But that night he hugged me and said "Son, I love you. We can get through this." Instantly, our relationship changed. Now life is about being the best man I can be. It doesn't matter about my achievements. It matters about me being a good dad. My family want me to be a better man, rather than me becoming the best fighter in the world but still corrupt and disturbed.

'I could be doing my old job, painter and decorator, work in retail, do scaffolding, and my dad would still be proud of me. He cares more about my real life than my boxing. So this will just be another fight for him – and me.'

I ask Benn if our probing of his past is distressing so close to the fight. 'No, because it made me who I am and I dealt with it. I've found my safety net, which is my son and my family.'

Did it help to have counselling? 'Definitely. Before then there were stages when I didn't know if I was going to tip over the edge. But my whole life's been a bit mad.'

That madness will carry a fresh edge in front of a fevered crowd when he walks to the ring to face Eubank Jr. 'You get butterflies in your belly,' Benn admits, 'but the only difference between good fighters and great fighters is the ability to perform under pressure. And, to me, he's just another man I've got to beat up. People keep talking about the magnitude of this fight, but you either fold or you rise to it. I've risen to him.'

The tears are long gone now and Benn smiles when I say that at least we avoided a predictable interview. 'Yeah, it was good and I've just got *Match of the Day* now.'

When I tell him, with a straight face, that I'll also be interviewing him for the BBC, a sudden look of alarm crosses his face. Benn then breaks into a laugh when he realises I'm joking. 'We will do another interview, mate,' he says. 'Just don't make me cry next time.'

Driving home in the autumn sunshine, I said a small thank you to boxing. It let me down so often, but it still had the capacity to surprise me in new ways. Fighters were special in their willingness to talk about the most upsetting periods in their lives with such candour. They were often loud and brash but, being so used to adversity, they could also show a disarming vulnerability. The way in which Benn opened up gave me hope that his showdown with Eubank Jr at a sold-out O2 Arena might elevate rather than diminish boxing.

Our interview was published on Monday 3 October. I began with the moment when Benn started to cry and the reaction towards the fighter was overwhelmingly positive and kind. He was described by readers online as being 'open and honest', 'remarkable', 'refreshing', 'surprising' and 'extraordinary'.

Despite some lingering misgivings about a manufactured scrap, I had begun to look forward to that Saturday. On a quiet, sunlit Wednesday morning, around half-past eleven, I left my shed in the garden and walked inside to make a coffee.

I can see myself now, standing in the kitchen, waiting for the kettle to boil and flicking through my messages. When I checked Twitter, the water boiled in a rumbling roll. I saw 'Benn' and 'drugs' and it took a few seconds to absorb the meaning.

Riath Al-Samarrai, of the *Daily Mail*, had broken the story that morning. The headline was in block capitals: BENN FAILS DRUGS TEST.

'Fuck,' I said out loud. Below the headline came the standfirst:

'Conor Benn FAILS a drugs test, plunging Saturday night's huge O2 Arena fight into doubt after he tested positive for a banned women's infertility drug.'

I scrolled through the content, my initial anger at being conned turning into curiosity. I had covered many press conferences and fights with Riath. He was a journalist I respected and liked, and we had shared a few conversations over the years about the idiocy and deceit of boxing. I also knew that Riath, who had written about doping in athletics for years, was an exemplary reporter. There could be no doubting the veracity of his story.

I sat outside in the hazy sun, drinking coffee and reading the jolting news that a drug test carried out by VADA had found clomifene in Benn's system. This was a new drug to me, but I soon became familiar with its use. A powerful female fertility drug, clomifene stimulates egg production in women and boosts chances of pregnancy. My bemusement, as to why a male boxer would take the drug, soon cleared when I learned that a daily dose of clomifene triggers the production of testosterone in men.

Testosterone increases the flow of oxygen and nutrients to repair an injury and enhances muscle growth. The most worrying aspect of testosterone is that it enhances strength and power. It helps a boxer hit his opponent much harder and for longer than usual. Remembering how shocked I had been by the way in which Benn poleaxed Algieri the previous December, I felt relief that he would not have the same opportunity to hit a severely weight-drained Eubank Jr.

It's actually a triumph for sport, and life itself, when a cheating athlete tests positive for performance-enhancing drugs. A small step in purifying a dirty river has been taken.

VADA was the best anti-doping outfit in sport and I knew Dr Margaret Goodman who had founded and still ran the organisation in Las Vegas. She had worked as a ringside physician in Las Vegas from 1994 to 2005, and tended to fighters in more than 500 professional bouts. Goodman was the president and driving force of VADA.

I began thinking more about Goodman, the venerable doctor, than Benn, the boxer accused of doping. I remembered why I trusted her implicitly when I reread our 2021 interview.

'Boxing,' Goodman had told me, 'is a beautiful sickness in so many ways.'

Goodman was so consumed by safeguarding boxers that she studied their previous bouts for signs of neurological damage. She had still been the ringside doctor when two fighters, Pedro Alcázar and Leavander Johnson, lost their lives. Finally, drained and exhausted, Goodman stepped away from the ring. I asked her if boxing should be banned.

'No,' she said firmly. 'I don't think boxing should be banned – ever. But we can make it safer.'

Goodman had witnessed the worst of boxing, but she sounded uplifted when she remembered working with boxers. 'Fighters were the best patients I ever had. I don't want to insult the patients I have now, but sitting with a fighter at the weigh-in, in the corner during a fight and then afterwards was more dramatic, amazing and educational than anything else. Oh my God, to be with a fighter after a fight? To see the emotion after winning or losing? It almost seemed inappropriate to be privy to that. So, from a medical and a personal standpoint, I never had anything I enjoyed more than boxing. We know the damage but, oh, the fighters are incredible. We just need to take care of them and help them take better care of themselves.'

Goodman was doing even more important work, with VADA, in caring for boxers. Doping in boxing mattered so much because, unlike athletes in other sports, the intention of most fighters is to render their opponents unconscious. We are not watching an athlete run faster or jump higher. We are watching highly trained professionals punch each other in the head. When an ordinary athlete cheats, he or she demeans the integrity of sport and robs their clean rivals of medals and prizes. It is far more serious, and life-threatening, when a boxer dopes.

I returned to my office and tried to work. It was difficult and, soon after 12.30 p.m., I searched for updates. My tangled emotions flattened into anger when I read a joint statement from Matchroom and Wasserman, the respective promoters of Benn and Eubank Jr. Incredibly, and knowing the seriousness of doping in boxing, they were still trying to proceed with the bout.

'We have been made aware that a random anti-doping test for Conor Benn conducted by the Voluntary Anti-Doping Association returned an adverse analytical finding for trace amounts of a fertility drug,' the statement began. 'The B sample has yet to be tested, meaning that no rule violation has been confirmed. Indeed, Mr Benn has not been charged with any rule violation, he is not suspended and he remains free to fight.'

I am not an angry person, but I felt rage then. The statement added that Benn had passed all the doping control tests carried out by the UK Anti-Doping Agency (UKAD), including one taken after the positive VADA result. Both boxers, and their promoters, had agreed to VADA testing in their contracts. But the British Boxing Board of Control relies on UKAD as its official anti-doping authority and so Hearn thought he had found a credible loophole to ignore the VADA result.

The Board had released a short statement to declare that the fight between Benn and Eubank Jr was 'prohibited and not in the interests of boxing'. Hearn acknowledged that he and Robert Smith, their general secretary, had been in discussion for more than a week, but he insisted the boxer could not be sanctioned because he had not returned any adverse findings in his UKAD tests.

'We saw the *Daily Mail* article this morning and we have just seen the Board's statement,' Hearn said in a video interview later that day. 'It is with the lawyers going backwards and forwards.'

Hearn was wriggling hard in a desperate attempt not to lose the vast amounts of money he expected to make from the bout. Benn also spoke later that afternoon on DAZN, the streaming service which bankrolls Hearn, and he was equally resistant to cancelling the fight. 'I've not committed any violations. I've not been suspended so, as far as I'm concerned, the fight's still going ahead. I've spoken to Chris personally and we both want the fight to go ahead. We've both taken medical and legal advice and we both want the fight to happen for the fans.'

When Benn wept during our interview, he knew about his positive test result for clomifene on 23 September, six days before we met. VADA had informed the fighters, the promoters and the Boxing Board. But he remained undeterred. 'I've signed up to every voluntary anti-doping testing there is under the sun. Throughout my whole career, all my UK tests have come back negative. I've never had any issues before. Even in the lead-up to this fight, my tests have come back negative. So my team will find out why there's been an initial adverse finding in my test, but as far as I'm concerned, the fight's still going ahead. I'm a clean athlete and we'll get to the bottom of this. I'll see you all on Saturday.'

Hearn worked hard all afternoon. Citing a case from 2018 when the British boxer Billy Joe Saunders had failed his VADA test and was banned in Massachusetts, Hearn pointed out that the British Boxing Board of Control had instead accepted a UKAD test, which cleared the fighter of illegality. 'So they need to make a decision on what they want to do,' Hearn said. 'If they don't suspend [Benn], which they haven't [done] and can't [do], he is clear to fight.'

Apart from being untrue, those phrases – 'free to fight' and 'clear to fight' – gave Benn license to ignore the fact that he had been found guilty of having a banned drug in his system. Hearn had said in the build-up that he hoped to sell around a million pay-per-views of the fight. It was an outlandish claim, but it explained why he was trying to railroad the Board or, alternatively, find another commission which might sanction the fight.

Social media can be a cesspit but, sometimes, it produces timely reminders. While Hearn spent all Wednesday trying to overturn the Board's ruling, a 2018 clip of the promoter went viral on Twitter. Embarrassingly for Hearn, he was captured talking good sense about doping and the fact that the Board ignored that positive

VADA test result for Saunders who had the banned substance oxilofrine in his system. 'What is the point in signing up for drug testing,' said Hearn, 'if, when you fail, everyone goes "Don't worry about it. Just let him fight"?'

At the time, Saunders was promoted by Frank Warren, Hearn's arch-rival, and so he went on the attack in that old video interview. 'The argument that it's all right with UKAD is totally irrelevant. You've signed for drug testing with VADA, the best testing agency in my opinion in the sport. If UKAD thinks in-competition should just mean the night of the fight, you are telling me a fighter should be able to take oxilofrine to cut weight and get faster and stronger. VADA's rules are quite simple. In-competition is 365 [days of the year]. You can't take performance-enhancing drugs in camp so you can be more dangerous in the ring. It's outrageous ... He failed a VADA test. You can't ignore it. Otherwise the sport's a mockery.'

Hearn had spoken this truth on 12 October 2018. Now, on 5 October 2022, he was trying to do the very thing he had warned against four years earlier.

Watching that revealing clip elicited another memory of Hearn. I remembered how, after Patrick Day had died, he'd cried in a video interview. Hearn had promoted the fight which took Pat's life in Chicago. The day after Pat's death was announced, Hearn wept on screen. I watched it again on YouTube.

On 17 October 2019, Hearn had spoken to Umar Ahmed, who introduced himself as being from 'iFL TV, MTK Global' and began their interview by suggesting 'there is only one place to start, Eddie. A very sensitive topic, the tragic news came through last night that Patrick Day has unfortunately passed away.'

A week on from the Day tragedy in Chicago, Hearn was promoting his next boxing show. It was in Newcastle and headlined by Lewis Ritson and Robbie Davies Jr. Their fight logo of 'Bad Blood', printed in red, could be seen behind Hearn as he spoke about a dead fighter. 'Yeah, I mean it's just tragic, you know. We know the saying that the sport of boxing saves more lives than it takes and that is true, but it doesn't make it any better when a tragedy like this happens.

'I met Patrick Day last Thursday for the first time and last night I was in absolute pieces. And I knew him for thirty seconds. You start thinking about Joe Higgins, his trainer and manager who he worked with for years and years. Of course, you think about his mum and dad. You think about his promoter Lou DiBella. It's heart-breaking. He was a man who didn't need to box. He had a family – he didn't need that search for money. He did it because he absolutely loved boxing.

'We need to make sure that the positive effects he had on the community live on because, if you look at the response from people, this is a guy that touched and motivated people. He touched their souls. He gave them positivity. He had that smile which would just light up the room. I feel as though I know the guy because of the responses and the way people have written about him. Last Thursday, I'll never forget. He came over to me before the press conference with Joe Higgins and he was so excited. He was . . .'

There was a long pause as, choked with emotion, Hearn blew out his cheeks and exhaled deeply. He looked away from the camera, his eyes swimming with tears.

Three years on, watching the interview again, I noticed that the letter D in the word BLOOD had started to peel off the poster behind him. Hearn also seemed to be unravelling.

'He just, uh . . .' he said before, bowing his head, he stopped talking again to cry some more.

'You all right?' Ahmed asked.

Hearn lifted his head. 'Yeah. I just remember talking to him and what he was saying . . .'

His eyes were glazed and his chin trembled. 'Sorry,' he said as he covered his eyes.

'Yeah,' Hearn finally continued. 'I knew him for thirty seconds. So it's terrible . . . It's the sport, it's everything.'

'Imagine how the family feel,' Ahmed said.

In that moment, I thought of how, two weeks before, to the very day, I had sat with Jean Day in the Imperial Diner in Freeport as he poured out his heart.

'Just terrible,' Hearn stressed. 'You can say it's boxing, but it's so hard to justify. It's been a rough year for the sport, so we need to make sure that we get together as a community, keep trying to evolve and make the sport safer. There are things we can do.'

Patrick had been the fourth of five professional boxers to die in fewer than four months in 2019. I wondered how Hearn could avoid this memory amid his desperation for Benn to fight Eubank Jr. This strategy, rather than making 'the sport safer', made boxing so much more perilous.

'Now it's a case of making sure that his name lives on,' Hearn continued as he praised Patrick. 'That's all we can do. I saw another heart-breaking interview that he gave and he was just talking about positivity. He was talking about making the most of your life. He was talking about doing what you love to do and he loved boxing. He *loved* boxing.'

Hearn wiped away the remaining tears. 'For him, it wasn't a case of it being a way out, or a way to make money. He was living his dream and it's so cruelly taken away. But it's deeper than that. It's the sport. It's knowing what these guys give, day in, day out and we have to make sure, as a sport, we do better. It's boxing, and it's very, very dangerous. There's so much more we can do. We need to respect these fighters. We need to make sure it's as safe as possible for them.'

Before they moved on smoothly to plug the 'Bad Blood' fight between Ritson and Davies, Hearn said, 'It's devastating. You could say "It's one of those things. It's boxing." But it's just brutal.'

Three years on and Hearn ended his Wednesday, at least in public, by stressing that the fight between Benn and Eubank Jr remained on track. There were rumours that he could take out a court injunction to prevent the Boxing Board of Control from stopping the bout. Meanwhile, the sports scientist Ross Tucker warned of the dangers for Eubank Jr in facing a fighter who had recently had clomifene in his system. Tucker explained that laboratory tests indicated that clomifene can boost testosterone levels by as much as 146 per cent.

The following morning, at 8.26 a.m., Fred Mellor from DAZN replied to my message asking for clarification. 'Yeah, fight week presser as normal,' Fred replied on WhatsApp. 'Canary Riverside, 1 p.m. I believe right now the fight is still happening.'

I had followed boxing closely for fifty years, seven years longer than Hearn had been alive, and written about it professionally for three decades. Yet my love of the sport had been compromised repeatedly by the fact that fighters can be maimed and even killed. So that Thursday morning, 6 October 2022, I was consumed by the fact that boxing, and my own writing about it, was stalked by the tragedies of the past.

The chaos of the previous twenty-four hours could not shut out the distressing memories that still haunted the Benn and Eubank families. Michael Watson ended up in a coma for months, and his life had never been the same again after he and Chris Eubank Sr met in the ring in 1991. Nigel Benn had shown such ferocity four years later that his opponent, Gerald McClellan, went blind and suffered brain damage.

Then, in 2016, Chris Eubank Jr's fists sent Nick Blackwell tumbling into a coma. I had interviewed Eubank Jr, Blackwell's trainer, Gary Lockett, and his friend and fellow fighter, Liam Williams, about that tragedy.

As a mere bystander, I had been shaken by those dark nights in the ring. I could only imagine the vivid scars marking the Benn and Eubank families. But there seemed less distress in the Hearn family, even though Barry had promoted the Watson fight and Eddie had put on the show which cost Pat Day his life.

Until the week of the Benn revelations, I had supported Hearn.

I thought he was a slick promoter who had been good for British boxing. Six months earlier, in April 2022, I had praised his promotion of women fighters and I still regarded that week in New York with Katie Taylor and Amanda Serrano, especially the night of that momentous bout, as a landmark occasion for boxing. There had just been a few moments on that trip which made me pause.

A few days before the Taylor–Serrano epic, I had interviewed Hearn in his swanky New York hotel. He was excellent when talking about Taylor and women's boxing. But he brushed aside my queries about Pat Day. After mouthing a few platitudes about the tragedy, he seemed curiously unmoved about the fate of a fighter over whom he had wept the day after his death. Hearn also described the fatality as being the result of a freakish knockout rarely seen in boxing. He seemed to have minimal interest in discussing the real story of Patrick Day's life and death.

In a way, I understood. Rather than linger over that terrible night, he had a positive story to tell about Katie Taylor and women boxers. A week later, when I again interviewed him about Canelo Álvarez in his vast suite at the MGM Grand, Hearn was full of cracking anecdotes. But I was struck by the different reaction of another writer. When we met later in the week, he told me how much he had disliked Hearn. He felt that there was something 'off' about him that his bonhomie could not conceal.

The writer said quietly: 'I just don't like Hearn. I don't believe him.'

Those short sentences summed up the way I felt about Hearn in October 2022. While Twitter was aflame with furious speculation that the fight was definitely on, I felt something harden inside me. Hearn had dragged boxing into unforgiveable terrain where doping and deceit, greed and hypocrisy prevailed. I had never felt angrier or more depressed about boxing.

At 10.02 a.m., Fred Mellor messaged again. 'Gone back to 3 p.m.,' he said of the press conference.

The news was soon all over Twitter with speculation that the additional two hours suggested a delay to help the lawyers find a way to ensure the bout proceeded. British boxing seemed close to slithering over the brink into lawlessness.

The British Boxing Board of Control had known about the clomifene test result for weeks and yet they had only prohibited the contest on the Wednesday of fight week. They also avoided all requests for further comment, despite the tawdry saga having opened up fresh questions relating to governance and regulation.

Arriving at the hotel for the press conference, I entered a sea of chaos. Undercard fighters, trainers, YouTubers and reporters were crammed into the lobby. The consensus was that the promotion would still happen and I was asked by numerous media outlets to go on camera to share my views of the fiasco. I declined them all. I'd had my fill of boxing.

Around 3.30 p.m., there was a shift. Someone had seen Benn leave the hotel with his bags and a stony expression. Talk escalated. The quiet suggestions that 'it could be off' grew in volume. By four o'clock, we had unofficial certainty. Benn vs Eubank Jr had, finally, been cancelled.

We waited another forty-five minutes before we were herded into a press conference room on the first floor. A media liaison man walked out and said Eddie Hearn and Kalle Sauerland would join us soon – but they would take no questions.

I actually shouted 'What?' in the muffled room. While I am used to asking questions, it is not my normal style to yell. But my disdain could not be contained.

Just after 5 p.m., Hearn and Sauerland appeared on a small stage. 'I was very tempted to slip out of the back door for a beer,' Hearn said in an attempted quip before making his statement.

'It's been a very difficult day, twenty-four hours, forty-eight hours. We were really looking forward to an event that had captured the imagination of the British public, a fight that had so much history ... But obviously we wanted to come here today and formally announce that Chris Eubank Jr against Conor Benn has officially been postponed.

'I want to make it clear that Conor Benn is not suspended by the British Boxing Board of Control and we do feel he hasn't been given due process, like many others in this situation before him. I also want to clear up so many different reports from journalists and outlets that we've seen today about us being in the High Court this afternoon, or considering other commissions. This is not true. We took time with Wasserman Boxing and we made a decision that we felt was in the best interests of the parties involved. This is a sport that is very, very dear to us, a sport that we have been around our entire lives and whilst we were desperate for this fight to take place for the fans, for the undercard fighters, we also made a decision that we felt we had to – especially considering the interests of the sport and the British public as well.'

Hearn turned to Sauerland to allow him to talk as Eubank Jr's promoter. 'Chris is hugely, hugely disappointed,' Sauerland said. 'He was ready. He was on weight and he was very much looking forward to this weekend. We now look at rescheduling it.'

Hearn stepped back in. 'For various reasons, we won't be taking questions today,' he reiterated.

That refusal, if nothing else, implied an awareness that the list of pressing queries was long and troubling. As the press conference emptied, I fired up my laptop and wrote with cold anger.

I wrote about the irreparable damage that would have been done to both families, and boxing itself, if either Benn or Eubank Jr suffered a brain injury in the ring. All the other previous calamities of boxing had been explained away as unfortunate tragedies. This was different. This was malicious. Questions of doping and damage in boxing could no longer be separated. This was how low we had sunk.

All the talk of the fight being built on the noble legacy of the two bouts between Benn Sr and Eubank Sr in the 1990s had been tarnished forever. The legacy of the week was more than embarrassment and humiliation. It reeked of greed and stupidity, incompetence and danger.

I wrote of the good and great fighters who work between the perilous ropes. They were the victims of a debased business in which the ghosts of the past were so hard to shake.

The room was almost empty when I hit 'Send'. I knew my words would not change boxing, but I felt calmer having written them.

Five days later, on 11 October, reports emerged that Benn was being investigated over claims he had failed another drugs test for clomifene. This one had been taken before the positive second test which had caused the cancellation of the fight. 'A few of us have known about this earlier test for some time,' said Frank Warren. 'This makes it even more of a scandal, more damaging to our sport than everyone thought.'

It emerged that Hearn and Benn had known about both test results for more than a month. They had spent weeks misleading the public, as well as Chris Eubank Jr, by only mentioning the second positive result. In trying to bury the first test, they deepened the case against them. The scandal rocked British boxing and confirmed that the sport's problems with performance-enhancing drugs and their regulation were insidious and entrenched.

On 26 October, three weeks after the clomifene story broke, Hearn said at a press conference: 'You become cold and emotionless in this business ... It's the worst business in the world and it takes away all emotion ... You go through fucking horrendous situations. All the stick I've had probably would have broken me four years ago. But you become immune.'

A day later, Benn conceded publicly that he had tested positive twice for clomifene. 'Trace amounts were found,' he said. 'The only thing I can think of is contamination.'

When an athlete is caught with dope in their system, the amount does not matter. The drug has been found. They then, almost always, protest their innocence with righteous fury. That amorphous word, 'contamination', is wheeled out often as an excuse.

But Benn had not failed one drug test. He had failed two tests taken weeks apart from each other.

15

The War Ground

Isaac Chamberlain's car was as cluttered as his mind. We sat in the front seats outside the Repton Boxing Club in Bethnal Green. Bags of clothes and stray shoes, empty energy drink bottles and sandwich wrappings, toys and sweet packets littered the old Range Rover. Isaac apologised for the mess, but he was tussling with problems far more troubling than an untidy car on the Friday afternoon of 18 November 2022.

It was the first time we had met since I'd watched him being taken to hospital in an ambulance after he fought Chris Billam-Smith. In the intervening months, he had been through surgery on his fractured eye socket and the psychological pain of defeat. His personal life had become chaotic because he and his partner Zalia had broken up in the aftermath of the fight.

'I know that it would have worked between us, 100 per cent, if I had a normal nine-to-five job where I'm not risking my life,' Isaac said. 'Imagine if I had been taken to hospital after the fight with a bleed on the brain, rather than just a busted eye, and then, boom, I end up not being able to talk properly or I'm in a coma and then dead. We know this can happen, but of course [Zalia] does not understand the sacrifice I am willing to make. You can't blame her, but I am not willing to settle for a mediocre career where I win some, lose some, get twenty grand here, thirty grand there and don't compete at world title level. I have to push myself to the limits and become super-obsessed by myself and boxing. People think it's unhealthy, and they're probably right, but I know what's best for me as a fighter.'

Isaac had moved away from Zalia and their son, Zion, even though he was still besotted with his little boy, and commuted to and from Faversham in Kent. It took him ninety minutes to drive to his more usual gym in Brixton on a good day, and the same time or more to get back. 'My petrol bills are ridiculous,' he said, and so he had just found a tiny studio flat in Putney which he would start renting in a few weeks.

'It's like a prison, bro,' he said, as he showed me images of the stark accommodation on his phone. 'Remember when I was on my own in Miami back in 2019? That's how it is going to be again. I will be alone and I will train and eat and sleep and train some more. I've never felt more dangerous than I did when I lived that lonely life in Miami. I want that feeling again.'

He and Zalia might have been arguing but, Isaac stressed, 'she knows I'm a great dad. I still see Zion almost every day and I will always be there for him. I know what it's like not to have a father, so we agreed I can see him all the time. I'm ready to sacrifice everything for Zion.'

I knew how much Isaac loved his son, but I felt uneasy hearing the extreme risks he was willing to endure. 'Bro,' he said quietly, 'this will sound crazy, but I am ready to sacrifice a little bit of my mind to be successful.'

His words settled in the gloom of late afternoon. Was he talking about his brain? 'Just a little bit of it,' Isaac said, laughing bleakly. 'Not fucking all of it. I don't want to end up loopy and helpless. I just need to make sure Zion is good, that he goes to a nice private school, and that he has all the opportunities I never had as a kid. If that means me living in a fucking shit studio prison, and risking the worst kind of damage in the ring, I'm willing to do that. I know it's crazy, but to make it as a world champion, you have to be ready to make the ultimate sacrifice.'

I was old enough to be Isaac's father and it seemed important to soften his outlook. I understood the addiction of boxing because it still held me in its grip. Boxing also had many redeeming features. The genuine hope and transformation it offered its fighters was tangible. I could not forget Isaac describing himself as 'a little peanut-head boy from Brixton who was never meant to be anything'. Without a stable family, and with poverty and low expectations undermining his chances of being the chemical engineer he believed he might have become in a different life, Isaac had found real purpose as a boxer. He became more confident and disciplined, and strived to fulfil challenging ambitions. So much was laudable about his boxing life – until he spoke about his willingness to absorb brain damage to reach his goals.

I attempted to voice these thoughts and I also spoke to Isaac about how much he meant to so many people, including me, and how Zion needed him as a happy and healthy dad rather than a damaged world champion. The boxer nodded and tried to smile. But his mood did not lift.

Isaac explained that he had fought with such anger in the opening rounds against Billam-Smith because he had been racially abused by spectators on his ring walk. He had not boxed the way they had planned and got caught up in a dogfight. 'But I can't remember much about what happened afterwards,' he said, 'except me telling them in hospital that I had the worst headache. So they gave me some kind of painkiller and three minutes later I was vomiting. They had to mop the whole room as I was sick so much.'

Were the doctors concerned about his concussion? 'I was so out of it I don't remember now. It's all so blurry. I was in hospital for a couple of days and then, when they let me go home, they said I would have to come back for eye surgery in a couple of weeks. Zalia, me and Zion were meant to go on holiday to the Dominican

Republic, but that got cancelled because I couldn't travel for eight weeks.'

Isaac brushed aside my sympathy. 'I was OK about it, bro. All I could think of was about me coming back. My mind was so messed up that I even thought if the surgery didn't go well, I would just get a dodgy doctor to pass me [fit] anyway. I didn't give a fuck then. I just thought: *I'm going to make this shit happen no matter what. Fuck the health, man.*'

He saw my reaction and then, suddenly, the old Isaac came back. 'I'm sorry, boss,' he said. 'I know I've been talking crazy stuff here.'

Isaac paused, shook his head and eventually continued. 'But I needed to get these thoughts out of my head. I know I did well in parts of that fight and people are saying how they have big respect for my courage and skill. They say, "You did amazing. It was one of the fights of the year." But I say, "Whatever. I still lost." So I got to start again.'

I felt better when Isaac said he would listen to his eye surgeons and avoid sparring until six months had passed. 'No sparring or blows to the head until the new year,' he said with a contrite smile. 'But the important thing is that all the docs say the eye will be good next year. It still really hurts sometimes and then, weirdly, I have parts of my face where I can't feel anything.'

His index finger traced a line from the corner of his left eye to a spot just below his nose. 'There's a nerve here that is damaged,' he said. 'I can't feel a thing when I touch it. The surgeons said the operation was successful, but that certain parts will never feel the same again. That's what boxing does. But I hear what you say, bro, and I want to avoid damage.

'That's why my whole life has to be like a training camp. I have to work harder than ever before. I have to eat right all the time. I can't be a normal person that just lets go. If you want to be a champion, you don't have that luxury of being normal. Sometimes people might be like, "Oh, it's not healthy or it's too extreme." But I know what I need to do right now.'

He stretched out his bunched hand. We bumped fists, but I did so a little reluctantly, as I told Isaac what Jean Day had always said to his brother before a fight: 'Protect the jewel.'

'I know,' Isaac said softly. 'But I promise to take care. Trust me.'

My interest in, and concern for, Isaac Chamberlain and Regis Prograis took precedence over their more famous contemporaries. I had shared meaningful moments with Canelo Álvarez, Anthony Joshua, Oleksandr Usyk and Tyson Fury, but the fame and wealth of that quartet meant I would never become close to them. It seemed more important than ever that I concentrated on those fighters I knew best and liked most of all.

In a similar way to Isaac, Regis had made mistakes and been let down. Defeat to Josh Taylor had knocked him off-kilter and he had lurched through a string of promoters: Lou DiBella, Triller, Probellum and MarvNation. They became more obscure as he moved down the list, but Regis was smart enough to make sure that the last three paid him a significant amount of money for each one-off bout they promoted. Probellum was the most problematic because it had a previous alleged connection to Daniel Kinahan. But Regis's sole bout with that company had been in Dubai in March 2022 when he stopped Tyrone McKenna in six rounds. Probellum was shut down soon afterwards in the wake of the FBI's pursuit of Kinahan. Regis had made a lucky escape.

MarvNation, the least known of them all, had won the $2.4m purse bid to stage his next fight for the vacant WBC world junior-welterweight title against Jose Zepeda in Carson, just outside Los Angeles, in November. The amount of money MarvNation would pay seemed far more than the fight could reasonably be expected to generate. But Regis was guaranteed $1,008,000, with an additional $240,000 that would be paid as a bonus to the winner. It showed again that, even if he was not being backed by an established promotional powerhouse who could build his profile methodically, Regis had the smarts to make lots of money out of boxing. These were the kind of purses and world title bouts which Isaac could only dream of while aiming for British and European belts at a contrasting stage of his career. Yet Regis had been in the wilderness, without a world title shot, for four years. I knew how much he wanted, and needed, it now. 'I can't wait for this fight and to become a world champion,' he said at the opening press conference. 'Zepeda's a real good fighter and I know what he brings. My last three fights were against OK opposition, but this will show that I'm elite. He's a killer, but I'm going to do my thing on November 26 and become a two-time world champion.'

Zepeda's record was 36–2, compared to Prograis's 27–1, and his pair of defeats had both come in world title bouts. This looked like his last opportunity to finally become a world champion and he sounded just as ready and as respectful. 'This is number one versus number two, the top two fighters in the division,' Zepeda said. 'We don't get to see that very often nowadays in boxing and this shows it's going to be a great fight. Both of us have a lot of knockouts, true punching power. I'm ready for hell and that's why there's not much need for trash talk between us. We're thirty-three years old and in our prime. Whoever wins this title will have a life-changing experience.'

The Mexican-American also knew the significance of the contest to those who cared about the sport. 'On social media, I keep seeing hardcore boxing fans saying that this is the fight. We see other fights where there's lots of trash talk, and then they don't happen or it doesn't end up being anything special. But, with me and Prograis, everybody thinks that this is gonna be a can't-miss Fight of the Year.'

Two days after meeting Isaac, I flew to Los Angeles, hoping that Zepeda was right but that Prograis would be just too good for him. I tried to ignore my worry for Isaac and the bleak chaos of the business – but it was hard. The last half of 2022 had been a mess. Alongside the Conor Benn scandal, there was little good news in boxing. The best fight of the year – a planned world welterweight title unification bout between Terence Crawford and Errol Spence – had been scheduled for 19 November. But this contest between two of the top-five pound-for-pound fighters in the world in Crawford and Spence, who held all the welterweight titles between them, had broken down amid contractual squabbles months earlier.

Most of the boxing stories on the internet, beyond Eddie Hearn insisting Conor Benn would soon be back in the ring despite failing to clear his name of doping, were taken over by YouTubers such as Jake and Logan Paul, KSI and Tommy Fury, and gossip as to when they might fight each other. Alternatively, there were reports of who John Fury, Tyson's dad, was threatening to beat up or snippets about the 'Legends' exhibition bout that had just been held between two middle-aged former fighters in Ricky Hatton and Marco Antonio Barrera.

It was depressing to see the reminders that, on the first Saturday night of December, Fury would defend his world heavyweight title against Derek Chisora in front of a 60,000 crowd in London. It would be the third fight between them and, despite having lost the first two bouts comprehensively years before, Chisora was being wheeled out again. His health was at serious risk; Chisora was already a battered old journeyman.

I was in a pretty dismal mood as, after a long flight from London, I stood in line for two hours at the Thrifty car rental office at LAX. I finally staggered into a cheap little blue car and drove through the dark to Carson. Taking exit 34 on I-405, I found my way to the Rodeway Inn, a low-slung motel which stood alongside a massage parlour, a tattoo joint, a liquor store and a Baptist church. Shutting the door to room 102, on the corner of the ground floor with a view of the car park outside, I wondered if I was nearing the end of the boxing road.

'I'm a historian,' Regis Prograis told me in his swish suite at the Hyatt Regency in Los Angeles, four days before he fought Jose

Zepeda. 'I've read so many books about great fighters and how their personal life was terrible. So I don't care how great I could be if it means my personal life is bad. I'd rather be happy than a miserable boxing legend.'

It was a relief to hear Regis talking good sense and I asked him which former fighter he identified with most. 'George Foreman had the same attitude as me,' Regis said of the once-frightening world heavyweight champion who, after he was shocked by Muhammad Ali nearly fifty years earlier, became a lovable and jovial figure who made an unlikely comeback to regain his title in middle age while operating a booming barbecue and grill business.

'I don't know George, but it seems he was always happy with who he was outside boxing,' Regis continued. 'He had a bunch of kids, made a lot of money and seemed so fulfilled. He is a legend but we think of him enjoying his life most of all.'

Regis was also an invaluable witness to the current ills of the fight game. When I asked him about Benn's two positive test results, he spoke with bristling intent. 'It's terrible, bro. I remember Conor Benn fought on the undercard to me and Josh Taylor. He was nothing special and people said "He's just not that good." Then, all of a sudden, Benn is destroying guys. He knocked out Chris van Heerden bad and no one did that before. I know Chris. I sparred with him a lot in LA. Chris also fought Errol Spence and Jaron Ennis, real good fighters, and they didn't do to him what Benn did. That was a chilling knockout – same as when Benn destroyed Chris Algieri. Those were his last two fights before he got popped. And now he just wants to box as if those failed tests don't matter?'

Regis and his trainer Bobby Benton both spoke openly about doping. 'It's crazy that so many fighters are willing to do this,' Regis said. 'For me, it's unfathomable to cheat in boxing because you could kill somebody. Bobby's been around the sport for over twenty years and he said, "Listen, most fighters cheat." I just didn't want to believe it for so long. But after a while, you see things with your own eyes. This Benn stuff showed us that the system is broken.' It would be Thanksgiving in two days' time, but boxing's anti-doping authorities had already settled into a holiday mood. Regis confirmed that neither he nor Zepeda had been visited by the drug-testers since the fight was announced months earlier. 'It's four days before the fight and we still haven't been tested. Why not? What is the WBC doing? I told them: "Test". Still nothing. This boxing business is so dirty and corrupt that, if I didn't love the sport as much as I do, I would walk away.'

Regis echoed the thought that had run through my head on a loop ever since Benn and Eddie Hearn tried to sidestep the two failed tests as if they were of no consequence. Regis was different. 'I'm even scared to take certain protein shakes,' he said. 'Who knows exactly what goes in them. The last thing I want is to have anything illegal in my system. If I'm out and people offer me food, I turn it down. I can't risk anything going wrong and unknown stuff showing in my blood. But so many fighters are looking for an illegal advantage they can hide. It's heart-breaking to even say this, but cheating and doping is a big part of boxing now and no one in power cares enough to rip it out.'

If Regis beat Zepeda, he would be in a position to set up an eventual rematch with Taylor, alongside other lucrative and significant bouts against star names, including Devin Haney, Ryan Garcia and Gervonta Davis, that would suit his charisma and talent. Such hopeful match-making depended on victory that Saturday night, but Regis was full of conviction. 'I'm definitely at another level to Zepeda. I'm a much better all-round fighter and he's going to be feeling more pressure than me. He has said this is do-or-die because this is his third title shot and he's fighting in his hometown.

'Zepeda's a decent guy but at the press conference today he said "Whoever wins this fight will be a real champion." I would never say that word "whoever". I know I'll win.'

After he had spoken about the books he was reading and his efforts to master Portuguese, his wife Raquel's native language,

Regis reached for his phone to show me an assortment of videos in which he clamped shut the jaws of a large alligator before having a scaly cuddle.

There was disturbing footage of the alligator biting the boxer's foot in swampland alongside his home in Texas. 'That was three weeks ago,' Regis said wryly. 'But I had my big old boots on so I was fine. He's a pretty big gator – ten feet long. We needed three of us to pick him up so I could play with him.'

Kidding around with an alligator was one way to prepare for a world title fight, but Regis just shrugged. 'I reckon it's because I'm from the south. If I came from up north, I'd be playing with a bear. It's just me being adventurous and having fun. Soon after I beat Zepeda, I'll take my family to Rio where I can speak Portuguese and enjoy life.'

But, first, he believed he was on the brink of becoming a two-time world champion. 'I will feel the nerves once we reach the arena on Saturday night. It will feel real as I have my hands wrapped, start hitting the pads and get ready to walk to the ring.'

Regis had already agreed to me joining him in the locker room before and after the fight and, as he smiled, a strange expression crossed his face. It fused contentment with relish for a defining battle. 'That's when I feel real good,' he said softly.

Every morning in Carson, I drove a few miles down the road to a diner called Norms, which carried a promise that it was here 'Where Life Happens'. The day before Thanksgiving, at 7.30 a.m., Norms was not exactly buzzing. Apart from one Hispanic family, and a couple of solitary older African American men having breakfast at a long counter near the kitchen, the diner was empty. I was happy as, after flicking through the news on my phone, I ordered some fruit, French toast and coffee.

It was low-key and peaceful. A cheerful waitress kept topping up my coffee. 'Mmm-hmmm, honey, it's a real pleasure,' she said when I thanked her. Half an hour passed in blissful reverie and, just before I left, she leaned over to replace the original bill with a new one. 'I have corrected the check for you, honey,' she said with a dazzling smile. 'You get the discount.'

After thanking her again, I thought, *What a generous woman. What a nice little diner.*

I strolled over to the cashier and looked down at the bill. At table eight, there had been one guest, me, and the server was Yessica. Below my order came the confirmation that I was being granted a 20 per cent senior discount. I wanted to say, 'Yessica, you're kind but, honey, this hurts.'

Yessica caught my eye with another smile, which she followed with a thumbs-up. I tried to show my youthful enthusiasm by grinning fixedly and offering her an exuberant two thumbs-up in appreciation of the 20 per cent cut. It had been another reminder to embrace such senior perks.

Charles Conwell was fighting on the undercard. He and the veteran Juan Carlos Abreu would meet in the ninth bout of a sprawling eleven-fight bill headlined by Prograis and Zepeda. Since the fateful night in October 2019, when his fists pummelled Patrick Day into a coma, Conwell had fought six times. He had won every bout and improved his record to 17–0. He was ranked number five by the WBC in the 154-pound division.

I didn't want to interview Conwell about his world title prospects as a super-welterweight. I wanted to talk to him about Pat Day. But I was asked to avoid that subject as much as possible and to be gentle. I also could not shake Jean Day's anger towards Conwell. Jean could not forgive the boxer for celebrating after he had knocked Pat down so savagely for the final time.

We sat down together in the hotel where all the fighters were based that week. I asked Conwell about his start in boxing in Cleveland. 'I was about eleven years old,' Conwell said. 'One summer me and my brothers were just bored and I saw how my dad loved the sport of boxing. He always watched boxing and he was entertained by it. Even before I actually started boxing, we kept a pair of gloves and me and my brothers would put them on, move the furniture and box in the living room. So there was always fighting in my household, but we really began when my dad took us to the gym. We started organised boxing and never stopped. My dad had heavy bags in the yard, heavy bags in the parking lot, heavy bags everywhere. We stuck to it and, you know, the hard work paid off.'

I mentioned I'd read that his father, Charles Sr, or Chuck, drove his boys to the graveyard in the early hours to run. Was that true? 'Almost,' Conwell said. 'He had us *run* to the graveyard and then we would run through it and back to our neighbourhood. And, like you say, it was real early. Four or five in the morning. I hated it when I was thirteen or fourteen, but it got better when a group of us, me and my friends, did it.'

Was his dad still a tough taskmaster? Conwell looked at the burly older man who sat close by, listening to our conversation. 'That's him over there,' the boxer said before his dad and I exchanged handshakes. 'He's still a tough critic, but he acknowledges my hard work. He knows if I keep following the yellow brick road, it'll lead to greatness.'

Yet he was still some way from being offered a shot at the WBC champion Jermell Charlo, who was a friend of Regis, and none of the other leading contenders seemed keen to fight him. 'They see me as high risk, low reward, so they try to avoid me,' Conwell said. 'But I will stay humble and quiet because I know my opportunity's gonna come.'

I could hear Jean in my head, pointing out the bitter truth that there would be no opportunity for him or his family to ever see Pat again. And so I asked Conwell about the day he heard that Pat had died. 'I cried,' he said, his face clouding. 'And I cried when I wrote that letter to him [which Conwell posted on social media], so it was real emotional. But I felt in my heart I had to let out all the pain and sadness. It was the hardest time of my life, going through something that tragic. Most people don't understand the toll it takes on you.'

I knew Jean would be disappointed, but I believed Conwell. His face was still wreathed in anguish, three years on, and I suspected he would never be the same again as either a fighter or a man. But I did not tell him how Jean and his family felt, and how they could not 'move on', even as Conwell explained that he had found ways to do so in his own life.

The boxer, who was not a natural communicator, explained that talking about the tragedy had helped overcome his depression. 'It was hard but I worked my way through that by expressing myself to my team and to my loved ones. It gets easier with time. I know it's not a normal thing and I tell myself [the tragedy] was probably a one-off in my career.'

Conwell looked up. He found it hard to say the right words as a boxer who did not want to sound callous or dismissive of death. It had not been his intention to damage Patrick Day and so I just asked one more question about his decision to wear Pat's name on his trunks and gown on his return to the ring. 'I wanted to do that, 100 per cent, because I'm never going to forget him. That's another reason pushing me so hard to become a world champion because I know that's what he wanted for himself. I think he would under-stand me wanting to do it.'

Dignity Health Sports Park, Carson, Saturday 26 November 2022

The winter sun slips away towards darkness when Regis Prograis arrives at the arena at 5.45 p.m. and the home of the LA Galaxy soccer team turns into the War Ground – as their boxing arena is known. There had been so many great battles here that the War Ground nickname seems fitting.

Regis knows that the definitive contest at the venue had occurred in March 2013 when Tim Bradley beat Ruslan Provodnikov in a savage bout. It had been *The Ring*'s Fight of the Year. The War Ground had produced three other Fights of the Year. Regis is now just three hours away from stepping into the ring to fight Jose Zepeda for the WBC's world super-lightweight title. It will be a brutal test to suit the short but riveting history of this outdoor arena.

Drifting past the David Beckham statue and moving into the basement, Regis and his team wear gleaming white tracksuits with an image of the Rougarou emblazoned on the front and back. Regis leads the way down an echoing corridor. Bright television lights throw eerie shadows across the slate floor and blue walls.

Steel lockers line his dressing room where, at the far end, a giant poster features a face-off between him and Zepeda above the promotional tagline 'Battle of The Best'.

Regis speaks to me in a typically relaxed way while, in contrast, his oldest friend shudders with trepidation. Ross Williams, a writer who has been close to Prograis since they were six-year-old boys in New Orleans, grips my arm when I ask how he is feeling. We have also become firm friends. 'It's like I've got a midnight storm moving through my body,' Ross says with a rueful laugh. 'And I'm not even fighting.'

Regis and Bobby Benton, meanwhile, are the epitome of calm even if the first hour drags as we watch the undercard on a television in a corner of the locker room. The sound is turned off, but the noise of the crowd outside erupts whenever a fighter is hurt or knocked down. Another reminder of the looming battle arrives in the company of the referee, Ray Corona.

'You could end up in deep water, but I will not let you drown,' Corona tells Regis during his pre-fight instructions at 6.40 p.m. 'This is a very dangerous sport. If you're hurt, I got to see you fighting back, otherwise I'm stopping it.'

Our attention shifts back to the muted television screen where Charles Conwell is caught up in a fierce struggle against Juan Carlos Abreu. Conwell was cut in the first round after an accidental clash of heads and the tenacious Abreu keeps resisting.

On the morning of Regis's solitary loss to Josh Taylor, on 26 October 2019, they had buried Patrick Day. I can't stop thinking about Pat as we watch Conwell win a majority decision. After the first judge calls the fight a draw, Conwell takes the two other scorecards 96–94 and 98–92.

Ten minutes later, modern boxing's most famous cutman strolls into the room. Jacob 'Stitch' Duran, the seventy-year-old Mexican-American in Zepeda's corner, needs to ensure that Regis's hands are wrapped correctly. Regis smiles and listens as his own cutman, Aaron Navarro, and Duran swap stories of bloody gashes and magic potions. Some of their anecdotes stretch back to the 1950s and, after the ritual hand-wrapping has been completed, Duran wishes Regis good luck. 'See you out there, man,' Navarro says.

Navarro's shirt carries an image of his daughter's face and the words 'In Loving Memory of Birdie Navarro'. The cutman tells me how she had been murdered in Houston eighteen months before. Birdie was just twenty-two. 'She was a beautiful girl,' he says. It looks as if his face might crumple.

But Narvarro lightens the mood as he then tells me about the best Indian restaurant he has ever eaten at: Dishoom on St Martin's Lane in London. 'I eat there so often that they absolutely love me,' he cackles.

In the corridor, an almighty racket breaks out as a posse of thickly set men move at a fast lick, chanting '*Yoka! Yoka!*' Their battle cry is in honour of Yokasta Valle, the young Costa Rican woman walking to the ring. Valle, a world champion, is moving up in weight to try to win the two light-flyweight belts held by Evelin Nazarena Bermúdez from Argentina. Ten two-minute rounds between the female fighters are all that separate Regis from his own ring walk.

Raquel speaks softly in Portuguese to her family in Rio while her husband makes cries and grunts as he hits the pads. 'Total domination, baby, total domination,' his imposing strength-and-conditioning coach Evins Tobler yells.

At 8.08 p.m., Tobler says more gently, 'It's almost time.' Raquel disappears to her ringside seat as Regis sips water from a bottle.

At 8.17 p.m., the hush is replaced by the arrival of Jermell

Charlo. The WBC world middleweight champion, who had been gym-mates with Prograis when they were teenagers in Houston, strides in with pizazz. Charlo hugs Prograis. 'Take his heart, baby.'

The white boxing gloves are pulled on and Prograis hits the pads. He makes a soft hiss as each punch lands while Tobler roars, 'Make that motherfucker pay for all the work you put in.'

Ducking low under Benton's swinging arm, Prograis smacks his blurring fists into the pads. He is hitting hard.

At 8.27 p.m., Navarro reaches into the small tub of Vaseline strapped to his wrist and rubs the filmy jelly around Prograis's eyes and over his cheekbones.

The last fight before the main event enters its final round at 8.29 p.m. 'Break this fucker's will,' Tobler growls.

Five minutes later, after a desperately close women's fight, Valle's hand is raised in victory. The first call comes for Prograis and Zepeda. 'Ten minutes to ring walk.'

At 8.35 p.m., a television technician attaches a small microphone to Bobby Benton's top so that his instructions from the corner can be heard on the live broadcast. Bobby then helps Prograis into his white gown with gold trim. Prograis would prefer to walk bare-chested to the ring, like Mike Tyson, but the late November night carries a chill.

The mood is pensive before the applause in the locker room starts. Ross Williams is the first to bring his hands together and then we all join him. The clapping rolls through the room, steady and insistent, becoming more moving the longer we keep applauding the impassive fighter.

Boxing is a lonely business and I know the men around him are trying to help Prograis as the enormity of his task takes hold. 'Your night, champ,' Tobler hollers. 'Your night!'

A television runner opens the door. 'Three-and-a-half minutes,' he shouts.

The cornermen do one last check to make sure they have all their gear, from steel buckets to medical equipment. Prograis bangs his gloves together.

At 8.42 p.m., the TV man is back in the room, gesturing us to follow him. 'I'm walking them,' he barks to his producer. 'We're on our way.'

Ross and I are at the back of the pack as Prograis marches down the echoing tunnel. A black curtain is swept open so we can move inside the War Ground without pause. Booing cascades from the bleachers as the locals make their antipathy obvious. I step away to my seat at ringside.

I have sat close to many fights, but it still remains difficult not to be affected by the harsh sounds and sights of professional boxing at world-class level. It is very different to watching a fight on television where the screen sanitises and even deadens the brutality. But it is also a privilege to see the astonishing skill and courage that define men such as Zepeda and Prograis.

The bell sounds for round one. It takes eighty seconds for the first meaningful punch to land and Zepeda's crisp right hand makes the crowd roar. Prograis takes it well and marches forward, snaking with concentration, as Zepeda steps back. Boxing as a southpaw, like Zepeda, Prograis settles behind his authoritative jab and lands a couple of hard lefts. He ducks under most, if not all, of the swinging punches coming his way.

Chants of *'Ze-pe-da, Ze-pe-da!'* and *'Me-he-co, Me-he-co!'* reverberate, encouraging the hometown hero. While the round belongs to Prograis, the left side of his face looks puffy as Navarro goes to work in the corner. Prograis seems calm.

From the start of the third round, he finds his range. Prograis nails Zepeda with his clubbing jab and jolting combinations. The pattern is set with Prograis's aggression and intent often making Zepeda seem passive in comparison. But the LA fighter, bolstered by the crowd, comes back with real grit. Zepeda is cut in round four and Stitch Duran has to work his usual magic to staunch the blood. It still seeps onto Prograis's once-pristine white trunks, turning them a dirty shade of pink.

A better round for Zepeda in the fifth encourages his supporters, but Prograis is undeterred as the action swings back and forth.

Puffs of steam float from the fighters' mouths in the cool night air and Prograis makes sweat fly from Zepeda's head whenever he catches him with a stinging blow. He also goes to Zepeda's body and absorbs some hard punches himself as they dig in for a long night. Yet, the tougher and harder the bout becomes in the middle rounds, the more clearly Prograis seems at home.

By round nine, Zepeda is struggling as Prograis tags him repeatedly with his right jab and sweeping left. Then, in the tenth, after he is buzzed by Zepeda, Prograis lets his hands fly. Zepeda stands his ground and both men fight valiantly. A right cross makes Zepeda hold on. Prograis has seen enough. It's time to close the show.

Early in the eleventh, Prograis backs up Zepeda and then stuns him with a scything left hand. Zepeda is stopped in his tracks and Prograis comes at him like a runaway train. He unleashes one punch after another as Zepeda totters towards the ropes. Another chopping left drops Zepeda to the canvas as the referee waves it to a merciful end.

Prograis whirls away, his face lit by exultation. Three years of frustration and hurt give way to joy. He is a world champion again.

Zepeda is helped onto a small stool while the doctors examine him.

Prograis is fulsome in his praise during his post-fight interview. 'I wanna congratulate Jose Zepeda. That dude is tough, tough, tough. He gave me one of my hardest fights.'

Turning to Zepeda, who smiles sadly, Prograis says, 'Bro, I got so much respect for you. I congratulate you. Don't stop. I feel like you still gonna be a world champion. You're real good.'

Jermell Charlo, his fellow WBC champion, is waiting for Regis in his locker room. 'Texas is takin' over!' Charlo yells as he embraces a beaming Regis. 'I'm so proud of you, dawg!'

I catch their hug on my phone and, when Regis retweets the photograph, he simply writes 'Brothas'.

Amid the bedlam I follow Regis and the doctor to a private area near the toilets. As the doc stitches shut a cut on the right side of Regis's face, the new world champion stretches out his hand to me. 'Thanks for being here, bro,' he says with typical generosity. When I congratulate him, Regis nods. 'I worked so hard. Three years I've been working for this moment.'

His trunks, damp with sweat and streaked with blood, are draped over a metal chair as the stitching continues in the War Ground. The needle going in and out of his skin doesn't seem to hurt Regis. He talks to me about how boxing has opened up to him again. Lucrative and fascinating fights await as Regis dreams of becoming one of the leading pound-for-pound boxers in the world.

Charlo is still shouting as he and an official argue about whether he and the twenty-odd people who had followed him should be allowed in the locker room. Regis gives me a wry smile as if to say: 'Boxing!' The stitching continues, but he looks serene.

I step back inside the locker room to find Ross Williams. Regis's oldest friend laughs when I mention the midnight storm that had moved inside him a few hours earlier.

'The storm is gone,' Ross says as he hugs me in helpless delight. 'It's all sunshine now.'

16

Butterflies and Promoters

'I've wanted to leave boxing a lot of times but it always drags me back,' Tyson Fury said as he explained why he had ended his fleeting retirement. 'It's like a massive drug and I'm an addictive person. The rush is unbelievable and it gives me the biggest highs ever, but also the lowest lows. Boxing is more addictive than any drug.'

Fury's return to the ring was the least surprising news of the year. The only shock, for me, was that Fury's words applied to my own habit. I couldn't walk away yet.

'For four months I was retired and life was very dark and very dull,' The Gypsy King said, 'so I'm back boxing because of this ...'

The heavyweight pointed to his head to suggest that the disciplined routine of training helped control his depressive tendencies. 'I've been in love with boxing for such a long time, from being a little boy, and I am thirty-four now, probably at the end of my career in the next few years. It has been a love-hate relationship and toxic at times. But when it's good, it is very good.'

Fury could not stop the words tumbling from his mouth. 'I don't think I can live a normal life. I need medical help to do that and if there is somebody out there who could help me, I'd love them to get in touch. I won't be able to leave this game and have a normal life unless I'm brain-trained to do that. I will just keep fighting.'

Fury had fought eight times since his first retirement ended in 2018. 'I'm like an old banger Ford Escort with 250,000 miles on the clock. Every part of me is battered to pieces – joints, elbows, knee, back. I've done some severe mileage.'

His next opponent was in far more serious danger. Derek Chisora was thirty-eight years old and had lost twelve of his forty-five professional contests. A year earlier, in December 2021, Chisora had suffered another beating against Joseph Parker. Frank Warren, Fury's promoter, spoke the blunt truth. 'Chisora should retire, end of story. The only way Tyson Fury fights Chisora again is if we were struggling for an opponent or if Tyson insisted on it. Chisora shouldn't be allowed anywhere near the ring, let alone in there with Tyson.'

On 3 December 2022, in a Warren-promoted show, Fury's insistence on facing his friend resulted in a predictable mismatch. I watched on television, rather than from ringside, and an outclassed Chisora was finally rescued in the tenth round when the referee, Victor Loughlin, brought the gruesome beating to a merciful end.

Fury kissed Chisora and led the crowd in singing his name. But the loser's right eye was sealed shut and he bled from the mouth. The crowd, some of whom booed shamefully when the fight ended, seemed to have little thought of the damage done to Chisora's brain.

Oleksandr Usyk, who held the IBF, WBA and WBO belts, was ringside and he and Fury had exchanged barbs during the fight itself – another example of how easy it had been for the champion to beat up Chisora.

They met in the ring afterwards and, while Usyk cut a picture of steely restraint, Fury insulted a man who had served in the Ukrainian army that year.

'Usyk, you are next, you little bitch,' Fury roared. 'You're next, rabbit! Prick. Fifteen stone little midget bodybuilder. I'm going to write you off.'

Usyk's silence spoke volumes. He only moved when, in an amusing moment, his phone rang and he answered it while still staring impassively at the man shouting in his face. Fury kept ranting. 'You ugly little man. Let's get it on, bitch. I'll end you, li'l sucker.'

I liked Usyk more than ever as he put his phone away and kept his gaze locked on the absurd figure of Fury. War, after all, is much more serious than boxing.

On Thursday 26 January 2023, at 12.30 p.m. in Ukraine, Oleksandr Usyk's face appeared on my laptop screen. He looked lean and fit as he said 'Hello, Mr Don' and asked how I was doing. I knew he was hard at work in his training camp as he prepared for his planned unification bout with Fury.

Our interpreter was based in Kyiv, which had been hit by yet more Russian shells a few hours earlier. Usyk tugged thoughtfully at his close-cropped beard while he listened to his fellow Ukrainian translate my own greeting and concern for his family.

'The walls were shaking and the dogs were hiding,' Usyk said in Ukrainian of the heavy shelling. 'I am outside Kyiv, but my wife and kids felt the attack this morning. But, thank God, everything is fine with the family.'

Usyk carried the gravity of a country under siege. He leaned forward, his head almost touching the screen, when I said it must be hard being away from his family while Kyiv was bombarded again. 'It's not that difficult,' Usyk said with a shrug. 'The anxiety starts but people are prepared. They're all thinking, *These dogs launched bombs or started shooting at us again.* They are used to it, so our people live with it. They go down into the bomb shelters.'

The war had been relentless for eleven months, with no end in sight, and Usyk admitted he could never quite escape the devastation of the Russian invasion. Instead of slipping into routine boxing chat about Fury, I just listened as Usyk told me how the war meant he would never see his friend Oleksiy Dzhunkivskyy again. 'Boxing brought me and Oleksiy together,' he said. 'He was a few years older than me and the first time I saw him was in Odesa. At the Ukraine championships in 2006. I was nineteen and became national champion for the first time. He was a silver medallist as a lightweight. We started talking and he showed great kindness and support. He believed in me and from that moment we always kept in touch.'

He was not a wizard of a fighter, but Dzhunkivskyy became a trainer. 'Oleksiy was very brave and bold,' Usyk said. 'He loved kids and his boxers had good results. He even trained European champions. When the Russians came, he did not give up.'

Dzhunkivskyy had set up a gym in the basement of an apartment block in Irpin. The gym resounded to the sounds of sparring and heavy bags being hit as intrigued boys and girls watched through the open doors. It was only in the last week of February 2022 that the gym fell silent. Reluctantly, Dzhunkivskyy stopped training once the first bombs fell on Irpin.

Even when an invasion by Putin's ground forces became inevitable, he resolved to protect his beloved gym from Russian soldiers.

Usyk's face darkened. 'Oleksiy was not tall, but he had the heart of a lion as he defended his gym. They killed him right in front of the building or inside the gym. I can't say for sure. All I know is that he fought hard to save the gym and they took his life.'

Usyk had begun helping the new Ukrainian government initiative, United24, to gain international support for the war effort. President Zelenskiy made the announcement. 'It is important to keep Ukraine in the focus of the world's attention. Oleksandr is now very popular both in the USA and Europe. His popularity already helps Ukraine.'

Usyk was also involved in a programme called Rebuild Ukraine, which aimed to restore eighteen shattered buildings in five cities close to Kyiv. Once the work was complete, 4,237 Ukrainians would return to their apartments. Usyk launched the programme by making a personal donation of $205,000, with a total of $333,000 needed to rebuild an apartment block in Irpin.

The Savenok family – Diana and Egor Savenok and their two daughters Sofia and Lili – were ordinary Ukrainians and their home would be among the first to be repaired. Usyk told me that he had been struck by a 'haunting coincidence'. It was hard to know what he would say as I waited for the next chunk of translation.

I could tell that the world heavyweight champion spoke with great intensity and emotion.

Once Usyk finished, he stared at me as I listened to the interpreter talking in English. 'I had eight different propositions to start the rebuild. I chose this one building randomly in Irpin. When we approached, I saw what was destroyed. A shell flew right into the building and tore off the roof and damaged five floors. I walked around and looked at everything. So much had been ruined, but I could tell that we could repair and restore the building with time and money.

'I was then deeply moved when we reached the basement where there was a boxing gym. There were no windows but I saw a sign saying "Gym Dzhunkivskyy". I turned to my friend, saying, "Brother, do you think this is the Hall of Oleksiy?" It's impossible to describe my emotions when I went inside.'

Usyk's understanding of English had improved greatly in recent years and, as soon as the translator said those last words, he began to resume talking in Ukrainian. 'It was where my good friend, Oleksiy Dzhunkivskyy, used to train children to box. Russian soldiers killed him.'

He paused to allow those sentences to be translated. And then Usyk found the right words. 'Once there had been children's laughter and the smell of boxing in that gym. All the passion of boxing. When I got there, it smells only of darkness and death. In that moment, I decided I want to return young athletes to this gym, and I want to return people to their homes.'

Usyk stressed that the coincidence of beginning the first restoration in a building which housed his friend's gym had 'redoubled my motivation. After this building is rebuilt, I choose another and one after that. I want to give people back the warmth of their homes before the invasion. I want to help in a human way because our people deserve it.'

War had made the bluster of boxing seem more ridiculous than ever. Usyk smiled when I said that I had admired his silent reaction to Fury when they met in the ring after the Chisora fight. Perhaps it even suggested that Usyk had won the first round of their psychological battle. 'I think I was able to get into his head a little bit. Mr Don, I have been watching Tyson Fury get into the heads of his opponents for many years. And then I got into his head.'

Did Fury act differently whenever he and Usyk were alone? 'When there are no cameras, he is completely different. He plays the bad guy for the cameras. In life, he is completely different. I think he likes movies about love and when he watches them, he cries a little. And that's not a bad thing. I can shed a tear too when I watch some sentimental movies.' He laughed before nodding when I said that the most difficult test of his career awaited. Fury's massive size advantage and ringcraft would not be easily overcome – even by a boxing master. 'I agree completely,' Usyk said.

Usyk wore a pristine white T-shirt. A beautiful black-and-white photograph of Muhammad Ali was printed on the front. The old promise of 'Float Like A Butterfly' rippled below the photo. Usyk grinned when he stood up to show me Ali on my Zoom screen.

'My friend gave me the shirt for my birthday last week,' he said. 'It's cool and I love it because, of course, I love Muhammad Ali.'

Usyk had just turned thirty-six and it seemed fitting that he and Ali shared the same birthday of 17 January. I thought Usyk was the most politically important world heavyweight champion since Ali. A Ukrainian flag, signed with messages for the champion by soldiers on the front line, hung behind him in a reminder that his training camp nestled on the edge of a war zone.

Usyk sounded as calm as he was certain of victory – against both Russia and Fury. He turned to look behind him. 'This flag was given to me by my friend and colleague when I was serving in the Ukraine border service. It is signed by the guys who are defending our country in Bakhmut. They gave me this flag and it is with me always. It gives me strength.'

Zelenskiy had spoken graphically of the besieged city of Bakhmut. 'Last year, 70,000 people lived there,' he said. 'Now only a few civilians are left. There is no place that is not covered with blood. There is no hour when the terrible roar of artillery does not sound. Still, Bakhmut stands.'

A fighter at his core, Usyk was forceful when I asked if the world was in danger of forgetting Ukraine. 'The world, it seems to me, is afraid of giving us the support we need. Ukraine is now a fence that holds back Russia and cannibals who want to seize half the world for themselves.'

How best could the world support Ukraine? 'Give us tanks,' Usyk said as he raised his fist. 'Give us arms and contemplate victory.'

Usyk and United24 arranged for me to speak to Diana Savenok in another video call the following day. Her home was about to be rebuilt thanks to the money raised by Usyk. I again needed a translator, but I could hear urgency and gratitude in her voice as she explained how much the boxer had helped her family. The thirty-four-year-old began by remembering the day the Russian invasion started.

'We were at home together and had not been awake for long when other family members called, letting me know war has come. When I saw the planes from my window, I realised it won't just be strikes against military facilities. The bombs will fall on civilians. We quickly packed and moved to the shelter. My husband hardly slept as he patrolled the area or tried to buy food. Most stores were closed and those that were open had kilometre-long queues.'

The Savenoks had to escape. Diana paused when I asked about the emotions tumbling though her as they fled to her parents' home far from Irpin on 4 March. 'We had no right to feel emotions. We knew we have to run as fast as we can. At the checkpoint, they let us go without checking documents. They just said "Faster, faster! Drive for your life." The kids were afraid but, in me, there was no fear. I just had a determination to drive to safety and survive.

'The next day our home was bombed. We escaped at the last

moment because, when we were evacuating, Russian troops entered Irpin. On March 5, our neighbours messaged me to say our building was on fire. A shell hit level 4 and our apartment was on level 5 – which was engulfed in flames.'

Her husband, Egor, had spent the last eleven months fighting in the war and Diana described how they all reacted when they heard that their home would be the first to be restored under the Usyk programme. 'The kids, my husband and I all cried from happiness. Oleksandr Usyk is our national pride. Just imagine what I felt when I found out that our family was under his patronage. I wouldn't say I'm a boxing fan, but we watch his every fight with family and friends. It's impossible to miss because this is a story of global Ukrainian success.'

Had she known Oleksiy Dzhunkivskyy? 'Our children knew him because of his boxing club in the basement. My girls are more creative. They didn't do boxing, but they always looked in the windows as they were very curious. They say Oleksiy was so kind. He never shouted at the kids, even when they were annoying and interfering with his training. There's terrible grief when wonderful people like him are taken away by this war.'

A few days later, two emails arrived from Ukraine. There were updates from Usyk and the Savenok family, who attached a photograph of a beautiful butterfly in their bombed apartment. The butterfly, with orange and black wings crested by white circles which looked like eyes, rested on the hand of Diana's youngest daughter. Against a pitch-black backdrop, the illuminated butterfly reminded me of Usyk's T-shirt of Ali, the world heavyweight champion who, amid great political adversity, could float like a butterfly and sting like a bee.

The words below the photograph were written in simple but moving English. 'The butterfly was in our apartment burned by Russian shells. We don't know how he ended up there. But we know that this is definitely a sign that life will win.'

*

I felt uplifted by Usyk. He was a world champion who transcended the modern staples of boxing and, instead of tedious trash-talking or cheating, Usyk undertook meaningful work during an unjust war. He was an immense force for good, while offering a reminder that boxing could still carry an inspirational social message.

The idea that Fury and Usyk might finally meet in a bout to establish the first undisputed world heavyweight champion of the 21st century was an additional bonus. My hopes for a rare burst of clarity, however, were kept in check.

Fury had stipulated that the fight needed to take place by 29 April, less than three months away. The days and weeks passed and the same old routine unfolded as promises of progress were undermined by opposing statements from Fury. He was either going to destroy Usyk – the 'gappy-toothed middleweight', the 'midget', the 'bum', the 'dosser' and the 'sausage' – or give up on their proposed fight entirely to resurrect talks with Anthony Joshua.

Usyk responded on his YouTube channel. 'I understand everything Fury says. I just don't pay attention. If I pay attention to anybody trying to offend me, I will feed my anger. Rage doesn't help when fighting. I'm motivated by the opportunity to fight this giant. Some people are not optimistic about my chances. But I will choose my way like a samurai.'

By mid-February, the once-likely destination of Saudi Arabia was no longer an option for the fight. The Saudis had apparently grown weary of the constant uncertainty and had grander plans to eventually try to sieze control of boxing. Wembley Stadium had become the only possible venue, but even the certainty of a 90,000 crowd would not compensate for the loss of Saudi money. But both camps insisted that they were ready to fight in London – until a fresh squabble broke out.

Alexander Krassyuk, Usyk's promoter, would not accept anything less than a 50/50 split. 'It is a fair deal when it comes to the undisputed unification,' he said, 'where one fighter [Usyk] has three belts and the other has one. If Tyson accepts, it means he's a real warrior and he wants to fight not just for money but for legacy in the biggest fight in heavyweight history.'

Fury made a counter claim. 'They want 50 per cent but, Usyk, you and your team are worth 30 per cent. If you don't want it, go fight Daniel Dubois for a few million dollars. If you want to make some real money, come fight The Gypsy King. I will also say, for every day from today that you mess around, I'm going to deduct one per cent until you take it. Tick-tock, tick-tock, pussies.'

Usyk addressed Fury directly on social media. 'Hey, greedy belly, I accept your offer. 70/30 split to fight you on April 29 at Wembley. But you will promise to donate to Ukraine immediately after the fight a million pounds. Every day of your delay, you will pay one per cent from your purse to Ukrainian people. Deal?'

The first undisputed world heavyweight title fight in more than twenty-three years teetered on the brink of possibility after Usyk agreed that drastic reduction. But Fury soon found another obstacle and, on Instagram, he refused to accept that a world champion's typical rematch clause should be allowed for Usyk. 'How about there is no fucking rematch clause for both of us? Let's up the ante completely. The winner takes the glory, the loser goes home with his dick in his hands.'

Usyk sounded frustrated in his reply. 'Greedy belly, rematch clause came from your side, not mine. Stop whining and ducking. Be a man and sign the contract or vacate the belt.'

His manager, Egis Klimas, stressed that the 70/30 split would only remain intact if the fight happened on 29 April. If they missed that date, Usyk would demand purse parity again.

On 22 March, the inevitable collapse was confirmed. 'The fight is off,' Krassyuk said in a radio interview. 'It went too far. There was a feeling that after Usyk accepted 70/30, Fury started to think that he could put a saddle around his neck and ride Usyk as much as he can. It's not right. Usyk accepted the 70/30 split as a courtesy. But there was a list of things Fury wanted in his favour which were absolutely unacceptable and completely disrespectful.'

Fury ripped into Usyk on social media. 'Always know, pussy, you were never man enough to tangle with The Gypsy King. You shithouse little coward.'

The fight game was yet another depressing mess.

After a four-month investigation into Eddie Hearn's contradictory responses to doping, I felt lost again. I was not an investigative reporter and picking holes in a promoter's reputation was not work which usually engaged or moved me. But it was hard to escape the scandal of Conor Benn.

On 15 October 2022, Benn had resorted to capital letters on Instagram: 'I HOPE THE APOLOGY IS AS LOUD AS THE DISRESPECT.' He was completely 'shocked and surprised' but, while he said his immediate priority was 'clearing my name because I am a clean athlete', Benn also spoke about rescheduling his fight against Chris Eubank Jr. Eleven days later, he confirmed the second positive result which he and Hearn had concealed until then.

Hearn was determined to help Benn return to the ring at the earliest opportunity. It seemed as if finding a way to resurrect the lucrative fight with Eubank Jr mattered far more than a proper investigation into the reasons for the undeniable presence of clomifene in Benn's body on 25 July and, again, on 1 September 2022.

Boxers I respected and liked spoke out. They understood the dangers of boxing better than anyone else. Fighters could be maimed or killed and so the presence of drugs not only cheapened the sport – it ruined boxing and obliterated lives. I could hear their anger.

Josh Warrington, then the IBF world featherweight champion, said: 'Obviously [Benn's] going to try and clear his name, but he's been caught with illegal substances in his body so, if you're guilty, you're guilty. I've spoken strongly against drug cheats for a long time. It's too fucking hard a sport, man. People die in the ring. It's barbaric, so it should be a lifetime ban.'

Chris Billam-Smith lamented the fact neither he nor Isaac Chamberlain had been tested before or after their gruelling fight.

'It was disgraceful. Boxing is already a life-threatening sport and if [doping] is as rife as people say, it's got to be more consistent than that.'

I'd also interviewed Eubank Jr in his ramshackle gym in Hove. 'Was I disillusioned?' Eubank said in January 2023, echoing my first question about Benn's failed drugs tests. 'No. Boxing is a ruthless, cut-throat game. If you're talking about the business aspect, much worse things have happened and will happen in the future. Any time money's involved, people are looking for an edge. So disillusion, no. Disappointment, yes. [Benn] messed up a lot of things.'

When did Eubank first hear about Benn's failed drug test? 'Ten to twelve days before the fight. People were shocked that I agreed to continue but, whether that was right or wrong, that's just who I am. It didn't change my mindset that I was going to win.'

Benn phoned him and, Eubank said, 'that was another reason why I didn't make a huge deal of it. He said: "I would never do anything like this. Trust me, this is bullshit."'

Eubank shook his head. 'The kid's a great fucking actor. He needs some type of Academy Award for the speech he gave me – but that was before we knew he'd already failed another test a few months before. Now I know everything he's saying is absolute bullshit. He's still trying to play the victim, but even when Eddie Hearn and his team bring "proof", quote unquote, that he's innocent, people are not going to buy it.'

Should Benn be banned from boxing? 'If you're setting an example to kids and the next generation. Then yes, absolutely. The selfish side of the coin, which is where I'm a fighter who wants to be in huge fights and get my hands on this kid for what he's done, doesn't want a ban.

'The fight is now twice as big. We would need a stadium with 60,000 instead of the O2. Does he deserve that kind of payday after being caught with illegal substances? Probably not. But it doesn't mean I'm giving up that payday. And, now, it's personal. I actually don't like this kid. He's done wrong by me. He lied to me.'

A more troubling question remained. I told Eubank about Regis Prograis's suggestion that between 60 and 70 per cent of fighters might be doping. Was that estimate too bleak? 'I pray it is,' Eubank said. 'But, absolutely, it concerns me.'

I believed in substantial punishment for boxers found guilty of cheating, including life bans, but it was obvious that the ineffectual anti-doping procedure in Britain would not implement such measures in the face of Benn's phalanx of hostile lawyers. Contrition and humility from Benn and Hearn would also have helped smooth the way for a more lenient sentence. But the boxer and promoter followed a different road – and it seemed as if money and ego drove Hearn.

After every press conference or weigh-in, he stood in the centre of a shot, looking straight at the banks of cameras as two fighters faced each other. It was his show so he could do whatever he liked, but did we have to see Hearn all the time when he never took a punch?

Some promoters did the same, but none sought attention with the voracious need of Hearn. At their own press conferences, other promoters chose a hired gun to ask questions of the fighters – or even allowed old-fashioned queries from the press. But at a Hearn press conference, he asked every question and he was in every photograph or television moment. I had interviewed Hearn many times and we had even done a joint interview with his father. Barry Hearn had been a successful boxing promoter in the 1990s, and had done outstanding work in snooker and darts. It had been difficult for Eddie to escape the burden of being the son of a famous father. His dad also pushed him hard and, during that shared interview in 2017, they told me how they had fought each other in the boxing ring.

'When I was growing up, I disliked people from better areas because I had a chip on my shoulder,' Barry said, before laughing. 'I might still have it. But I didn't want my son to grow up like one of those rich kids. I thought the easiest way was to have a little set-to.'

Eddie chipped in to tell me that their fight 'was due to happen when I was eighteen. But it happened at sixteen because I got so big. He came out, his teeth gritted. He was really going for it.'

'I wanted to find out what you were like,' Barry said to Eddie before turning back to me. 'I hit him with a proper shot. It was great because he came back and dropped me twice in the second round. It was the best defeat I ever had. That competitiveness is how we run our business.'

Shrugging off his public-school education, Eddie swapped his boxing gloves for selling double-glazing on the phone. 'I worked for Weatherseal in Romford,' he told me. 'I'd go there after college at night and do telesales. It's the worst job in the world, but the best training for sales. For every rejection – from "I've just lost my husband" to "I've just done my double-glazing" – we always had a reason to make an appointment. I was on £3 an hour, but for every appointment, you got a £5 bonus and your money went up by £1 an hour. But then I did work experience for dad at seventeen. I was selling sponsorship in fight magazines, which was a doddle compared to phoning some geezer about double-glazing who says "Fuck off".'

Hearn Jr brought the tenacity of the double-glazing salesman to his media hustle and I had written positively about his promotional talents for years. But his hypocrisy and greed gnawed away at me and I knew I had to write in detail about him and Benn. In early December 2022, I began the laborious task of addressing the inconsistencies in five doping cases involving Hearn over the previous four years.

The first two showed Hearn in a positive light. I already knew that, in 2018, when Billy Joe Saunders prepared to fight again after his positive test result for clenbuterol that year, Hearn had made that unforgettable statement: 'It's outrageous . . . He failed a VADA test. You can't ignore it. Otherwise the sport's a mockery.'

Six months later, Hearn also claimed to be on the side of clean sport when Jarrell Miller's VADA test returned a positive result for GW1516, a peptide with similar effects to anabolic steroids. Miller had also tested positive for human growth hormone and EPO.

Hearn was in the midst of promoting Anthony Joshua's world title defence against Miller, but once the American was denied a licence by the New York State Athletic Commission, he was emphatic. 'This leaves no doubt. Miller is out. AJ's new opponent for June 1 will be announced next week. Clean fighters only need apply.'

In February 2020, Hearn rejected an approach from Miller. 'He was desperate to sign with us. I couldn't do it. I know I can be hypocritical at times, but this guy failed three drug tests.'

But Hearn's response to positive drug test results became murky when his own fighters were involved in controversy. I dug deeper and learned more.

On 17 July 2019, Dillian Whyte, another Hearn heavyweight, had tested positive for Dianabol before he fought Oscar Rivas three days later. UKAD, the UK anti-doping agency, officially informed Whyte's team, which included Hearn, and the British Boxing Board of Control. But they didn't share news of the positive test with Rivas or his management. The anomalies of the British approach to anti-doping mean that a fighter who fails a test is not perceived to be in initial breach of any performance-enhancing drug protocol. Following the testing of a B sample, the boxer has a right of appeal which can drag on for a year. So the BBBoC decided that, while Whyte had failed a drug test, he could fight Rivas. Out of concern for Whyte's 'privacy', it would not share word of the positive test result with the public or Rivas.

Hearn also did not tell Rivas or his promoter, Yvon Michel, about the test. Instead, he hinted that Whyte might be struggling with an injury and that the fight could be postponed. Then, having invited Michel to breakfast on the morning of the fight, Hearn told him that Whyte's unspecified injury had cleared and the fight was on. That night Rivas lost the decision to Whyte.

Four days later, Thomas Hauser, the esteemed American journalist, broke the news of Whyte's positive result – to the shock of Michel and Rivas. A December 2019 statement from the British Boxing Board eventually declared that 'UKAD has accepted the explanation provided by Mr Whyte ... the charge has been withdrawn.' Whyte's explanation has never been made public.

But Leon Margules, Michel's lawyer, told me he was astonished the fight went ahead. 'The really shocking thing was here's Eddie Hearn, one of the biggest promoters in the world, willing to take the risk – because if something happened to Rivas the liability would be immense. If there ever was a case where a fighter tested positive and was allowed to fight, and the other boxer got severely damaged, it's probably a criminal act.

'I'm a promoter and a lawyer. A fighter died on me. [In January 2000] Teddy Reid fought Emiliano Valdez. It was brutal – and both fighters were severely damaged. I remember going to hospital with Valdez. He was in surgery when I saw Teddy. He had broken ribs, a broken jaw, his head was swelled up and he was the winner. Valdez was in a coma for a couple of years before he passed.'

The dangers of boxing should mean that any positive drugs test ensures the immediate cancellation of a fight. Margules agreed, but he knew how the business worked. 'Eddie had a problem no matter what he did. How can he stop the contest if saying something about the drug issue subjected him to liability? But how could he allow the contest which would have subjected him to potential liability? I would have said "Sue me, go fuck yourself. I'm not allowing this fight."'

Margules did not like Hearn. 'Eddie is one of the most arrogant human beings I've ever met. I'm sixty-nine and been in the business over thirty years and I've never met a guy who more people at the highest levels dislike.'

Hearn was soon caught up in another doping saga, also in late 2019.

Victor Conte, who had seen, heard and done so much in the dirty world of doping, was briefly involved in this case. In 2004, Conte had admitted to distributing tetrahydrogestrinone [THG], known as The Clear, and other prohibited substances to high-profile athletes including Marion Jones, Tim Montgomery and

Dwain Chambers. Conte told ABC Television that 'the whole history of the [Olympic] Games is full of corruption, cover-up [and] performance-enhancing drug use'. In this jungle of deceit, he helped his clients cheat.

Conte was also accused of supplying Barry Bonds, the renowned baseball player, with steroids. He denied this, but the scandal became one of the most notorious cases in American sporting history. In October 2005, Conte was jailed for four months on a separate charge.

He had since become one of the most informed and passionate advocates against the use of illegal performance-enhancing drugs in sport. Anti-doping entities around the world relied regularly on Conte's expertise and he had also advised leading boxers including Andre Ward, Nonito Donaire, Mikey Garcia, Devin Haney, Danny Jacobs and Joshua Buatsi.

Conte told me his involvement in boxing convinced him it was the most corrupt of all sports.

On 9 November 2019, he was surprised when Hearn approached him in Los Angeles. Hearn was promoting a scrap that night between KSI and Logan Paul, a couple of boisterous YouTubers, and traditional boxing fans were outraged that seasoned professional fighters had been consigned to an undercard headlined by two novices.

Hearn, according to Conte, had something else on his mind. One of his fighters, Danny Jacobs, was scheduled to box Julio César Chávez Jr in Las Vegas the following month. However, Chávez Jr had fallen foul of VADA. At the outdoor weigh-in area near the Staples Center, Conte told me, Hearn approached him. They must have made a curious sight as the then forty-year-old promoter from Essex towered over the bespectacled Californian who would soon turn seventy.

Conte told me that 'the Chávez Jr case was the first indication that Eddie may be willing to do whatever it takes to make a fight happen, even if a boxer is not following agreed anti-doping rules.

Chávez had enrolled in VADA and agreed to be randomly tested. When the doping control officers went to the gym, Chávez refused to give blood and urine samples. This was a violation of the VADA agreement. Eddie said: "I want you to help me find another anti-doping group aside from VADA. We want to take the fight to Arizona and they're saying they will do it if we have a credible anti-doping programme." I said: "What Chávez did is the same as a positive drug test. I can't do that." It seemed crazy he was asking me, of all people. But, sure enough, they jumped commissions and went to Arizona and the fight carried on.'

More than three years later, I knew that Hearn was trying to find a new boxing commission which would grant Benn a licence to fight. A trusted source tipped me off that Hearn's company, Matchroom, had approached numerous commissions in the US about Benn.

Just after 9 a.m. on the morning of 1 March 2023, I emailed Hearn. He phoned within a minute of my message being sent and told me that they had 'spoken to a number of commissions about moving forward with licensing Conor, but have not made any official applications yet'.

I asked him to clarify whether he had spoken to Jeff Mullen, the executive director of the Nevada Commission. 'It's not my field,' he replied. 'I believe our legal team may have had a conversation with Nevada. I honestly don't know. But, ultimately, [Benn] will be licensed in the next couple of weeks.'

It was still a case of commission-jumping and trying to circumvent the British Boxing Board, which did not believe Benn could fight again while the UKAD investigation continued. 'Conor is not licensed with the British Boxing Board of Control,' Hearn countered. Yet Benn was a licensed BBBoC fighter when he tested positive for clomifene. 'Yeah,' Hearn said, 'and they never asked for any information [about clomifene] from us at all other than very simple stuff.'

I called Robert Smith at the Board of Control and he was sceptical that Benn would be licensed by a credible US commission. 'The biggest problem with boxing is that there is no world governing body,' he said. 'However, the big state commissions in Nevada, California, New Jersey and New York tend to do the same thing as us.'

On 23 March, I texted Hearn to ask if he 'could spare me some time on the phone today. I am writing an article about you, Conor Benn and a few other cases where positive test results have emerged.'

Hearn called me back within an hour. We were still on relatively good terms and we discussed the cases involving Billy Joe Saunders, Dillian Whyte, Julio César Chávez and Conor Benn.

I asked Hearn if he still endorsed his 2018 statement when he said ignoring a VADA test result would make a mockery of boxing. 'Yes, I think so,' he replied. 'In terms of the available testing agencies, I would say they are the best in the world.'

Did his contrasting approach with Benn make him feel like a hypocrite? 'No, I'm not. The VADA results haven't been ignored. The [British Boxing] Board have precedence and they do not acknowledge VADA testing.'

These quotes were just a small portion of a long and rambling answer which reminded me of the way Hearn had a prepared answer for every rejection he received as a double-glazing tele-salesman for Weatherseal in Essex.

Conte had told me that Hearn sometimes texted him for information about illegal drugs. 'It's happened a few times when Eddie says: "Tell me about Dianabol". A day or two later, bam, I realise one of Eddie's fighters [Dillian Whyte] tested positive for Dianabol.'

Hearn, on our call, repeated that confidentiality protocols meant he could not divulge this truth to Whyte's opponent, Rivas, or his promoter, Michel. So I asked a simple question about the Jacobs–Chávez Jr bout in 2019. Which drug testing agency did they use in Arizona?

Hearn hesitated. 'We didn't. I don't think we did. I think if you're referring to the test where he didn't –'

He paused again. I explained that I did not mean the VADA test that Chávez Jr had missed, causing him to be sanctioned by the Nevada State Commission. I was talking about Arizona and the testing agency he used in that state.

'No, I don't believe that was our testing for that fight,' Hearn said. He was blustering. 'I don't believe it. I believe that was a commission test or something. They turned up to test him and he left the gym or he wasn't in the gym, or – I don't know the full, because it wasn't reported to us, because we didn't – that wasn't part of our contracted testing programme.'

As if attempting to salvage a fragile double-glazing deal, Hearn tried to blur the fact that there had apparently been no drug testing for Chávez Jr and Jacobs in Arizona by waffling on about the first missed test. We would return to the subject of this controversial fight in person and so I switched to the Benn fiasco.

He had known that Benn tested positive twice the previous year. But for more than a month, Hearn had spoken only of one positive test. Why did he not share the full facts with Eubank Jr, his team and the public?

'Because we were bound by legal confidentiality,' Hearn said, gliding over the reality that he could have persuaded Benn to admit the truth. 'Because, ultimately, for Conor and also for us, [VADA] was not part of the testing under the contract. At the time of receiving the test [result], I spoke to Robert Smith who confirmed this is confidential, subject to the hearing. Then we left it in the hands of the Board and said: "What are you going to do? You don't acknowledge VADA testing, but obviously you've got this information." It was, "OK, we'll look into it and come back." When we received the second test [result], same thing. I don't throw the Board under a bus. They had a difficult decision.'

Hearn was right to reiterate that anti-doping procedures in British boxing were hopelessly flawed. But he also used these problems to deflect attention from the role he and Benn played at the heart of the story. 'How it took five weeks [for the second test result to be made public] is beyond me,' he continued. 'I wish it didn't, because that's the sole reason we're still talking about this now. And it's the sole reason we lost so much money on the event.'

Benn still hid his own defence from UKAD, the media and the public, despite stressing his anguish that his innocence was not widely believed. Benn's legal team had hired scientific experts to produce a 270-page document, exclusively for the WBC, which the boxer insisted cleared him of all wrongdoing. Yet if the report was scientifically credible, it was hard to fathom why it stayed shrouded in secrecy.

In February 2023, the WBC had said it would return Benn to its world rankings because of a 'reasonable explanation' that the positive results for clomifene had been caused by a 'highly elevated consumption of eggs'. Benn made an immediate protest. 'In my defence to the WBC, and the 270-page report provided to them, at no point did I indicate that I failed any VADA tests because of contaminated eggs ... The WBC statement did a disservice to my defence which was based upon a comprehensive scientific review of the testing procedures, which set out a number of reasons why we believed the results were completely unreliable, and proved beyond any reasonable doubt that I am innocent.'

One of my sources had seen the mysterious report. It alleged that the Salt Lake City laboratory, which recorded both positive results, was guilty of fraudulent behaviour, including the deliberate manipulation of test results. Yet the public statement from the WBC, in explaining why it was reinstating Benn to its rankings, dismissed this, concluding there was 'absolutely no fault attributable to the laboratory'.

I asked Hearn to help me understand it all. 'Yeah, Don,' he began before pausing. 'This is nothing to do with me, mate. You're asking stuff about Conor Benn's case and defence, which I don't need. I mean, honestly, [I've] not even read the document. Aware of, you know, [what Benn said to] Piers Morgan. I think one sample's tested [negative] three times and then tested [positive]. I'm not qualified to give you that view.'

We were coming to the end of our version of a Weatherseal cold call. Hearn and I knew that no bonus or double-glazing was due for either of us. I reminded him that a *Mail on Sunday* investigation suggested that, in the first ten months of 2022, 30 per cent of all fight cards promoted by Hearn involved at least one boxer who had failed a drugs test or been sanctioned for an anti-doping offence. That figure did not include fighters who used micro-dosing or other techniques to avoid detection of PEDs.

Hearn replied that he had 'no idea' if the *Mail* figure was accurate, but he conceded that there had been a card in Saudi, among the 'forty shows I do a year', when 'three or four fighters out of twelve had previously dealt with doping controversies. But he stressed that the *Mail*'s suggested percentage 'certainly did not' apply to 'my contracted fighters'.

The call ended and I mulled over the fact that, in October 2022, Hearn had said 'I could have put [the rescheduled] Benn–Eubank Jr on November 5 in Abu Dhabi, but that would have looked terrible. [Benn] has to go through a process to be cleared to fight. I'm telling you now I am not prepared to stage the fight until he has gone through some kind of hearing ... I believe he is innocent. But you have to take responsibility, whether you're unlucky or not, that something has been found in your system.'

Five months on, despite deep concerns about doping in boxing, it felt as if there was a new desperation in Hearn for Benn to fight again without clearing his name first. 'I've never seen so many people contacting us, trying to land the Benn fight,' Hearn said. 'It's going to be one of Kell Brook, Chris Eubank Jr or a couple of big-name Americans. That's up to Conor and [his trainer] Tony Sims. It will be in June and I think it will be announced next week.'

17

Back Home

I was three days from publication of my investigation into Eddie Hearn. Anthony Joshua, his most famous fighter, had last won a bout two years and three months earlier and would face Jermaine Franklin that Saturday – 1 April 2023. Having suffered successive defeats to Usyk, Joshua's career was on the line. But I was more interested in Hearn.

As I walked into the crowded reception room for the Joshua–Franklin press conference in a London hotel it took me a while to find him. But I knew to look for the cameras, as he was sure to be talking into one of them. Eventually I saw Hearn and a familiar face – Louis Theroux was working on an interview series which featured Joshua as his first guest.

Theroux talked to Hearn for another ten minutes and I inched closer. As soon as they finished, I walked over to Hearn. 'Mate,' he said, 'you're becoming relentless, you know that?'

He did not mean it as a compliment and so I got down to business. Had he met Conte at the KSI–Logan Paul fight?

'Victor?' Hearn asked. 'Probably. I mean, I've met him.'

When I asked him to confirm he had asked Conte for advice about moving the Chávez Jr–Jacobs fight from Nevada to Arizona,

Hearn said, 'Never. No, no, no. I've had one or two conversations with him in my life. I think I've messaged him before, once, about a fighter.'

I had screenshots of multiple text messages which Hearn and Conte had exchanged. They related to Hearn's questions about illegal performance-enhancing drugs and two fighters.

'No,' Hearn repeated as he spoke about the Chávez situation in 2019. 'I would never say to [Conte] "How should I handle this?" It's got nothing to do with him. He's very knowledgeable about substances, not about commissions.

'We never applied for that [Chávez Jr–Jacobs fight] in Las Vegas. We'd never booked anything in Las Vegas, so we didn't move anywhere. We had an option of about three different venues. One was Las Vegas. We hadn't secured the date with the commission officially.'

But Hearn's company Matchroom Boxing had notified the Nevada State Athletic Commission (NSAC) that, on 20 December 2019, it planned to stage Chávez Jr–Jacobs at the MGM Grand in Las Vegas. That notification led to a request from Nevada that VADA test both fighters.

On 24 October, a VADA collection officer went to the Wild Card Gym in Hollywood where Chávez was training. The collection officer arrived just before 2 p.m., but Chávez refused to provide a sample.

Matchroom was made aware of the awkward situation. Frank Smith, Matchroom's CEO, and Shaun Palmer, the company's lawyer, contacted VADA's president, Dr Margaret Goodman, to ask that her collection officer remain at the gym while they tried to convince Chávez to provide the sample. At 4.35 p.m., Chávez left the gym without doing so.

On 30 October, Bob Bennett, executive director of the NSAC, suspended Chávez temporarily. There was no chance that Chávez's fight against Jacobs could take place in Vegas and Hearn chose Arizona as an alternative.

I had access to all the documents, but Hearn wanted to move on. He had a fight to promote between Joshua and Franklin. We shook hands and drifted apart.

I felt as sick of boxing as Joshua did when, an hour later, the former world champion spoke wearily. 'I'm wiser and more numb to the expectations of others. I just do it for me now.'

My long article ran in the *Guardian* on the Saturday morning of 1 April 2023 under the headline of 'Eddie Hearn, Conor Benn and the poison at the heart of British boxing'.

Every fact was watertight, backed up by more than one source and included Hearn's right-of-reply responses to various questions I had asked. It was a long, arduous and often grim process, but my last three lines were the easiest to write.

'This is boxing. But even here, in this perennial wasteland, the inexcusable is no longer acceptable. Resistance to doping and deceit, evasion and hypocrisy, is now the only antidote to the poison at the heart of British boxing.'

It was published online at noon and I tweeted a link which said: 'I've loved boxing a long time. But that love is compromised by corruption & damage. I wrote this because Eddie Hearn is planning Conor Benn's return even though the boxer has not cleared his name. This is boxing. But the inexcusable is no longer acceptable.'

I knew it was self-righteous, but my relief at having published the monster got the better of me. The response to the article was overwhelmingly positive, but I turned my Wi-Fi off. I was driving to the O2 late that afternoon to cover the Joshua–Franklin fight.

At 5.17 p.m., I received a text from Hearn.

'Hi Don, really disappointed with your article – especially as you didn't let me know about this article or give me a right to reply. I am even more disappointed by your tweet which accused me of corruption which I will not take or accept. My lawyers are across this, your tweet is completely unacceptable and damaging.'

While I had no concerns about the article itself, I had made one stupid mistake. I walked into the kitchen and, as Alison turned to me, I said 'Fuck!'

Hearn had zeroed in on a single word in my tweet: 'corruption'.

I slapped my forehead as if I might knock some sense into my thick head. 'I'm so fucking stupid!'

In my haste, I chose the wrong word. Instead of 'corruption', I could have suggested hypocrisy. But, in allowing myself to be swept away by emotion, I had left myself open to a legal attack by seeming to have alleged on social media that Hearn was corrupt. That had not been my aim. Instead, I wanted to highlight his contradictory approach to positive test results.

In light of my loaded tweet, it seemed sensible to remove it and, at 6.39 p.m., I texted Hearn:

'Hi Eddie

Thanks for your text. I did give you a right of reply. We spoke on the phone in detail. I told you I was working on an article about these five different cases and we discussed the various issues the article raises. Your replies were considered carefully and are incorporated throughout.

You also seem concerned about my tweet and you say I'm accusing you of corruption. I am not and I'm sorry you think that. The tweet was just trying to stress that my love for the sport has been compromised by the things I've seen in the 50 years I've followed it. That being said, and out of consideration for your concern, I have removed the tweet.'

I left for the O2 and the first hour of my journey passed smoothly before I hit a sudden jam. My car slowed to a crawl and then, after another ten minutes, ground to a standstill. The Blackwall Tunnel had been closed and traffic was blocked.

Dan Barnard, the head of Matchroom Boxing Media in the UK, texted me. 'Are you coming, Don?' I called him back and he listened to my predicament sympathetically. He said more than half the press row was still empty as the tunnel closure had caused havoc. After another half-hour of slow progress, I phoned him again to explain that I had decided to turn round and try to reach home before the fight began so I could cover it from the television.

The roads away from the O2 were clear, but I still felt clogged in my head and heart. Why was I spending another Saturday night thinking about boxing and my curdled love for it?

I made it back in time to see a pedestrian fight. Joshua won a wide decision on points, but his disappointing performance matched my mood.

The following morning, I woke to various messages that Hearn had spoken out against me at the post-fight press conference. I clicked on the link, which, of course, was on iFL's YouTube channel. The headline said: '"That article was a joke!" – Eddie Hearn goes off on one.'

Hearn was in full flow. 'It was a hatchet job from Donald McRae,' he said. 'I've already written to him because it was a snide piece because he never asked me for a comment based on what people had said or incidents.'

I thought of my questions he had answered in regard to comments made by Victor Conte, Leon Margules, Robert Smith, Billy Joe Saunders, Jarrell Miller, Chris Eubank Jr and Conor Benn. Hearn kept talking. 'He came up to me on a few separate occasions. If you want to talk about the Chávez fight, Chávez was not my fighter. The contract was not signed for Chávez against Danny Jacobs. The Nevada commission turned up to test Chávez who hadn't signed any agreement for the fight, wasn't on any testing programme and basically said "What are you doing here? I'm not being tested. I've not even signed the contract." Not my fighter, not my responsibility.

'From there, Las Vegas had an investigation. Chávez said "Whatever. I'm not fighting in Vegas. You can all do one." We made the fight in Phoenix. He didn't want to work with VADA. He asked for a reputable body and I asked for the opinion of Victor Conte who now seems to be the saviour of sport – the biggest drug cheat in the history of sport. And he now seems to have a vendetta against me. I've never even met him.'

Hearn had answered me clearly on my recording that week when I asked if he had met Conte before the KSI–Logan Paul fight in 2019. 'Victor?' he said. 'Probably. I mean, I've met him.'

Hearn kept talking on the iFL clip. 'Leon Margules, I texted him earlier. He said some nice words. I'm the most arrogant, hated man in the industry. He texted me and said "But I do like you . . ." They're all snides, do you know what I mean? But that article was a joke because he never even asked me to comment on what was said. That's why he deleted his tweet, if you go and check what Donald McRae did. He's a fantastic writer. You're free to ask me any questions about the comments Donald McRae made.'

The short video ended at that point. Hearing Hearn's accusation, and memory lapses, I felt I had been right to work so hard on the piece. But my love of boxing had soured even more.

Two days later, I was writing another drugs story after news broke that Amir Khan had received a backdated two-year ban from UKAD. He had tested positive for ostarine, an anabolic agent, after being stopped by Kell Brook in Manchester on 19 February 2023. It had been such a brutal defeat that Khan had since retired.

It was the same old story. I liked Khan and I thought he was a talented and courageous fighter who had lost his way. He had been dignified in defeat, but he now suggested that perhaps ostarine had inadvertently entered his body after he had shaken hands with someone.

'It makes me feel sick,' Brook said. 'It is a fucking joke and it's the same for everyone who has been caught out: "I didn't know, it was this or that." At the end of the day, it was in you and you were going to fight and hurt me in a sport where you can legally get killed. It is in your system and it could have been a completely different story. I could be in a wheelchair now, him seriously destroying my life.'

*

Isaac Chamberlain burst into laughter at my suggestion. We sat on the floor of his Brixton gym. His challenge for the British cruiserweight title on 27 May had been confirmed and, seven weeks from fighting Mikael Lawal, his unbeaten rival with whom he was engaged in a vociferous slanging match, Isaac told me he would be in supreme shape.

He had just mentioned his 6 a.m. runs in Putney, which took place before strength-and-conditioning sessions with his fitness trainer Rory Lynn. A sudden idea lit up in my head. Would he mind if I ran with him early one morning?

His laughter was exuberant, but I chided him for being so doubtful. I might look like a slightly rotund white-haired geezer, but I went running two or three times a week. I loved it even if it caused mild skirmishes in our house as, when I got home forty-five minutes later, drenched in sweat and wheezing cheerfully, Alison was worried I'd drop dead. 'You're sixty-one,' she would remind me with exasperation.

I jogged sedately, but my T-shirt would darken with sweat and the long old hill on the way back always left me breathless. But the real truth was that I felt better than I looked. I felt alive and full of light after that time in the fresh air, away from my desk and this book. I felt happy.

Isaac kept laughing as I kept talking. I just liked the idea of writing about meeting Isaac at 5.30 a.m. on a cold April morning and then running along the River Thames with him. It wouldn't matter if I couldn't keep up for more than five minutes. I would be content to see him disappear into the distance while I finished my own run.

'Of course, bro,' Isaac said. He was smiling. 'You're always welcome.'

We settled on Monday 1 May. It was a bank holiday, but Isaac joked that boxers, and maybe even ageing writers, are too disciplined to take a break. More importantly, it gave me a couple of weeks to do some proper training.

While it would not take much stamina to complete a five-mile run, I was worried about the speed at which Isaac ran. I could run easily for forty-five minutes, but I hated the idea of Isaac having to adjust to my tortoise pace. The better option would be for me to run faster than normal to keep up with him and then ease off so he could forge ahead.

One morning in mid-April, I set out on a more concentrated run. It was a mild day and the ground was dry and firm. My mind turned blank, as it so often does when running, and I ran faster than normal. But, after twenty minutes, I felt a tweak in my right knee. It was sharp enough to make me curse and slow straight away. I turned around and jogged home laboriously. The knee did not feel too bad after a shower and I decided that one day off would suffice.

Two days later, I hobbled along for a while, but I was back home after twenty minutes. Maybe a week of rest would help.

In another sign of belated maturity, I bowed to my family's urging and did something I had put off for two years. A couple of days before I turned sixty-two, I logged on and, with a resigned sigh, registered for the dreaded Senior Railcard.

I thought it would make everyone happy if I marked the moment on our family WhatsApp group. Of course, my efforts to take a screenshot of the digital railcard failed dismally. Even more than the railcard, this made me feel seriously old.

The knee worsened rather than improved, but Isaac didn't laugh when I told him I would not make our run. 'No problem, bro,' he said. 'We'll do it next time.'

I wasn't sure if there would be a next time but, three weeks later, it was me consoling a far more dejected Isaac. His title challenge had been postponed after Lawal withdrew from the fight for 'medical reasons'.

Isaac was indignant. 'It's just an excuse. He's too scared to fight me.'

Bobby Mills, Isaac's trainer, believed the fight would still happen but that Lawal needed more time to prepare. Lawal insisted on social media that 'I look forward to getting a new date and defending my British title once I'm fully cleared to do so'.

Isaac was deflated. 'It's all bullshit, bro.'

At least he had been promised by Ben Shalom and his promotional company Boxxer that he would still fight on the 27 May bill
at Bournemouth's Vitality Stadium. He and Lawal had been ear-
marked as the chief support to Chris Billam-Smith's WBO world
cruiserweight title challenge against Lawrence Okolie. They were
the only two men to have beaten Isaac.

'We'll find a decent opponent,' Isaac said more brightly, 'and I'll
spend all week calling out Lawal.'

It was just another let-down that Isaac needed to overcome on
his long, slow journey to the British, European and world titles he
hoped to win before he left boxing.

I flew to Dublin early on the morning of 20 May. My mind was
distracted after Regis Prograis signed a contract with Eddie
Hearn. He had turned down Top Rank to join Matchroom and
I felt a pang of regret at this latest twist. 'I am so excited to
welcome Regis to the Matchroom team,' Hearn said. 'The 140-
pound division is fast becoming the most exciting in the sport,
littered with big names and glamour fights, so to have the WBC
king in the team is a massive coup for us. Regis's fights always
promise action and, along with his charisma and personality,
there's a perfect blend that makes him one of the most market-
able and fan-friendly fighters.'

Their first fight together would be on 17 June, when Regis would
defend his world title in his home city of New Orleans against Liam
Paro of Australia.

The fact that one of my favourite fighters had forged an alliance
with a promoter against whom I had just clashed seemed like a
typical boxing experience. But I didn't like it.

There were persistent rumours that Daniel Kinahan was still
involved in boxing despite being hunted by US law enforcement
agencies. If we had been talking about any other sport apart from
boxing, it would have been hard to believe – but so many credible

sources told me that Kinahan continued to make deals for various fighters. It seemed especially troubling on the morning I flew to Dublin to watch Katie Taylor's first professional bout in Ireland against Chantelle Cameron. She had been blocked from fighting at home for so long precisely because of Kinahan's involvement in boxing.

Taylor was thirty-six years old. She was the undisputed world lightweight champion and carried a flawless 22–0 pro record into her homecoming bout. But Taylor was about to be tested like never before. She had chosen to move up a division to challenge Chantelle Cameron, the imposing and unified super-lightweight world champion, at the 3Arena – fewer than three miles from the Regency Hotel where David Byrne had been killed by the bullets meant for his friend Kinahan in 2016.

There had been no major boxing promotions in Ireland since then.

The Regency shooting was headline news again in May 2023. Gerry Hutch, who led the gang that had been at war with the Kinahans for ten years, had been acquitted of murdering Byrne and released from prison in April. But the day before I arrived in Dublin, two men were found guilty of providing getaway vehicles from the Regency and sentenced to lengthy jail terms.

The Taylor–Cameron bout dredged up other uncomfortable reminders of Kinahan's involvement. Jamie Moore, Cameron's trainer, had been shot twice in August 2014 outside Kinahan's home near Marbella. The authorities eventually established that the shooters had been aiming to kill Kinahan. A month later, while convalescing at home in Manchester, Moore told me how lucky he had been as one bullet missed an artery by millimetres. Moore added that Kinahan was 'a good bloke' as he supported boxers.

At the press conference in Dublin, Moore was asked whether he regretted his interaction with Kinahan. He stonewalled. 'We're not here to talk about that. We're here to focus on the fight.' And yet the fight was taking place in the north inner city where most of the nineteen people in the Kinahan feud had been killed. It was also the first big fight since the Regency shooting.

After Cameron became the undisputed world champion in Abu Dhabi, she had been joined in the ring by Anthony Fitzpatrick, who had once held a key managerial role in MTK. The Criminal Assets Bureau in Dublin had taken possession of a mansion owned by Kinahan in Dublin and they revealed in court that Fitzpatrick had lived there. Cameron was clearly not involved in any of this, but Fitzpatrick being at her side posed unanswered questions.

I was back at a Hearn show for the first time since our dispute. I sat on the opposite side of the ring to the promoter, who was happy next to Conor McGregor, the UFC fighter whose reputation had plummeted after multiple scandals. But I was offered a good view of a stony-faced Conor Benn walking past before he became embroiled in a scuffle with Kell Brook.

Hearn's certainty that Benn's comeback fight would be announced in the first week of April had faded. Seven weeks later, the disgraced boxer, whom UKAD had provisionally suspended, appeared no closer to a return. Benn was still full of big talk after the fleeting altercation with Brook had been broken up by security men. 'It's personal when you lay your hands on me like that,' Benn said. 'Let's handle this in the ring. I don't care what Kell Brook has left – I stop him in two rounds. If you choose to fight me, it's your death wish.'

Taylor and Cameron provided a more admirable spectacle. The 3Arena was crammed two hours before the main event as the crowd celebrated the return of big-time boxing to Ireland. It was very different in Taylor's hushed dressing room. While having her hands wrapped, Taylor wore a grey T-shirt which promised that 'It is God who arms me with strength'.

Even though Cameron was the defending champion, the near deification of Taylor in Ireland meant that the thirty-two-year-old woman from Northampton walked first to the ring to a cacophony of boos. Taylor soaked up her own euphoric reception as she was home at last. Her face shone, with sweat and rapture.

The introductions seemed interminable, but Cameron was ready. She was aggressive at the outset, pushing Taylor back and landing some solid blows. But Taylor responded with a few sharp combinations in a competitive opening round. Taylor moved with alacrity in the second, making Cameron miss, but the champion powered forward.

The danger Cameron posed was clear in round four as her percussive punching intensified. For the first time, the older woman from Bray looked ragged, her hair streaked with sweat.

At the halfway stage, it was obvious Taylor would need to dig deep as Cameron nailed her with a hard left. In the centre of the ring, they traded with unrelenting pressure. A dogfight, which Taylor can seldom resist, bit hard as the two women hurt each other in see-sawing exchanges. Taylor still refused to sit down at the end of the sixth.

It was desperately close in round seven with Cameron shading it as she finished strongly. Her left hook to the body kept hurting Taylor. Cameron's strength and determination seemed unflagging as the fight continued, but near the end of the eighth Taylor's blurring fists caught Cameron, whose face had begun to swell and mark up.

In the penultimate round, Cameron went to the body again only for Taylor to match her ferocity. The crowd were on their feet as the last round began. The action was fierce, but Cameron had done just enough to snatch the decision. Her narrow victory on points secured the sweetest win of her career by scores of 96–94 twice, with the third official ruling it a 95–95 draw.

It had been an outstanding contest which stunned the crowd. They roused themselves to boo Cameron, which was grossly unfair as both women had shown immense courage and skill. 'Congratulations to Chantelle and thank you for this opportunity. I'm looking forward to the rematch,' Taylor said afterwards. 'It was a close fight but this is boxing.'

Cameron said she had been 'petrified' before the scorecards were revealed. 'I've seen results go the other way. It was a close fight and Katie is a great boxer, pound-for-pound the best. But my strength is putting the pressure on. I don't mind getting hit so my corner let me off the leash.'

Once again, two of the world's best women boxers had set a riveting example to their male contemporaries.

Outside, there were no taxis and so, at one in the morning, I began the forty-five-minute walk to my hotel. There were the usual signs of Saturday night revelry as I trudged past drunken men and women singing and staggering along. The River Liffey flowed, dark and steady, while I walked painfully alongside it. My injured knee throbbed.

Fifteen minutes from my hotel, I slowed to a heavy limp. The thought of running again seemed as distant as the prospect of any lasting happiness in my fractured relationship with boxing.

I finally made it back, like a lame old donkey, and soon lay in the dark, unable to sleep.

A week later, I was in Bournemouth. Following the postponement of his British title challenge, Isaac Chamberlain was scheduled to fight a decent if uninspiring opponent in Dylan Bregeon, a durable French cruiserweight. It was a beautiful late spring evening when I arrived at the Vitality Stadium where a sold-out crowd had arrived to watch their local hero, Chris Billam-Smith, fight Lawrence Okolie.

Isaac had ended up in hospital after he fought Billam-Smith, but there had been moments early in the bout and late in the last round when he looked close to forcing a stoppage. But the harsh difference between winning and losing was accentuated on 27 May 2023 when, with Billam-Smith about to fight for the WBO world cruiserweight title that night, Isaac was reduced to his role in a 'floating' bout which would fill any gap in the television scheduling.

I sat with him in a crowded dressing room, shared with six

undercard fighters, as he waited to be told when he and Bregeon would walk to the ring. He was scheduled to be either the sixth or seventh fight, but after four of the first six bouts went the distance, and the two others only ended in the last or penultimate round, the programme was running late.

Isaac looked heartsore when hearing the news that he might go on as the last fight of the night if Billam-Smith and Okolie produced an early finish. It meant he would fight in front of a near-deserted football stadium as most of the 12,000 crowd would stream out of the arena as soon as Billam-Smith left the ring.

In an ugly scrap, Okolie was knocked down three times and docked points twice for his illegal brawling. Billam-Smith won the fight by huge margins on two scorecards to become a new world champion. At ringside, I knew how Isaac would be feeling as, with a different slice of luck and better preparation, he could have been in Billam-Smith's place. Instead, he had spent the whole night waiting for his floating bout to finally land on the undercard. As the Bournemouth crowd roared their delight, and Billam-Smith tearfully embraced his wife, Mia, my phone pinged with the news that Isaac's fight was definitely off.

Having imagined just two weeks earlier that this would be the night he would celebrate winning his first British title, Isaac had been bumped completely from the card. All his months of sacrifice felt wasted on another night of disappointment.

Far darker, if familiar, problems had returned to the ring an hour earlier in the boxing heartland of Belfast. At the SSE Arena, the Liverpool featherweight Nick Ball had faced the unbeaten South African Ludumo Lamati. Ball, despite being only five-foot-two, was winning clearly against the much taller and rangier Lamati. He landed hurtful shots, but Lamati was resilient and kept fighting back. But in the twelfth and last round, Ball opened up and, reeling beneath the sustained punishment, Lamati was rescued by his corner.

Before he could even reach his stool, he collapsed. The ringside doctor, Martin Duffy, ducked swiftly between the ropes and an oxygen mask was strapped to Lamati's face. They were still attending to the stricken fighter when Ball was interviewed in the ring. He said, 'The main thing is Lamati's health. I hope he's all right because boxing is no joke. You have got some people not taking it seriously and you can lose your life in here.'

The thirty-one-year-old South African was wheeled away on a stretcher and taken to the Royal Victoria Hospital. He was placed in an induced coma and the following morning Boxing5, his promoters, released a short statement: 'Ludumo is currently under hospital care and the latest feedback from the medical team is that his vital signs are stable. We will provide further updates as soon as they become available. Please keep him in your prayers.'

Another anxious boxing vigil had begun.

Hugh O'Halloran messaged me two days later. With the trademark generosity of ordinary boxing fans in Northern Ireland, where the fight game is treated with passion and reverence, Hugh had set up a GoFundMe page for Lamati. The boxer was alone in hospital as his team's visas had run out and they had been forced to return to South Africa.

Frank Warren and Bob Arum, as joint promoters, were in the midst of arranging flights for Lamati's family to join him in hospital. But O'Halloran wanted to raise funds which could be used to 'help ease the burden on his family. We still have no way of knowing the outcome, but we know Ludumo is getting the best care anyone could ask for at the Royal Victoria.'

On Friday 16 June, Isaac Chamberlain finally stepped into the ring against Dylan Bregeon on the undercard of a low-key bill at the venerable York Hall in Bethnal Green.

The heat was searing and, over-trained and drained of enthusiasm, Isaac performed listlessly in an eight-rounder. He was never in danger and the referee, acting as sole judge, gave him the verdict by a comfortable 78–74, but it was an uninspiring display. Isaac was dejected in victory and his trainers and I, and Mick Hennessy, tried to boost him in the dressing room.

But the mess of boxing, like life, was a struggle.

That same weekend, early on Sunday morning, I got up at 3.30 a.m. to watch Regis Prograis fight for the first time under Hearn's promotion. It was another bad night for one of my favourite fighters as Regis faced a late replacement, Danielito Zorrilla, in New Orleans. He did more than a hundred interviews in the weeks leading to his homecoming and told me how he was being run off his feet tending to ticket requests from family, friends and acquaintances.

The chaos and stress did not help and Prograis was knocked down in the first round by Zorrilla. He got up quickly, but the rest of the fight was ugly as he struggled to catch his awkward opponent. When they went to the scorecards, one judge scored the fight 114–113 for Zorrilla. The two other official cards were far more lop-sided, giving Prograis the split decision win by 117–110 and 118–109.

Regis looked an even more disconsolate winner than Isaac had done. He remained a world champion but the fight had been a stinker.

I had entered a ridiculous period of mourning for my wounded old knee. A consultation with an NHS physiotherapist had not gone well. After working on my right knee, while making ominous noises, he explained that an X-ray would be the only way to clarify the extent of the damage. We would then decide what to do next. I could consider cortisone for temporary relief with the more drastic option of a knee replacement down the line.

Only one question really mattered to me. *Will I run again?*

'You actually go running?' the incredulous physio said. 'You're doing well.'

I smiled politely, but felt crushed when he stressed that there would be no running in the months ahead, or perhaps ever again.

'You can still exercise,' he said encouragingly. 'Can you swim?'

'Like a shark,' I wanted to reply. But I simply nodded.

'Swimming is low impact and good for the heart,' he said as he printed off a series of daily exercises to help strengthen my knee.

I joined my local leisure centre the next day and, amid mild gnashing of teeth, began my sessions in the pool. When I first slid into the warm, chlorine-scented water, I cursed the contrast with running under a vast sky in the fresh air, alongside the canal where I'd pass a family of swans, the occasional kingfisher and solitary heron. I would pant past friendly walkers and their dogs and feel lucky to be alive.

It was different in the pool. I had new trunks, goggles and ear plugs. It's hard to feel like a shark wearing all that paraphernalia. But I thought of the great white and hammerhead sharks as I tried to power through the water. It was all going well until my third length.

My lungs were burning, my arms felt heavy and my heart was pounding. I committed sacrilege in the medium lane and stopped swimming to catch my breath in another small humiliation.

The tired old shark slid beneath one lane divider, and then another, and I found my place. I was in the slow lane. I began again. I swam like a sluggish basking shark that needed a five-second breather every other length. I followed pool etiquette and, after a few weeks, I was on nodding terms with the unknown gang of slow swimmers.

As my swimming improved, I liked seeing the sunrise glow behind the giant windows at the far end of the pool. I set little goals of additional lengths and timed myself against the wall clock.

After two weeks, I waved goodbye to the slow-lane gang and re-joined the medium swimmers. The aim now was to make it to the fast lane before autumn descended. Every Monday, Wednesday and Friday, between 6.30 and 7 a.m., I swam up and down and thought of boxing and this book, of life and death, of Isaac Chamberlain and Regis Prograis, of Tyson Fury and Oleksandr Usyk, of Patrick Day and Ludumo Lamati in hospital in Belfast.

I also thought of my sister, Heather, and my parents, Ian and

Jess, and how as a family we had loved to swim in the sea. As a kid in South Africa, I was scared of sharks, but that didn't stop me racing into the sea to body-surf rolling waves with Heather and my dad, as my mom sped down the roaring banks of water on her boogie board.

Five decades later, I swam harder, secretly racing the fast swimmers in the adjoining lane, as I yearned to spend just one day with my lost family.

On Wednesday 5 July, I climbed out of the pool and limped to the showers. I stood beneath the hot jets of water and, having closed the cubicle door behind me, came close to letting the tears roll down my wet face. But I knew it was hopeless. Crying would not change anything.

I would never see my parents or sister again. They were gone forever.

A few minutes later, I dried my face and forgave myself for the sudden deluge of emotion. I understood the reason. Alison and I would fly back to South Africa the following night. It would be the first time I had been back to my old home since my father's death nearly three years before.

It was winter in Bedfordview, on the edge of Johannesburg, and South Africa shivered in the cold. Even Alison and I thought it was freezing in the early morning and at night but, most days, the sun still shone. We were there to sort out my parents' remaining possessions and documents rather than to have a holiday. Covid had stopped me from returning for a very long time. After my dad's death, when the lockdown was so stringent, I had not been able to go back to clear their rooms at the care home.

My cousin Brian and his wife, Kate, had taken charge and a spare room in their house in Johannesburg had been given over to books, paintings, photographs and boxes of paperwork which once belonged to my parents. We lingered longest over the photographs and the letters where Ian's and Jess's handwriting still stood out so clearly on the page. It was painful, but strangely comforting to feel close to them again.

I also felt their presence when we drove through my old home-town and returned to the same B&B where I had always stayed when they had been so ill near the end. We sensed them again when we visited the care home and embraced Tryphinia Kelitlilwe, the nursing sister who had looked after my parents for so long while sharing deeply political conversations about the state of the world with my dad. I thought of my mother and father when Tryphinia lamented the difficulties of life in South Africa and, again, when another middle-aged Black woman cried and poured out her heart to us about the injustice she experienced every day.

We felt Ian and Jess when we saw two of my oldest friends from school for lunch – and when we visited my parents' friend who had lost her husband soon after my dad. We laughed and almost cried as we spoke about everything we had all gone through.

I imagined my parents' faces on the morning it snowed. The last time it had snowed in Johannesburg had been in 1981 on the day we buried my one-armed grandfather, Alec, my mother's father. He had come to South Africa from Scotland and so the snow seemed fitting when his coffin was lowered into the ground. It again felt surreal, if moving, to witness the frozen joy of South Africans as the snow drifted down on us.

Of course, the snow did not last and it was nowhere to be seen by the time we were out in the bush in the Pilanesberg, less than three hours from Johannesburg. A rush of memories, for my parents had so loved Africa, brushed up against the present as elephants walked slowly past us or we watched a pride of overfed lions finish off the carcass of the kudu they had dragged down the night before. I heard my father's voice in my own warning to Alison that we had better back away from the skittish rhino who had made a mock charge at us just as the sun sank across the reserve. I saw my mother's kind face as we watched a hippo nudge its seemingly dead baby along the length of a dam. I imagined what they would say, and how my dad would explain these small matters of life and death in the bush.

But the closest we came to them was in St James's Church in Bedfordview. Alison and I are not churchgoers, but it felt important to be there that Sunday morning. My parents had been members of this congregation for a very long time and both their funerals had been held here. We had stayed in touch with Gavin Lock, the minister who had conducted their final services. Gavin had helped my dad and I bury my mom's ashes in the garden of the church in January 2020, on the second-to-last day I saw my father.

I had not had the chance to say goodbye. So Gavin met Alison and I, and Brian and Kate, in a private part of the garden. Brian had brought my father's ashes with him. It was quiet as we took turns to tilt a small scoop each into a hole in the ground, next to the spot where my mother's ashes had also been buried.

Gavin spoke beautifully about my parents and then the four of us each said some words about all that Ian, and Jess, had meant to us. When it was my turn, I cried a little. I could feel the sun on my tear-streaked face, and the love of everyone around me. But then my words flowed more easily. I said the tears had come not just because I still missed them, and Heather too. They fell because these were tears of acceptance and gratitude – 'happy tears' as my mother always called them – because I knew how lucky I had been to have them for so long.

There was relief and happiness, too, when Ludumo Lamati was finally able to return to South Africa after being placed in an induced coma following his fight in Belfast. A week after his brush with catastrophe, he had been eased back into consciousness and his manager Larry Wainstein confirmed that Lamati could walk again and dress himself in hospital.

Hugh O'Halloran, who had raised £8,000 for Lamati, told me that the boxer's girlfriend and mother had been overwhelmed by the kindness they experienced in Belfast. When they tried to buy food for themselves, their money was waved away by people who recognised them.

And then, on 16 July 2023, a day short of a month since he had been rushed from the ring on a stretcher, a beaming and seemingly healthy Lamati, accompanied by his girlfriend and mother, met with Carl Frampton, Jamie Conlan and others from Belfast's boxing community.

'Unbelievable to be able to sit and have a meal with Ludumo Lamati and his friends and family today,' Frampton, the former world champion, said as he posted photographs on social media. And then, as if to remind us that there could still be happy endings in boxing, Frampton added just two words: 'Miracle man.'

18

Champions and Dissidents

Mikael Lawal was just thirteen when he watched his mother die in front of him in Lagos. 'That hit me really hard,' the boxer said, before explaining to the writer Paul Zanon that, having previously spent eleven years of his life in London, he went to stay 'with my real dad, who I'd never met before, and my stepmom, who was quite evil. She used to tell lies about me and my dad beat me.'

He ran away and, for a while, he was homeless on the Lagos streets. 'I was so sad and in a terrible situation,' he remembered. He eventually went to the British High Commission where 'I showed them the marks on my body from the beatings I'd taken and they could see I was malnourished. They put me in an orphanage for a few months while they tried to sort out my papers. Then, finally, the great news came that they'd got me a temporary passport and a flight back to the UK. I was sixteen.'

My interest in Lawal had grown since he agreed to defend his British cruiserweight title against Isaac Chamberlain. There had been an edge to their London rivalry, with Lawal coming from Shepherd's Bush and Chamberlain from Brixton, but the acrimony deepened. After Lawal withdrew from their scheduled fight in May 2023, citing those 'medical reasons', Isaac was irate. 'You're not going to believe this, bro,' he told me. 'He says he's got *toothache*!'

The bout had been rescheduled for October and I worried about the threat Lawal posed. He carried serious power and had won all seventeen bouts in his pro career. Twelve had finished inside the distance. He also had a backstory forged in adversity.

After his mother's death, Lawal returned to London where he stayed briefly with a family friend. He then moved to a hostel. 'It was a bad time of my life,' Lawal said. 'I had a lot of anger and was getting involved in fights. In the end, my key worker referred me to boxing. It got my interest straight away.'

Life was given hope and meaning after Lawal joined the Stonebridge Boxing Club in Wembley. 'The moment I walked in, I loved the energy, how it looked,' he recalled. 'But it got to the point where I couldn't afford to go.'

Aamir Ali, the head of the gym, told Lawal: 'Don't worry about the money. Just train anyway. You've got great potential.'

Lawal was deeply moved; 'You don't forget those things,' he later said. He believed 'boxing saved me' and 'gave me hope and discipline, and helped me with depression. If it wasn't for boxing, I don't think I'd have any structure in my life and I'd probably still be smoking and drinking. Most importantly, boxing provided me with dreams and aspirations.'

Lawal had become British champion in November 2022 and, along with defending his belt, he knew that either he or Chamberlain would also win the vacant Commonwealth title. The victor would then be in a prime position to fight for European and world titles.

Defeat, however, would be devastating for Isaac. He had already lost twice and a third setback would end his grand plans. 'I cannot lose,' he admitted to me. 'But he ain't beating me.'

The first Chamberlain–Lawal press conference in May 2023 had culminated in the traditional face-off with neither fighter prepared to look away.

'One fist up to the camera, Isaac,' a photographer yelled. 'Mikael, start looking this way.'

Chamberlain and Lawal refused to move.

'C'mon guys, we're on a tight schedule,' the publicist said.

Lawal raised his right fist but Chamberlain remained motionless.

The publicist tried again. 'Turn fully this way and look at the camera please.'

Chamberlain suddenly grinned and turned. Lawal followed his lead with a tutting sound.

'You can do that, kissing your teeth,' Chamberlain said to Lawal, his face creased in a familiar smile as they looked at the cameras. 'That ain't gonna do nothing.'

'Shut up, man,' Lawal warned. His face was stern as the cameras clicked. 'I'll slap your face.'

'Slap who?' Chamberlain said, his smile gone as he spun away from the cameras. 'You think you're a bad man,' Lawal sneered. 'What are you on, bro?'

'What do you mean?' Chamberlain said. 'Stop this rubbish talk.'

A burly man held Chamberlain back. 'Leave it for the ring, bro,' he urged.

In September 2023, the feud escalated. Lawal vs Chamberlain would be the main support to another all-London showdown between Joshua Buatsi and Dan Azeez on 21 October at the 02 Arena. The four fighters shared the top table and the Sky Sports boxing pundit Andy Scott asked Chamberlain to describe his feelings towards Lawal.

Chamberlain laughed. 'We found him. Bloody hell, bruv. He'd gone MIA. But we're here finally. I don't want to jinx anything but, please, no excuses this time. No toothache with no doctor's report.'

Lawal snapped back. 'There was a doctor's report. I've given it to Boxxer, to the Board.'

Scott, hosting the press conference on behalf of Sky, asked Lawal to explain his dental injuries.

'Yes, please,' Chamberlain interrupted. 'Tell us, cuz!'

Lawal replied cryptically. 'They've got the reports. If there was an issue, they would have stripped me of my title. That's all I want to say.'

Ben Shalom, the promoter, stressed that the British champion had overcome every obstacle he'd faced. He then turned to the challenger. 'We all know about Isaac Chamberlain. He's been very unlucky in his career and has taken fights possibly at the wrong time for him, without the right preparation, and he believes he's one of the best cruiserweights in this country, if not the best. But it's one of those fights that could go either way. Mikael Lawal has so much power that, if he connects, it's going to be very interesting. It's a crossroads fight.'

Scott asked Lawal if he felt disrespected. 'Honestly, I'm used to it. It's me against the world.'

'Everyone has a sob story, bro,' Chamberlain said with a shrug.

'It's me against the world,' Lawal repeated.

'Are you a Tupac fan?' Chamberlain said as laughter lightened the atmosphere.

'You're a comedian,' Lawal sneered.

Scott asked if they had a final message for each other. Chamberlain smiled. 'Don't pull out of the fight. Please.'

On 7 October, two weeks before the fight, Isaac texted me. 'My brother, can you come to the gym on Monday as Sky is coming to film a documentary? It would be great to have you in it.'

I found it a curious experience to watch Isaac being interviewed on camera with lights and microphones. He was nervous. 'Some of the stuff I saw when I was growing up was a bit crazy,' he said. 'Gang violence, stabbings, killings, police raids. But if you grow up with it, you don't really think it's crazy.'

He described the work he did for the gangsters when he was twelve. 'Selling drugs or delivering a package or coming back with whatever they give you. But then you start carrying knives. It gets real deep.'

But, he continued, 'boxing really changed me and gave me confidence. It made me believe I can be someone.'

Isaac stressed how much fatherhood had also transformed him. 'I love my little man, my little dude,' he said of Zion. 'He reminds me of what I wish I was like when I was younger. I wish I had his self-confidence because, when I was young, I really had very low self-esteem. I was very shy. I wasn't able to express myself.'

We headed outside for filming. Isaac and I walked with Zalia and Zion to his car. It was much less cluttered than when he had been so distressed and telling me that he was willing to suffer minor brain damage to fulfil his boxing dreams. Isaac had dragged himself out of that hole and he and Zaila were together again. If he could become British and Commonwealth champion, he would move even further away from the shadows.

The Sky crew were waiting at the Hillyard Street bus stop where Isaac's life had changed. The 133 bus still ran along this route and they began filming on an autumn afternoon in Brixton. Isaac described how 'my heart froze' when, while carrying drugs, he saw the police outside his bus. 'I know if I get caught, I am finished,' he said.

At that very moment, in a timely coincidence, a police car raced past, its siren screaming.

Isaac pointed to the estate across the street. He had run through it and escaped – to boxing.

As the past and the present blurred, Isaac scooped up little Zion. His son squealed in delight as he was lifted high in the air. The late afternoon sunshine streamed across Brixton and I thought of the moment when the gym had been blacked out an hour earlier. Just the glare of television lights remained as Isaac stood alone on the apron of the darkened ring.

Isaac had held his phone so that he could read his words into the camera. It was quiet as, after a deep breath, he said, 'Letter to my Younger Self by Isaac Chamberlain'.

The boxer paused and then began to read aloud.

'Dear Isaac

I don't even think I can tell or put into words the things that are going to happen in your life. There are going to be some crazy highs and some low lows but you will bounce back because God put the spirit of resilience inside of you. Stay on the right track, no matter how it looks now. Your loving heart will attract the ones that are meant to be in your life, but also the ones that will try and use you.

It will all work out in the end. And your character will be tested but your resilience, courage and determination will see you until the very last bell and beyond. Always believe that you can be the best you can be and more. You are destined for great things. Just see until the very end.

Isaac paused and then, looking into the camera, he said one last sentence to his younger self.

And, if no one has told you yet, I love you.'

The fight was off. I felt a surge of disbelief, as well as disappointment for Isaac, on Tuesday 18 October, four days before he was meant to face Lawal.

Dan Azeez had been due to face his friend and now rival Joshua Buatsi in that Saturday night's headline bout. But Azeez had injured his back near the end of his very final sparring session. He would not be able to fight for months.

I texted Bobby Mills, Isaac's trainer, who answered immediately. 'Hi Don, just heard the news. We are trying to clarify our end.'

Conor Ward, his co-trainer, kept me updated over the next few hours, but I felt dejected for Isaac when one last text arrived that night. 'Nothing yet,' Conor said simply.

Finally, on Wednesday afternoon, fresh news arrived from Conor. 'It's going ahead, mate.'

An hour later, Boxxer made the official confirmation. 'This Saturday's undercard will now relocate to York Hall in London, headlined by Mikael Lawal defending his British Cruiserweight Championship against bitter rival Isaac Chamberlain.'

At Friday's weigh-in, after Chamberlain scaled 199 pounds and Lawal a pound lighter, they did their final interviews. 'Thank you to everyone who came out to support me,' Chamberlain said to the Sky camera. 'It's going to be a great night to remember at the prestigious York Hall.'

He suddenly turned in the direction of Lawal. The champion and his crew were staring at him.

'What are you looking at?' Chamberlain said, matching their hostility with his own. 'All that stuff don't scare me. Who're you trying to intimidate?'

Lawal remained quiet and Andy Scott, conducting the live interview, cut in with a joke. 'I thought you were talking to me.'

Chamberlain laughed and then pointed at Lawal. 'He's still looking at me. Why are you staring at me? It's going to be a great atmosphere tomorrow night and I will do everything to win.'

Could it be the toughest night of his career? 'It's never easy. It takes a lot to get into that ring and fight in front of thousands of people. The pressure is high, but I'm winning.'

It was soon Lawal's turn. 'I think the pressure is getting to him,' the champion said. 'All his talking doesn't bother me. We'll let our fists talk. It's time to put an end to it.'

York Hall, Bethnal Green, London, Saturday 21 October 2023

The rain lashes down in east London as I trudge from the Tube. York Hall rises up in the deluge like an old castle of dreams and nightmares. There has been so much glory here over the past fifty years, and so much pain, that my stomach tightens as I approach the stately building.

I head to the rear, to pick up my credentials, and I see three ambulances. They are here to avert tragedy, but they look ominous. Almost fifteen months before, I had watched Isaac being swallowed up by an ambulance in Bournemouth. I don't think I can bear another such night.

'Wait, wait,' a strident voice calls out. 'The champ is here. Let him through . . .'

I turn to see Mikael Lawal and his entourage. Lawal looks ready, but he stops to accept a handshake and an embrace from a friend. And then he sweeps past me.

I have special dispensation to be in Isaac's dressing room, so I slip through the crowd and pass the ring to reach the opposite side of the hall. The double doors swing open and I walk down a maze of corridors, past the swimming pool, before reaching the same dressing room Isaac had used for his last fight against Dylan Bregeon.

Bobby Mills has already wrapped Isaac's hands and pulled on his gold boxing gloves. Isaac smiles. 'Bro, yes,' he says to me. 'You're here.'

He wears a black T-shirt which says 'R.I.P. Perm' in honour of a friend who had recently been murdered in south London. The seriousness of life, and boxing, fills the space.

I go around the room, quietly saying hello to everyone, from Bobby and Conor to Jon Pegg and Mick Hennessy. I talk to Zalia and to Andy Knuth, Isaac's great friend who wears the body bag in training and absorbs so many punches. Rory Lynn, Isaac's strength-and-conditioning coach, reassures me. 'Isaac's ready. He's in great shape.'

The Atlanta rappers Lil Baby and Money Man boom out as Isaac hits the pads. He will be in the ring in fewer than twenty minutes.

I leave the dressing room for a breather and look down at the Olympic-sized swimming pool, covered by a blue tarpaulin for the winter. Standing on the iron gantry which will lead Isaac to the ring, I hear the muffled din of the crowd on the other side of a cream-coloured wall. This is a very lonely place.

Time disappears fast in the dressing room. The usual five-minute warning comes and goes. Isaac hugs and kisses Zalia and then calls his team together in a circle to pray.

Isaac sees me in a far corner. 'Don,' he shouts. 'Join us, bro.'

I'm not sure I belong, but it is an honour to be included. I find a place in the circle between big Andy and Bobby. We link arms and bow our heads. Isaac speaks quietly, expressing his gratitude for having reached this moment with everyone who has helped him. He asks for strength, resilience and safety. He thanks God for watching over him in the ring and then, humbly, he asks for victory too. Everyone says 'Amen'.

The circle breaks open and the applause begins, as Andy shouts, 'And the new . . .'

Andy and Isaac lead the way, followed by Bobby and Conor, with Jon and Mick, the two most experienced boxing men near the back. I walk a few steps behind them. The crowd noise gathers in intensity.

We reach an opening to the arena. The wait grinds on and then the door opens and Isaac walks out to a roar.

Lawal makes his own ring walk from the opposite entrance. Time speeds up again.

Bob Williams, the referee, tells both fighters to protect themselves at all times. Then, with brusque efficiency, he orders them to touch gloves.

'Seconds out,' Williams shouts. The bell rings and the two fighters move towards each other again. Lawal wears white trunks, and Chamberlain gold with black trim.

It's a predictably cagey opening, but Chamberlain, twitching and moving, is more aggressive. His jab is slick and, after a minute, he pins Lawal in a corner and opens up with combinations. Lawal deflects the punches with his arms and gloves, but he looks strangely passive. Even when Lawal throws a couple of big punches, Chamberlain ghosts away.

Chamberlain opens up in the second with a series of blurring combinations. Lawal is caught hardest by a chopping overhand right and he draws Chamberlain into a messy clinch. When they break, Chamberlain keeps pumping his jab to the body. It's an effective punch which seals a second straight round.

Lawal, knowing that he needs to change the tempo, comes out fast for the third and stuns Chamberlain briefly with a hard right. But the challenger settles back behind his jab and, when Lawal begins to brawl, Chamberlain is the more impressive in-fighter. He clips and cuffs Lawal with uppercuts and short hooks.

Chamberlain wins the first six rounds but Lawal still carries a threat.

A left and right make the sweat fly from Chamberlain's head midway through the seventh, but he takes the combination well. Lawal is nailed by an even harder combination just before the bell. Chris Billam-Smith, sitting in front of me on the Sky broadcast, says Lawal is seven rounds down and in real trouble.

The reminder comes in round eight. A huge overhand right catches Chamberlain on the chin but, anticipating the blow, he moves his head fractionally away. He's still been tagged, but the worst of the blow is softened by his deft head movement. Lawal's cornermen are excited. 'You catch him one more time like that,' his head trainer shouts, 'you'll get him.'

Chamberlain's corner is calmer after a relatively even ninth round. 'He's running out of ideas, Isaac,' Mills says. 'All you've got to do is watch the right hand when you're throwing. You're so close, but watch what the fuck is coming back. He's still dangerous.'

Lawal's corner is agitated. 'You've got to wake up,' a co-trainer urges. 'It's now or never.'

Billam-Smith and Matthew Macklin, on commentary, have given every round to Chamberlain. He just needs to avoid being knocked out to win both titles. The tenth is closer as Lawal lands a couple of meaty punches and Chamberlain complains to his corner that he has torn his right bicep. Mills and Pegg gloss over the injury and stress that he just has to use his left jab to keep out of trouble.

He cruises through the penultimate round and, after Lawal misses with a wild swing before the bell, Chamberlain does a little dance of delight.

'This is the twelfth and final round,' Mills reminds him. 'He's desperate because he knows he's behind. Look at me, Isaac! Do not back up or give him the confidence – stay tight.'

Lawal's corner sound as forlorn as their fighter looks. 'Fight, fight!' they plead.

Chamberlain is too professional and canny. He moves easily around the ring, popping out the jab, and, whenever Lawal closes in, Chamberlain smothers him in a clinch.

When the wooden clappers sound to signal the final ten seconds, Chamberlain ducks easily under one last swinging right hand. He skips to his corner as the former champion pursues him without landing another blow. At the bell, Chamberlain climbs the ropes and hammers his chest in exultation. He screams at the rafters while his damaged right arm points skywards.

The recognition Chamberlain craves has come, as the fighters Anthony Yarde, Chris Eubank Jr and Billam-Smith all praise the new British and Commonwealth champion at ringside.

Lawal looks desolate and Chamberlain offers him consolation. All the bitterness is gone and Lawal taps the glove of the man who has outclassed him. The scorecards are clear: 119–111 and 118–111, twice. Chamberlain had cried and covered his face with a glove while waiting for the result. It is only when the words '. . . and the new . . .' are shouted that he raises both arms in triumph.

'Every dog has his day,' he says when Andy Scott interviews him in the ring. 'I kept going. It's all you can do. Everybody fails in life. We just happen to fail in front of the whole world. But, whatever failures you have, you can always bounce back, baby.'

The dressing room erupts when, finally, Isaac walks in, his face lit by joy. Zalia runs to him as his friends cry out, 'And the new!'

Isaac wipes away the sweat and tears as he shouts: 'We've done it, man!'

He looks down at his dangling right arm, over which two belts hang. 'My bicep is torn, man.' But it will heal far quicker than it took his broken eye socket and cracked heart to mend after he lost to Billam-Smith.

Isaac and I clutch hands and embrace. His black T-shirt is soaked in sweat. But neither of us care as I say how proud I am of him.

'You know what I've been through, bro,' he says.

Isaac beckons Zalia to him again. His arm wraps around her and she pats his stomach before he kisses her. There are whoops as Zalia stretches up to hug him. He holds her tight and beams.

An hour later, in the back of an Uber, it is dark and peaceful as the silent driver takes me home. I gaze out of the window and remember an old truth: boxing can be this joyous and meaningful.

Boxing, of course, does not offer refuge for those seeking lasting happiness. It is too greedy and too damaging to allow more than fleeting euphoria.

Twenty-eight hours after I arrived home from the glorious night at York Hall, I called Lina al-Hathloul, a Saudi Arabian woman in exile, in Belgium. Her sister Loujain al-Hathloul was the most renowned female activist in Saudi Arabia. Loujain had led the protests against the state ban which prevented women from driving a car. She was arrested numerous times before, in March 2018, she was kidnapped in the United Arab Emirates and brought back to Saudi Arabia, where she was jailed.

Loujain went on hunger strike to protest against being denied contact with her family. After her parents were finally allowed to visit her, they heard that Loujain suffered beatings, electric shocks and waterboarding while being threatened with rape and murder. She was nominated for the Nobel Peace Prize in 2019 and 2020, but her plight remained distressing until her release in February 2021.

Boxing did not care about Loujain al-Hathloul or any dissident persecuted in Saudi Arabia. Instead, it was ready to do business with the Kingdom of Saudi Arabia and gave grovelling thanks to 'His Excellency', Turki Alalshikh, the chairman of Saudi Arabia's General Entertainment Authority, who had as much cash as he wanted to splurge on attracting the world's best fighters to the glittering kingdom.

Many ageing footballers, from Cristiano Ronaldo to Jordan Henderson, had already received obscene amounts of money to play in Saudi. A gang of professional golfers had also left the conventional PGA Tour to join the Saudi-backed LIV Golf for billions of dollars.

Turki Alalshikh, had settled on boxing to push the line that Saudi Arabia was a modern and changing country which should be added to your list of future holiday destinations. It was not a hard choice for him as no sporting business cared less about morality or justice than boxing. He did not have to convince boxing's promoters and fighters to join him in Saudi. He showed them the money and they came.

I was not much better. I was about to fly to Riyadh to cover Tyson Fury's bout against Francis Ngannou, the mixed martial artist and former heavyweight champion of the UFC, who had never boxed professionally before. It looked like a stunt before Fury faced Oleksandr Usyk for the undisputed heavyweight championship of the world in Riyadh on 23 December 2023.

I was being sent to cover the boxing by the *Guardian*. It was important to remember that I was not dragooned into travelling and, if I had taken a moral stand and refused to go to Saudi Arabia, my editor would have been supportive. But I reluctantly agreed to go; the choice was mine.

Such hypocrisy was embedded in my boxing writing. I lamented the damage and death that boxing caused. I complained about doping and gangsterism in boxing. I railed against the corruption and chaos of boxing. Yet I still came back for more, again and again.

The great boxing writer Hugh McIlvanney had advised me thirty years before that hypocrisy and ambivalence would be my constant companions. He warned that boxing would also lead me to various hellholes, whether it was Las Vegas or a country led by a dictator or a fascist regime.

Hugh had felt compromised when he flew to Zaire (as the Democratic Republic of the Congo was known in 1974) to write about one of the greatest fights in history. Muhammad Ali shocked the world all over again when he defeated George Foreman, but the bout was used by Zaire's dictator, Mobutu Sese Seko, to drum up cheerful publicity for his totalitarian regime. Hugh had also been in the Philippines when Ali beat Joe Frazier in the Thrilla in Manila in 1975. He had written about one of the greatest and most savage fights in heavyweight history, but he could never forget that the bout was a publicity stunt, too, for Ferdinand Marcos, who ruled the Philippines from 1965 to 1986 with a mixture of corruption, brutality and greed.

Saudi Arabia's move into boxing came straight from the repressive state textbook and so Hugh would not have been surprised. He made it clear that I always had a moral choice but, if I chose to ride with the devil, it was important to try to write with clarity and truth.

The Saudi state had lifted the ban on women being able to drive in June 2018, but Loujain and Lina al-Hathloul claimed that far more serious oppression had escalated. 'It's very difficult,' Lina said as she explained that her sister's five-year travel ban, and being barred from talking in public, had recently been upheld. 'Loujain is always hopeful, but it's not easy knowing she's under constant surveillance. She's isolated while our family also have the travel ban.'

Lina continued to campaign against the guardianship policy which meant 'a woman is considered a minor and subject to the will of a man until the end of her life'.

In March 2022, the Saudi state passed the Personal Status Law, perpetuating the male guardianship system and codifying expectations that women will obey their husbands. Loujain started a campaign called I Am My Own Guardian. Her sister stressed that, 'since Mohammed bin Salman came to power, many changes have been applauded in the West, including the fact that, for example, a woman does not need the prior consent of a male to travel. Ironically, since the lifting of this law, there's been an explosion in Saudi women refugees in the West because women are still not safe inside the kingdom. Women flee because the fundamentals of male guardianship are still there, including the disobedience law. A male guardian can consider anything as disobedience and get her arrested. We have become a police state. We are now like Iraq under Saddam Hussein.'

Despite the opening up of Saudi Arabia, and investment in sport and tourism, human rights were restricted. Salma al-Shehab, a Leeds University student, had been given a thirty-four-year prison sentence for tweeting about women's rights in 2022. That same year, there had been 196 executions, including eighty-one people on a single day. More than 100 executions had occurred in Saudi from January to September 2023, with many of those people having been tortured and denied legal representation after criticising the government.

Before packing my bag for Riyadh, I asked Lina if she felt increasing concern for her family? 'Absolutely,' she said. 'I haven't seen them since 2018. It's very hard.'

The next night, just before 10 p.m. local time, I stood in a long line at passport control at King Khalid International Airport in Riyadh. My laptop contained two files called 'Saudi Oppression' and 'Saudi Dissidents'. There were over a hundred pages of rudimentary research on each file. They were in a folder called 'Tyson Fury', which was tucked away in a primary folder named 'Boxing Book Research'. It would take a while for the Saudi authorities to find such material.

But, in a side panel of the case, my recorder contained various interviews about Saudi Arabia and the most recent was identified clearly: 'Lina al-Hathloul 23.10.23'. My phone also held the contact details of various Saudi dissidents.

I was wary rather than apprehensive as I edged towards the front of the queue. I had felt embarrassed when I'd asked Lina if I needed to be careful when writing about her family and other dissidents while in Saudi Arabia. It was important not to put her sister in any further danger, but Lina understood I was also asking about my own safety.

After she had stressed how important it was to write about Loujain, she said: 'They will not do anything bad to you. The last thing they want is bad publicity for locking up a writer from the West. The worst thing that might happen is that they will kick you out of the country or maybe stop you going back to Saudi.'

I apologised for even asking the question, but Lina was gracious when I said my wife was a little concerned. 'It's important to think about this. We are talking about seriously bad people.'

When my turn came to show my passport, a woman wearing a burqa gestured to me impatiently. She flicked through the passport as she spoke in Arabic to her colleague. Her stamp came out and she pressed down on one of the pages and then, without another look, returned the passport. I was through and, officially, in the Kingdom of Saudi Arabia.

My first day in Riyadh started early. The noise was shuddering as construction workers drove their pneumatic drills into the bleached earth. They were laying the foundations for two new hotels that were part of a relentless modernisation programme.

The dust and the heat outside were already rising, with the temperature climbing towards 34°C. I turned left down the dirt street leading away from the hotel. I was on the hunt for a café for breakfast, but as soon as I found the main road, a soon-to-be-familiar problem emerged. They did not seem to believe in pavements in Riyadh and so walking was a hazardous experience.

On the main drag, I was pinned to the very edge of a wide road, full of cars speeding along multiple lanes. There seemed a fair chance of being run over, but I kept walking until I found a couple of hotels. Some of the staff spoke English and they shook their heads mournfully when I asked if there was anywhere close by where I could get a coffee or breakfast.

So back I plodded to my own hotel, counting the thirty-one construction sites I passed. It was hard to know what the planned influx of tourists would do if and when they eventually arrived to watch Frank Warren's, Bob Arum's and Eddie Hearn's immensely wealthy fighters.

I wanted to get back to my room to write about the fact that it was difficult to be indignant about sporting greed, or the ludicrous Battle of the Baddest between Fury and Ngannou, when something terrible was lodged in the heart of Saudi society. I didn't care that Cristiano Ronaldo had given Ngannou a watch worth £87,000 when they'd recently met in Riyadh – or that so many celebrities, from Kanye West to Eminem, were flying in for the money and the fight.

The morning flashed past as, alongside the drilling and hammering, I wrote about Loujain and Lina al-Hathloul. Just after 2 p.m., I went back outside. The heat and the glare were intense and I ended up at a dingy Starbucks. My piece on the dissident sisters was not due to go online for hours, but I felt paranoid – even if I knew I really was not on the list of Saudi's most wanted.

When I arrived at the plush fight hotel, I was reduced to smiling queasily when a boxing PR person welcomed me to Riyadh and said 'Isn't it great?' We were soon herded onto buses which provided the only permissible transport to the fighters' open workout at a new stadium on a patch of scrubland on the fringes of Riyadh.

We had a long wait. Finally, just before 9.15 p.m., Francis Ngannou walked to the ring at an open-air venue that had been built in sixty days. The main arena next door had still not been completed and it smelt of fresh paint.

Ngannou threw some lumbering punches to the slinky thud of Nigerian singer Burna Boy. His public workout did not bode well as the MMA grappler looked a boxing novice. 'I haven't got any respect from the boxing community,' he said wistfully. 'But if that big shot comes, anything is possible.'

At 10 p.m., Tyson Fury lifted his long legs over the ropes as if striding across a low fence. He danced and shadow-boxed in the ring to a bizarre soundtrack stretching from AC/DC to Depeche Mode. Fury looked as if he could hardly believe the gigantic purse he would earn for fighting an amateur boxer. And so he kidded around through his final preparation.

'I was in there floating like a butterfly,' Fury exclaimed afterwards. 'Nineteen stone, six-foot-nine and moving like that! He's the bull, I'm the matador and, 99.99 per cent of the time, the matador wins. Francis Ngannou is a big, fat sausage. That's why he won't take his top off. He's embarrassed by his body. If it was up to Francis, he'd fight with his T-shirt on. Facts!'

The more salutary facts of nationwide repression, imprisonment, torture and state executions were swept aside as Fury shouted, 'Thank you for turning out to see me tonight in the Kingdom of Saudi Arabia. What a place.'

Fury grinned because not even Saudi Arabia could curb his crass character. 'I'm on fire,' he hollered. 'I feel fantastic. I'm thirty-five years young and ready to knock the motherfucker out.'

His profanity left numerous Saudi dignitaries in flowing white robes shuffling their sandals in dusty embarrassment. The awkward combination of Fury and Saudi Arabia had a few more nights to run before we reached Saturday's circus.

'To be a fighter, you have to have a little screw loose,' Tyson Fury said calmly in his dressing room late on Thursday night, forty-eight hours before he climbed back in the ring. 'Who on earth would want to go and fight against a highly trained athlete, time and time again?'

A shirtless Fury wore a fawn waistcoat and wildly patterned green trousers. He pushed back his green cap as he explained his obsession. 'But I love everything that comes with this game. I don't think there's anything else where you can get happiness, sadness, fear, nerves and excitement all in one night. Going in there on Saturday night will be, for me, as daunting as going up against Deontay Wilder.'

The world heavyweight champion sat with five of us. He had known us all for many years. We were granted a private audience, but it meant that, among fellow writers, my questions about Saudi were compromised. He would wave them away, but there was also a risk he'd terminate the conversation and leave my colleagues without any copy. I shelved them for a while.

But the old Fury, the more interesting and likeable man he had once been, suddenly re-emerged. I reminded him of how, after the third Wilder fight, he had wept.

'It takes a lot of emotion, guts, physicality, spirituality, to keep going even when you've been knocked down twice, like I was in round four,' he said. 'Every time he hit me clean, I was hurt. Then, round eleven, bang! Chinned him. Get up from that. That's my favourite knockout because it was a perfect shot. I ran away and jumped on the ropes, looking at him on the floor.'

This was not just bluster. Fury was thoughtful as he remembered being knocked down twice earlier in that fight. 'Against real punchers like Wilder, you wake up on the floor and, if you're lucky, open your eyes as [the referee] says "Four ...". I remember the referee looked like an alien and said, in an alien voice: "Are you OK?" I was like: "Yeah, let's go!" But I didn't know what had hit me.'

I pointed out that Saturday night would probably be very different as Ngannou seemed to have few boxing skills. 'I hope you're right,' Fury cackled. 'I'm intent on punishing him for a while, putting on a show, then bang! He might be tough as a brick, but he's never been hit by a proper puncher. There's MMA punching and boxing punching.'

I was far more interested in Fury's bout against Usyk in December. The winner would become the first undisputed world heavyweight champion since 1999. 'It's the fight of the century,' Fury said.

Usyk was also a masterful boxer. 'Is he?' Fury asked me. 'Is he any better than the rest? I'm not sure. He had a 50/50 fight with Del Boy [Derek Chisora]. Even Daniel Dubois had a lot of success against him. Without being rude to those guys, they're little more than a heavy bag on legs. Even AJ had lots of opportunity and he didn't do anything. Just walked forward with his hands up around his head, terrified of what's coming back and didn't use his advantages. Do you really think, after all these years of knowing me, I'm going to lose against a guy like that? Oh my God. Please.'

This was typical Fury – a showman capable of describing the 'daunting' challenge of facing a man who has never boxed before and then trashing an outstanding champion in Usyk.

He had already slipped into amusing detail about his daily

routine at home. 'I wake up every morning at six, having gone to bed at nine. It's not stuff you think the heavyweight champion of the world will be busy with. But it's Groundhog Day and keeps me very grounded.'

Fury listed his schedule of tasks: dressing and feeding the kids, taking them to school, getting down on his hands and knees to collect everything the dogs had shredded overnight, picking up teddy bears and cushions before going to the tip to dump the rubbish his seven children accumulated. And then, he said, 'I go to the gym at 4 p.m. every day.'

As a way of cutting down on his chores, Fury had sold more than a hundred properties in the north-west. 'Too much headache, although the rents are good. Imagine dealing with your own family's problems. Times that by a hundred.'

He had just made another small fortune after allowing Netflix to feature him and his family in a reality show. But he claimed he would not box anywhere apart from Saudi Arabia as he had signed a rumoured four-fight contract worth £200m. He also insisted that the one that really mattered, against Usyk, would be a certain victory. 'I will stop him. I guarantee it.'

Fury grinned again, looking utterly at home in the madhouse of boxing.

We stepped into the open-air arena and, while waiting for the final press conference to begin, I received a message. Two young Saudi men, Abdullah al-Derazi and Jalal Labbad, had been sentenced to death for taking part in anti-government protests when they were under eighteen. The teenagers faced the same fate as 112 people who had already been executed in Saudi that year.

I felt a surge of self-contempt for not asking Fury the important questions. He might have offered a stock 'none of my business' reply, but at least I would have tried.

A journalist from the UK came across to say hello. He also asked how I was enjoying my time in Saudi. My evident lack of enthusiasm prompted his next question as to whether I planned another outdated sportswashing feature. He told me about the nightclub he had been to in Riyadh earlier in the week and how the men and women there looked happy and liberated. They did not need alcohol to free themselves. He suggested I stop talking to organisations such as Amnesty International as they painted a distorted image of Saudi.

'I've turned to the East,' he said mysteriously as he stressed that the female members of his family could walk around Riyadh safely at night, and that would not be the case in London or New York. He railed against Western hypocrisy and pointed out problems of addiction and poverty, crime and injustice. He didn't see me writing about such issues when I covered boxing in the US or Britain. Why was I so negative about Saudi?

I asked if he knew about Mohammad bin Nasser al-Ghamdi, a teacher sentenced to death for tweeting innocuous criticism of the state to his ten followers on Twitter.

He had a question of his own. How did I know it was 'innocuous' when I did not speak Arabic? 'Don't believe all you read,' he urged. 'Just open your heart while you're here.'

At the dismal press conference which followed, the promoters and fighters made obsequious tributes to 'His Excellency', Turki Alalshikh, and the glorious Kingdom of Saudi Arabia. Fury and Ngannou then kept being interrupted by a loud, rasping voice. John Fury, Tyson's dad, screamed abuse at Ngannou and, especially, Mike Tyson, who looked bemused. Tyson was meant to be training Ngannou, but his well-paid presence was also a sop to boxing history.

John Fury had named his son after Mike Tyson. But Big John now whipped off his shirt and had to be held back from fighting his old hero. The fifty-seven-year-old Tyson smiled at the lunacy. His reaction infuriated Fury Sr and, in those surreal moments, it was easy to understand why Saudi Arabia and professional boxing seemed made for each other.

Just before midnight, on the bus back to the fighters' hotel, I sat on my own near the back as we rattled through Riyadh. I listened to the heckling voices of some well-known boxing people who had made their names, and money, on YouTube channels. They mocked each other and railed against my colleague who now saw me as a lost soul.

'Have you seen his fucking hotel suite?' one YouTuber exclaimed. 'It's bigger than Fury's.'

While the gossip and bile spilled out, I wondered how much longer I could stay in this world.

On Saturday 28 October 2023, the Rugby World Cup final between New Zealand and South Africa unfolded amid high drama in Paris. But I was stuck in Riyadh with the boxing undercard.

I'd spent the first twenty-three years of my life in South Africa, growing up under apartheid when racism and repression deformed the country. Rugby was the chosen sport of our white minority. But the Springboks were now captained by a remarkable Black man, Siya Kolisi, and their racially mixed team had become a symbol of hope and unity in a nation still scarred by apartheid.

My dad would have been immersed in the game, willing on the Springboks. Even my mother would have set aside her usual antipathy to rugby and cheered. Trapped by boxing, I relied on text updates from Alison at home and Jack wearing his Springbok shirt in a London pub. The game was compelling and the boxing was pedestrian.

It needed a corpulent heavyweight, Martin Bakole, to break the tedium. After he stopped Carlos Takam in a crude slugfest, Bakole alluded bashfully to his weight. He said he looked so out of condition because an injury meant he had barely trained. 'I wanted to thank Anna for helping me get this victory,' he said of his physiotherapist. 'Without Anna, I would not be here.'

The crowd, which had watched the boxing in virtual silence, roared. It was only later that we learned the Saudis were exultant as they thought Bakole had shown deference to Allah rather than the hard-working Anna.

With eight minutes left, South Africa led 12–11. My phone pinged again. Penalty to New Zealand.

I looked up at the black desert sky and imagined my dad burying his head in his hands.

Time passed in slow agony. Finally, the phone pinged again. Missed! Still 12–11.

I was part of a small pack waiting to be led to the main arena. My eyes were fixed on my phone until exuberant messages arrived from Alison and then Jack. South Africa had clung on. They were world champions again. I thought how happy my dad would have been – and I missed him and my mother all over again. They were gone, and I was here.

Sporting happiness and personal loss were soon swamped. After a long concert featuring American rappers and dancers, and spectacular pyrotechnics, a boxing ring rose up magically from beneath the dance floor. It stood resplendent in the suddenly darkened arena. The Saudis were determined to show the world what their money could buy.

Ngannou had told me before the bout that he faced a mountainous challenge against Fury. But he also stressed that, 'I am not afraid of mountains – I have been climbing them all my life.' Born into poverty in a village in Cameroon, Ngannou had begun working in a quarry when he was just ten. Life was no easier when, aged twenty-six in 2012, he left for Paris in the vague hope he might learn how to become a boxer. He was jailed briefly as a refugee before he found work as a nightclub bouncer. Ngannou then began fighting on France's low-key MMA circuit and, with talent and grit, eventually earned himself a contract with the UFC in 2015.

Apart from being immensely likeable, Ngannou proved against Fury that he was also brave and skilled. He almost shocked the world on his boxing debut. Fury looked strangely listless and, in the third round, a big left caught him heavily on the temple and he tumbled to the canvas. Fury got up, but Ngannou surged with confidence.

As they entered the last three rounds, both men were marked and puffy around the eyes. Ngannou landed a long left as he maintained the pressure in the eighth round. He then hit Fury with a hard left and a clubbing series of combinations.

Fury seemed flat in the final two rounds. Weariness also took its toll and he didn't attempt to force the pace. It was almost as if he believed that the judges would favour him.

It had been a poor performance from Fury, and an astonishing display by Ngannou. The first judge believed Ngannou had won 95–94. A second card had the exact same score in Fury's favour, while the third official gave him a 96–93 win. In their ten-round, non-title fight, Ngannou had tarnished Fury's reputation by fighting with fire and purpose while earning $10m. But, as gracious as he was in defeat, Ngannou had been unlucky.

A non-boxer had proved again that boxing could produce drama at the most unexpected times. Fury, with a cut on his head and a swollen face, did not look like a man who could step back into the fire in fewer than eight weeks.

I succumbed to selfishness. 'Thank you, Francis Ngannou,' I murmured.

If Fury's fight against Usyk on 23 December was off, Christmas had been saved. We would still be without an undisputed world heavyweight champion, but I didn't care that much anymore. I would be far happier being home for Christmas. On the hushed and mostly empty last bus back to Riyadh, relief flooded through me.

I had chosen life over boxing.

19

The Test

They fit a clamp into my mouth as I lie on my side on the narrow hospital bed. It stretches my lips wide apart in a grim parody of a smile. Dread spreads through me as a nurse checks I am comfortable.

This is my fourth time and I know what's coming. I fix my gaze on the screen that will show grainy images of my insides. A second nurse reminds me I will gag instinctively and then, the deeper they move, a feeling of fullness will settle inside me despite my having not eaten for twelve hours. It will be bearable, but it will also be tempting to wave in surrender. They will stop and ask if I want to be sedated after all.

If this happens, I might just gesture for them to remove the clamp so I can say 'Sorry, I'm not doing this.' I will leave the state of my gullet to fate.

But I want to live and so I nod when the first nurse asks if they might begin.

She gives my shoulder a reassuring squeeze and then, with a hiss and a gurgle, they slide the tube through the narrow opening of the clamp. A tiny camera is attached to the tube, or endoscope, and as soon as it touches the back of my throat I gag and heave.

It's a horrible feeling, but the endoscopist, a kind Spanish woman, reassures me the worst is over. She is right because I no longer need to retch. The endoscope has begun its journey and I sense the tube being fed inside me. I have swallowed a camera and begun my latest uncomfortable endoscopy.

Six years ago, on holiday in the US with my wife and three teenage kids, my life changed even before I lost my sister and parents. On a sultry late summer evening, we had a barbecue in the rolling green yard outside our apartment. Bella, our eldest, was about to begin university. She would be the first of the kids to leave home and Alison and I knew life was about to assume a different rhythm. We felt proud of them and it was a happy evening as the kids took the piss out of me with deadly accuracy.

And then the slow choking began. An innocuous piece of chicken snagged at the back of my throat. I could not dislodge it, let alone swallow it, and I stood up to find a way of freeing myself of the choking sensation. Everyone was distraught, but I kept reminding them that I could breathe and even talk. This was not a terrible death by suffocation and there was no need for Alison to wrap her arms around me and produce the Heimlich manoeuvre. But I would have taken her cracking a couple of my ribs if it meant I coughed up the rogue chunk of chicken.

We calmed down, because I was still breathing, and I set off for a little walk around the garden in an attempt to loosen the blockage. But nothing worked. An hour later, I agreed I needed to be taken to hospital by the manager of the complex where we were staying.

The kids were close to crying, and Alison looked anxious, as I climbed into the car while wanting to claw at my throat. It was a long journey and the woman driving me to hospital understood I was in too much discomfort to talk. I had to fight back feelings of suffocation as we raced through the dark. But I concentrated on my breathing and banished thoughts of dying because a piece of chicken, lightly basted with soy sauce, honey and garlic, was jammed in my constricted throat.

I must have looked in trouble because they rushed me through reception and straight into an emergency room without checking my medical insurance. The doctor came from the Bronx and his gruff efficiency reassured me. He told me that they would open my windpipe, relax my oesophagus and allow the chicken to disappear down my gullet. The doc said I would feel better in about twenty minutes.

He was right. I texted Alison to say all was OK and that they would just keep me in for a couple of hours to make sure I had recovered completely.

The doctor asked if I had experienced similar problems before. I admitted that, in the preceding months, I occasionally felt an urge to clear my throat repeatedly after eating. It was strange rather than painful.

'If it was me,' the doctor said pointedly, 'I would definitely have this checked out.'

Five days later, I sat in front of my own very serious doctor as she read the notes from the US.

'I'm sending an emergency referral for an endoscopy,' she said.

I reverted to the time-honoured language of such fraught conversations and asked if she thought there might be something 'sinister' to investigate.

She hoped not, but it was important that they were thorough.

I took another breath and asked if they would check for cancer. She nodded before adding that we should not look too far ahead and I needed to avoid Googling my symptoms.

'It could be something minor,' she suggested.

The hospital offered me an endoscopy on a dismal Sunday afternoon. Alison and I left the kids at home, telling them not to worry, and we went through a protracted procedure.

My first endoscopy was a jolting experience, but the staff were caring and attentive. After three hours, I was told that I suffered from a condition called Barrett's oesophagus, where excess acid means that cells in the oesophagus start to change and grow abnormally in a process called dysplasia. Cancer of the oesophagus can result but, with medication and a restricted diet, it is possible to control the spread of dysplasia. They explained that, apart from taking anti-acid pills twice a day, a more drastic change would entail me avoiding so much good stuff, including alcohol, spicy food, coffee and chocolate.

They did not add boxing to the banned items as it is probably too marginal an activity these days. I left hospital feeling relieved and, for the next few years, I was rigorous in sticking to a sober diet.

My third endoscopy, which took a long time to arrange because of Covid, occurred in 2020 and my condition seemed stable. I was advised that I only needed to be checked every three years from then on – and I should stick to decaf coffee, few spices and little alcohol.

'But you've got to live,' another endoscopist advised me when saying that the odd drink on a special occasion should not be forbidden. I just needed to be sensible while enjoying myself on birthdays or anniversaries. No mention was made of getting a little drunk after a great fight or a big win for Arsenal.

All seemed fine until now.

I can feel the endoscope moving down inside me and, embarrassingly, I burp loudly and expressively. My burps come in a rumbling chain and I belch out gassy air like a huge bullfrog who has drunk champagne rather than pond water. I would laugh if I did these at home, out of the earshot of anyone apart from my howling family.

But, in a muffled hospital room, it feels pitiful. While the endoscopist monitors the screen and utters medical terms I do not understand, I keep burping uncontrollably. Each eruption of noise brings some respite from the uncomfortable sense of being filled to the brim.

I wave my hand in apology and the kindest nurse rubs my back. She tells me how well I am doing without sedation.

The endoscopist explains that, as I have a particularly elongated stretch of Barrett's, they need five biopsies. She counts the segments where the camera pauses so that small samples of tissue can be examined in a lab.

Down we go – stopping at 30cm, 32cm, 34cm, 36cm, 38cm and further – and my brain becomes a fog. The nurse pats my back every now and then while ominous words are said quietly by the endoscopist to an assistant recording her observations on a computer.

I think about everyone I love, including one of my closest friends who is deep in treatment for prostate cancer, as it's hard to avoid her words.

The endoscopist says, softly, that there is 'post-acetic acid staining' at 36cm and 'different pigmentation on NBI'.

I have no idea what she means, and no way of asking. My mouth is still clamped shut in its rictus grin. I try to think about the fact I will soon fly to the US to talk to Jean Day and watch Regis Prograis fight Devin Haney in one of the most intriguing bouts of the year.

It helps because, in another few minutes, the endoscopist confirms that they have taken the last of the biopsies. She just needs to move the endoscope down into the second part of the duodenum, which is the first part of the small intestines leading to the stomach. It is important that she scans this area for any irregularities.

Time drags amid her discreet murmurings.

'You've been very good,' the endoscopist eventually says to me, 'and very brave.'

I don't feel good or brave. My head swims, instead, with acid staining and changing pigmentation.

The tube comes up much more quickly than it had gone down and, at last, I feel a surge of relief as it leaves my body. They unclamp my mouth and ask if I am OK. I apologise for my compulsive burping and they smile and remind me that it's totally normal. Then, beyond such niceties, I sit up and ask the endoscopist what she has seen.

She explains that she took more biopsies than usual as they need to rule out 'anything suspicious'. It had been a longer period of surveillance because of a difference in pigmentation.

'That sounds ominous,' I say.

'Maybe not,' she replies. 'It's probably nothing, but we want to make sure. I am hopeful all will be well.' She adds that as soon as my throat recovers, and I have shown them that I can drink a glass of water again, I am free to leave.

There is nothing more I can do now but wait for the life-shaping news.

On 7 November 2023, a month and two days before he stepped into the ring in San Francisco to defend his world title against Devin Haney, I woke Regis Prograis. It was mid-morning in Texas and, on a rest day at home before he headed to Los Angeles for the last three weeks of camp, Regis had gone back to sleep. He dismissed my suggestion that we reschedule our call. 'No, bro,' he said, stifling a yawn. 'I need to get up because this is the biggest fight of my career. Fighting Haney is the one I've been waiting for.'

Haney was the only man to have become an undisputed world lightweight champion in the modern four-belt era. Six months earlier, he had successfully defended his titles in a desperately close battle against Vasiliy Lomachenko. Haney had struggled to make lightweight for years and he name-checked Regis as the best champion in the next division, the 140-pound super-lightweight ranks. He agreed to move up in weight and accept the bout.

'He only took this fight because I looked bad last time out [outpointing Danielito Zorrilla in June],' Regis said. 'Haney is twenty-four, so he's ten years younger than me. I turned pro at twenty-four while he did at seventeen. But he has the mentality of a kid and no idea of the deep waters he will get into with me. I think Bill [Haney's father and head trainer] knows, but the kid doesn't comprehend it. He's cocky and arrogant and thinks it's gonna be easy. But I'm gonna hurt him bad.'

Regis seemed eerily confident against a fighter as good as Haney, so I asked him about his promotional partnership with Eddie Hearn. 'So far everything has been cool, man. The only thing is that he's got a little favouritism towards Haney because he's dealt with him a lot in the past. But, on December 9, I'm gonna break their hearts.'

A drenching rain fell on Freeport early that Saturday morning. The 2nd December 2023 was miserable as I ran slowly away from my motel. I didn't care. It felt beautiful to be running again. After six months, the last residue of pain in my right knee had eased and so, on a much lovelier early afternoon in November, I had gone for my first run.

I followed my old route, through the fields, down the hill and along the canal. I was even slower than usual as I kept waiting for the moment when my knee collapsed beneath me. But it felt like a small miracle. I completed the run I had given up believing would ever happen.

It made sense to keep swimming more than running, and allow my knee to recover fully, and so I still visited the local leisure centre for my 6.30 a.m. slog in the pool three mornings a week. The old fast-lane crew remained and I came to almost love it. I even appreciated the bruises from smacking my hands against the heavy lane dividers.

But I was not a sufficiently keen swimmer to check out the public pools in Freeport and it gave me a good excuse to run instead. I ran down to the main drag, turned left and jogged past the Imperial Diner where I would soon meet Jean Day. I crossed the road and ran alongside the Word of Life Ministries church where Patrick Day's funeral had been held four years before.

I was lucky to be fit and well. When the letter from the NHS arrived on a murky autumn morning, I'd scanned it apprehensively. It had been written by the Spanish endoscopist and the key words came in the Management and Aftercare section.

Long Barrett's oesophagus, C8M10. No suspicious areas but noted

different pigmentation on NBI and poor staining post acetic acid at 36cm,
target samples done. Quadrantic biopsies taken on the remaining segment:
38, 36, 34, 32, 30cm. Pathology results and surveillance plan will follow.

I was in the clear for another three years, unless there was a sudden flaring of my symptoms. So that reprieve, and the fact I was running again, meant a hard rain in Freeport didn't matter.

Four hours later, at the Imperial Diner, Jean slid into the booth with a smile. After everything we had discussed a year earlier, and by staying in close contact and sharing some of my writing about Pat with him, it felt like we knew each other well.

Jean and his twin Bernard had been twelve, and their brother Mike was four, when Pat was born in August 1992 in Freeport. 'Coming back from school every day, I'd feel the joy of knowing you have a baby brother waiting at home,' Jean said. 'You go in and you're peeking in the crib, looking at this little baby. I loved watching him grow. It's crazy because, soon after he learned to talk, he made us laugh. In later years, the kindness inside him was obvious. But his sense of humour won people's hearts.'

When Jean was seventeen, in his senior year of high school, and Pat was five, their parents separated. 'It was tough because you grew up with the mindset of your whole family being together forever. But we loved them and they wanted us to have the next best thing to all being together. So we lived with my mom and, on weekends, we'd hang out with my dad.'

Jean looked across at the church where he had read his remarkable eulogy. 'One thing stands out vividly in my memory. When my dad moved out, he took the dog with him. I remember Pat sitting there crying and speaking to our American bulldog, Duke. He was such a great dog – and Pat loved him. Patrick and I had a lot in common. We both looked like my dad's side of the family and shared a love for animals. So whenever we went to my dad's new place on weekends, we spent so much time with Duke and another dog called Tyson in the backyard.'

The Day boys bonded with their father over boxing. 'Our dad

always loved Mike Tyson. I remember my twin Bernard and I were introduced to boxing by my dad in that Tyson era. We'd have parties and my dad would invite lots of people over for the fight. He'd pour himself a drink, sit down and then, man, the fight would be over even before he finished his drink. But we loved Tyson. He was such a force.

'That curiosity grew in the family when Bernard became the first one to train in a boxing gym. Pat then went to Joe's gym and he encouraged Bernard and I to join him. I remember my mind being blown by the fact that my little brother was boxing. It was exciting but, of course, we had no idea it would eventually take his life.'

Jean looked desperately sad and so I asked him who had been his brother's favourite boxer. 'Pat really liked Sugar Ray Leonard. There was a passing resemblance between the two of them. Both were good-looking, charming guys who were intelligent. Pat also admired Sugar Ray Robinson from the old days – but the fighter he liked most of all was Terence Crawford.'

I thought Crawford had become the best fighter in the world, with his claim to that position rivalled only by Naoya Inoue, the undisputed super-bantamweight world champion. When I began this book, I'd hoped to include Crawford in these pages, but he's a pretty aloof man who doesn't like interviews. So I have yet to meet him, or write about him in detail, which is a source of regret. But I liked hearing Jean recall his brother's only encounter with Crawford.

'I guess Pat was figuring out how to talk to him,' Jean said. 'He just went up to him and because he was a humorous guy, and Crawford's nickname is "Bud", he used a really weird voice and was like "Buuud!"'

Jean imitated his brother's goofy, high-pitched greeting to the formidable Crawford. 'Pat was trying to break the ice. But Crawford looked at Pat as if he was crazy. We were laughing so much and I was like, "Why did you do that?" Pat said: "I have no idea! Crawford was not impressed."'

Jean grinned again. 'I told Pat he would have been better off just saying "Hey, what's up? I'm a big fan." But he was trying to make Crawford laugh. He didn't care that lots of people thought Crawford was mean and hard. He wanted to bring some light to their exchange.'

In July 2023, Crawford knocked out his great rival Errol Spence in a blistering performance in Las Vegas. Both men had been unbeaten and held different versions of the world welterweight crown. A unification contest had been mooted for years without happening. I remembered Jean had once told me that, for all the hurt boxing had caused his family, one of the few fights he'd watch would be a showdown between Crawford and Spence.

So, when it finally happened, had he tuned in? 'Oh yeah,' Jean exclaimed. 'I watched the fight with Mike and my dad. Bernard watched it with a friend at his house, but me and my dad went to Mike's place. We were all shocked at how easily Crawford dispatched Spence.'

Boxing had taken Pat from them but, still, they appreciated the brilliance of Crawford as he stopped Spence in the ninth round. 'We watched the fight as people who understand the brutal art of boxing,' Jean said. 'We are never going to forget what it did to Pat, but we admire Crawford as an incredible fighter. We knew Pat would have been whooping for Crawford.'

When we met again the following day, for another lunch at the Imperial Diner, I said to Jean that it sounded as if he had reconciled himself a little to the old ambivalence that boxing generates in most of us who follow it closely. 'At first, after Pat's death,' Jean said, 'I didn't watch boxing at all. It was too painful. But after that Crawford fight, I started to think about the happier boxing memories I shared with Pat. I remembered all the times it was just me and him, and we'd jump on the train at Freeport station. We would catch the Long Island Rail Road and go into the city, to the Barclays Center, to watch boxing. We had some special times.'

Jean's eyes opened wide. 'One night, we were at the Barclays

Center when Spence fought Chris Algieri [in 2016]. What I remember most is hearing Spence's shots landing. I turned to Pat and said: "Man, he's punching so hard. That's no joke.'"

Boxing always dragged us back to its violent finality. It meant that, no matter the drama and the excitement, we could not avoid the danger and ruin. It was one of the reasons why his parents preferred not to talk about Pat's death.

'They are incredible,' Jean said. 'My mom, especially, because I was scared that she would break. But one day she told me she'd had enough. This was three years after Pat was gone. She said that she couldn't stay stuck in the same place. It was doing her no good and Pat would not want her to be this way. My mom did not want to grieve forever. She wanted to live again.'

Jean looked up. The diner was quiet as lunch had ended hours earlier. 'I was so proud of her. I saw her strength and wisdom. I'm not there yet. I still want to expose what boxing did to Patrick, but I remember the joy and the laughter he gave us more powerfully than ever.'

Flying from New York to San Francisco on the Monday of fight week, I felt intrigued and hopeful for Regis Prograis. Victory over Devin Haney would elevate him into the top ten in the mythical pound-for-pound rankings, with huge fights to potentially follow against boxers such as Ryan Garcia and Gervonta Davis. But Haney was a gifted technician who would give Regis the most testing fight of his life.

The fight-game rollercoaster had surged wildly through 2023. In late July, a National Anti-Doping Panel ruled that the provisional UKAD suspension of Conor Benn should be lifted. The boxer had not been cleared of doping and no explanation was made for the presence of clomifene in his system on two separate occasions the previous year. UKAD would appeal against the decision, but Benn released a statement: 'I have now been vindicated for a second time. Hopefully the public and various members of the media can now understand why I have maintained my innocence so strongly all the way through.'

Benn and Hearn claimed that the investigation had 'formally ended' and he was now 'free to fight'. This was not strictly true. On 17 August, UKAD confirmed that it had lodged its appeal against the lifting of Benn's suspension. The British Boxing Board of Control also stressed that they would not license Benn to fight in the UK until he had cleared his name.

But Benn could box abroad and the Florida Boxing Commission approved a request for him to fight in Orlando. It was announced only in the week of the bout that he would face an obscure Mexican, Rodolfo Orozco, on 23 September. I chose not to write about the fight, or watch it. Instead, I read the following day that Benn had produced a laboured performance while winning a unanimous verdict on points. His career had resumed, but the shadows remained. He would not be allowed to fight in Britain for the fore-seeable future.

A week later, I got up in the early hours of Sunday 1 October to watch Canelo Álvarez dominate Jermell Charlo, Regis's friend from Houston, and retain his four world super-middleweight titles in a crushing performance. But the hold Canelo had once exerted over me had slipped. I felt, like me, he was no longer in thrall to boxing.

I was more enthused by Katie Taylor. She had led the remark-able rise of women in boxing. There were still a few female fighters whose celebrity status was built as much on the skimpy lingerie they chose for the weigh-in as their limited fistic prowess. But Taylor defined the new seriousness of women's boxing.

Most people wrote her off and she seemed unusually spiky before her rematch against Chantelle Cameron in Dublin on 25 November. 'I hate all the talk,' Taylor said a few days before the bout as she dropped her typical politeness and showed how much she needed to defeat Cameron, the only woman to beat her as a pro.

The pain Taylor had been through could be heard in her dis-missal of the fripperies surrounding the fight. 'I hate all these press conferences, there's nothing to say. The only people I listen to are my team, my family, the people I trust.'

The thirty-seven-year-old bristled when asked if she would consider retirement if she lost again to Cameron. 'Don't insult me,' Taylor murmured.

The odds were stacked against her, but Taylor spoke with renewed urgency. 'I'm ready to dig deep and that's why I put my body through the trenches week in, week out. I understand this is a must-win fight for me. I'm like a woman possessed.'

There was something magnificent in watching Taylor roll back the years once more to preserve her remarkable career. In a gruelling and compelling bout, she was awarded the justified decision by margins of 98–92 and 96–94, while the third judge scored it as a 95–95 draw as Taylor became the new undisputed super-lightweight champion of the world. She also retained her status as the world lightweight champion. Taylor had proved again that she was an exceptional fighter.

After that uplifting victory, and Isaac Chamberlain becoming British and Commonwealth champion, I just needed Regis Prograis to prevail in the fight of his life to seal the end of another boxing year with fresh hope and light.

'I'm calm, but I'm also a little anxious, and definitely nervous,' Regis Prograis said in his room high up in a ritzy hotel in downtown San Francisco. Books, bags, shirts, shoes, water bottles and boxing gloves were swept to one side as he made space for me to sit next to him on a sofa. As a boxing historian and a champion fascinated by the psychology of elite sport, Regis was more interested in embracing the tension and fear all fighters experience before a brutal test. 'These nerves give you an edge,' he added as he recalled Mike Tyson's legendary first trainer. 'Cus D'Amato used to say if you're not nervous, then you're lying or you're crazy. You need this nervous energy. I visualise the outcome and I see a real good night for me, and the destruction of Haney, but until we get to the arena, I have this anxiety. I want to fight now.' For D'Amato, 'fear is like fire. It can warm you, cook your food and give light in the dark. But let it get out of control and it can hurt you, even kill you. Fear is a friend of exceptional people.'

Haney had just turned twenty-five and was regarded by many pundits as the likely winner. The Dream, as Haney called himself, had great skill and he was returning to the city of his birth.

Regis seemed to like Haney's dad and trainer, Bill, more than the fighter himself. When he was twenty-two, Haney Sr had been sentenced to five years in prison for possession and conspiracy to sell cocaine. He spent forty months at Lompoc Penitentiary in California before being released a year and eight months early for good behaviour. Haney Sr, realising that he would be killed on the streets or end up back in jail if he did not change, had turned his life round.

'Bill is like everybody I knew coming up on the street,' Regis said. 'He has the lingo and I've been around these guys my whole life. Devin has had a different and very privileged life and he needs his dad to be the big dog. My whole team comes from that street environment, so all this trash talk don't mean nothing to us. But we're not going to allow them to treat me like the challenger. I'm the champion.'

Regis was one of the most interesting men I'd met in my thirty years of writing about boxing. No other fighter spoke about boxing literature with his knowledge and insight, and I was curious to hear how he would control his fear. 'You know me,' he said. 'I'm always reading and right now I'm deep in this one.'

He picked up a dog-eared and heavily underlined copy of a book about psychology. 'I read this two times already, so I'm just going over stuff. I've been training four months for this fight and now I'm just anxious for time to pass so I can reach my destiny.'

We revisited the years since he lost to Josh Taylor in London, in October 2019. 'I was in boxing purgatory,' Regis said. 'The first fight back [after Taylor] was on the undercard and none of those three opponents in three years made me nervous. But all that frustration made me stronger and I have a good family. I have my wife and three kids and we travel a lot and I'm a good husband and father. So I kept that life separate and I never stopped believing in myself even when things felt shitty in boxing.

'That's how it's been since [Hurricane] Katrina. My daddy always says I had a harder route than everybody but I just keep going.'

In examining his past adversity, and admitting his nerves against Haney, Regis showed real courage. He believed 'you learn more in failure or defeat' and he had been steeled by his spell in the wilderness. Haney seemed untouched by life in comparison.

'I've tasted defeat and frustration,' Regis said. 'I've been in a locker room after I lost and never want to go there again. When you taste failure, it makes you much stronger. Devin's never had failure so it's hard to know how he will react. So far he's been winning [with a 30–0 record compared to Regis's 29–1 résumé], but when it gets hard on Saturday he could fold.'

I asked Regis again about the way in which Eddie Hearn appeared to favour Haney by treating him like the A-side fighter. Even in fight week, Hearn had turned to Regis first, as if he was the challenger, when introducing the fighters. Regis insisted on being called second.

'It's cool. I said, "Eddie, I know Devin's your boy, but I'm gonna whup him bad."'

The fighter was an amusing trash-talker, but he had allowed Evins Tobler, his rumbustious strength-and-conditioning coach, to shout down Haney Sr in street-style slanging matches. Regis was just as profane and vocal at Thursday's final conference when his usual humour was lost in a blizzard of swearing.

He was much more thoughtful in his hotel room and opened up amid the ravaging weight cut. 'We're getting to the hardest time now,' he said, 'which is the night before [Friday's] weigh-in. It's a miserable night.'

Regis described how he took one steaming bath after another, with the temperature so hot he could barely stand it, while starving and dehydrated. 'Last time, the night before the weigh-in, I was 146 pounds, so I had to lose six pounds that night. This time will be easier.'

He looked briefly pensive. 'You have to come from a certain environment because it's so hard. You have to be so disciplined, so dedicated, to put up with this pain. I'm not even talking about the emotions of boxing, when you have so many feelings running through you. You get doubts when you're losing all that weight because you don't feel like yourself. But once the weigh-in is done, and I can eat again, I feel like myself. It's showtime.'

Regis offered a contrast to most boxers in his willingness to talk about taboo subjects – from hidden vulnerabilities to systemic doping. But he was also determined to gain the recognition he deserved as the most crucial night of his career loomed. 'I had a dream last night and it was after the fight. I was with Eddie Hearn.'

He laughed. 'Sounds like a nightmare but I'd just beaten Haney. We were in the car and I'd won the fight. That's what I see all the time – me being victorious. I am locked into that vision. When it happens, I'm going to be super-happy, so much so that I might cry a little, because I'll be grateful to show the world what I've always known – that this is my destiny.'

Chase Center, San Francisco, Saturday 9 December 2023

Devin Haney walks to the ring in a black tunic as the announcer David Diamante hollers his welcome to *'Devin "The Dream" Hanneeeyyy!'*

Haney, concentrated and gleaming, bounces around the ring. Diamante rips through the next introduction while Regis Prograis, wearing a massive Rougarou mask in honour of his Cajun heritage, appears on the giant screen above my ringside seat. He is followed by his little boy, Ray, dressed in an identical costume. Diamante yells: 'Fighting out of New Orleans, Louisiana, here is the reigning

and defending WBC super-lightweight champion of the world ...
Regis "Rougarouuu" Prograis!'

The referee Jack Reiss brings the fighters together. 'Fight hard, fight clean,' he says. 'Good luck to you both.'

Haney lands the first meaningful punch, snaking out a fast and slippery left jab as they both start cautiously. Prograis, fighting as a southpaw, looks to use his right jab but Haney moves fluidly. He stays out of the way until, deep in the first round, he unleashes a flurry of punches.

Prograis goes downstairs early in the second, but Haney responds with sneaky little uppercuts and cuffing overhand rights. I lean forward in hope as Prograis tries to slow his rival with a series of combinations, but Haney ghosts away. Prograis's wild swing with his left hand, which misses by some distance, is answered by a short, shuddering right cross from Haney. It lands squarely on Prograis's jaw. It makes me wince, and the sold-out 20,000 crowd roar.

Haney boxes with swaggering confidence. Prograis moves forward aggressively, but his punches don't connect and Haney nails him again with a right uppercut. A worrying pattern takes hold. In the last ten seconds of the round, Prograis lunges forward and, as he slips, Haney pushes him to the canvas. The referee rules, correctly, that it is not a knockdown. He wipes Prograis's red-and-black gloves on his powder-blue shirt.

In the corner, Bill Haney praises his son and tells him to stick to their game plan. The fight is unfolding just as they expected.

Haney throws a rapid and accurate combination to welcome Prograis to round three and then, with jolting impact, a decisive moment comes. A hard straight right detonates against Prograis's chin. The champion tumbles to the canvas. He sticks out his right glove to break his fall and, rather than stretching out on his back, he manages to spin himself around and then push himself up onto his feet. But it had been a peach of a punch and Prograis nods in acknowledgement. He walks to a neutral corner.

The referee, having shepherded Haney away, picks up the count. 'Four,' he barks at Prograis, holding the same number of fingers in the air.

'Five,' he shouts, flashing all five digits on his right hand.

I feel sick and anxious. 'Six,' Reiss counts, but he can tell Prograis is ready to fight on. He looks over his shoulder to check Haney is still on the opposite side of the ring.

'Seven,' he continues.

Prograis looks alert as they are allowed to resume the fight with two-and-a-half minutes left in the third round. Haney carries a mean look as he closes in, looking for the opening to land another big right. Prograis ties him up and drives Haney back to the ropes. It seems as if his head is already clearing but, still, Prograis finds it immensely difficult to catch Haney, who clips him with contrasting ease.

I can feel hope draining away. Prograis is meant to be the venomous puncher, while Haney is supposed to be a light-hitting stylist who has not stopped any of his last seven opponents. But a salutary realisation creeps up on me. In moving up in weight, a stronger Haney now has real power to match his speed and dexterity. As they work on Prograis in the corner, trying to reduce the swelling around both eyes, I feel for a fighter I know so well.

Haney comes out like a sleek train in the fourth. Moving in and out, back and forth, from side to side, he lands blows and evades their replies. He looks supreme while Prograis flounders. The backs of both fighters gleam with sweat under the hot lights, while Prograis tries desperately to close the distance and force a change in momentum. But Haney keeps popping off fast combinations to add to the slow swelling of Prograis's face.

There is more of the same in the next round as Haney's crisp punching and sumptuous movement dominate. Then, with fifty seconds left in the sixth, a hard left jab sets up a short right cross that makes Prograis stagger backwards. He waves Haney back in and sees out the round. But Prograis is in dark trouble.

The fight is halfway through and it's been a landslide for Haney. Prograis needs a knockdown of his own, and to win the remaining rounds, to match Haney on the scorecards. The chances of this happening seem, as Don King used to say, slim and none, and slim is out of town.

Haney switches to bodywork in round seven, before mixing it up by going upstairs again. He seems able to land at will. At the end of the round, the doctor steps into the corner to make sure Prograis is not taking too much punishment. The champion waves him away.

Bill Haney sounds contemptuous. 'Let's get this clown outta there,' he tells his son.

Prograis looks nothing like a clown to me. He is losing badly, but he's still brave and determined. He has not resorted to dirty tactics, protests or looked for a way out of the beating. Even when Haney rocks him again in the ninth, and Prograis stumbles when he misses with a big punch near the end of the round, I sense his resolve.

In the eleventh round, he is still trying and still throwing punches. Haney has not been able to extinguish his will.

The final round starts and Prograis looks noble in his lonely defiance. He marches forward and briefly backs Haney against the ropes. Prograis snaps out the right jab and looks for an opening to land a thunderous and fight-saving knockout blow. Haney slides away.

At the sound of the last bell, Prograis embraces Haney and talks quietly to the man who has just beaten him in such painfully emphatic style. Prograis then crosses the ring to congratulate Bill Haney. They had exchanged bitter words in the build-up but, now, Prograis places his gloves on Haney Sr's chest while the trainer nods in appreciation.

Haney doesn't celebrate wildly as the scorecards have already told the story of the one-sided fight. All three judges have scored it a 120–107 shutout for the new champion. It has been a shattering night for Regis Prograis.

*

The terrible marks of battle cover the face of the fallen champion as he comes out first for the inquisition in the basement. An hour earlier, Regis spoke with raw honesty in the ring.

'That motherfucker's good. He's better than I thought he was. I just couldn't get to him. I thought he was a soft puncher, but he does have power. I was down and I was like, "What the fuck happened?"'

Regis's face is bruised, cut and swollen, while red blotches are smeared across his forehead and beneath his left eye, like lipstick applied in a drunken daze. But his grace is clear as he praises Haney's sublime performance. 'I was trying and trying but I couldn't get to him,' Regis says, lauding Haney's 'quick and sneaky power' and dazzling footwork.

The thirty-four-year-old cuts a moving figure as, rather than hiding away in sorrow, he faces us. An American reporter speaks solemnly but compassionately as he urges Regis to 'hold your head up high, walk tall. You're still a champion to the people and I wouldn't give up if I was you.'

Regis nods as the old fire in him blazes again. 'Thank you for the words, but I'm definitely not giving up. Like I said, three-time world champion, that's my goal right now. I told all my people in the dressing room, while they were crying: "Bro, pick your head up. It's a fight. You're gonna win or lose." For this fight, I trained my ass off for four months, and it just wasn't good enough. Sometimes that's gonna happen in life.'

Eddie Hearn wraps up the press conference by saying 'Well done, Devin'. He quickly realises his slip of the tongue and corrects himself, a little sheepishly, by turning to the deposed champion and saying his correct name: 'Regis'.

Regis glances at him, shakes his head with a bleak laugh, and sighs. 'Goddamn, Eddie . . .'

While others wait for Haney's regal arrival, I follow Regis out of the interview room and down the corridor towards the cold night outside where the cars are waiting to take him and his team back to their hotel. He walks ahead of his trainers, friends and family.

He would be alone, but for the fact that his seven-year-old daughter, Khalessi, clutches his left hand which had failed to do any damage to Haney.

Regis turns when I call his name. He smiles and walks over to extend his right hand. It had also not hurt Haney, but none of that matters now. I tell him how much I'd admired the way he had conducted himself amid the heartbreak.

'Thank you, Don,' Regis says. 'I tried, bro, but he was too good.'

As we clench hands, I remember how much you learn about the character of a man in defeat.

Regis will soon travel through the darkened streets of downtown San Francisco. But at least he is not alone. He has his family and team around him as well as the consoling knowledge that, in accepting a devastating loss with such class and composure, he had looked more like a champion of a man than ever before.

I tell him as much and he grips my hand. 'I appreciate it, man,' he replies. 'It's boxing. It's life. Sometimes we lose and it hurts like fuck. But, bro, we get up and we go on.'

20

Resolution

Riyadh, Saudi Arabia, Monday 13 May 2024

Just after five o'clock that morning, at the very start of fight week, a beautiful and hauntingly insistent call to prayer rang out as I walked through the city. The voice of the muezzin was steady and profound, echoing through the mostly empty streets with the power of his delivery accentuated by those moments when it drifted into fleeting silence.

In the dry stillness the adhan resumed soon afterwards, with the call sounding even fuller, as if a yearning had strengthened the reverberating voice. My parents were suddenly with me, at least in my head. Unlike me, they had been churchgoers, full of faith in God until the early morning hours when, less than a year apart from each other, they had drawn their final breath. I sensed their presence more clearly than I'd done in a long time.

As the solitary voice kept calling, I remembered how adrift I had felt nearly six years before when Heather died and my parents were so ill. It was then that I turned back to boxing. On 2 December 2018, I rose at 3.45 a.m. to watch Tyson Fury haul himself up from years of confusion and despair for a riveting world heavyweight title fight against Deontay Wilder.

I slipped deep into boxing's shadowy world of courage and deceit, glory and grime, and soon remembered the bracing truth of the great old trainer Brendan Ingle. Long before his death in May 2018, he had suggested that 'at its worst, boxing is a dirty, rotten, prostituting game. But, at its best, it's the most beautiful thing that you'll ever see.'

So, at the outset of a historic week for boxing in Riyadh, it felt right to carry seemingly contradictory ideas simultaneously. As the muezzin approached the end of his beseeching chant, I was intrigued and even excited by the prospect of Fury and Oleksandr Usyk fighting for the first undisputed heavyweight championship of the world this century. But I also thought long and hard about Turki Alalshikh, the man who had made Saturday night's bout possible.

I'd been unable to sleep, having arrived nine hours earlier in the oppressive heat. The night passed fitfully, even though the humming air conditioner cooled my hotel room. I stared into the darkness and recalled how I would have once been wildly smitten by fight week and the overblown words Norman Mailer had used before Muhammad Ali fought Joe Frazier in 1971.

Mailer had suggested, with a kind of drunken fervour, that 'the closer a heavyweight comes to the championship, the more natural it is for him to be a little more insane, secretly insane, for the heavyweight champion of the world is either the toughest man in the world or he is not, but there is a real possibility that he is. It's like being the big toe of God.'

The old braggart of American literature added with absurd grandeur that 'when the heavyweights become champions, they begin to have inner lives like Hemingway or Dostoevsky, Tolstoy or Faulkner, Joyce or Melville, or Conrad or Lawrence or Proust'.

After thirty-five years of being around world heavyweight champions, I was no longer a sucker for such romantic bullshit. Boxing, like life itself, made its greatest fighters feel glorious and desolate, elevating and eroding them at different stages of their career, even if their complex and vulnerable inner lives were little like those of Dostoevsky or Proust. Mailer's riff seemed the lofty equivalent of some hopeful YouTuber ending an interview by asking for a selfie with a champion while they both hold a fist in the air – as if the non-boxing mug in the pic could feel like he, too, was a fighter for a few moments.

After the last echo of the adhan subsided, I turned down a side street, away from the road where the traffic would build with the heat. I felt a sudden longing for Fury and Usyk to produce a gripping contest which rekindled the lost majesty of boxing. For the first time in years, there was genuine mainstream interest in a heavyweight title fight. But even with Turki Alalshikh's lucrative backing, there had been doubts. After Fury had nearly lost to Francis Ngannou almost four months before, his bout with Usyk was pushed back to 17 February. Then, fifteen days before the fight, Fury was cut in sparring.

The wound required 'significant stitching' and Egis Klimas, the abrasive manager of Usyk, suggested the cut had been self-inflicted. 'Tyson Fury is a fucking coward who will do anything not to face Usyk, and he asked his bitch to hit him with a frying pan in his brow.'

Alex Krassyuk, Usyk's promoter, was more politely barbed when he messaged Fury. 'Wish you soonest recovery. God sent you a sign. Think of retirement, brother.'

Fury, for once, limited himself to a mild outburst. 'I ain't retiring,' he said as he promised to have at least five more fights, starting with two against Usyk, the first of these on the rescheduled date of 18 May.

It would take another seven hours for the temperature to climb to a high of forty-two degrees, so there was time to think about more than a world heavyweight title fight. But even a quiet stroll soon after dawn meant a sheen of sweat made my skin prickle. I felt a strange chill too.

On 2 October 2018, Jamal Khashoggi was murdered in the Saudi Arabian consulate in Istanbul. A prominent Saudi journalist who wrote a column in exile for the *Washington Post*, Khashoggi was an outspoken critic of Mohammed bin Salman and his assassination had made headline news around the world. I read about his demise in a blur, as just seventeen days had passed since Heather's death.

Khashoggi had entered the consulate to obtain a document which would enable him to marry his fiancée. A hit squad was waiting for him. Turkish intelligence officers said that a team of fifteen Saudi agents had arrived in Istanbul a few days before the murder and that they had removed the surveillance cameras from the consulate. Irfan Fidan, Turkey's chief prosecutor, concluded in late October that Khashoggi had been suffocated soon after his arrival and that his body had been dismembered.

The Saudis, including bin Salman, initially denied that Khashoggi had been killed. But they soon alleged that a 'rogue' operation had taken place without official approval. Finally, in mid-November 2018, Saudi Arabia's deputy public prosecutor Shalaan al-Shalaan said the plan was instigated by the head of a 'negotiations team' sent to Istanbul to bring Khashoggi back to Riyadh 'by means of persuasion' or 'force'.

In December 2019, the Riyadh Criminal Court sentenced five men to death for 'committing and directly participating in the murder of the victim' and three others were sent to prison. The death penalties were eventually overturned and the Kingdom of Saudi Arabia was accused of ignoring the culpability of those in power. Meanwhile, the CIA and the United Nations concluded that 'credible evidence' showed that Mohammed bin Salman had sanctioned the execution of the fifty-nine-year-old journalist.

When it became obvious in 2023 that Turki Alalshikh was planning to take control of boxing, I learned that, under a name spelt slightly differently in some foreign reports, he had been well-known to Khashoggi. The French news agency AFP reported in October 2018 that 'Jamal Khashoggi criticised Crown Prince Mohammed bin

Salman's "authoritarian rule" shortly before his death . . . Speaking off the record to a *Newsweek* journalist, he insisted that "I'm not calling for the overthrow of the regime, because I know it's not possible and is too risky. I'm just calling for reform of the regime."'

Khashoggi described bin Salman as 'an old-fashioned tribal leader' who still 'wants to enjoy the fruits of First World modernity and Silicon Valley and cinemas and everything, but at the same time he wants also to rule like how his grandfather ruled Saudi Arabia'.

AFP said that 'Khashoggi described two of the prince's aides – sports chief Turki al-Sheikh and the since-dismissed media adviser Saud al-Qahtani – as "very thuggish. People fear them. You challenge them, you might end up in prison, and that has happened."'

Khashoggi's last column for the *Washington Post*, filed on 18 September 2018, was headlined: 'Saudi Arabia wasn't always this repressive. Now it's unbearable.'

In November 2019, the *New York Times* reported that 'when Crown Prince Mohammed bin Salman of Saudi Arabia convened an outdoor banquet this spring for his fellow Arab rulers, seated among the kings, princes and presidents were two friends with few qualifications other than their closeness to the young prince himself: a poet who has become known for orchestrating ferocious social media campaigns, and a former security guard who runs the Saudi sports commission. The two men had each played pivotal roles in many of the brazen power plays that have marked Prince Mohammed's sprint to dominance of the kingdom.'

The newspaper added that 'even Saudi royals have come to fear the prince's two friends — Saud al-Qahtani, 40, and Turki al-Sheikh, 37 ... Now the killing of the Saudi dissident Jamal Khashoggi by Saudi agents has focused attention on their roles as enablers of the crown prince's impulsiveness and aggression.'

It was suggested that 'Mr Sheikh was a bodyguard in Prince Mohammed's security detail who charmed the prince with his sense of humor and intense loyalty. Roughly the same age, they developed a personal rapport, and the prince rewarded Mr Sheikh with a seemingly limitless budget to make the kingdom an international contender in tennis, boxing, soccer and other sports.'

The *New York Times* claimed to have proof that the ambitious sports minister had 'splurged on a $4.8 million limited-edition Bugatti Chiron sports car' in September 2018. More seriously, it alleged that he and al-Qahtani 'acted as interrogators, demanding that the captives confess to corrupt self-enrichment and pledge to surrender vast sums, according to relatives and close associates of several detainees. Although blindfolded during some interrogations, detainees told relatives that they saw the two men or recognized their voices from broadcast interviews. Others said that through hotel room windows, they saw Mr Sheikh coming and going surrounded by armed guards.'

Saudi and Turkish sources told Reuters that Qahtani had made a Skype call to the Istanbul consulate on the day of the murder and 'began hurling insults at Khashoggi'. The US Treasury also sanctioned Qahtani and described him as being 'part of the planning and execution of the operation that led to the killing of Mr. Khashoggi'.

Qahtani was relieved of his official duties and disappeared from public view, but he was later cleared of the charges by an internal state investigation.

Mohammed bin Salman had been appointed as crown prince by his father, King Salman, in 2017. He had succeeded his father as prime minister in 2022 and tried to drive significant social and economic change while bolstering his family's grip on power. The crown prince believed that Saudi Arabia's vast financial resources needed to rely less on oil and, instead, broaden its economic might by making the kingdom more appealing to foreign investment and tourism. The Saudis had the money to be patient while pouring billions into sport as a lever of change.

Ed Caesar pointed out in the *New Yorker* that 'between 2016 and 2023, Saudi Aramco, the state oil company, made profits of seven hundred and twenty-two billion dollars, making it, by some distance, the most profitable company in the world. (During the same period, Apple reported only five hundred and fifty-eight billion in profits.) Mohammed bin Salman foresees a future without oil, and hopes to diversify the economy. The Public Investment Fund, which is dedicated to that end, is worth nearly a trillion dollars. Such numbers make the giant purse for the Usyk–Fury bout—a hundred and fifty million dollars —seem like pocket change.'

Saudi Arabia had opened its arms to sport and allowed some liberalisation. Music was no longer banned in elevators and restaurants and, instead, concerts and festivals were supported by the Public Investment Fund. Women could file for divorce even if, to do so, it often involved withstanding intense family pressure not to undermine a traditional subservience. But these changes could not hide the fact that the country had actually become more repressive in its clampdown on dissent. Sweeping laws against 'terrorism' meant that the state could still detain and execute people.

The previous week, Fawzia al-Otaibi had spoken about her sister Manahel being jailed in Riyadh for eleven years by an anti-terrorism court. Manahel had been arrested for 'her choice of clothing and support for women's rights' and Fawzia told the *Guardian* that 'for the first time, I hated the fact that I was created a woman in my country, a country that had destroyed me and my family and turned our lives into an unbearable hell for the crime that we are women who want our right to life'.

Manahel was charged on a number of criminal counts, which included supporting women's rights on social media and posting Snapchat photos of herself shopping while wearing dungarees rather than the traditional abaya. The situation worsened when the case was moved to a court specialising in terrorism-related offences.

The twenty-nine-year-old's fate only became known in May 2024 when Saudi officials confirmed her sentence for 'terrorist offences' to the UN. On 1 May 2024, Fawzia, responding on X to her sister's imprisonment, asked: 'Can you believe they have imprisoned her, tortured her, broken her foot, terrorised her, and accused her of terrorism? Just because she is a woman advocating for women's rights. Why have my rights become terrorism, and why is the world silent?'

Back in my hotel room, and preparing to write an article about Saudi Arabia, I did an online search. Manahel al-Otaibi was held in al-Malaz prison which Google Maps confirmed was less than ten miles from the luxurious Hilton Hotel and Residences in downtown Riyadh, where I would talk to Fury and Usyk later that afternoon. I started another search and discovered that the hotel was forty miles from al-Ha'ir prison where Mohammad bin Nasser al-Ghamdi was incarcerated after he had been sentenced to death by the special-ised criminal court on 10 July 2023. He had since been moved to Dhahban prison in Jeddah.

Al-Ghamdi was found guilty of terrorism for posts on two dif-ferent X accounts. The first account had eight followers, while the second was followed by two people. He criticised the crown prince, but most of his posts apparently focused on the need for economic reforms and complaints about rising prices and supermarket queues.

His brother Dr Saeed bin Nasser al-Ghamdi told me that 'the worst thing is that he was arrested for a few tweets, which were barely seen by the police officers, and they were tweets criticising the increase in milk prices'. I asked him if Mohammad, a retired schoolteacher, could be saved from execution for a series of seem-ingly innocuous posts. 'It is part of our Islamic religion not to despair and to submit to God's will. If [execution] happens, we are prepared.'

A Saudi academic and dissident exiled in Britain, Saeed al-Ghamdi was far more politically outspoken than his brother and he argued that 'repression in Saudi Arabia has not diminished. It's increasing. Manahel al-Otaibi was sentenced to eleven years for charges that the authorities say are related to "terrorism". Most of the peaceful detainees are charged with terrorism. The so-called terrorism law is written in a way that is not Islamically or legally correct because it is broad and vague.'

I asked for his thoughts on the boxing that weekend. 'If it happens that some of them [involved in the promotion] did not know about the oppressive situation of the regime, or were tempted by money, they can reclaim their humanity by abandoning their participation while they are in Saudi Arabia – or by publicly demanding that the state abolish the security trials and these imprisonments.'

Of course, the undisputed heavyweight championship of the world would not be derailed by a sudden fit of political conscience. There was too much money and personal glory at stake. But, in the heat and looming tumult of fight week, the grim fate of Mohammad al-Ghamdi, Manahel al-Otaibi and other political prisoners in Saudi Arabia remained unchanged.

Mayhem broke out in the Hilton Hotel that afternoon in Riyadh. Tyson Fury and Oleksandr Usyk were tucked away, in the midst of television interviews, and I chatted to Frank Warren with some British reporters. It was all very routine, even when a dozen members of Team Usyk kicked up a racket and chanted '*Uuu-sykkk … Uuu-sykkk … Uuu-sykkk …*'

We had heard it so often that we only looked across when the small posse of Fury's brothers and their father began shouting. After John Fury had hollered '*Fuuy-ryyy … Fuuy-ryyy … Fuuy-ryyy*', while the camera crews jostled to film the stand-off, there was a lull. But, then, one of the youngest Ukrainians, Stanislav Stepchuk, resumed a cheerful chant of Usyk's name.

John Fury suddenly smashed his head into Stepchuk's face.

Ironically, Fury Sr was left bleeding heavily from a gash across his forehead while Stepchuk sustained just a tiny cut. Hefty security men struggled to hold back the belligerent Fury brothers while their dad dabbed forlornly at his wound with a tissue. 'I live for this fucking shit!' he roared. 'I live for blood, guts and horror!'

It was easy to understand why Fury Sr had spent four years in prison after being found guilty of grievous bodily harm in 2011. He had left his victim blind in one eye.

He was handed a small white towel so that he could wipe the blood from his forehead and face and he did not initially see Alex Krassyuk, Usyk's promoter, walk over.

'I'm here to say apologies,' Krassyuk said in a classy touch.

'Do not disrespect our champion,' Fury Sr growled. 'We did not disrespect your man.'

'Apologies,' Krassyuk said, 'in a very respectful way.'

The Ukrainian's diplomacy softened even old man Fury. 'No problem,' he told Krassyuk.

'Fuck them all,' Krassyuk said, knowing how to speak to Fury as they embraced.

A few minutes later, the headbutt was already on the internet and footage from the clearest angle made the young Ukrainian look mightily impressive. When Fury's head cracked into his face, Stepchuk was unflinching. It was as if a mere headbutt was nothing compared to everything else he and all Ukrainians endured in the war against Russia.

Stepchuk was asked whether he wanted to fight back. 'Yeah,' the twenty-eight-year-old said with a little smile, 'but because of the age difference, it would not be very fair.'

Boxing shenanigans mattered little amid a new tragedy. Sherif Lawal, a British middleweight, had made his professional debut the night before when he fought Malam Varela at the Harrow Leisure Centre, just north of London. Varela was born in Portugal but based in Manchester and had a poor record. After winning his pro debut, he then lost all four of his subsequent bouts. Lawal was knocked down in the fourth round and the fight was waved over. He had been badly hurt and, despite being rushed to hospital, he died later that night.

Tyson Fury was surprised when we told him the news. 'God rest his soul, poor old fella,' he said. 'You know getting into this sport that it's dangerous. You're getting your brains knocked out, you're not there to tickle each other to death. I've known the risks my whole life. If it's God's will, then I'll die. If not, I'll live.'

As happened so often when I sat down with Fury, away from the cameras and the crowds, a thoughtful and complicated man emerged. Having just witnessed the needy rage of Fury Sr, I thought Tyson had turned out better than most of us might have done in his circumstances.

Forty-five minutes earlier, he'd been shocked by the bloodied sight of his father. 'What have you done to your head, you silly cunt?' he asked.

He could be boorish, but Fury was never violent outside the ring. I could do without his demeaning insults of Usyk but, the closer we came to the fight, it was striking how he no longer used words like 'dosser' or 'midget'.

Fury spoke more about his life with a simple candour. 'Fame is a curse, for sure, not a blessing,' he suggested. 'There's a lot to be said for a normal nine-to-five [job]. No one asks you any questions, no one is coming up to you all the time. I can't go anywhere. I'm tortured. I can't even have a dinner. People round my neck taking pictures. People have no respect when it comes to someone they know on telly. They're straight over: "I know you're having your dinner but . . ."'

Fury grimaced. 'It's horrible. I wouldn't wish it on my worst enemy.'

When was the last day that Fury felt at peace? 'I've got thirty-four gates at my house and a twenty-foot wall, so every day when I'm there. My idea of a good day is getting up early, going for a run, dropping the kids off at school, and then I found this really long walk. There's nobody on it so I take the dog for a walk in privacy. I'm very cautious because a dog is an animal. It can jump up to somebody and, all of a sudden, you've got a lawsuit: "Tyson Fury's dog's tried to bite me!" When you're in my position, everybody's hunting you. They want a few quid off you.

'So I go to a secret location where I walk for miles with the dog. Man's best friend, loyal, loves me to death, never gives me any lip. He's the best, a Rottweiler called Cash.'

I liked the fact that Fury spoke about so much more than boxing. But the fight was close and I asked him if he sensed Usyk's conviction that he would win their bout on behalf of Ukraine.

'I don't know,' Fury said reasonably. 'But we are both getting paid very well. The biggest payday there is. He's had 350 amateur fights and twenty-one professional fights. I've had thirty-five pro fights and thirty-five amateur fights. Are we bothered about another fight? I don't think so. If it's destined for me, it will be. And if it's not, will I cry about it? No. I'll thank God for the good and bad times and I'll roll on, collect me money and go home. Back to picking up the dog shit.'

Frank Warren had just spoken of the constant struggle Fury had with his bipolar disorder. I asked Fury if the black dog of depression still came for him? 'All the time. No two days are the same for me. Up and down like a rollercoaster.'

When was his last bad day? 'A couple of days ago. But I know how to fight it more than I did before. Short-term goals, keep training, eating healthily. I know tomorrow's going to be a new day so, even if I'm feeling absolutely shit tonight, I'll start again. It's a brand-new day.'

Someone asked Fury if he worried that he might wake on Saturday morning, just hours before facing Usyk, feeling desolate? 'No, because I'm bulletproof on fight day. I can't be affected because it's not Tyson Fury. It's The Gypsy King – different mentality completely.'

Fury leaned forward. 'Here's the thing. If you give me another £500 million, it wouldn't make [life] better or worse. It's all a big game of Monopoly. However, and there is a big however, I would never go into a job and be underpaid. It's my principle. People say: "You can fight for $5 million, why do you want a hundred [million]?" But I know my worth.'

In the extravagant circus of boxing, the thirty-five-year-old was worth hundreds of millions of dollars. Mike Tyson, had just announced that he would fight Jake Paul later that year at the age of fifty-eight. Would Fury also remain addicted to boxing in his late fifties?

'I can't see myself hanging around for the next five years, never mind twenty years. I gave all my youth and young adult life to this game. All the things I've done and all the accolades and money I've earned? I've got to have time to enjoy them.'

The big man shrugged. 'It's only a short life, innit? We're here today, gone tomorrow.'

Oleksandr Usyk, we were warned, was exhausted and fed up. He was in no mood to talk for he had spent all afternoon being shunted from one room to another and made to suffer the tedium of countless television and YouTube interviews as he answered the same old questions.

Our small group of boxing writers in Riyadh quickly reached a joint agreement that we would leave Usyk in peace. We knew that Ukraine was in trouble. Kharkiv, its second-largest city with a population of more than a million, was being bombed heavily as Russian troops advanced. The previous day, Oleksandr Syrskyi, Ukraine's chief military commander, admitted that the 'situation is difficult' and 'we are fighting fierce defensive battles'.

Ukraine was hampered by chronic shortages of soldiers and weapons, and by damaging delays in funding from the West. Yet it seemed as if the world had, for the most part, moved on.

The horror of Gaza dominated the news. Palestinians were being bombed mercilessly, with nowhere to flee as the rising daily death toll soared. Reports from Ukraine had become much more sporadic as compassion fatigue set in and the Russian invasion ground on out of sight.

Most of us had known Usyk for years. We liked him and we respected him. It seemed almost insulting to expect him to sit down and answer yet more repetitive boxing questions. Stepping away from our scheduled round-table felt reasonable.

But then, in a blur of colour and a din of noise, Usyk and his dozen soldiers strode towards us. He looked cheerful and, before gesturing to his comrades to fall silent, he smiled and shook everyone's hand. Usyk then chided a member of his team who was about to take my seat and he settled down next to me. The conversation flowed and he seemed amused and energised by the earlier headbutt.

'It's just bad behaviour from Tyson's team,' Usyk said in English. 'We are professional athletes, not street fighters, and this is a big event for our people in Ukraine. If they want to destabilise my team, it's not possible because I don't just have professional coaches and trainers. I have professional soldiers.'

Usyk grinned, like a proud father looking at his brood. 'My team is very good at wanting to fight – not boxing but street fighting. But I said: "Hey, guys, get back." We had to behave properly. I am not disappointed by my team, but they are disappointed because I stopped them fighting. They were looking over at me, waiting for the thumbs-up, but I gave them the thumbs-down. The situation doesn't matter to me. It's just more motivation for my team.'

I reminded Usyk that Fury Sr ended up with blood pouring from his head while Stepchuk had hardly winced. 'My friend did not bleed because he is a powerful guy, a street guy,' Usyk replied with a chuckle. 'He was like a pit bull, ruff!'

The thirty-seven-year-old sounded full of serene conviction when he stressed his belief against Fury. 'I will definitely win and take the belts back home. I have four belts coming for four children, two for my sons and two for my daughters, one each.'

Fury, in contrast, had just told us that, if he won, he would give all four belts to Turki Alalshikh.

Usyk waved his hand in the air and slipped into the cry of an American ring announcer: *'Oleksandr "Undisputed world heavyweight champion, The Cat" Usyk!'*

But Usyk sounded deadly serious when suggesting that becoming the undisputed world champion could never match the Olympic title he had won at London 2012. 'My gold medal will always be better than undisputed. Everyone who does sport dreams of the

410 | THE LAST BELL

Olympic Games. I know men with three world championship medals but no Olympic gold. I did two Olympics and only got one medal. It takes four years of work. In 2012, my opponent in the final, [Clemente] Russo, had done four Olympics and still no gold medal, after sixteen years.'

Professional boxing, Usyk argued, 'is just a business for lots of people. It's money, belts, fame. But for me, first, it is a sport.'

It also means something more profound in a time of war. Usyk paused when I asked if the gravity of the situation at home would spur him to even greater heights. 'I really appreciate the support from my Ukrainian fans and soldiers,' he said. 'It's a big motivation.'

He briefly fell silent. 'Maybe I motivate my people,' he eventually murmured. 'Maybe.'

He had ignored the signals from various media people that his time with us was up but, in respect for him and all that he would soon face in the ring, it felt enough to thank him for our little chat. 'Of course,' Usyk said, rising to shake everyone's hand again, 'always.'

In that moment, away from the clamour and the madness, it was easy to remember that the best fighters bring light and meaning to boxing.

On Tuesday morning, at 10 a.m. in Riyadh, my article was posted online. The headline read: 'Saudi money has reshaped boxing but how do we justify the human cost?'

There was nothing heroic in writing about repression from within Saudi Arabia, and the impact of many supportive comments online was minimal, but I knew the article would be read by a few people close to those in authority in Riyadh. I did not feel in any personal danger, but there was still a twinge of unease. The PR representative of the Saudi government in London had not replied to my request for any comment on the allegations.

I logged off and the rest of the morning and early afternoon passed slowly.

That evening, we were driven by shuttle bus to Boulevard City, in north Riyadh, for the 'grand arrivals' of Fury and Usyk. I sat at the back and read notes from the Boulevard City website which promised that, apart from global brand stores, a dance fountain, cafés and restaurants, the venue was an 'enchanting realm ... where every moment is a jubilant celebration ... that shines like a diamond in the Arabian desert'.

Boxing people were starting to call Riyadh 'the Vegas of the East' – when they were not fawning over Turki Alalshikh and thanking 'His Excellency' for his vision.

I was more interested in the fighters. As a man naturally inclined to a comfortable body shape, with small rolls of flesh cushioning his torso, Fury looked leaner than usual in the face. His skin glowed with obvious good health and fitness. Usyk looked even better and there was a glint in his eye which suggested he was ready to dazzle the far bigger man who stood six inches taller and weighed forty pounds more.

The Ukrainian was the first to make his 'grand arrival' at Boulevard City. He wore the same snazzy white, blue and yellow tracksuit while walking down an entrance lined with flames that shot up into the air. He dealt with the stock opening question from the onstage interviewer as to how he was feeling with a three-word answer: 'I feel good.'

He was pressed as to whether this was really his only emotion. 'No, because after this event I go to sleep.'

Fury followed soon afterwards, wearing multicoloured trousers adorned with large stamp-sized images of his face, a black waistcoat and a black fedora which might have been worn by a pimp or a gangster in 1970s New York City. He was shirtless beneath the waistcoat and, arriving on stage, he removed his hat and bowed extravagantly.

He was also more expansive than Usyk. 'It feels fantastic to be here in the great kingdom of Saudi Arabia, *two thousand and twenty-four*! I'm feeling fantastic. I can't wait to put a good show on. There are so many people coming. It's such an event, all the big stars are here. Ah, it's just gonna be epic. I cannot wait for Saturday night.'

Fury was asked what winning a fight of such magnitude would mean to his legacy. 'Every fight I've ever had is important to me. Every left and right turn I've ever taken, every time I've fell over, every time I've climbed up, was all leading to this moment. It was destiny.'

By a quirk of fate, Usyk stood close to me near the back. For once, he was alone. His entourage waited ten feet away and no one approached him for a soundbite or a selfie. Usyk locked his attention on Fury. It was fascinating to feel the intensity of his gaze, and to sense the closeness with which he listened, as if he might learn one tiny snippet which he could store in that chess-playing brain of his and use at a decisive moment in the ring.

Fury started singing an old Tinie Tempah ditty. 'Written in the stars, a million miles away,' he crooned.

Usyk, motionless and concentrated, monitored and measured his unusual opponent, trying to see beneath the comic façade. His eyes never left Fury, who was given a chance to say the final words when asked for his prediction.

Fury grinned and, in an American accent, drawled, 'I predict that somebody's O has got to go!'

He looked out into the dark, searching for Usyk. 'I'm coming for you sucker,' he warned.

Usyk didn't blink, let alone smile, even when Fury offered his pet name: 'Sausage.'

Usyk still didn't move. Conviction seemed to surge through his very stillness.

Fuck, I thought, *this is boxing. This is why I still love it.*

An hour later, while the stragglers were shepherded back to the shuttle bus, I was taken aside by one of the boxing media officers. We were always friendly but, then, he looked serious.

It was unsurprising when he said the Saudis were not happy with me. This was not my first offence either. They raised the fact that I had written critically of Saudi Arabia the previous October. My card was marked.

It seemed as if they gave my colleague a little roasting. He defended me and told them that I was 'a good guy' and that I would concentrate on writing about boxing from then on. I pointed out that I had to cover all aspects of the promotion, including political issues and the abuse of human rights, alongside the actual fight. He understood, but he urged me to stick to boxing for the rest of the trip – for both our sakes.

As the shuttle gathered speed, I gazed at the dusty, moonlit landscape. More than ever I wanted the fight to light up boxing and remind me why I had given up so much of the last fifty years to this battered old business. I wanted to feel proud I had loved boxing this long, and this hard.

I took Wednesday off the boxing conveyor belt and missed the public workout. I really didn't need to see Tyson Fury slap the pads held up by SugarHill Steward while he sang along to 'Mr Brightside' by The Killers. I certainly did not need to hear any more praise for His Excellency.

Instead, I worked quietly in my room. I ate my meals in the hotel as I had become friendly with some of the staff. My favourite was the restaurant manager who liked talking in a mock-Cockney accent to me. He would grin and say 'Lovely jubbly' or 'See you later, alligator'. In between such greetings, he told me a little about his life and his family while he went out of his way to make sure I was happy. It was a relief to chat to someone who had nothing to do with boxing or political repression.

I went for a walk that sweltering night. I liked seeing people chatting in the local Starbucks where a young woman worked hard on her laptop. She was on her own and looked content, much like any other twenty-something woman getting her stuff done in a café. Dressed in jeans and a top, her head covered loosely by an elegant scarf, she could have been in London or Istanbul, New York or Cape Town.

Passing a coffee shop, filled with men of all ages talking intently or playing a board game, my new neighbourhood only felt strange when I saw one pet shop after another. There were four in a single block and I looked away from the cats, dogs and birds in cages.

There was a more interesting café on the other side of the road and I wanted to cross over and drink a cup of dark, intense Saudi coffee. But I was soon reminded that, as on so many roads in Riyadh, there were no pedestrian crossings or traffic lights which I could use to get to the other side. I was stranded as the metallic sea rolled on with waves of cars.

So I walked back to my hotel. I'd had enough excitement for the day. After three restless nights, with little sleep, I was out for the count soon after I lay down in the dark.

The WhatsApp message arrived at 10.33 a.m., Riyadh time, on Thursday morning.

'Hey Don.

You have been requested to attend an off-the-record media briefing with HE. This will take place in Boulevard City. Please note this is strictly *invitation only and would appreciate you keeping this confidential.'*

For a moment, I was tempted to text back and say, 'Sorry, I am confused. Is "HE" actually Oleksandr Usyk? If so, I'm really keen.'

But it felt churlish to be so mocking. I just said 'Thanks' and wondered what it would be like to meet the mysterious Turki Alalshikh.

I woke early on Friday and decided to skip the weigh-in. I felt good about saving my last burst of boxing fervour for the fight itself and went for a run.

I passed the hotel gym and, briefly, wondered if I should opt for running instead on a treadmill in the air-conditioned cool. But the message alongside the gym entrance made my decision:

IN HOUSE GUESTS

Female Timings
06:00 AM – 08:00 AM
04:00 PM – 06:00 PM

Male Timings
08:30 AM – 03:30 PM
06:30 PM – 05:30 AM

I ran slowly down the deserted side streets, adjusting to the heat, and found a steady rhythm. It felt as if I was running towards a kind of ending, not only of fight week, but to a fork in the road. One way would take me down the same old narrow boxing furrow while the clearer, healthier path would lead me somewhere new. But I was ready for one last mighty dance in the ring. I was ready to hear the last bell.

My slow thud ate up the road. I ran like I hadn't run in more than a year.

I only felt like keeling over when, drenched in sweat and relief, I made it back to the cool of the hotel lobby. The restaurant manager, seeing me stagger in, clapped his hands and exclaimed, 'Lovely jubbly.'

The Kingdom Arena, Riyadh, Saudi Arabia, Saturday 18 May 2024

I sat at a desk close to ringside, cabled up to the ethernet, reading the live blog that Jack, my twenty-three-year-old son, had begun. Jack was writing about fight night for a sports website in London, watching the feed from Riyadh on a pay-per-view screen, and getting used to covering live boxing. He did well, finding the right tone as he followed the undercard while drawing in readers to the prospect of Fury vs Usyk. At the same time, Jack wrote about Cristiano Ronaldo having an awkward conversation with Neymar.

In between his quick-fire postings, I marvelled at the fact that, just as I was getting ready to escape boxing mania, my son was writing about this very fight. But Jack's interest in boxing was far healthier than my own addled relationship with it. He liked football, movies and music much more, but he recognised the singular power of boxing. Jack was keen to watch and write about it when it really mattered to him – rather than trying to cover every aspect of it, week after week, year after year, as I had done for more than three decades.

I resolved, after the night was over, to be a little more like my son in this regard.

There was a tap on my shoulder. I looked up to see the publicity man who had messaged me two days earlier.

'It's on,' he said, 'the briefing with His Excellency.'

I told him that it was not a good time, ninety minutes before the fight, and I was busy getting my head into gear. 'No problem,' he said.

As I watched him walk away, I felt torn. When else would I get a chance to meet Turki Alalshikh in person? What would he be like? Would we talk properly about boxing and Saudi?

I called out to the publicist. 'Wait for me,' I said. 'I'll come.'

A dozen of us, from the UK and the US, were led out of the arena and down a long corridor. We were ushered into a plush enclave where numerous men welcomed us effusively. They showed us to our seats, a semi-circle around a chair reserved for Alalshikh.

Tea was poured and plates of the most delicious dates I had ever tasted were offered. It only felt uncomfortable when we were then each presented with a gift. I tried to wave mine away, but the man handing them out was insistent. It would have been blatantly rude to have kept refusing and so I accepted. Inside a green box was a fancy pen.

A stern reminder was given to us, by a British woman who worked for Alalshikh, that our ensuing conversation was off the record.

We waited, chomped a few more stuffed dates and then,

suddenly, he was there. Wearing a white robe and sandals, Turki Alalshikh swept into the room. He was loud and friendly and made a point of coming to each of us in turn so that he could shake our hands and welcome us.

It was a curious experience, having so many questions tumbling through me, while knowing that the one-way traffic would be controlled by the new master of boxing. Alalshikh swore a lot, with gusto, as he promised that he would take boxing to a far higher plane. He wanted to work with us, to talk to us, to learn from us, and he said we would make a great team as long as we opened our hearts. He knew some of us were critical of him and the kingdom, and that we doubted his motives, but he hoped that he could, in time, convince us of his sincerity.

He would help us spend time with all the fighters on the Saudi roster, so we could use our skills to tell their stories. We would work together to make boxing better.

Alalshikh then told us how he disliked the UFC but that the mixed martial arts juggernaut had found the right formula. Saudi Arabia would be a better version of the UFC in boxing. Promotional squabbles and sanctioning body politics would become redundant. Anti-doping programmes would be introduced and boxing would be cleaned up. At the same time, he would ensure that the best fighters were pitted against each other and that the greatest boxers in the world thrived beneath the benevolent support of Saudi Arabia.

Alalshikh promised that great boxing cards would soon be staged in Los Angeles and London. He wanted to make boxing relevant and riveting, easy to follow and full of drama and entertainment. He wanted one world champion in each division and fewer weight categories because boxing deserved to become a mainstream sport again.

He pointed out that he had already set a template in making fights which hardcore boxing fans around the world had craved for so long – with Fury against Usyk to be followed by a world light-heavyweight unification contest between two great unbeaten champions in Dmitry Bivol and Artur Beterbiev. He had also changed British boxing because Frank Warren and Eddie Hearn, who had refused for decades to even speak to each other, let alone meet, were now working happily together under his guidance.

In different circumstances, in a country where human rights were enshrined rather than shredded, I would have thought Alalshikh spoke some good sense amid his radical scheme to fund the best 200 male fighters in the world under the auspices of one entity. It was a plan but, still, it carried worrying uncertainties. What would happen to boxing if, and when, Saudi Arabia had had enough and decided to move onto more useful terrain? Who would run and support boxing then if all the major promoters and powerbrokers had sold up to Saudi? And, right now, what would happen to all the great women fighters who had yet to be mentioned? Were they to be jettisoned along with all those male boxers outside the top 200?

Most of all I wanted to ask Alalshikh about Jamal Khashoggi, Manahel al-Otaibi and Mohammad bin Nasser al-Ghamdi. What did he think of Khashoggi and his murder? Would al-Otaibi and al-Ghamdi be spared from prison and death row? Would ordinary Saudi people, like boxing, be saved?

Instead, there was a world heavyweight title unification fight to watch. His Excellency roared around the room, shaking hands and promising that we would meet again and work together.

I knew then, more than ever, that it was time to leave.

Michael Buffer, a ghost from my boxing past, wears a white suit as he stands in the centre of the ring and makes his ancient call to fight. 'From the Kingdom of Saudi Arabia,' Buffer croons and then pauses. He draws breath deep down into his seventy-nine-year-old frame and lets rip with his trademark howl: '*Let's Git Ready To Ruummmmbbbllleeeeeeee* . . .'

Turki Alalshikh, sitting next to Cristiano Ronaldo at ringside, pats the impassive footballer on the leg before reaching over to clutch the forearm of Anthony Joshua. At least the boxer laughs at

Alalshikh's quip as Buffer rolls on. 'Fighting out of the blue corner, wearing blue and yellow . . .'

Joshua claps enthusiastically, Alalshikh pumps his arms in excitement and Ronaldo remains as mute as a waxwork. Buffer builds to a crescendo, stretching out the details of Usyk's ring record. Finally, he introduces 'the reigning, defending, unified IBF, WBA, WBO heavyweight champion of the world, from Ukraine, the undefeated *Olexandrrrrr Uuuuuuusssyyyk*!'

Usyk crosses himself and then, with a sombre expression, raises his right arm high.

Buffer looks across the ring to Fury. He hollers out the fighter's credentials and hails him as 'the reigning, defending, undefeated WBC heavyweight champion of the world . . .'

John Fury lifts the WBC belt high and his son throws flurries of punches, making eerie little cries as Buffer reaches his climax.

'The Gypsy King . . . *Tysonnnnnnnnn Fuuurrrrrrryyyyyy!*'

After the ring empties, the referee Mark Nelson calls the fighters and their trainers together. 'Alexander and Tyson,' Nelson says, sounding very American as Fury bounces up and down while Usyk looks piercingly at him, 'you had your instructions in the dressing room. You know what I expect. A clean, professional fight for the undisputed heavyweight championship of the world. Protect yourself at all times. Touch gloves, good luck to both of you. Touch 'em up.'

Usyk embraces his trainer Yurii Tkachenko and then crosses himself. Fury also makes the sign of the cross. They are about to enter brutal terrain.

I stare at the two lonely figures in the brightly illuminated square. The rest of the arena is lost in darkness and it's almost as if the last six years have brought me to this moment. I am suddenly greedy rather than reflective. I want Fury and Usyk to be safe, but I also want them to produce an epic fight which reminds us that boxing can be thrilling and noble, ferocious yet inspirational. I want Fury to dazzle, but I want Usyk to win, both for himself and Ukraine. I want to forget about Saudi and doping and damage for a while. I want it all to feel worthwhile. I want something heroic rather than grubby before I slip away.

'Seconds out,' the ring announcer barks. 'Round one.'

Fury, skipping lightly, comes out fast. Usyk joins him in his familiar southpaw stance. They both snap out the jab with easy fluidity, the left for Fury and the right for Usyk. The height and reach difference seems vast, but Usyk moves in and out to jab effectively to the body. He bobs and skitters while staying close to the centre of the ring. Fury is smart, too, and he answers with his own jab to the body. He then uncorks a meaty right which Usyk deflects cleverly.

Usyk's supporters chant his name with rhythmic precision as, on cue, a series of jabs to the gut drive Fury into his corner. But The Gypsy King is ready. He places both gloves on the adjacent ropes and wags his head furiously, opening his mouth wide in mockery, as if tempting Usyk to take another crack. Usyk backs away, strategically, and Fury looks to the crowd on his right, his jaws opening wider in delight, as if he has scored a psychological blow.

Usyk cuffs Fury for his impudence with a left cross. Fury is no longer mugging. He looks suddenly concentrated as he tries to fend off the smaller man. And then, after a double feint, he snakes out a long, slippery jab which connects. Fury then goes downstairs only for Usyk, The Cat, to pounce and catch him with a hard left.

There is a roar as Fury, still playing the clown, bizarrely punches his own head as if to suggest he is unfazed by his rival's power. Fury is caught by two more lefts and a right before he spins away and raises his arms as if he has been landing, rather than taking, the blows.

Five seconds into round two, Usyk follows a right jab with another hammering straight left that catches Fury. The chant rises again. 'Uuu-sykkk . . . Uuu-sykkk . . .'

Usyk remains implacable, while Fury mugs again and dabs at his nose. The Ukrainian reverts to a double jab to the body and Fury responds with a decent pair of lefts. Yet Usyk, 'the midget', forces the giant to retreat. He marches forward resolutely while throwing combinations from different angles. Fury digs in a shovel uppercut to the body, but Usyk does not flinch. They swap more body blows and Fury grins. He is in the ring with a real fighting man.

Fury comes out forcefully after the break. His jab is a slick, point-scoring weapon which keeps landing. They clinch for the first sustained period and Fury leans down on Usyk, hoping his huge frame will drain some of the relentless energy from his fellow champion. He then pops out a fast combination before Fury reverts to fighting off the back foot. Usyk complains to Nelson that he is being hit to the back of the head. But the round belongs to Fury.

Fury is in the groove now and body blows flow from him, interspersed with crisp jabbing up top in round four. He looks a master boxer. As the weight and accuracy of Fury's punching increases, the voice of his trainer, SugarHill Steward, echoes, 'There you go ... there you go ...'

A powerful left seems to unbalance Usyk, but Fury keeps fighting on the back foot. After another sharp combination, Fury resumes his needless showboating, waggling his hips and pulling faces. An accidental clash of heads stops the japes and Fury uses his glove to check that he has not been cut. He needs to remain concentrated.

But a beautiful right uppercut from Fury, followed by a lovely string of jabs, as pretty as a pearl necklace, seduce The Gypsy King. He is so impressed by himself that he raises his arms. Usyk pummels him and Fury clowns yet again. But he is up against a skilled stoic who refuses rest. Usyk's work rate is admirable, but Fury is in full flow and, after a third of the contest, the scores are level.

Usyk gathers himself in the corner, gulping down water, while his cutman Russ Anber works on the nick above his right eye. There's little blood, but it's a sign that Fury, after a slow start, threatens to take over.

I am tense and absorbed as something extraordinary is brewing. This is what happens when the two best fighters in their division test each other. This is the promise and fascination of boxing at the highest level.

Fury's consummate bodywork in the fifth is followed by a straight right down the pipe. The body punches keep sinking into Usyk's gut but, halfway through the round, he makes a legitimate complaint that Fury has caught him with a low blow. The King of the Gypsies doesn't care. Soon after they are waved back into action, he goes downstairs again and lands a hard and fair right hand just above Usyk's beltline. These are sapping punches.

Fury produces a bolo punch, blending a hook with an uppercut, which lands with sickening impact. He then cuffs Usyk around the head followed by a left-right combination to the body to finish off his best round of the fight, so far, with a flourish.

Halfway through round six, Usyk looks unsteady after a right uppercut from Fury. He back-pedals and then he is caught with another withering uppercut which makes him stagger. Usyk is hurt and on the retreat with a minute left in the round. Fury goes back to the body and then the head as his control tightens. He seems able to land at will, but then, rather than pouring on the pressure, he hides his hands behind his back. It looks wasteful rather than clever, but Fury is ahead by four rounds to two.

Usyk's eye needs attention, as he and his trainer Tkachenko try to work out how to stem the massive tide.

Fury whips the right hand into Usyk with impunity and, early in the seventh, the smaller man takes in deep breaths. Usyk composes himself and tags Fury again – but with light clips to the head rather than hefty blows to the body. Fury then makes Usyk wince with a big right hand to the gut. The Ukrainian comes back with a sharp left and, just before the bell, he nails Fury with a left. Usyk is back in the fight.

In the eighth round, Usyk looks light on his feet and quick and determined to land first as they circle and pummel each other. A right and left, as slick as they are thunderous, crash into Fury's face, damaging his nose. With fifty seconds left, Usyk catches him with another shuddering left hook. Fury paws at his right eye, as if he can feel it swelling beneath the skin, and Usyk finds another big right. Two thirds of the way through, on the scorecards, the two champions are locked together at four rounds apiece.

Fury, now, needs to be replenished for Usyk clearly has restored his bounce and zip.

The Ukrainian crosses himself once more as he rises for the ninth. He also looks skywards as if asking for fresh courage. Halfway through a seismic round, Usyk thuds a left into the puffy right side of his rival's face. Fury is no longer breathing easily, but he comes back with two rights, first to the body and then the head. A left hook detonates off the side of Fury's head.

Fury fights on, but Usyk soon backs him against the ropes. A short right hand opens up Fury and, then, the punch of the fight comes twelve seconds before the end of round nine.

A brute of a left hand looks ruinous. Even from my seat twenty feet away, I can see the light dim in Fury's eyes as if the punch has hit a trip switch that shuts down his system. His head rolls back, his arms fall helplessly to his side and he slumps against the ropes as Usyk unfurls a barrage of punches. Fury reels away and lifts his hands in front of his face but, as punch after punch land, he looks like a hapless drunk who cannot control his legs on a slippery bar-room floor. He spins from one corner to the other, his zigzagging lurch looking increasingly dazed as Usyk keeps hitting him. Finally, a short right and scything left make Fury fall, like a giant oak, into the ropes. He looks close to unconsciousness as he then smacks against the ring post.

The referee jumps between them. A standing count booms around the arena as Fury just manages to hold himself up by clinging to the ropes. 'Four ... five ... six ... seven.'

As the referee approaches him, Fury nods. This is the eighth time he has been down in his career and, as if in confirmation, the count of 'eight' is heard.

Referee Nelson asks Fury if he is ready to fight on. The big man, blood pouring from his nose, raises his hands just before the bell rings.

Usyk looks searchingly at Fury to see if he has anything left. Fury has often shown astonishing powers of recovery but, now, he looks in worse trouble than since the moment six years ago when Deontay Wilder seemed to have knocked him into oblivion during their first fight.

'Are you OK?' John Fury asks his son, pressing a blue ice compress against his head. 'Where are ya?'

'I'm here,' Tyson Fury slurs.

I count the punches in a replay on the big screen. They come in a dark and steaming train of unanswered blows. Usyk keeps chasing and throwing, with punch after punch racing past, even in slow motion, like a long chain of blurring carriages. Fury is lucky that some of these carriages are empty and unlit, and they don't crash into him, but he is still hit by fourteen big punches, some of them so heavy that they land with the impact of railway sleepers.

Usyk comes out for round ten. Calmly, methodically, he backs up Fury and hammers him again. Fury tries to move his feet in a sad shuffle, but Usyk remains patient. Two lefts and a right are blocked by Fury who is still coherent enough to parry and give himself more time to recover. Usyk mimics Fury by showboating in the centre of the ring. It seems a strange tactic when he might hunt down a vulnerable Fury with more venom.

Fury, incredibly, snaps out a jab and then returns to the ropes where, rather than clutching at them like a drowning man, he teases Usyk by resting his arms against their knotty fibre while offering a queasy smile. Fury lands a decent right hand which Usyk answers with a left. It has been a notable recovery from Fury.

Before the fight, the consensus had been that the judges will almost certainly favour the more famous Fury. A draw or even a late victory for him is still on the cards if he can be competitive in the last two rounds.

A left cross from Usyk is the first meaningful punch of the

penultimate round. Fury responds well, but Usyk then lands a solid right. A snapping jab cannot dent Usyk and he clips Fury again. Nelson has to separate them as they clinch wearily. Just before the bell, Usyk lands a right jab and a long left.

After the break, they rise to their feet once more. Nelson brings them together and, before the final round, they touch gloves.

Usyk lands first, but Fury fires back. In Fury's corner, Usyk nails him again and then pushes the big man away to avoid giving him the respite of another clinch. Fury slips back into the old routine, his jab once more a thing of beauty that allows him to then connect with a hefty left to the body. But Usyk ducks under a chopping right hand and forces Fury to the ropes. The punches are mostly coming from Usyk, the best of which is a right hook which makes the sweat fly from Fury's bald head.

Fury is still not beaten. He uncorks a big right which catches Usyk. When they clash heads accidentally, Fury raises his right glove in apology. Thirty seconds are left. Fury connects with a straight right, but Usyk throws a sequence of punches. Fury hides his hands behind his back as if he has already done enough to snatch the win. It seems fitting that the bout should end with Usyk landing punches from a variety of angles before Fury wraps him up in a bear hug.

It's over and, in relief, Fury kisses Usyk on the top of his head before he raises his own arm high. Usyk, meanwhile, sinks to the canvas in a silent prayer. He spreads his arms wide and gazes to the heavens. Helped to his feet, Usyk is engulfed by his exultant team. He looks like a man who believes he has won while Fury, more quietly, drinks deeply from a plastic bottle of water.

Then, in a typically moving moment of tenderness, the boxers embrace. Fury again kisses Usyk, this time on the forehead. They look at each other, in admiration, and share a few words. Fury ruffles Usyk's sweat-streaked hair and leans down to kiss him for a third time.

I stand and watch, in appreciation and gratitude. The fight had everything I wanted – and now I just need the right result. It had been an engrossing battle, but the two-point swing of a knockdown in round nine, when Fury came so close to being counted out, surely sealed the result in favour of Usyk.

As they wait for the scorecards, Fury seeks out Usyk again. He places his hands gently on the side of his smiling opponent's head, holding him by the ears, and steals his fourth kiss on the head. Usyk speaks intently to Fury while Turki Alalshikh, standing alongside them, beams.

Finally, after an agonising wait, the verdicts are ready. 'Ladies and gentlemen,' Michael Buffer says in his velvety way, 'here in Riyadh, Saudi Arabia, we go to the scorecards.'

I take in a deep breath. 'Manuel Oliver Palomo,' Buffer says, 'scores it 115 to 112 for Usyk.'

The Ukrainian is typically impassive as his gloves are unlaced. He looks as if he knows that, from the way Buffer is reading the cards, we are in for a twist.

'Craig Metcalfe scores it 114 to 113 for Fury.'

The King of the Gypsies pumps his right hand in relief. He then raises his arm in anticipation of victory.

I groan inside. This is boxing. A draw or a controversial win for Fury looms.

'Mike Fitzgerald,' Buffer says calmly, 'scores it 114 to 113 to the winner by split decision ...'

Buffer keeps us hanging before he finally relents. 'From Ukraine ... *Olexandrrrrrr Uuuuuuusssyyyk*!'

I lift my bowed head and look up. Fucking hell. Boxing has got it right. After a rollicking fight, in which Fury boxed beautifully at times while showing incredible grit, Usyk has been given the justified decision for his magnificent performance.

Somehow, the boxing gods have saved this one for us. Relief and exhilaration surge through me. What a way to end it all, free of bitterness or controversy, dissent or rancour. It really has been worth it. I feel sure that this is the last time I will be invested so deeply in boxing. The ending could hardly be sweeter or more meaningful.

Inside the ring, as tears roll down his face, Usyk lifts up a new belt. Rather than being covered in the gaudy logo of a sanctioning body, it carries two words: Undisputed Champion.

At 2.45 a.m. on Sunday morning in Riyadh, the UK print deadlines have long since passed. Such leeway allows me my moments of reflection. But, now, it's time to work.

I hunch over my laptop and bang out my online report. I write of the brave and admirable Fury, and of the imperious Usyk joining the heavyweight pantheon. I tap away in silence while the Kingdom Arena slowly empties. The words fly in a giddy rush and, the closer I come to the final sentences, I feel a strange kind of freedom, and even joy.

I arrive late for the Fury press conference as I had been one of the last to finish writing. The fighters had already spoken in the ring in the immediate aftermath and, before packing up, I went online to check what had been said. Usyk had spoken simply. 'Thank you so much my team. Thank you so much my God, Jesus. Mister Excellency, thank you. It's big opportunity for me, for my family, for my country. It's a great day.'

Usyk was asked if he would be prepared to honour his contract and fight Fury again. 'Of course. I'm ready for a rematch. Listen. We do a good fight, yes?'

Fury was more churlish. 'I believe I won that fight. He won a few of the rounds, but I won the majority. What can you do? [It's] one of them decisions in boxing. We've both put on a good fight. Best we could do. And, you know, his country's at war. So people are siding with a country at war. But make no mistake, I've won that fight and I'll be back. We've got a rematch clause. I thank Jesus for all the victories he's given me. I've dropped a split decision to the good little man, and I thank him again in the mighty name of Jesus. We go home to our families and we'll run it back in October.'

Wladimir Klitschko, the Ukrainian who had been world heavy-weight champion until he was shocked by Fury in 2015, admitted he had been nervous. 'It was very difficult for [Usyk] due to the size difference and mobility of Fury. In the ninth round, Oleksandr turned it from zero to 100, all of a sudden. That was unbelievable. I'm surprised Fury got up – so respect to him. But Oleksandr showed once again that, with technique, you can get much further than just with power. His power is his heart, his belief, and that he's Ukrainian. I'm really proud of Oleksandr and really proud to be Ukrainian.

'Every day and night, Putin's Russia is bombarding us with kamikaze drones and rockets. Tonight, Ukraine was suffering. Lives were lost, I'm sure. But we Ukrainians had the chance for forty-eight minutes to enjoy the performance of Usyk, and that gave peace to our hearts and souls.'

At the heaving press conference, Frank Warren stresses that Fury's comments about war in Ukraine affecting the scoring should not be taken out of context. They had been made soon after the fight when he was churning with emotion.

Fury sits next to his promoter. He wears a white baseball cap and his face is bruised and cut. A purple mouse makes the skin bulge beneath his right eye. He sounds more magnanimous than forty minutes earlier. 'It was a close fight. I thought I did enough, but I'm not a judge. I'm not going to sit here and cry and make excuses. Have you seen my face? It's pretty busted up and he's just gone to the hospital with a broken jaw. We've punched the fuck out of each other for twelve rounds. So we'll go home, eat some food, drink a few beers, spend some family time, walk my dog, go to the tip, and me and Frank will talk about the future.'

I stand outside in the dark at 3.46 a.m. I am not sure if I should hang around, look for a shuttle bus or book an Uber. Usyk is apparently in hospital having his jaw scanned for a fracture.

Most of the press pack will head to the airport in a few hours; almost everyone I know is getting out of Riyadh as fast as possible. I have two articles to write and so I will be awake for another fourteen hours. Then, early on Monday morning, it will be time for me to leave Saudi Arabia.

As people amble around, I hear variations of the same refrain. 'What a night, what a fight.'

There is a sudden commotion. Two camera-wielding crews run across the tarmac. We follow and, around the corner, an empty ambulance waits with open doors.

The news comes quickly. Usyk will delay his hospital visit until after he speaks to us.

'What a guy,' someone says.

The Kingdom Arena, Riyadh, Saudi Arabia, Sunday 19 May 2024

At 4 a.m., Oleksandr Usyk walks into the room. The swollen skin above his right eye has been stitched shut and he raises his left arm in greeting.

Applause breaks out spontaneously. Usyk wears a stone-washed T-shirt, emblazoned with a boxing glove on the front. He carries a Ukrainian flag and Eeyore, his eldest daughter's favourite cuddly toy, under his right arm.

'Hello, everybody,' he says.

Usyk drapes the flag over the back of his chair and places the toy in front of him. Poor old Eeyore, looking exhausted, keels over on the desk. Usyk also seems depleted and, as he sits down, he groans. In that muted exclamation, all the brutality of a monumental fight rises up.

Usyk focuses on Eeyore. He makes sure the old donkey sits upright again.

The boxing questions came first. Had he been concerned when Fury was announced as an unjustified winner on the second scorecard? 'No, I don't worry,' Usyk says. 'I believe I won.'

Had a knockout been stolen from him because, in the unforgettable ninth, a reeling Fury had been held up by the sagging ropes
as the referee gave him such a long count?

Usyk's face splits into his familiar gap-toothed smile. 'I don't
think about it because we have a winner. No knockout, no problem,
but for twelve rounds it's a big drama.'

Would Fury avoid their contracted rematch and accept an easier
bout against Anthony Joshua? Usyk starts to reply, only for the room
to darken.

'Oh,' Usyk says in puzzlement, before realising that someone had
accidentally leaned against the light switch. Picking out the culprit
he says, jokingly, 'Don't play, please.'

He keeps going above the laughter. 'I don't think about boxing
now because my [training camp] start was September 2023.' Usyk
counts the months. 'September, November, December . . .'

Alex Krassyuk politely reminds Usyk that he has forgotten
October. Krassyuk lists the months correctly, snapping out a finger
for each one.

'Yes, nine months I work,' Usyk agrees, as he explains how he'd
missed the birthdays of each of his three eldest children, as well as
the birth of his youngest daughter. 'All the time, training, training,
training. Now I am happy. I want to go to my church, pray and say:
"Jesus, thank you", because it's not for me. It's for my God, my
supporters, my country, the Ukrainian soldiers, Ukrainian mothers and fathers, children. I want to go home, to rest, eat, sleep,
kiss my wife.'

Then we reach the moments that matter most. Usyk had lost his
father, Sasha, just days after he became the Olympic heavyweight
champion at London 2012. In the build-up to this fight, Usyk had
explained that 'he watched me become an Olympic champion, but I
didn't make it on time to show him the gold medal. When I arrived,
he was already lying in the coffin. I put the medal in his dead hand,
and left the room.'

Usyk had also explained that he'd recently felt the presence of his dad in a dream. Someone asks if the dream had returned in the past few nights and helped him beat Fury.

'No,' Usyk begins, only to pause. 'I miss my father.'

The breath catches in the back of my throat as that simple sentence resonates. I know what Usyk means. Nearly four years since I lost my dad, I still miss him too.

Usyk looks up as he remembers that dream. 'I say to my father: "Hey listen, you live there …"'

The fighter stretches his arm skywards as if reaching towards the unknowable afterlife. And then Usyk begins to cry as, speaking again to his father, he says, 'I live here. Please, no coming for me. I love you.'

His face crumples. 'It's hard when my father is coming for me, because I remember how my life …'

Briefly, it sounds like he is choking back laughter. But, instead, Usyk cries with quiet persistence.

Krassyuk squeezes his shoulder. A grimace of a smile crosses Usyk's bruised face. Then, a solitary tear slides from his wounded eye and trickles down his cheek.

In a broken voice, Usyk says, 'I know … he is here.'

He rises to his feet, bunches his arms in a fighting salute and then, with glistening eyes, glances at Eeyore. He picks up the toy, places him under his arm and brings his hands together in a prayer of gratitude.

'How do you feel?' someone shouts.

'I feel!' Usyk exclaims, turning a worn-out question into a stark statement.

His knuckles look raw and sore, but I ask him about Eeyore. I'd been surprised that he had accompanied Usyk to the ring and that the toy is still cradled in his arms now.

Usyk smiles. 'My daughter said, "Papa, please take it with you. It gives you power."'

He stretches over to introduce his daughter's favourite toy to me. 'This is Leeloo,' he says.

I think of all the conversations I've had with Usyk over the years and how he spoke about war and the death of some of his closest friends. He had found the words to talk about devastation, and how he felt as if he might never joke or dance again.

Now, with dawn about to break across Riyadh, he has made us laugh, before he cried. He has just become the first undisputed world heavyweight champion this century, but the IBF, one of the four main sanctioning bodies, will soon strip him of their belt for not agreeing to fight their mandatory challenger.

Usyk will pay more attention to his family, and even to Leeloo, than to such chicanery. He is exhausted, but serene, as he slips away into the dark. The great world champion carries the look of a man who has faced both death and glory and learned to savour life above all else.

Riyadh, at 5.30 a.m., is lit by yellow and pink streaks in the sky. In the Uber, I wish I could hear the haunting call to prayer as the road flashes past, but a new day has begun. Usyk and Fury have given us a fight for the ages and there is no point in harking back to the past glory of the fight game, or worrying about the troubling future of boxing. It's time to take a new direction.

I will sometimes still watch boxing, and write about it, but I am no longer hopelessly in thrall to its addictive chaos. Rather than following it obsessively, in a ravaged fixation, I will pick and choose the times when it matters to me. In this new transaction, I will interview fighters because they talk much more about real life than sport. But I am done with the rest of my habit. I will be happy to be less disappointed and less frustrated and less informed too. I might not know the coming sensations, or the latest crooks and fiends, but I will always remember how much boxing once meant to me.

Now, I will try something different. It might sound as deluded as an alcoholic saying that he will give up hard liquor while, when clean and sober, enjoying the occasional social drink with a meal or good company. Maybe it's just not possible when you have been addicted to drinking or boxing for so long. Perhaps it always is all or nothing.

But I feel hopeful. I think I can like boxing at a distance. How can I be bitter or unyielding when boxing, despite its ugly realities, has shown me so much about life?

The Uber races through Riyadh. My young driver has been on his phone most of the trip but, following a long call, he has started texting relentlessly. He looks up and down, but far more time is spent staring at his screen than the weaving road in front of us. There is more traffic now than when our journey began and, after scowling at him for a few minutes, I actually shout 'No!' when he almost hits another car.

The driver glances into the rear-view mirror. 'In Riyadh,' he tells me with a grin, 'we drive on the phone.'

His cackle dies away and he resumes texting. 'Excuse me,' I say prissily, 'can you just drive?'

'Don't worry, mister,' he replies. 'We all do it.' He points at a driver alongside us who is also clutching his mobile.

I shake my head forlornly and he laughs again. 'OK, my friend,' he says. He hits send and the WhatsApp message is delivered.

We drive quietly for thirty seconds and his phone pings again. But, rather than looking down at the reply, he asks why I am in Riyadh.

When I say the word 'boxing', he laughs again and holds his fists up in the time-honoured fashion. The car veers to the left before he brings it back under control.

'Who win?' he asks.

'Usyk,' I say, keeping my gaze on the road ahead in my best example-setting way.

'The big one?' he exclaims.

'No, the other guy,' I say. 'The Ukrainian.'

'The small one?'

I am tempted to point out that Usyk is six foot three and the new undisputed world heavyweight champion. But this is not the time or the place. I just nod.

'You like it?' he asks.

'I like being alive more.'

The driver bangs his hand in delight against the wheel. 'OK, my brother, we will be safe.'

Peace and quiet return to the Uber and the last five minutes of our journey are almost restful. The driver finally eases the car into the hotel courtyard.

'Inshallah,' he says, 'we are alive.'

'Beautiful,' I say, as I open the door and step outside into the heat of dawn.

The driver rolls down his window. 'Mister, mister,' he calls out. I turn to see him bunch his hands into clenched fists again. 'You like the boxing?'

One last word tells the simple truth. 'Sometimes,' I say as, with a little wave, I walk away.

The Last Dance

King Khalid International Airport, Riyadh, Saudi Arabia
Sunday 15 December 2024

The woman in a black burqa looks bored as she flips through the pages. In her booth at passport control, she glances at me a couple of times before reaching for the stamp granting entry into Saudi Arabia. Then, just as I expect her to hand back my passport, she turns to her computer and something shifts in her gaze. A stillness settles over her.

Eventually, she gestures to me to follow her. Dread rises inside me as she walks to an office and points to a bench. The woman walks away with my passport and talks to a man in Arabic.

I sit down on the bench which is shared with another passenger who is here for boxing work. Her passport has also been taken, but her visa was only issued after our plane left London. She is unsettled, but her delay could be a mere administrative check.

My visa arrived yesterday, but the woman knows I have written critically of the Saudi government on my two previous visits. She smiles sympathetically and we chit-chat nervously before she's called to the office. Her visa has been ratified and she is free to go.

'Would you like me to stay?' she asks kindly.

I reassure her that I will be fine. She wishes me good luck and says she looks forward to hopefully seeing me tomorrow when I'm part of a small group of writers due to meet Oleksandr Usyk and Tyson Fury before their rematch this weekend.

It seems possible I might be sent back to London as Oliver Brown, of the *Daily Telegraph*, had been denied entry to Wembley Stadium three months ago. He had also written sceptically of Saudi and there was a mild uproar when he was not allowed to cover Daniel Dubois' surprise knockout of Anthony Joshua in a London fight marketed as part of Riyadh Season.

There had been no place for me at ringside that night, but I was given a seat up in the gods, watching the fight on a screen because I was so far away.

My family has asked me to keep a low profile this time and to delay talking to relatives of Saudi dissidents who are imprisoned or on death row. They just want me home in time for Christmas. But all the key bouts in boxing are now brokered by Turki Alalshikh and the overwhelming majority are held in Riyadh. Alalshikh is the reason that this riveting rematch between Usyk and Fury is taking place. The man hailed as 'His Excellency' sweeps aside the obstacles imposed by rival promoters and sanctioning bodies as he sets about restoring the glory of boxing.

Alalshikh has also bought *The Ring* magazine – the great old 'Bible of Boxing' which had ceased its print edition two years earlier, reduced to being a digital publication. Signing up boxing writers from around the world to work for *The Ring*, he promises that the revamped, relaunched magazine will devise a ratings system which identifies the best fighters and propels them towards captivating contests with each other. Boxing will be stripped of chaos and corruption.

Three hundred and six people, meanwhile, were executed in

Saudi Arabia between 1 January and 5 December 2024 and, earlier this week, FIFA matched boxing's cavalier attitude when the country was confirmed as the host of the 2034 World Cup. Twenty-one global organisations issued a statement condemning the decision as a 'moment of great danger' for human rights.

Four days ago, I called Bissan Fakih of Amnesty International. She's based in Beirut and works with Dana Ahmed, who has helped me before with my writing about Saudi. Dana is part of a small Amnesty delegation which has been given diplomatic immunity to attend the annual United Nations Internet Governance Forum this coming week in Riyadh.

Despite the fact that Dana and her colleagues can travel, and their safety is guaranteed, it seems bizarre that Saudi Arabia should accommodate a forum on internet governance and 'advancing human rights and inclusion in the digital age'. Amnesty has documented the cases of eighty-five people prosecuted for expressing their views of the country online. Forty-eight of these detainees are still imprisoned.

Bissan shared a press release in which she said: 'While Saudi authorities lead discussions on shaping the future of internet governance, they continue to lock up, forcibly disappear and impose decades-long prison sentences and travel bans for people's online expression. Now is the time to demonstrate their commitment to respecting and upholding freedom of expression.'

'Even foreign visitors to Saudi Arabia can be at risk of being imprisoned solely for expressing their views online. Saudi authorities detained Dutch-Yemeni citizen Fahd Ezzi Mohammed Ramadhan on 20 November 2023, two days after he arrived from the Netherlands. He told officials from the Dutch embassy in Riyadh that he had sympathised online with a critic of the Saudi royal family and believed, based on interrogations, that was the reason for his detention.'

I am shown into the office. A man holds my passport and talks into the phone, in Arabic, but nothing is said to me.

Finally, after about forty minutes, a different man leads me back to passport control.

'Is everything okay?' I ask when he returns my passport.

'Go,' he says, waving me into the Kingdom of Saudi Arabia.

Since I was last in Riyadh, I have followed boxing at the distance I'd agreed to in that silent pact with myself. I only wrote about the big fights and spent meaningful time with the fighters I liked. My heart still snagged as I watched Isaac Chamberlain and Regis Prograis both lose defining bouts.

On 30 August 2024, which was my sister Heather's birthday, almost six years since her death, I visited Isaac in Clapham. In mid-June, at Selhurst Park, he had lost a gruelling fight for the European and Commonwealth cruiserweight titles. Jack Massey was awarded the decision, with two judges giving him the verdict by a one-round margin of 115–113.

I had been with Isaac in his dressing room before and after the fight. He had cried and it made one of the saddest sights I'd seen in all my years of boxing. Ten weeks on, Isaac wanted to discuss his future. But, really, he just needed me to listen as he wondered out loud whether he should keep fighting. It was not my place to tell him what to do and so he talked and I offered a few Dad-like observations on his options.

Isaac said I had lifted his spirits and that he felt good again.

On 11 October, he sent me a photo of Adam Booth, the vastly experienced trainer. It was Isaac's way of telling me that he had left his old team in Brixton and moved to Adam's gym. 'It wasn't easy,' he wrote, 'but I needed the change to make me better. I'm learning so much already.'

Two weeks later, I was in Manchester with Regis. On the afternoon of Saturday 26 October, I sat with him as, quietly, he prepared to fight Jack Catterall.

It was a hard night. Regis scored a flash knockdown in round five, but Catterall took charge and, in the ninth, he threw a crunching left. Regis went down heavily. He was dropped again just before the bell, but fought to the end of a bout which Catterall won by wide margins. Regis was a model of dignity in defeat and admitted it was time to retire.

We kept in touch and, when I went to Texas in November to cover the circus scrap between Jake Paul and Mike Tyson, Regis reassured me. He felt ready for new ventures – even though he would change his mind and be back in the ring in February 2025.

Donald Trump had just swept the US election and Texas seemed almost as bleak as Saudi as I wrote about the most hyped boxing event of the year. Paul, a 27-year-old social media huckster, beat a 58-year-old man with a long history of health problems, both physical and mental. The fact that Tyson, a once-great world heavyweight champion, was defeated so comprehensively on points was meant to give Paul authenticity in boxing. But it didn't mean much – even if more people watched the event on Netflix than any other fight in 2024.

It mattered far more that, in the main support bout, Katie Taylor and Amanda Serrano fought a blistering rematch. Taylor won their bloody and controversial battle 95–94 on all three scorecards, almost matching their 2022 epic. I enjoyed interviewing Taylor before the rematch and then seeing her and Serrano display the courage and skill which makes boxing so distinct.

Boxing and I had drifted further apart, but I found a strange peace. After my return from the US, our three kids sent me their work about boxing in the same week. Bella had written a beautiful interview for *The Big Issue* with the boxer Cindy Ngamba who had become the first member of the Refugee team to win an Olympic medal.

Jack wrote a moving and insightful blog on Robbie Chapman, a journeyman boxer, while Emma sent me the inspired outline of her plans for Southpaw – the boxing-influenced brand she'd created as a fourth-year fashion student. Regis and Isaac had been interviewed about boxing and fashion for Emma's work.

Everyone in my family understood why I had given so much of my life to the ring. They also proved that it was possible to be interested in boxing, and write about it, without falling into a fevered obsession.

After my bumpy start at the airport, I concentrated on the boxers during fight week in Riyadh. It made sense because my re-immersion in boxing had begun six years before, to the month, with Tyson Fury's first fight against Deontay Wilder in December 2018. Since then, there had been tumult and strife in boxing and life. Fury and Usyk had also suffered.

I was among the little band of boxing writers in whom Fury confided the upsetting truth that his wife, Paris, had endured a stillbirth six months into her pregnancy. She lost the baby the day before he fought Usyk in May. Fury then sat down with four of us in Riyadh, on 16 December, to reveal that he had not seen or spoken on the phone to Paris for the past three months. He was locked in training and nothing could dilute his focus on Usyk.

The great Ukrainian had become the fighter I admired most. He carried himself with such a light touch that it was possible to forget the burden of responsibility bearing down on him. As the war against Russia ground on, Usyk knew that millions of Ukrainians relied on him to spread another flurry of good news when he defended his world titles against Fury that weekend.

In our company, Usyk had to be prompted gently to discuss his impact on Ukraine's morale. 'I will tell you one story,' he said. 'The soldiers on the second line have special communications connecting them to the frontline of the battlefield. They have nicknames like "Rocket".'

Usyk grinned as he acted out the warzone conversations after he defeated Fury in May. 'They would say: "Rocket, Rocket, can you hear me?". Their intonation was very serious when they first took the phone. They were like: "Yes, yes, what's going on? What do we need to do?" They were thinking it was an emergency to do with the war, but then they heard I was the undisputed champion and they started cheering. *"Oh yeah! Okay!"'*

The mood of the country was lifted, at least for a while, by Usyk. There was similar joy among his three eldest children who stayed up to watch the fight on television. But, before his narrow win over Fury in May was confirmed, they went through an ordeal. 'They were very afraid and nervous, my two boys and my daughter,' Usyk remembered. 'When I got home, they said I'm now a real legend. I said: "Hmmmm, no." Legend is very high-class. I don't like it. I like to be a simple guy.'

It was a suitably low-key fight week in Riyadh for Usyk. He seemed unfazed, even when he and Fury gazed menacingly at each other for more than eleven minutes in the face-off at the final press conference. Usyk smiled after Fury promised that 'I'm going to put this fucker into the hurt locker. I am going to do some fucking damage here.'

'Do not be afraid,' Usyk murmured to Fury. 'I will not leave you alone.'

There was more supportive mirth among the boxing media that I was the only writer not to be invited to a 'gala dinner' or to receive a gift of a traditional Saudi robe and a scarf from Turki Alalshikh, who had promised Usyk that Fury was about to cook him like 'a rabbit in the pot'.

I liked being on the outside in Saudi as I yearned for another Usyk win.

The Kingdom Arena, Riyadh, Saudi Arabia
Sunday 22 December 2024

As Oleksandr Usyk walks towards us soon after three in the morning, while holding Eeyore, his promoter lets slip a gentle cry: 'Here he comes, the best man in boxing . . .'

Alex Krassyuk is not a traditional boxing promoter, being much more understated than most in this riotous business. But his pride is understandable after Usyk's second straight defeat of Tyson Fury.

Outweighed by more than fifty pounds, Usyk used an irresistible combination of grit and dazzle to seal a thrilling victory. The imperious way in which he stood up to Fury before out-thinking and out-fighting him offers compelling evidence that Usyk should be regarded as the best pound-for-pound fighter in the world. But, as he speaks with humility and wit, it's easier to savour his human qualities as an ordinary man, as a son, a husband and a father.

Boxing is full of unsavoury and highly suspect people. But it also produces extraordinary men such as Usyk. While Fury refuses to praise Usyk, the world champion is the epitome of grace. 'He is my best friend,' Usyk says wryly of Fury. 'I really respect this guy. Tyson Fury is a *great* opponent. He is a good man.'

Fury argues that Usyk had been given the unanimous decision – 116–112 on all three scorecards – as a Christmas present. Frank Warren, Fury's promoter, suggests the verdict was 'nuts'.

'Uncle Frank?' Usyk says cheerfully. 'I think he's blind. If Tyson says it's a Christmas gift then, okay. Thank you, God. Thank you, my team. Frank is a crazy man. But it's okay. I win.'

He dedicates his victory to 'my Mama and all Ukrainian mothers' as he highlights the bond with his war-ravaged country. He also tells us about the inspiration he received that afternoon from his sons who won their judo competitions and called him to say: 'Hey Papa, you're next to win.'

Usyk shouts out his love to his eldest daughter who again loaned Eeyore to him for luck. He says that returning to his wife Yekaterina and their four children matters far more to him than discussing his boxing future. 'Today my wife sent me a video message. My little daughter Marisa say "Da-dee . . . Da-dee". She is ten-and-a-half months. I have looked at my little daughter for only two months, maximum. Now I want to go home, rest, stay off my phone and sit like this . . .'

Usyk stretches out his legs and spreads his arms wide. 'I want to lie back and look at the sky. *Mmmmmm.* I want to look at a tree and see how it is growing. I want to rest, not think about boxing. *Bleagghhh!* I want to play with my children.'

Before he slips away, the best man in boxing stands up and bows to us with respectful gratitude.

I want to return the gesture to thank Usyk for this happy ending and for proving again that boxing, despite everything, can still elevate the soul. It is enough to have had this beautiful moment, and all the others, both good and bad, because boxing will always be part of me, and I shall continue to follow it at this safe distance.

I also want to be with my family. I want to lie back in a chair and look at the wintry sky and the skeletal trees. I want to live and not think about boxing and where it goes from here.

It's time, now, to leave all this behind and head for home.

ACKNOWLEDGEMENTS

The death of Patrick Day lies at the heart of this book. I owe so much to his brother Jean Day and Patrick Artisthene, his best friend, who helped me understand the kindness, intelligence, wit, courage and sheer spirit which made Pat so special. Thanks to Patrick A for talking so openly to me from the moment we met, just six weeks after Pat's death, and especially to Jean who gave up so many days over the years to remember his youngest brother's life and death with fire and passion. There was anger towards boxing but, most of all just great love for Pat.

I appreciate the whole Day family, and their friends, including Sean Monaghan, the former fighter, who spoke movingly about Pat.

Isaac Chamberlain was the fighter I became closest to over the five years I worked on *The Last Bell*. We became real friends and Isaac was so generous in sharing his hopes and fears, both in person and through his own writing. He also made me proud to be with him in the dressing room before and after all his fights since 2020. Thanks, Isaac, for showing me again what boxing really means.

Regis Prograis was another fighter who went out of his way to help me. We got to know each other first through email and then countless interviews. Regis and I share a love of books and boxing, despite our agreeing it is a dirty business, and I am so happy we now have a mutual friend in the great Ross Williams. Thanks also, Regis, for allowing me inside your locker room on the unforgettable night you became a world champion again.

The fighters make boxing compelling and meaningful and so a sincere thank you to Tyson Fury, Oleksandr Usyk, Katie Taylor and Canelo Álvarez for all the interviews over the years.

So many people in boxing helped or spoke to me: They include Bernie Bahrmasel, Dan Barnard, Bobby Benton, Dmitry Bivol, Victor Conte, Charles Conwell, Jane Couch, Lou DiBella, Eric Donovan, Eddie Hearn, Fran Hennessy, Michael Hennessy, Mick Hennessey, Joe Higgins, Paddy Hobbs, Anthony Joshua, Evan Korn, Andy Knuth, Anthony Leaver, Andy Lee, Rory Lynn, Buddy McGirt, Barry McGuigan, Fred Mellor, Bobby Mills, Jon Pegg, Brian Peters, Matt Rich. Ed Roff, Diana Savenok, Claressa Shields, Sugarhill Steward, Melissa Takimoglu, United24 in Ukraine, Conor Ward and Frank Warren.

I enjoyed the support and friendship of other boxing writers including Rick Broadbent, Matt Christie, Kieran Cunningham, John Dennan, Tom Kershaw, Chris McKenna, Sarah Shepherd, Wally Swift, Declan Taylor and Declan Warrington – and those shared transcripts, moans and laughs sustained me.

Tris Dixon, Jonathan Drennan, Thomas Hauser and Elliot Worsell were great friends and they all spent so much time reading and making excellent suggestions to improve various drafts. Thanks to Jonathan for all those early readings and to Elliot, Thomas and Tris for their work near the end of the book.

Ian Marshall and Ian Chapman at Simon & Schuster commissioned *The Last Bell* and I appreciate all their belief and backing over the years. Kris Doyle was my editor and he made me think deeply about boxing with his intelligence and insight. It has been such a pleasure working with Kris and everyone at S&S including Sophia Akhtar, Suzanne Baboneau, Joe Christie, Amy Fleming, Craig Fraser, Oli Hunt, Frances Jessop, Alice Twomey and Rich Vlietstra.

Jonny Geller, my agent, always helps me write the books that matter most to me ... much to my gratitude.

I couldn't have asked for more supportive editors, colleagues and friends at the *Guardian* who helped me write about boxing. Will Woodward, my editor, sent me to cities as different as Las Vegas, Dublin, New York and Riyadh while also making me feel that even a business as chaotic as boxing deserved to be covered properly. Huge thanks to Will, Steve McMillan and Claire Tolley – and to Andy Martin and Philip Cornwall for handling all the live reports amid wonky Wi-Fi and late deadlines.

I always wanted this to be a book about more than boxing and so it meant so much when writers I really admire took time to read the book with such generosity. Thank you Ed Caesar, Adrian Duncan, Keiran Goddard, Ben Myers, Barney Ronay, Dina Nayeri and David Whitehouse.

Amanda Kelley painted James Toney for the US cover of *Dark Trade* – and I always wanted her boxing art to be the first thing readers saw when they picked up *The Last Bell*. Amanda found the image of Tyson Fury and Deontay Wilder and, working so hard with great skill, she brought that extraordinary moment to life with her incredible painting. Her vast boxing knowledge, and eye for a great story, also meant that she encouraged me to interview and write about Isaac Chamberlain and Regis Prograis. So a special thank you to Amanda for her support and belief in this book.

My other close friends Hilton Tanchum, Jay Savage and Diane Coetzer were great allies. They all faced difficult times but kept encouraging me and proved the depth of our friendship again and again.

The audio version of *The Last Bell* has been read by Ronald McIntosh – the brilliant radio commentator I have known for the past twenty-five years. It's always a pleasure to see Ronald at ringside and his work as the BBC's boxing commentator is exemplary. It's an honour to have worked with him on the audio book.

My sister-in-law Anna Fisher, and my brother-in-law Tim

Musgrave, allowed me to write about their mum, the mighty Pat Musgrave, and they read those pages with compassion and kindness.

There was much loss in my family during the early years of this book. I still miss my parents, Ian and Jess, my sister Heather and my mother-in-law Pat, and so thank you to my wife Alison and our kids Bella, Jack and Emma. Having the four of you with me gave me light and hope.

It has been a thrill to see how Jack, Emma and Isabella have sometimes included boxing in their own work with such skill. As fellow writers Isabella and Jack made such constructive comments about improving my book – while Emma opened my mind, and forgotten fashion sense, with Southpaw.

Alison read this book so many times with such a clear gaze and a sharp editing pencil. She might not follow boxing as closely as she did back in our *Dark Trade* days but her attention to detail, care and love shone through each new reading. And she supported me, and looked after me, with typical patience as I gave up so much time to this book. Thanks, as always, to Alison.